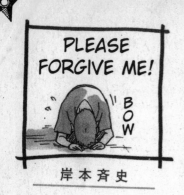

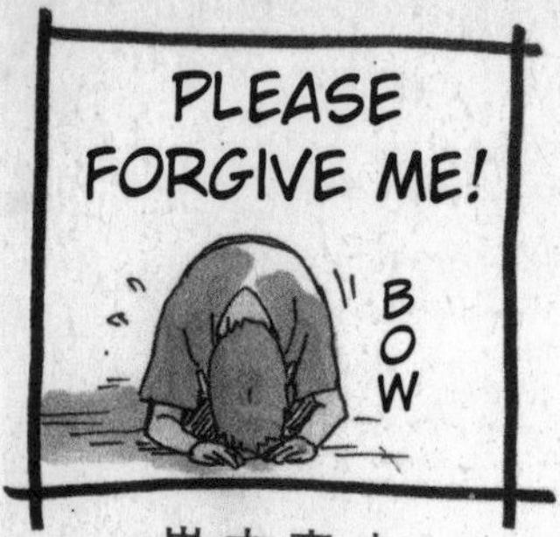
PLEASE FORGIVE ME!
BOW

岸本斉史

450 yen (with tax)...
I truly apologize for this affront. I had decided that this (241) was the right number of pages to bring you, the readers, the Sasuke vs. Itachi arc. But this resulted in the price of the tankobon [graphic novel] going up, for which I feel absolutely terrible. This volume is also a bit thicker but I do hope that you will read it to the very end.

—Masashi Kishimoto, 2008

Author/artist Masashi Kishimoto was born in 1974 in rural Okayama Prefecture, Japan. After spending time in art college, he won the Hop Step Award for new manga artists with his manga **Karakuri** (Mechanism). Kishimoto decided to base his next story on traditional Japanese culture. His first version of **Naruto**, drawn in 1997, was a one-shot story about fox spirits; his final version, which debuted in **Weekly Shonen Jump** in 1999, quickly became the most popular ninja manga in Japan.

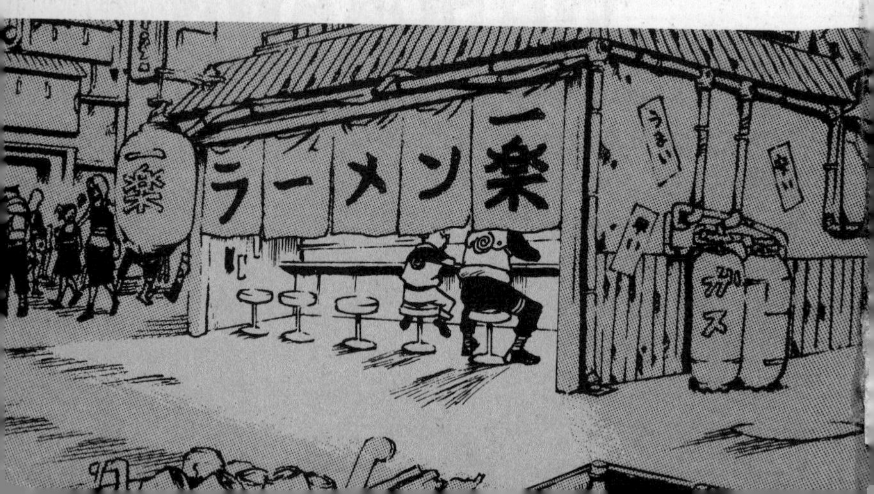
一楽
ラーメン一楽

NARUTO VOL. 43
The SHONEN JUMP Manga Edition

STORY AND ART BY MASASHI KISHIMOTO

Translation/Mari Morimoto
English Adaptation/Deric A. Hughes
Touch-up Art & Lettering/Inori Fukuda Trant
Design/Gerry Serrano
Editor/Joel Enos

Editor in Chief, Books/Alvin Lu
Editor in Chief, Magazines/Marc Weidenbaum
VP, Publishing Licensing/Rika Inouye
VP, Sales & Product Marketing/Gonzalo Ferreyra
VP, Creative/Linda Espinosa
Publisher/Hyoe Narita

Printed in the U.S.A.

Published by VIZ Media, LLC
P.O. Box 77010
San Francisco, CA 94107

SHONEN JUMP Manga Edition
10 9 8 7 6 5 4 3 2 1
First printing, April 2009

SHONEN JUMP MANGA EDITION

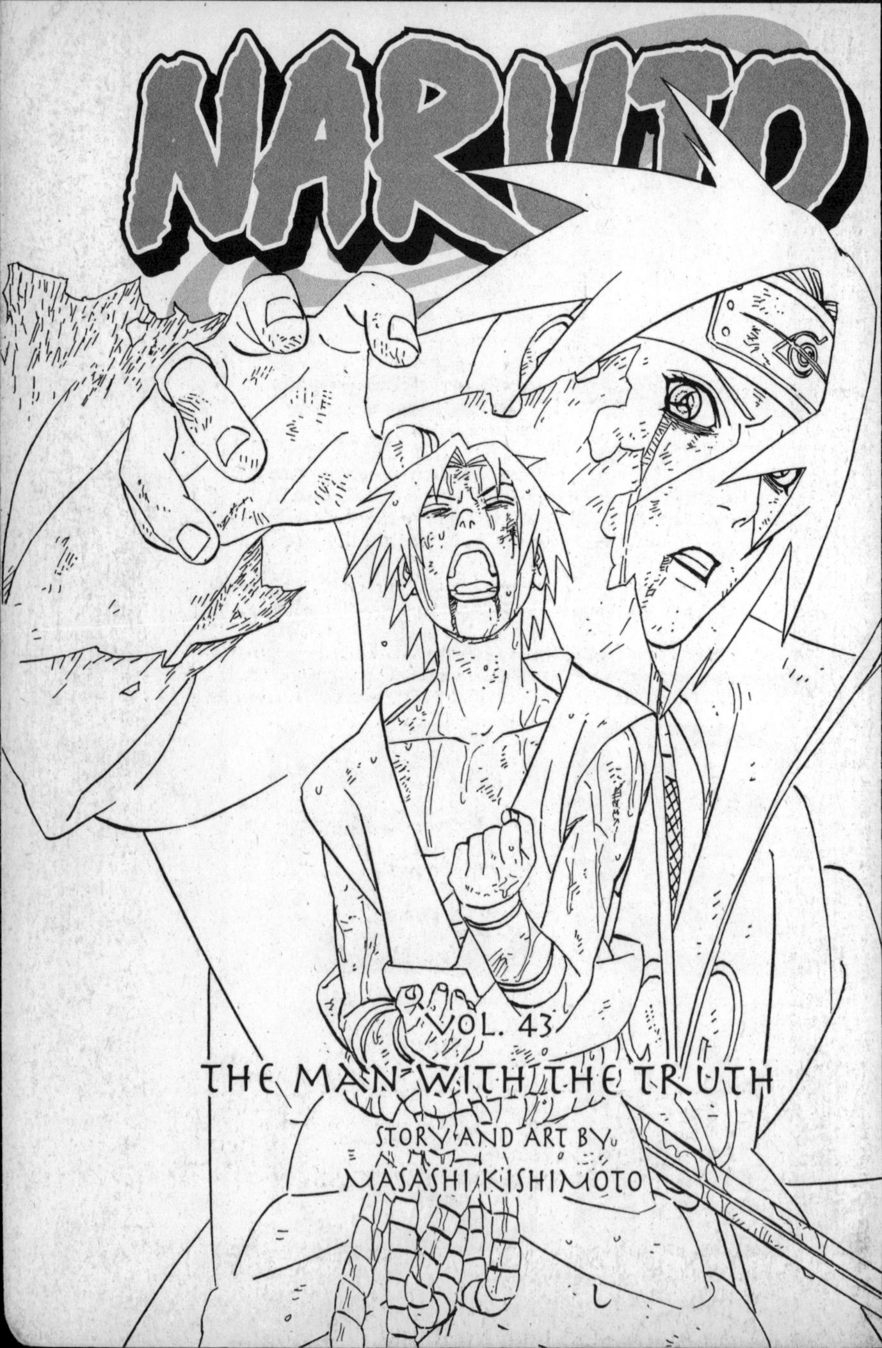

NARUTO

VOL. 43

THE MAN WITH THE TRUTH

STORY AND ART BY

MASASHI KISHIMOTO

CHARACTERS

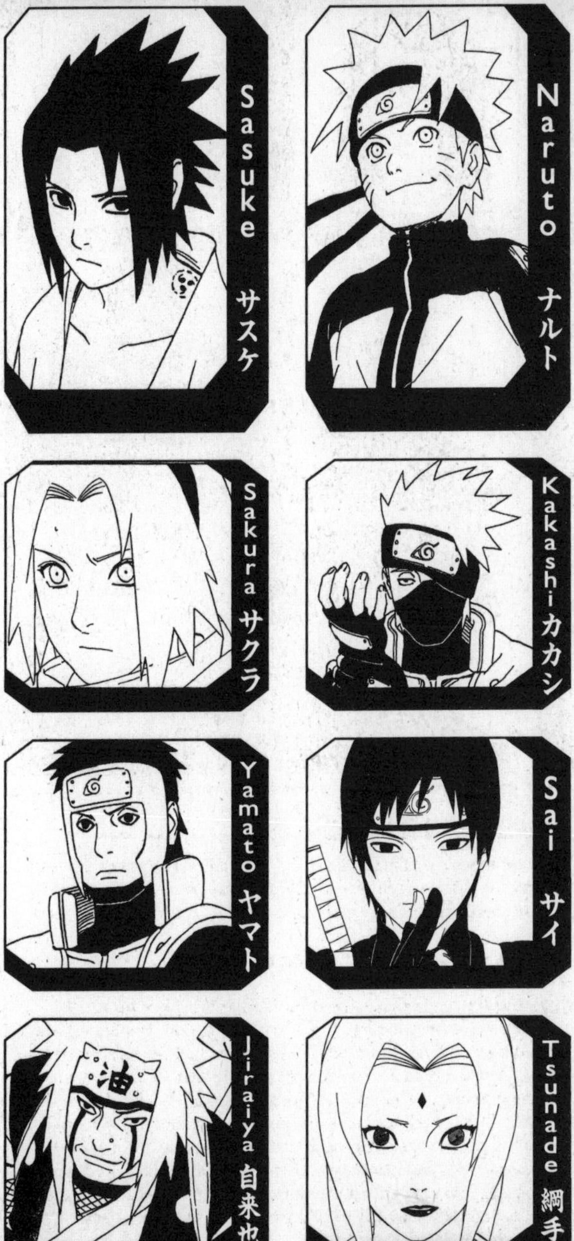
Naruto ナルト
Sasuke サスケ
Kakashi カカシ
Sakura サクラ
Sai サイ
Yamato ヤマト
Tsunade 綱手
Jiraiya 自来也

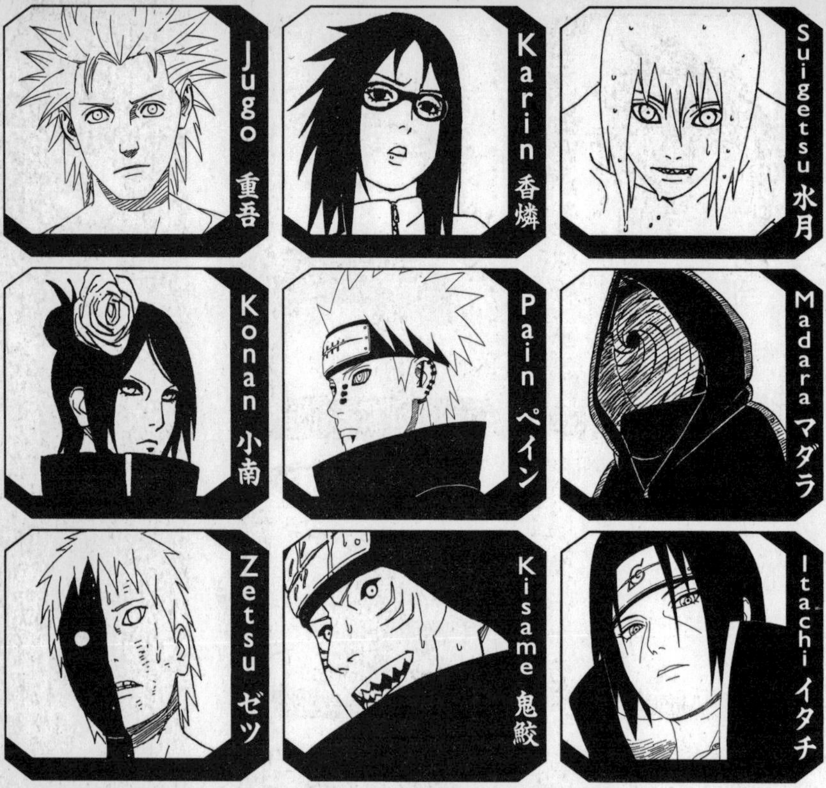
Suigetsu 水月
Karin 香燐
Jugo 重吾
Madara マダラ
Pain ペイン
Konan 小南
Itachi イタチ
Kisame 鬼鮫
Zetsu ゼツ

THE STORY SO FAR...

Once the bane of the Konohagakure Ninja Academy, Uzumaki Naruto now serves dutifully among the ranks of the Konoha shinobi—an illustrious group of ninja sworn to protect their village from the forces of evil seeking to destroy it from without and within...

However, Sasuke, unable to give up his quest for vengeance, leaves Konohagakure to seek Orochimaru and his power...

Two years pass. Naruto and his comrades grow up and head out once more. As their fierce battles against the Tailed Beast-targeting Akatsuki rage on, Sasuke rebels against Orochimaru and takes everything from him. Sasuke then gathers new companions and chases after Itachi. Jiraiya, the man who has trained Naruto for more than two years to deal with the impending attack of the Akatsuki, finally discovers the identity of the Akatsuki leader, Pain, and the secret is then bequeathed to Naruto—after Jiraiya's untimely death. Sasuke once again confronts his brother Itachi and learns not only about his brother's true intentions, but also about the Uchiha Clan's past. And to slake his vengeance, Sasuke challenges him to a battle. Confident that he can win, Sasuke appears to overpower and corner his brother... but then Itachi begins to unleash the full power of the Amaterasu...

NARUTO

VOL. 43
THE MAN WITH THE TRUTH

CONTENTS

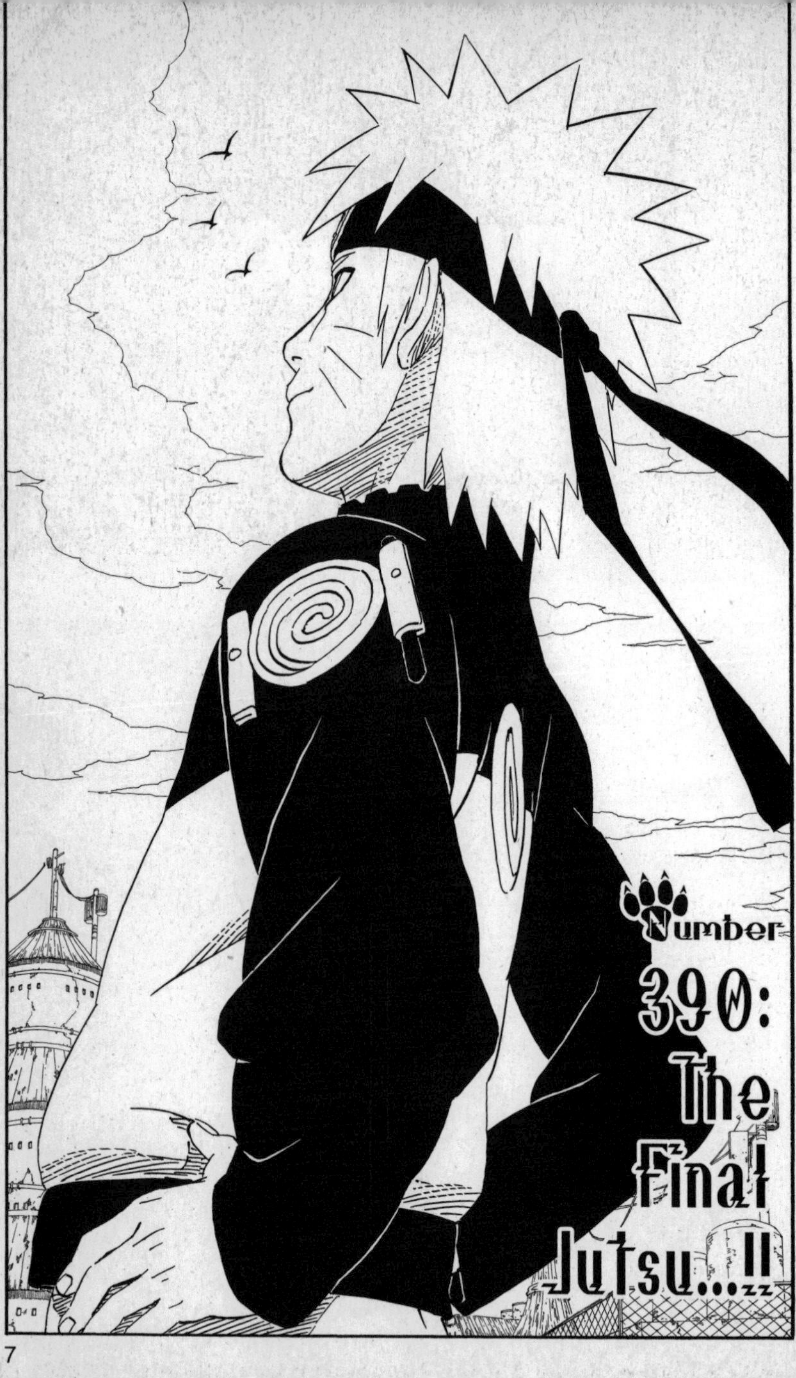
Number 390: The Final Jutsu...!!

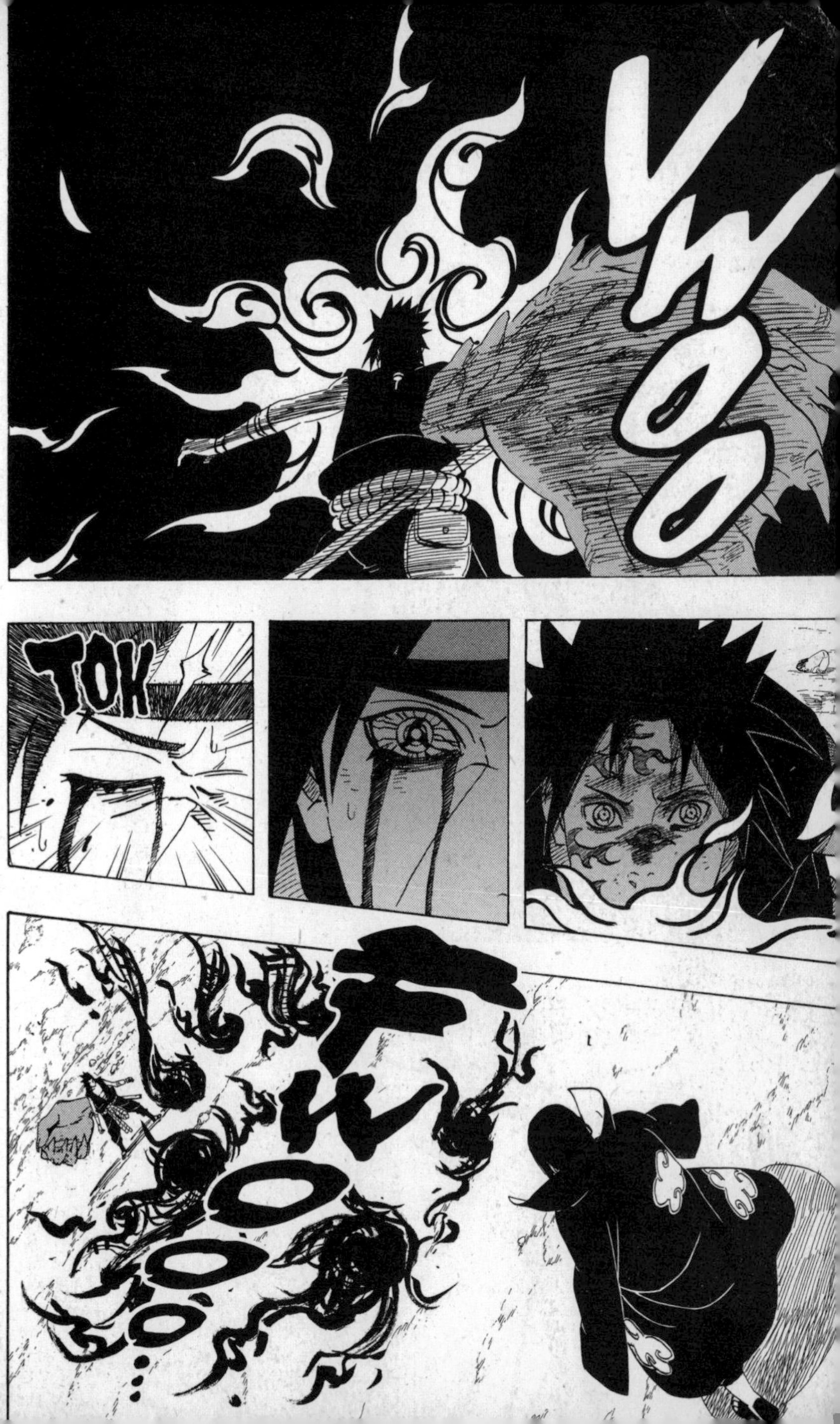
VWOOO
TOK
FWOOO...

READ THIS WAY

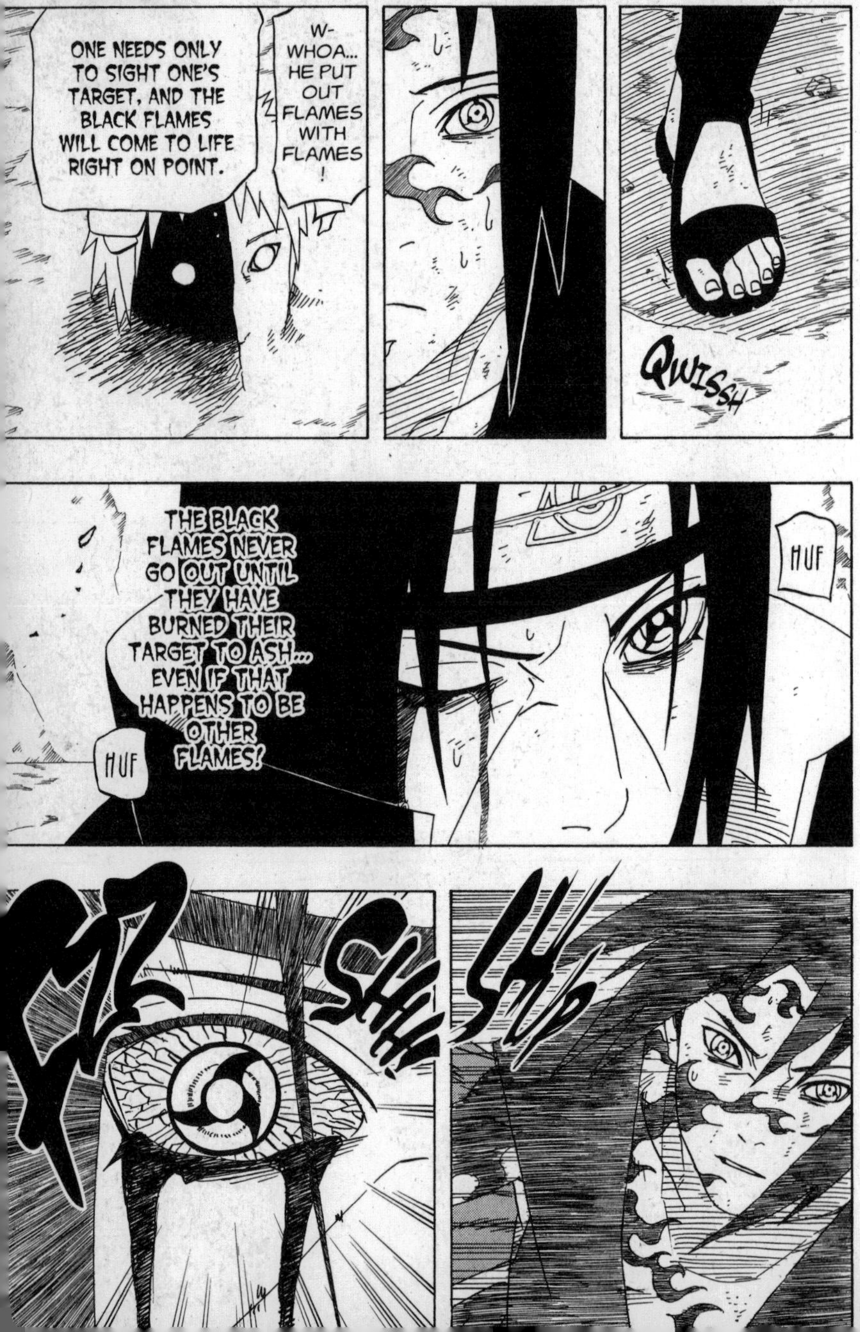
QWISSH
W-WHOA... HE PUT OUT FLAMES WITH FLAMES!
ONE NEEDS ONLY TO SIGHT ONE'S TARGET, AND THE BLACK FLAMES WILL COME TO LIFE RIGHT ON POINT.
HUF
THE BLACK FLAMES NEVER GO OUT UNTIL THEY HAVE BURNED THEIR TARGET TO ASH... EVEN IF THAT HAPPENS TO BE OTHER FLAMES!
HUF
FZZ SHH!

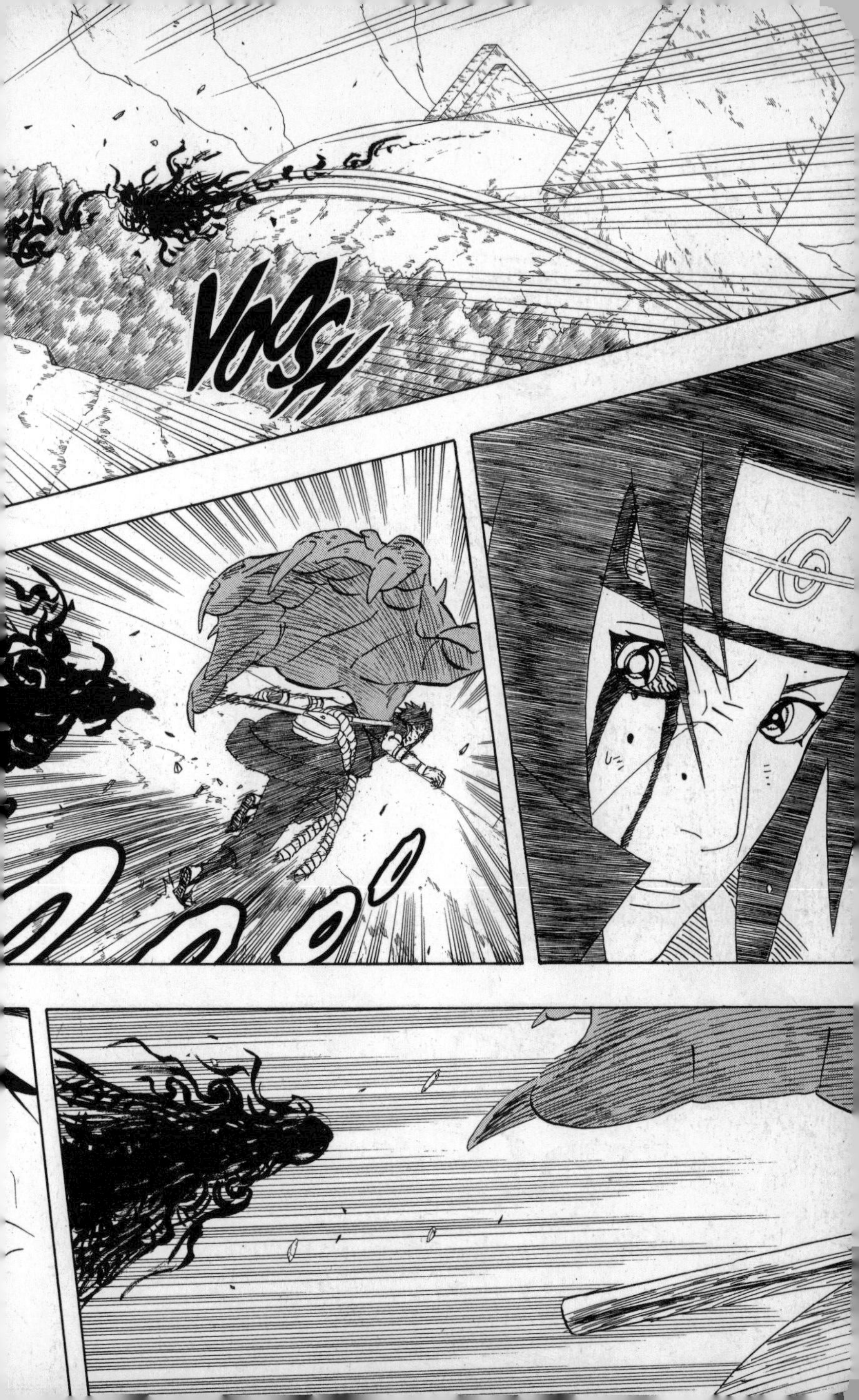
VOOSH

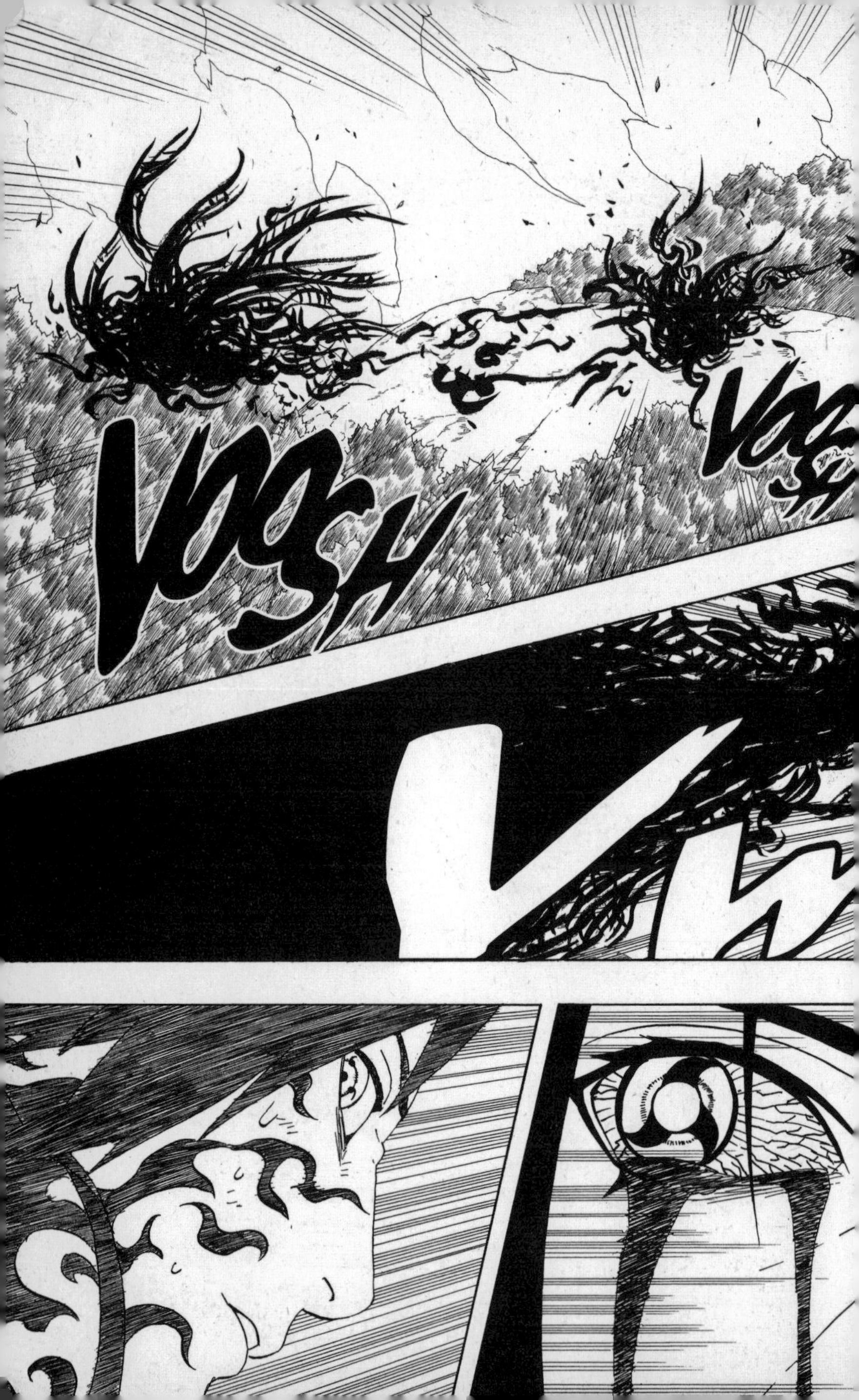
VOOSH

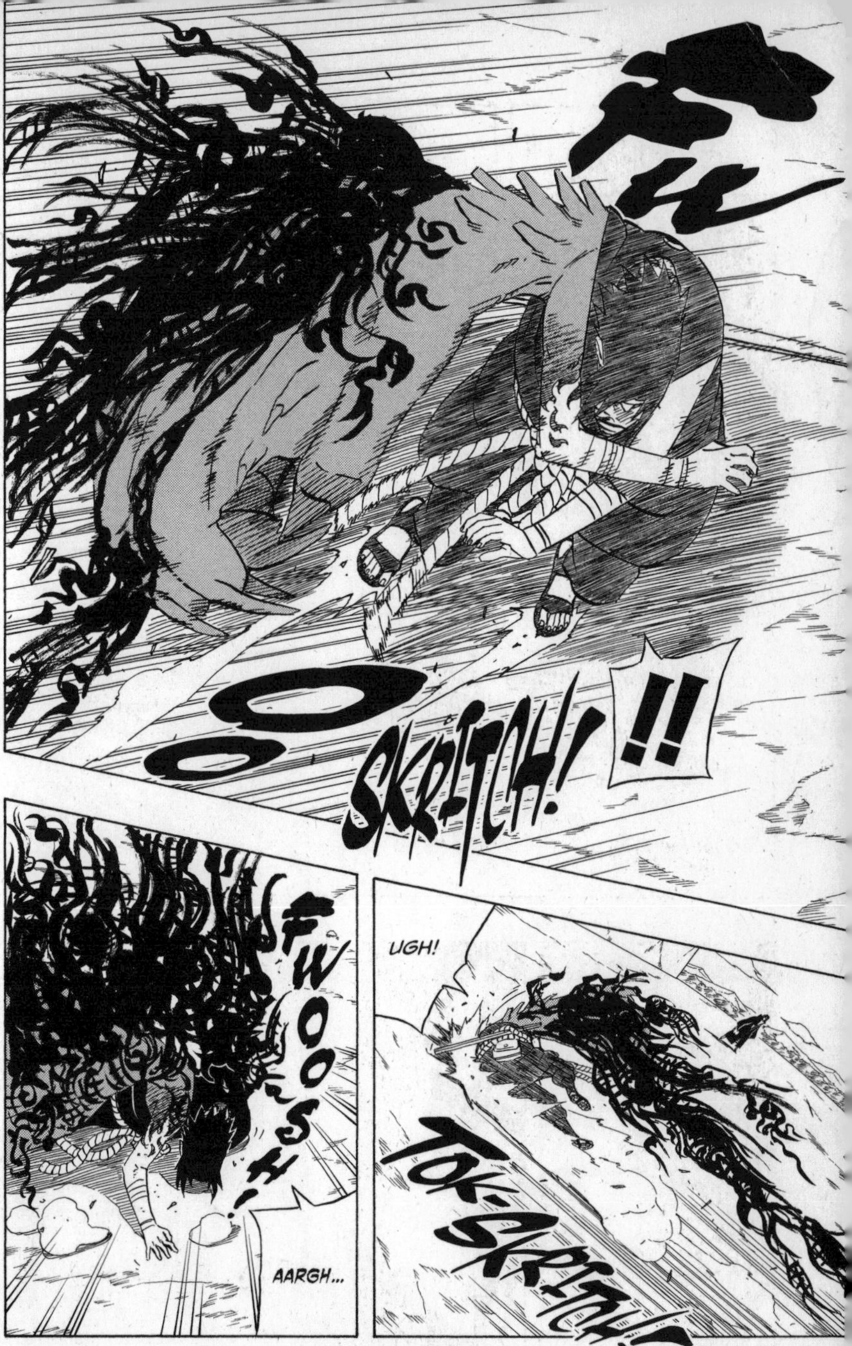
SKRITCH!
!!
UGH!
TOK-SKRITCH!!
FWOOSH!
AARGH...

READ THIS WAY

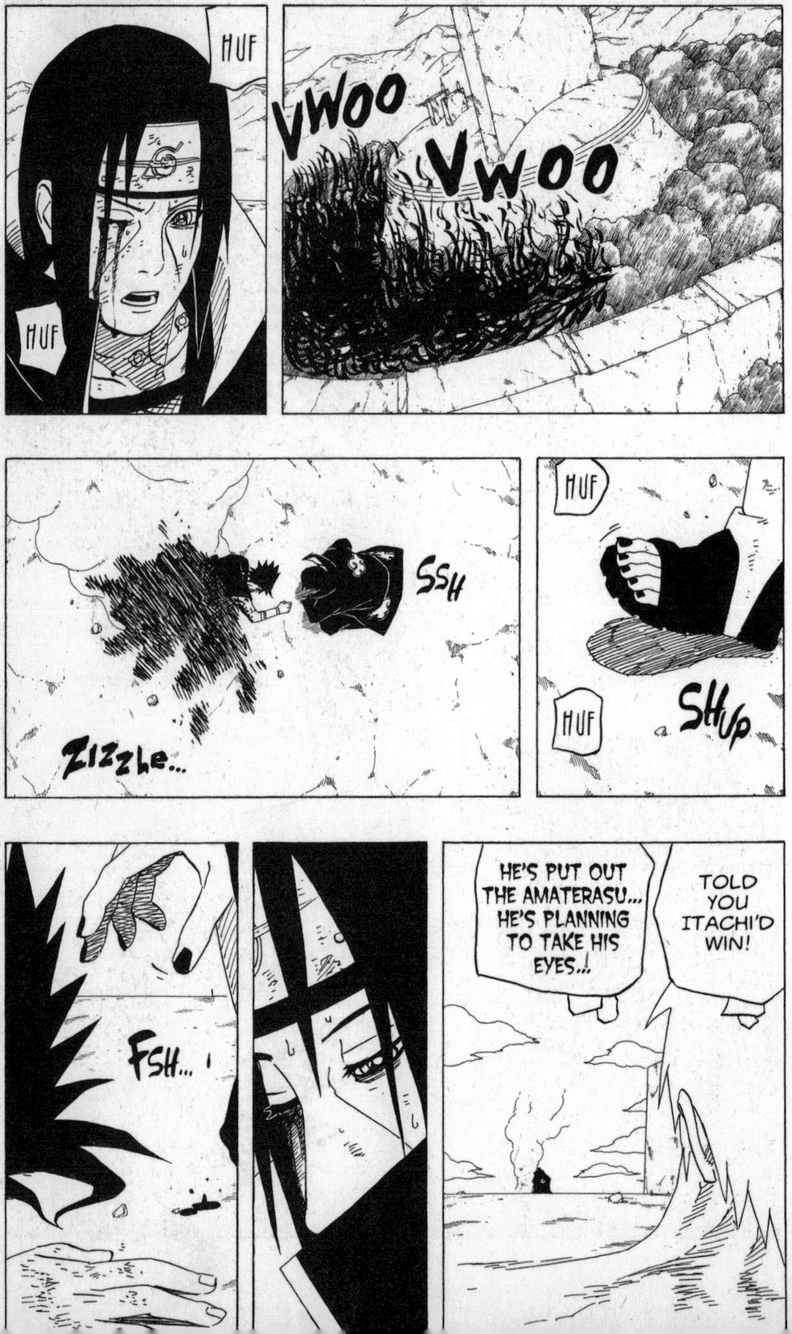
VWOO
VWOO
HUF
HUF
HUF
SHUP
HUF
SSH
ZIZZLE...
TOLD YOU ITACHI'D WIN!
HE'S PUT OUT THE AMATERASU... HE'S PLANNING TO TAKE HIS EYES...!
FSH...

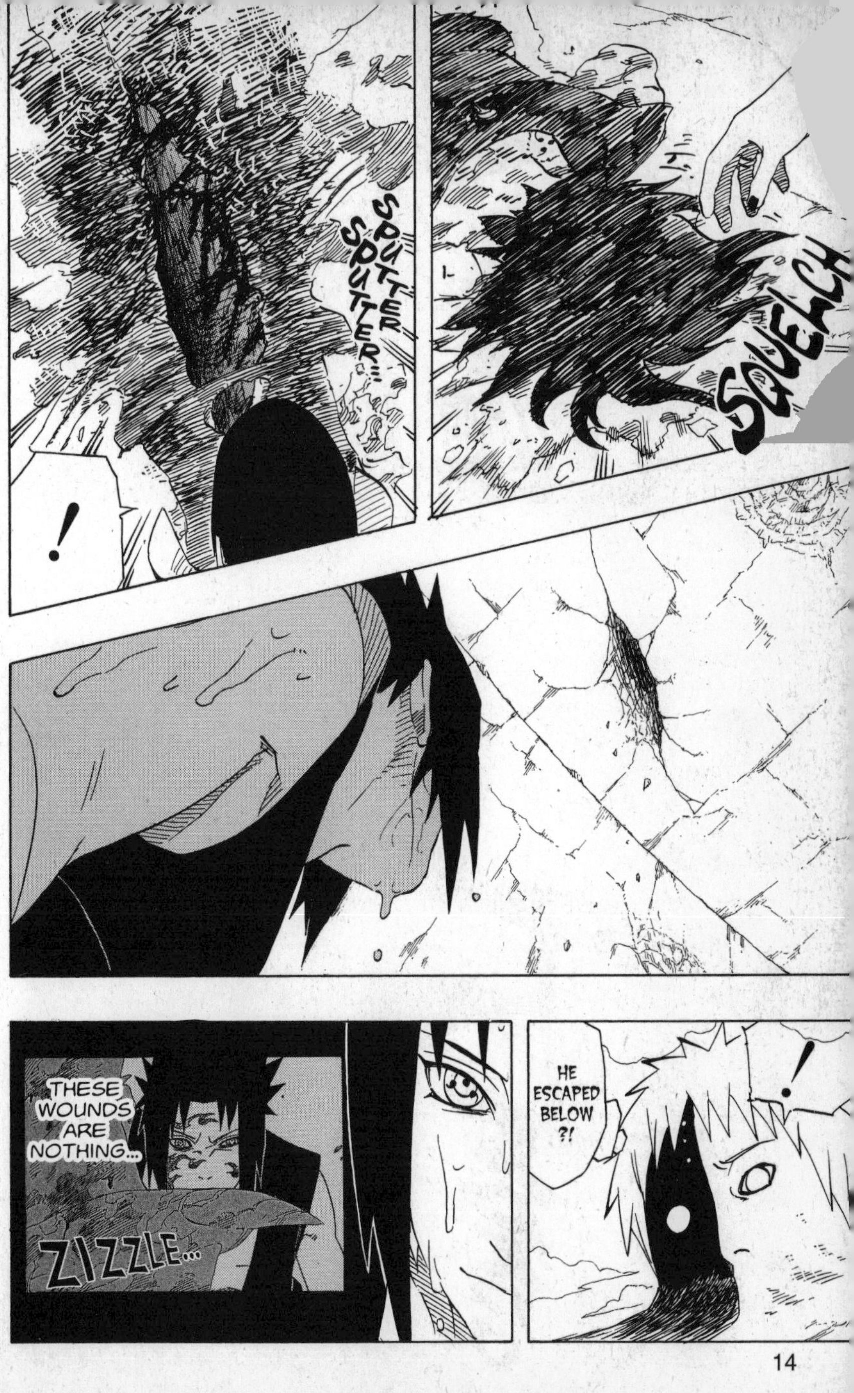
SQUELCH
SPUTTER SPUTTER...
!
!
HE ESCAPED BELOW?!
THESE WOUNDS ARE NOTHING...
ZIZZLE...

READ THIS WAY

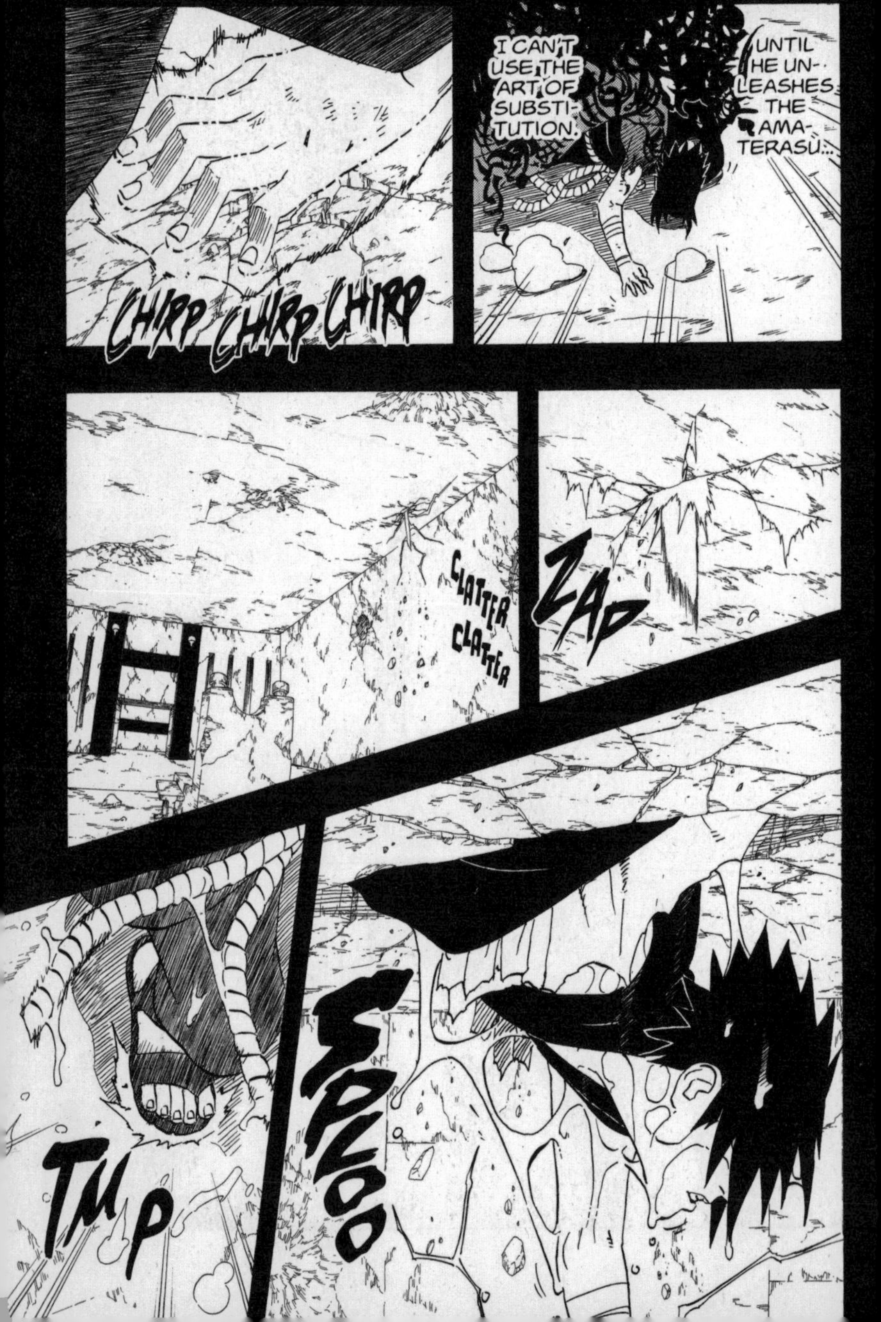
UNTIL HE UN-LEASHES THE AMATERASU...
I CAN'T USE THE ART OF SUBSTITUTION.
CHIRP CHIRP CHIRP
ZAP
CLATTER CLATTER
SPLOO
TMP

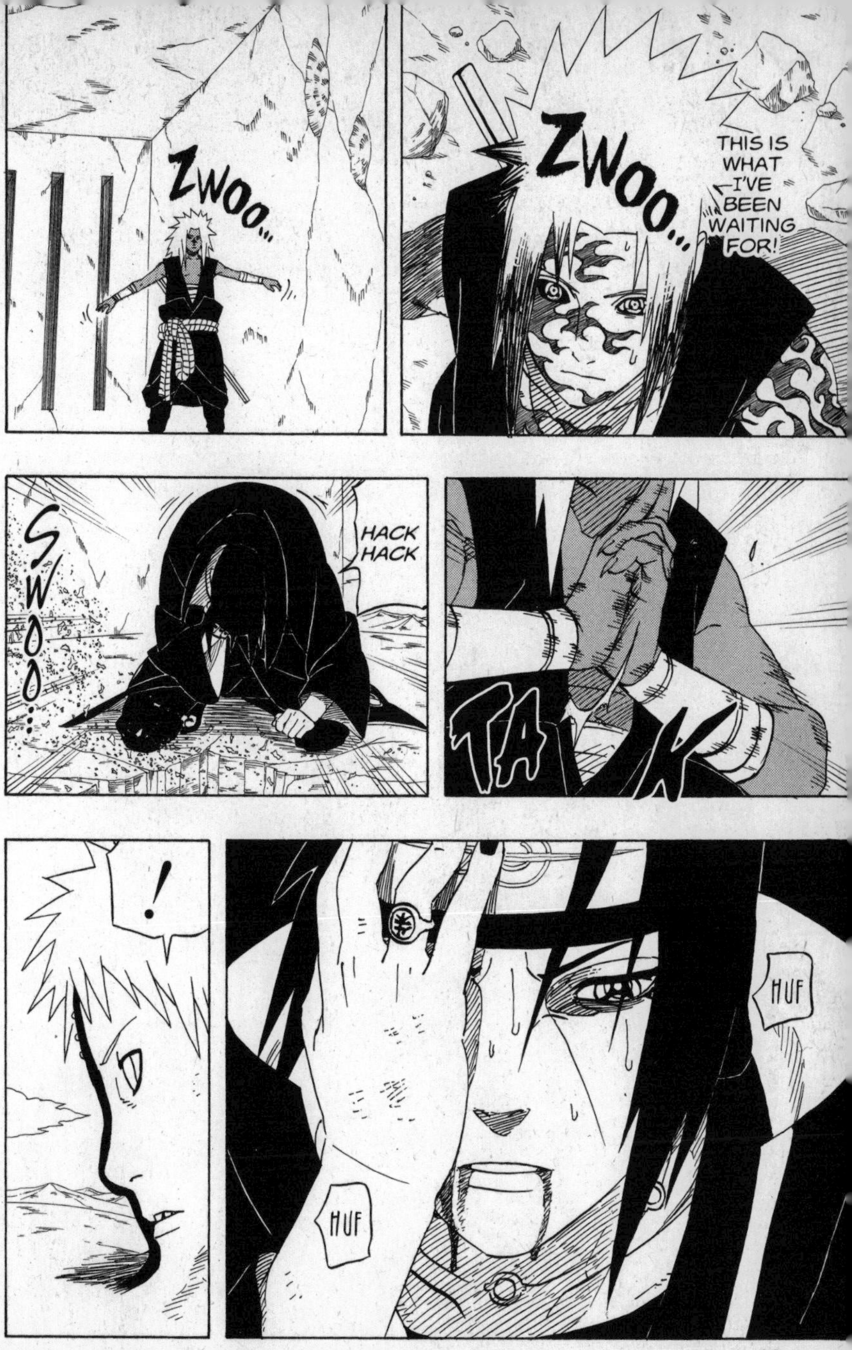
ZWOO...
THIS IS WHAT I'VE BEEN WAITING FOR!
ZWOO...
TAK
SWOO...
HACK HACK
HUF
HUF
!

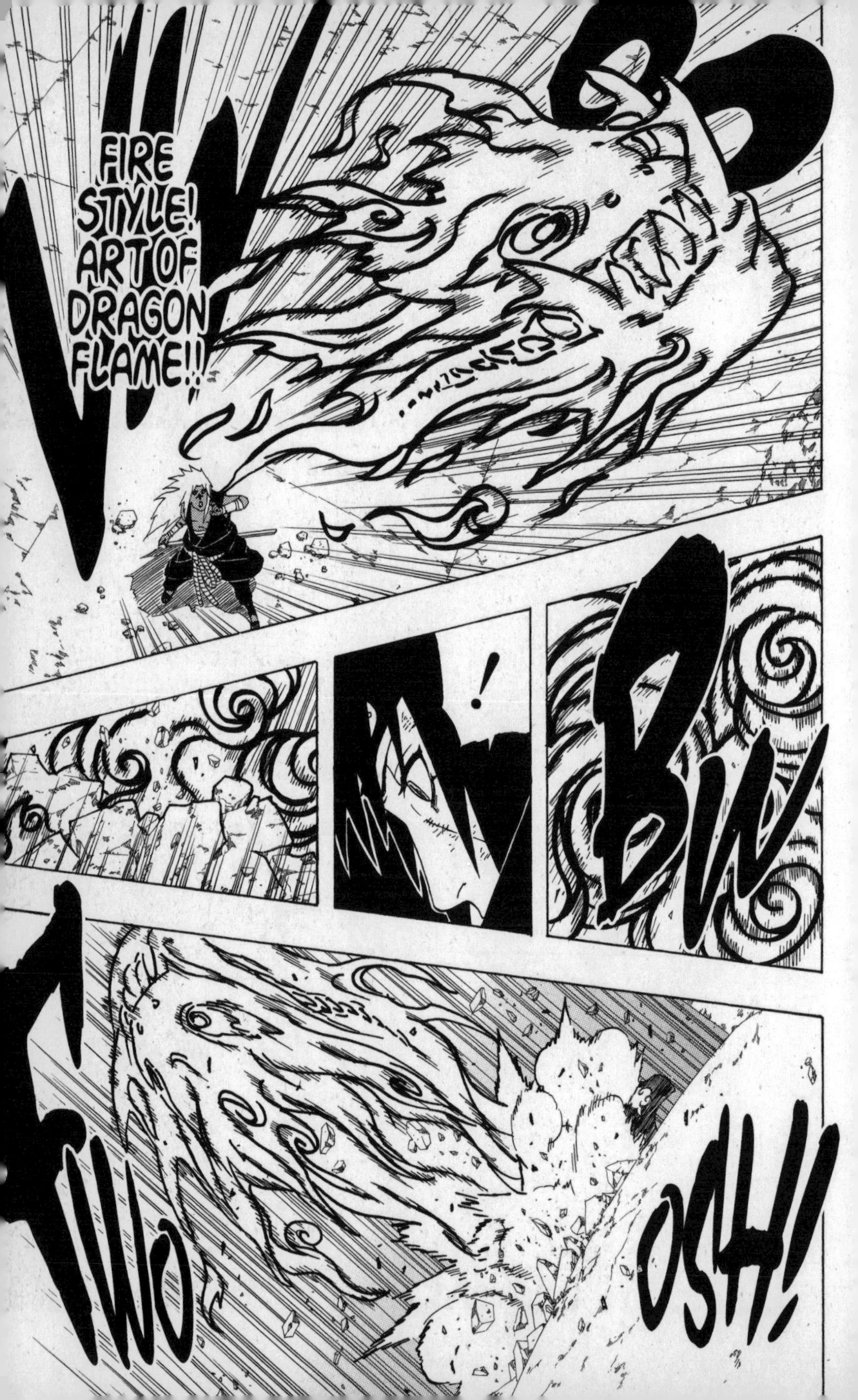

FIRE STYLE! ART OF DRAGON FLAME!!
!
FWOOSH!!

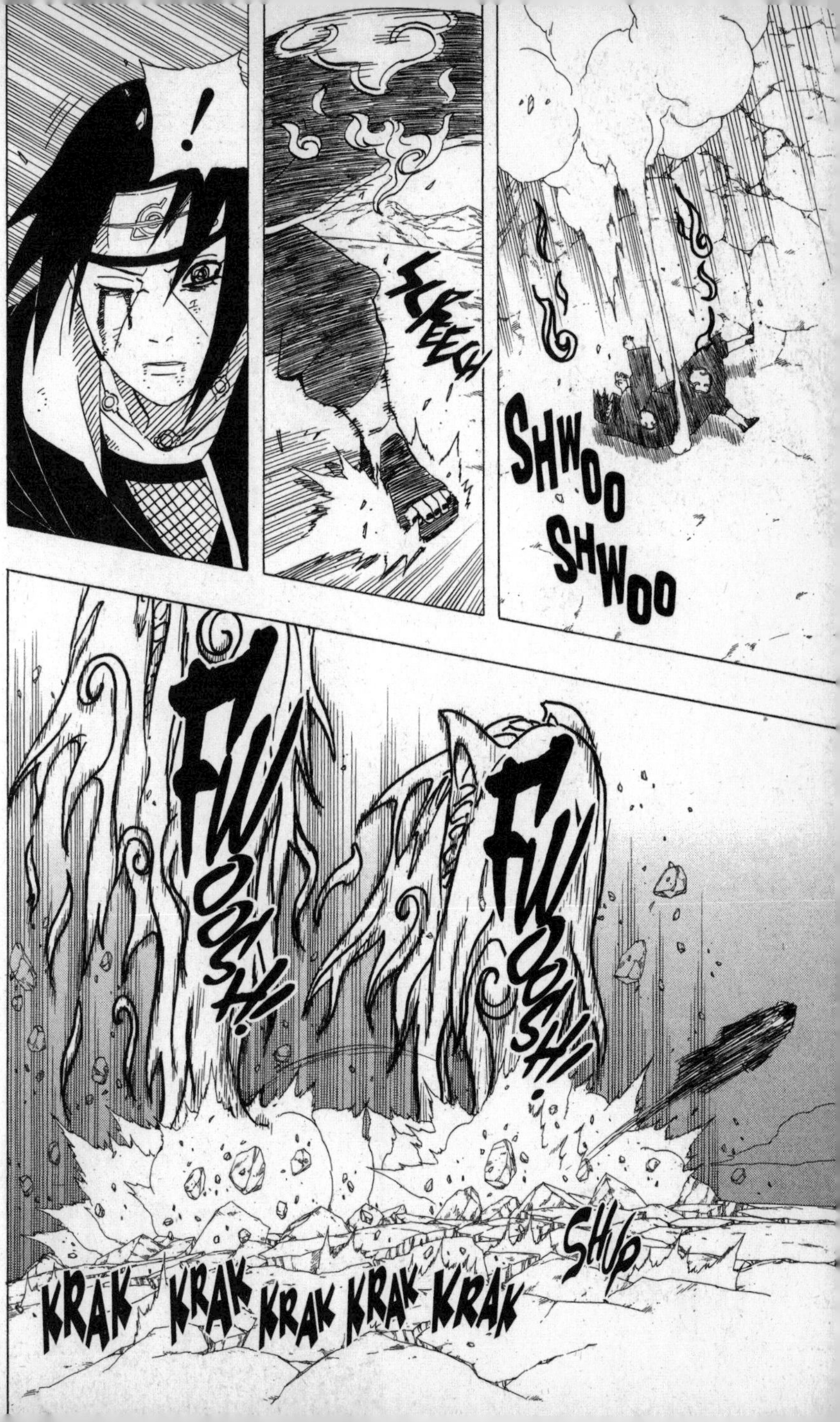
SHWOO SHWOO
SKREECH
!
SHUP
FWOOSH!
FWOOSH!
KRAK KRAK KRAK KRAK KRAK

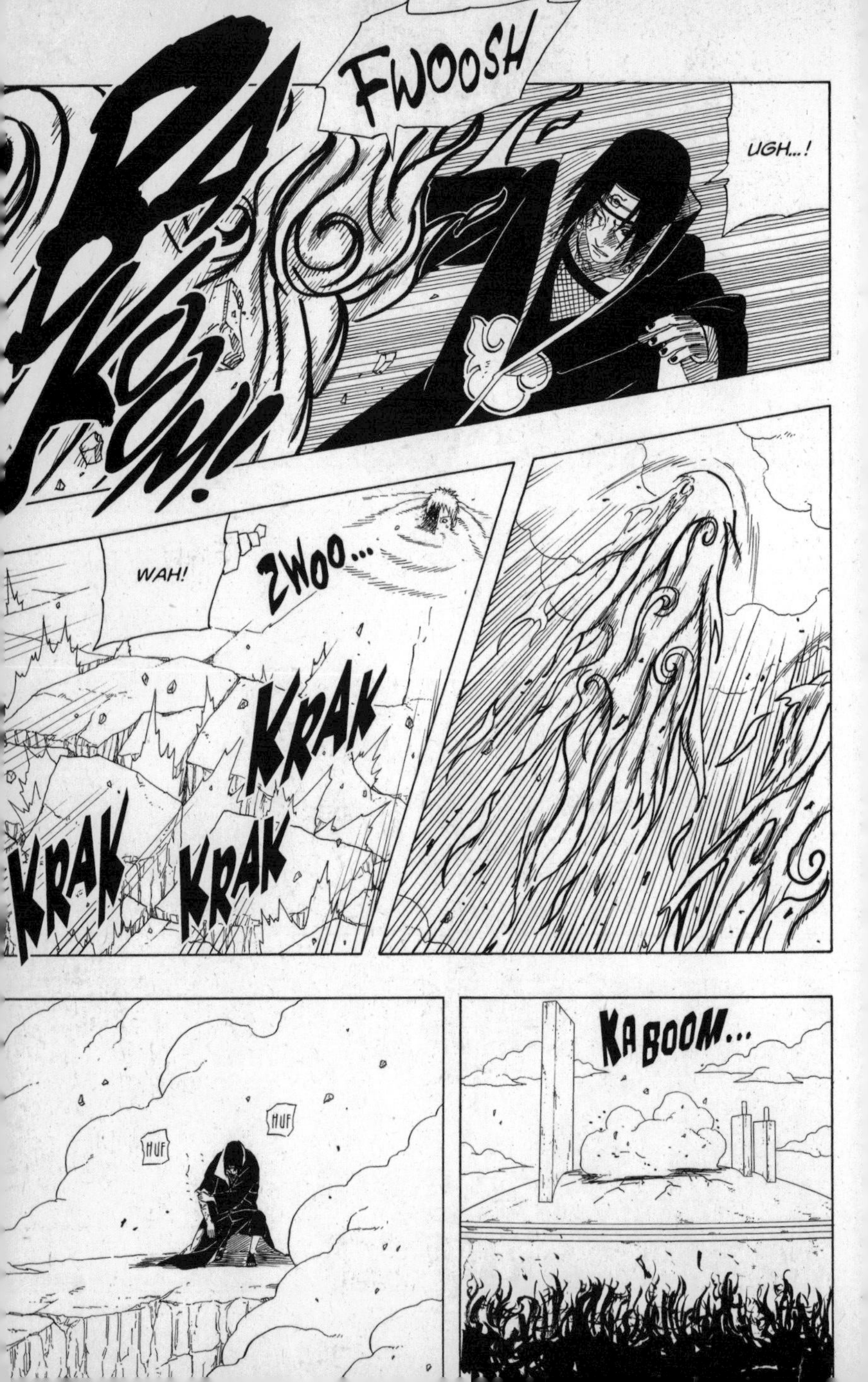
UGH...!
FWOOSH
BA-BOOM!
ZWOO...
WAH!
KRAK
KRAK
KRAK
KABOOM...
HUF
HUF

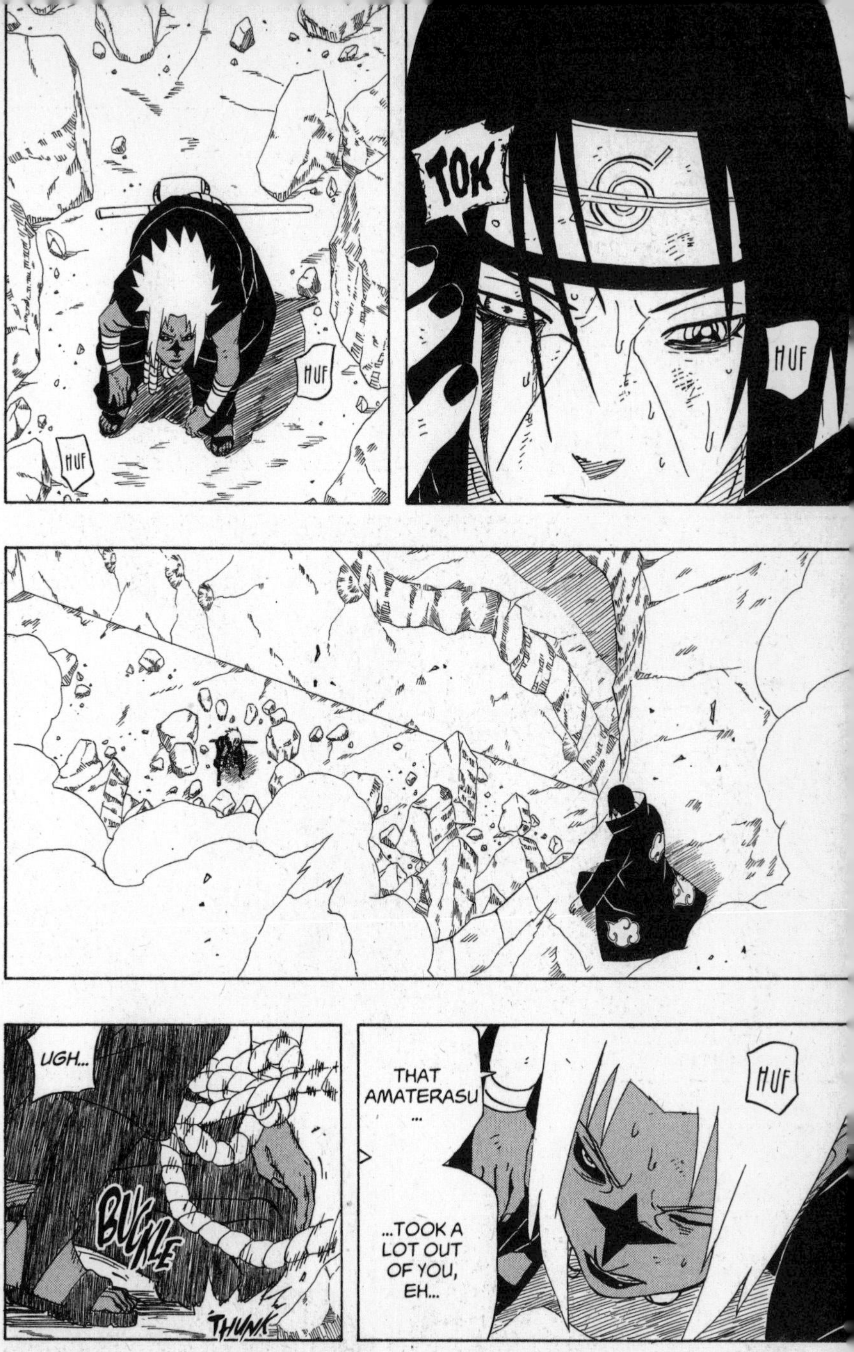
TOK
HUF
HUF
HUF
HUF
THAT AMATERASU ...
...TOOK A LOT OUT OF YOU, EH...
UGH...
BUCKLE
THUNK

READ THIS WAY

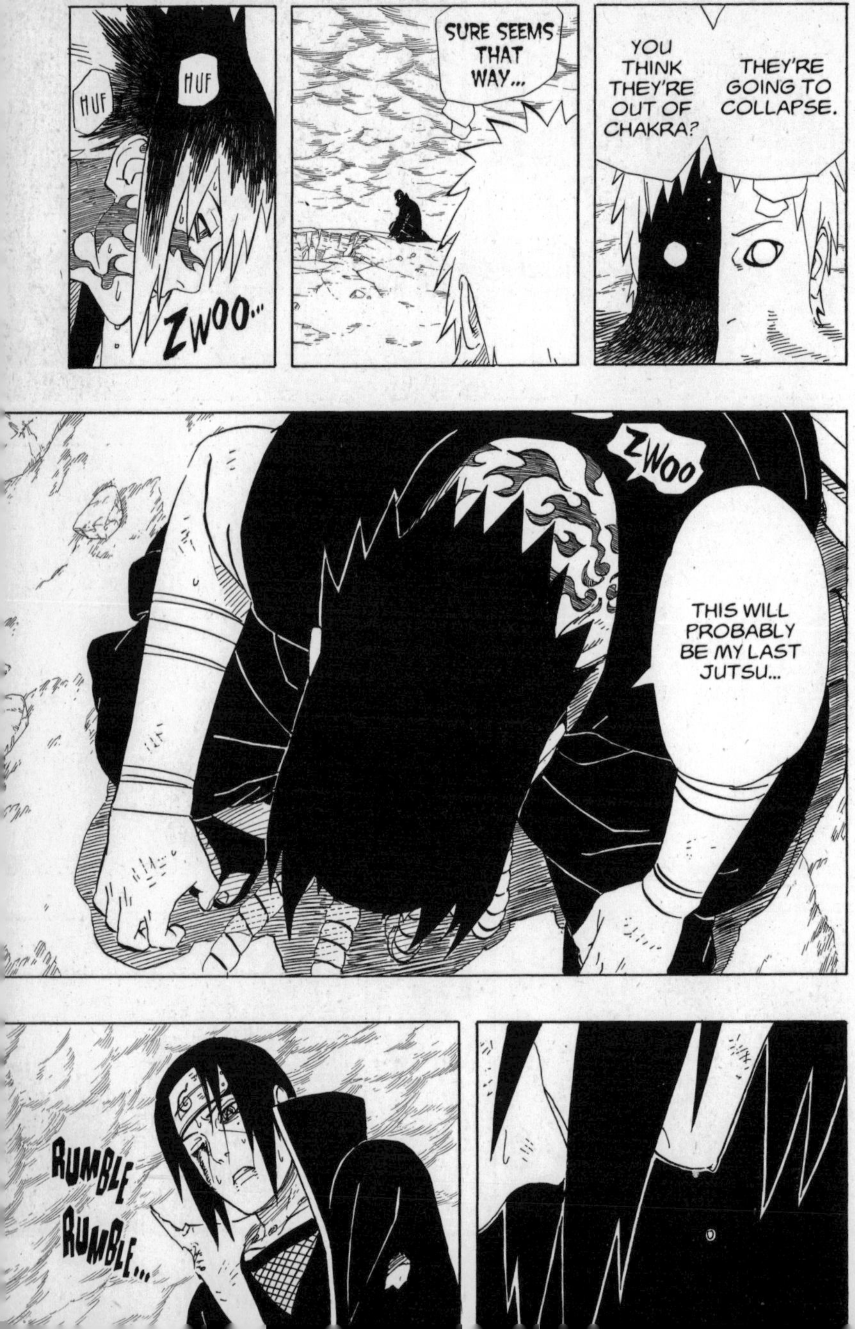
THEY'RE GOING TO COLLAPSE.
YOU THINK THEY'RE OUT OF CHAKRA?
SURE SEEMS THAT WAY...
HUF
HUF
ZWOO...
ZWOO
THIS WILL PROBABLY BE MY LAST JUTSU...
RUMBLE RUMBLE...

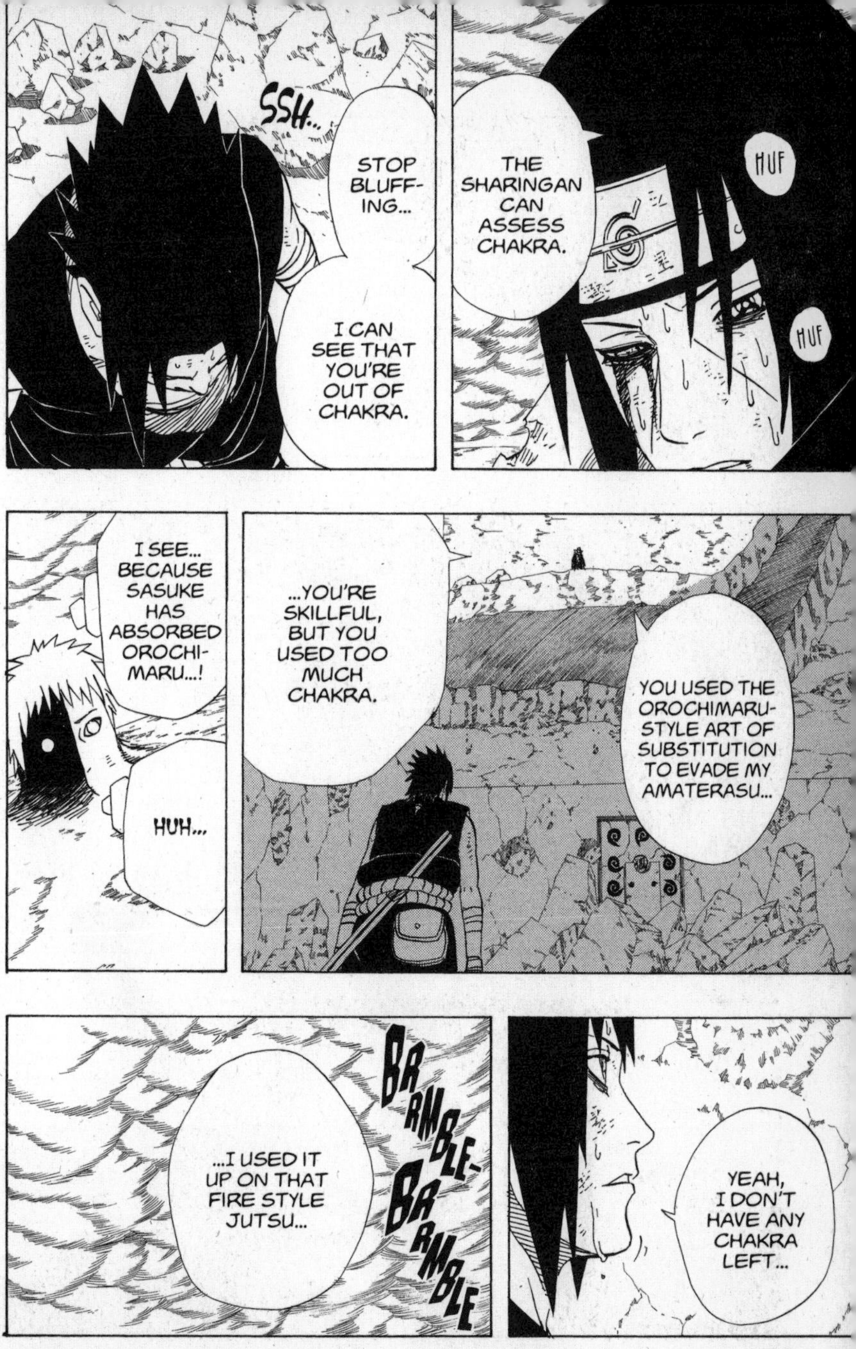
HUF
THE SHARINGAN CAN ASSESS CHAKRA.
HUF
SSH...
STOP BLUFF-ING...
I CAN SEE THAT YOU'RE OUT OF CHAKRA.
YOU USED THE OROCHIMARU-STYLE ART OF SUBSTITUTION TO EVADE MY AMATERASU...
...YOU'RE SKILLFUL, BUT YOU USED TOO MUCH CHAKRA.
I SEE... BECAUSE SASUKE HAS ABSORBED OROCHI-MARU...!
HUH...
YEAH, I DON'T HAVE ANY CHAKRA LEFT...
BRRMBLE-BRRMBLE
...I USED IT UP ON THAT FIRE STYLE JUTSU...

READ THIS WAY

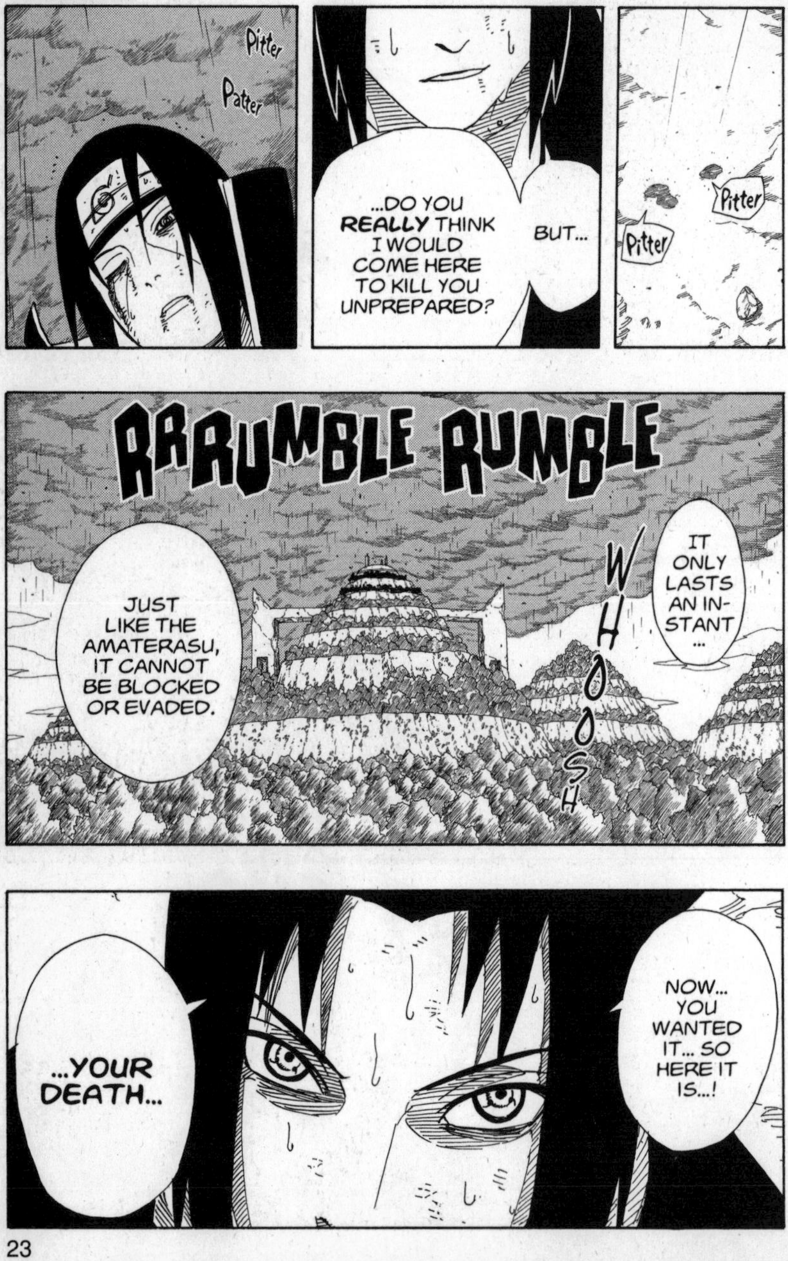

Pitter
Pitter
BUT...
...DO YOU REALLY THINK I WOULD COME HERE TO KILL YOU UNPREPARED?
Pitter
Patter
RRRUMBLE RUMBLE
IT ONLY LASTS AN IN-STANT...
WHOOSH
JUST LIKE THE AMATERASU, IT CANNOT BE BLOCKED OR EVADED.
NOW... YOU WANTED IT... SO HERE IT IS...!
...YOUR DEATH...

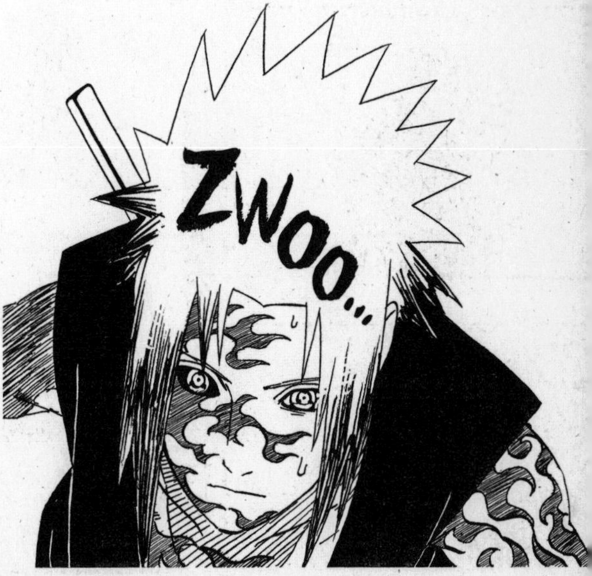
ZWOO...

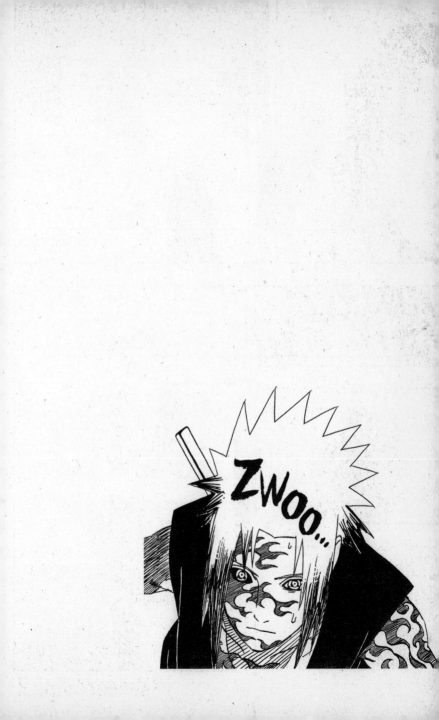

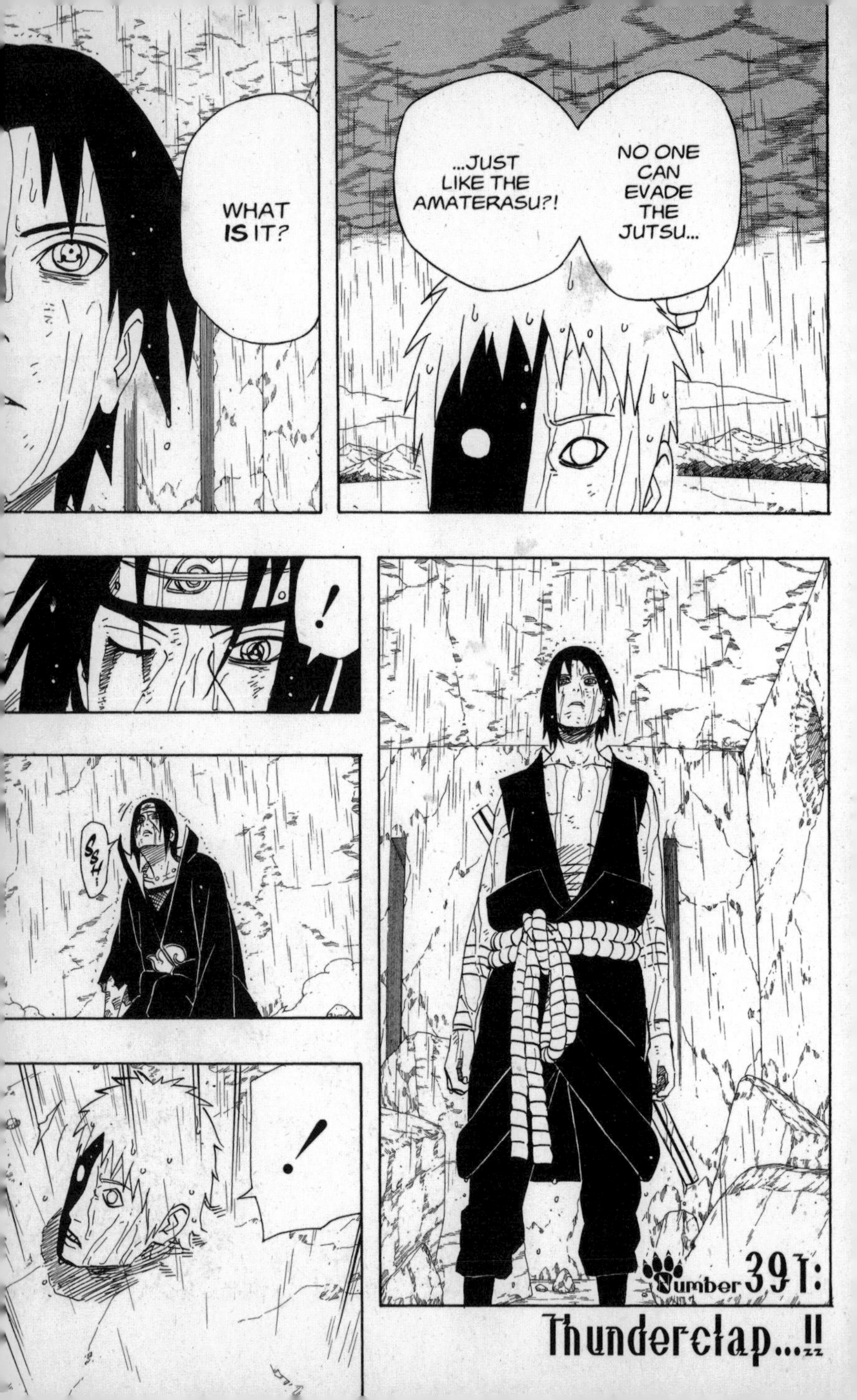
NO ONE CAN EVADE THE JUTSU...
...JUST LIKE THE AMATERASU?!
WHAT IS IT?
Number 391: Thunderclap...!!
!
SSH...!
!

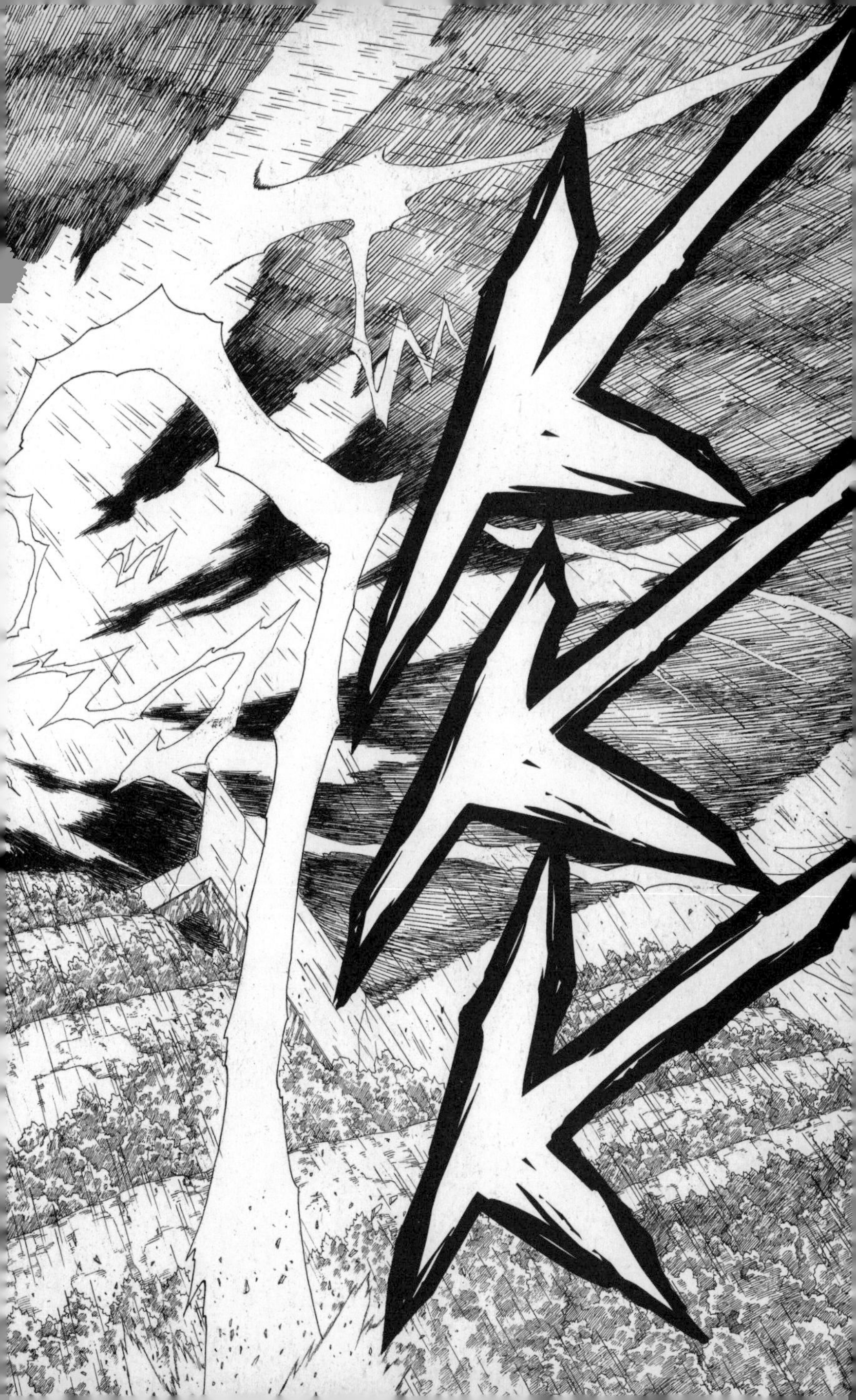

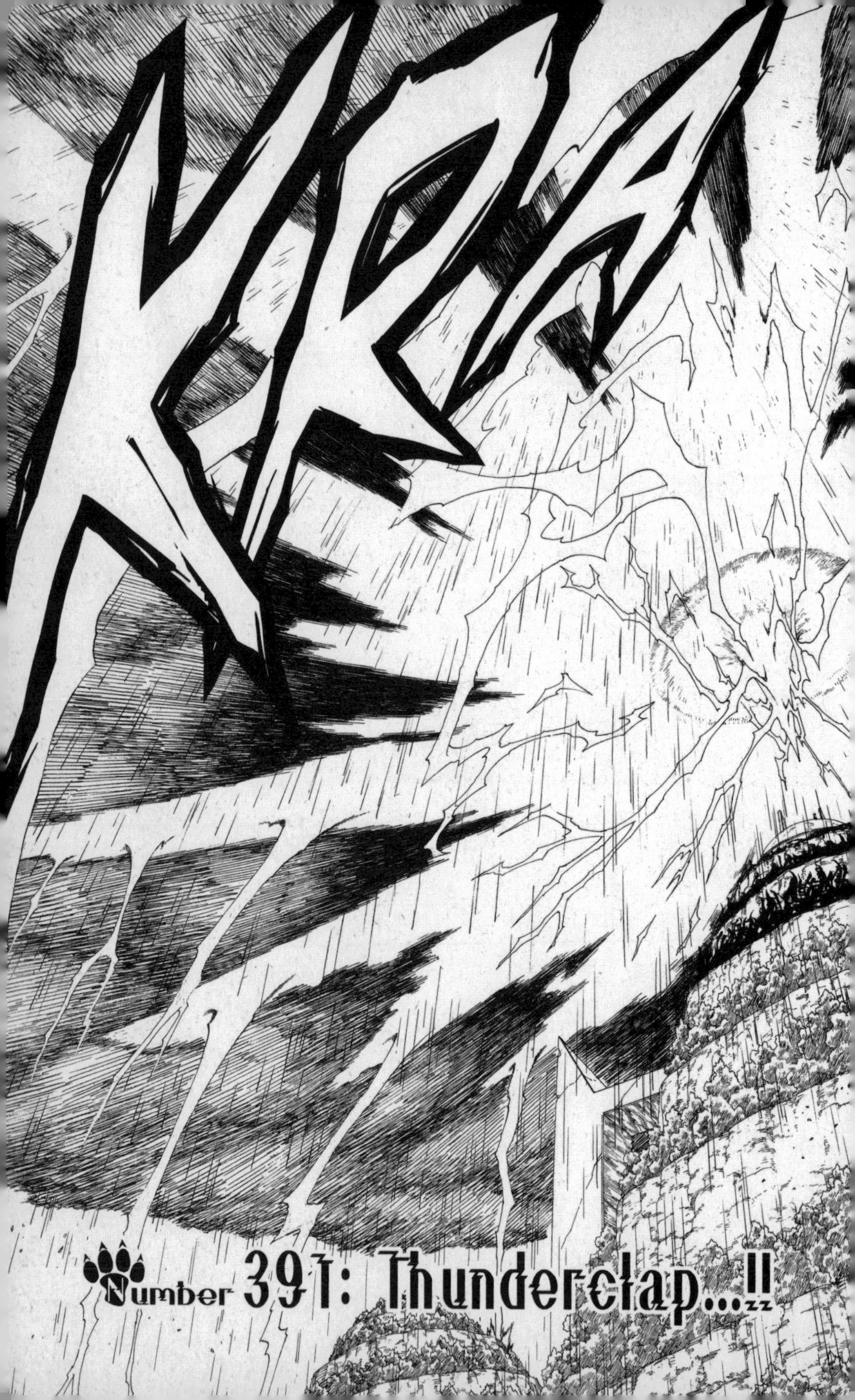

Number 391: Thunderclap...!!

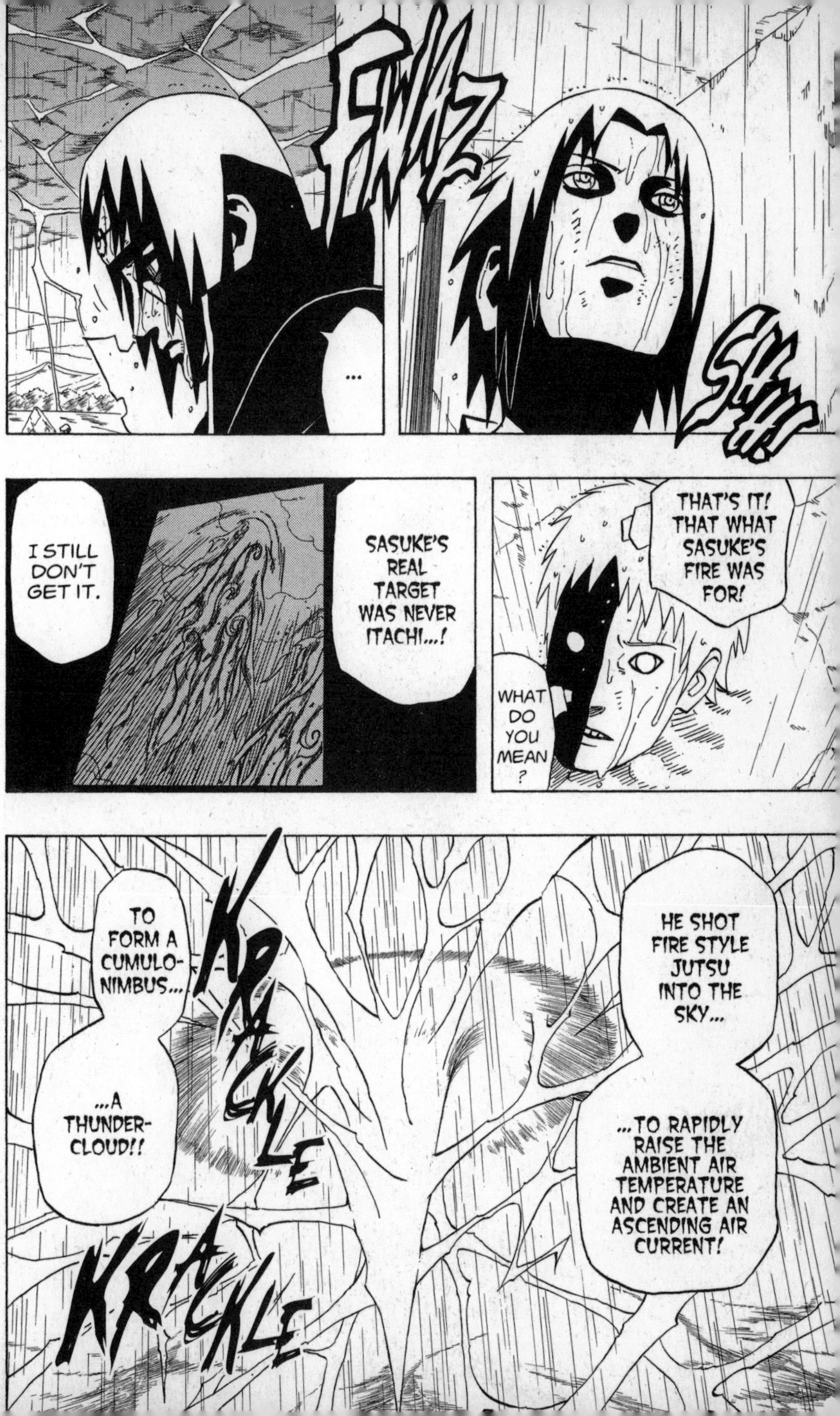
...
THAT'S IT! THAT WHAT SASUKE'S FIRE WAS FOR!
WHAT DO YOU MEAN?
SASUKE'S REAL TARGET WAS NEVER ITACHI...!
I STILL DON'T GET IT.
HE SHOT FIRE STYLE JUTSU INTO THE SKY...
...TO RAPIDLY RAISE THE AMBIENT AIR TEMPERATURE AND CREATE AN ASCENDING AIR CURRENT!
TO FORM A CUMULO-NIMBUS...
...A THUNDER-CLOUD!!
KRACKLE
KRACKLE

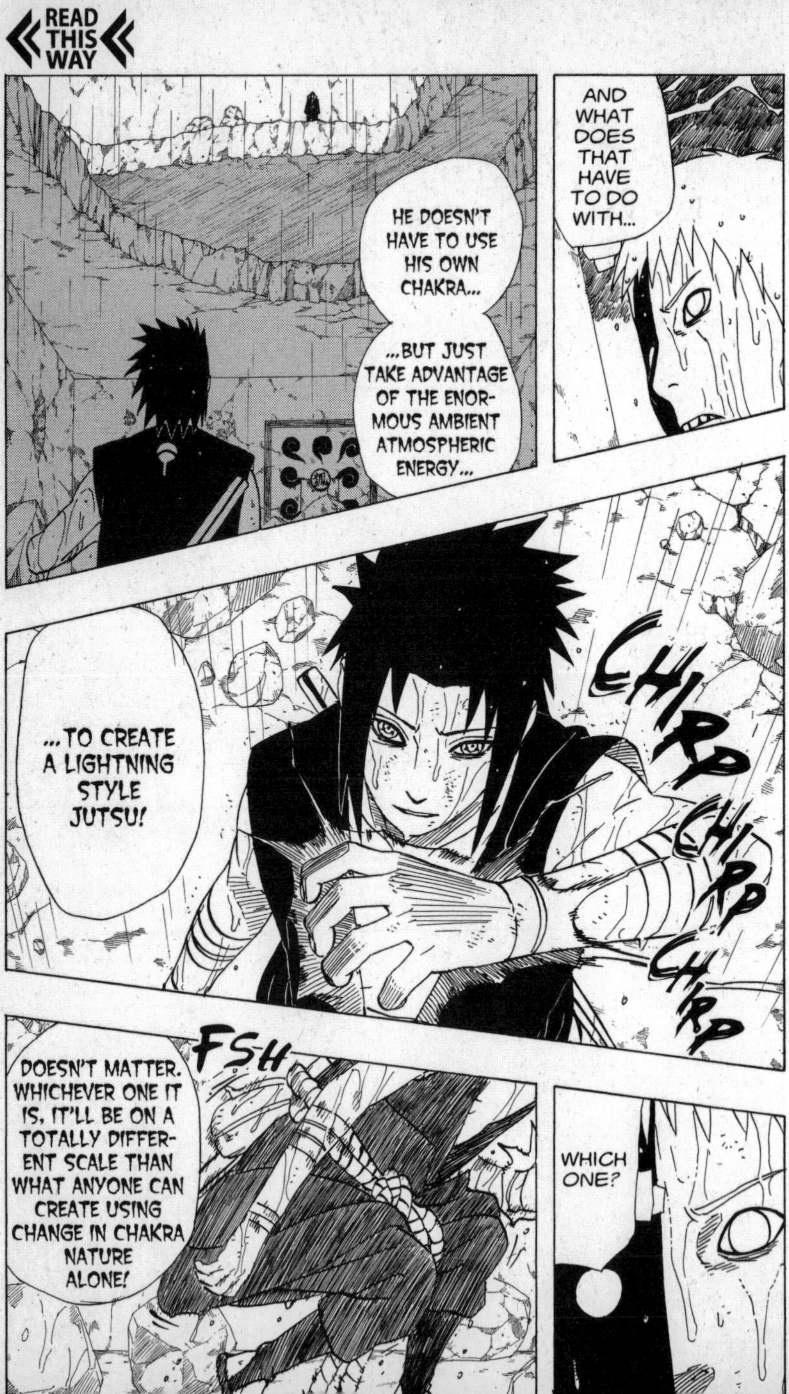
READ THIS WAY
AND WHAT DOES THAT HAVE TO DO WITH...
HE DOESN'T HAVE TO USE HIS OWN CHAKRA...
...BUT JUST TAKE ADVANTAGE OF THE ENORMOUS AMBIENT ATMOSPHERIC ENERGY...
CHIRP CHIRP CHIRP CHIRP
...TO CREATE A LIGHTNING STYLE JUTSU!
WHICH ONE?
FSH
DOESN'T MATTER. WHICHEVER ONE IT IS, IT'LL BE ON A TOTALLY DIFFERENT SCALE THAN WHAT ANYONE CAN CREATE USING CHANGE IN CHAKRA NATURE ALONE!

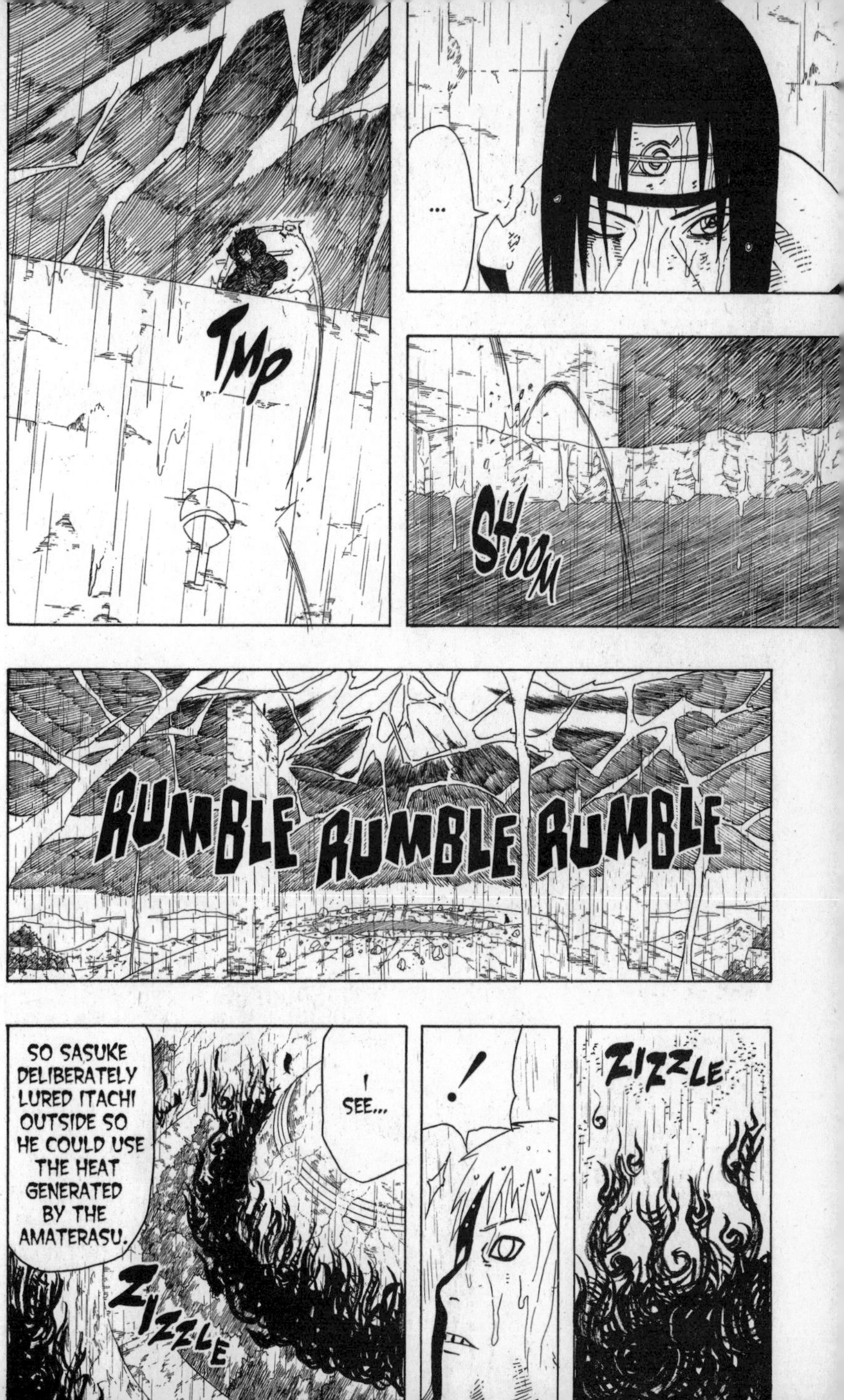
...
SHOOM
TMP
RUMBLE RUMBLE RUMBLE
ZIZZLE
!
I SEE...
SO SASUKE DELIBERATELY LURED ITACHI OUTSIDE SO HE COULD USE THE HEAT GENERATED BY THE AMATERASU.
ZIZZLE

READ THIS WAY

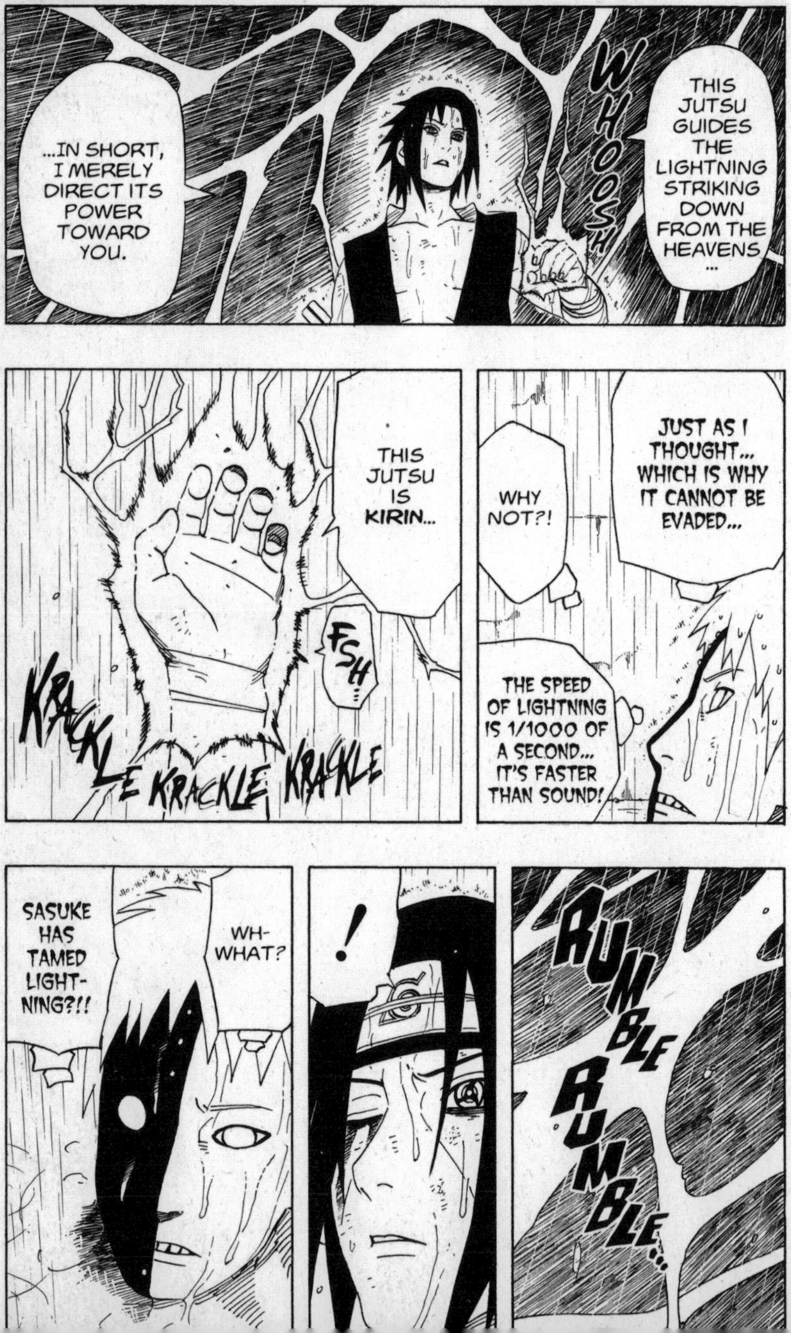
THIS JUTSU GUIDES THE LIGHTNING STRIKING DOWN FROM THE HEAVENS ...
WHOOOSH
...IN SHORT, I MERELY DIRECT ITS POWER TOWARD YOU.
JUST AS I THOUGHT... WHICH IS WHY IT CANNOT BE EVADED...
WHY NOT?!
THE SPEED OF LIGHTNING IS 1/1000 OF A SECOND... IT'S FASTER THAN SOUND!
THIS JUTSU IS KIRIN...
FSH
KRACKLE KRACKLE KRACKLE
RUMBLE RUMBLE...
!
WH- WHAT?
SASUKE HAS TAMED LIGHT- NING?!!

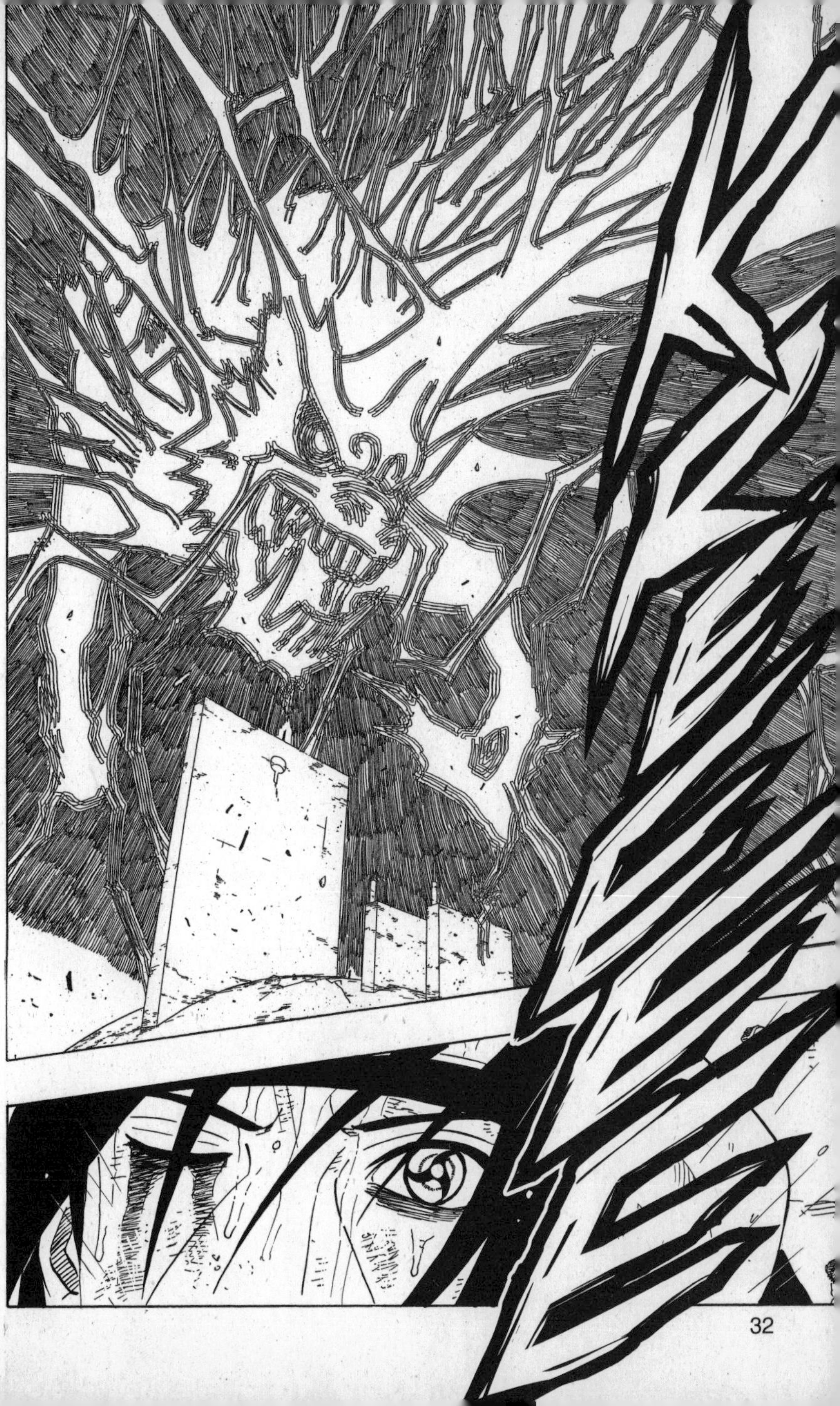

READ THIS WAY

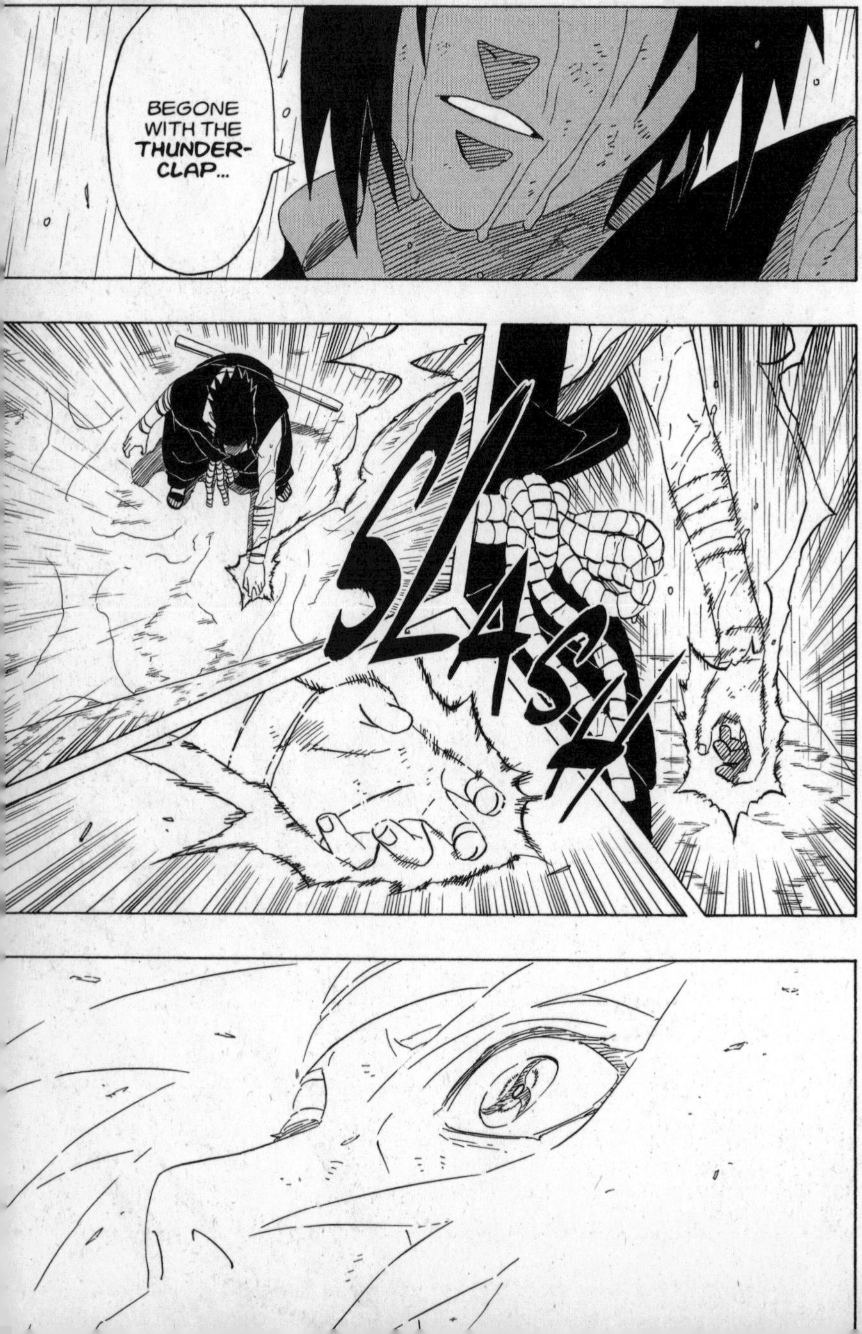
BEGONE WITH THE THUNDER-CLAP...
SLASH

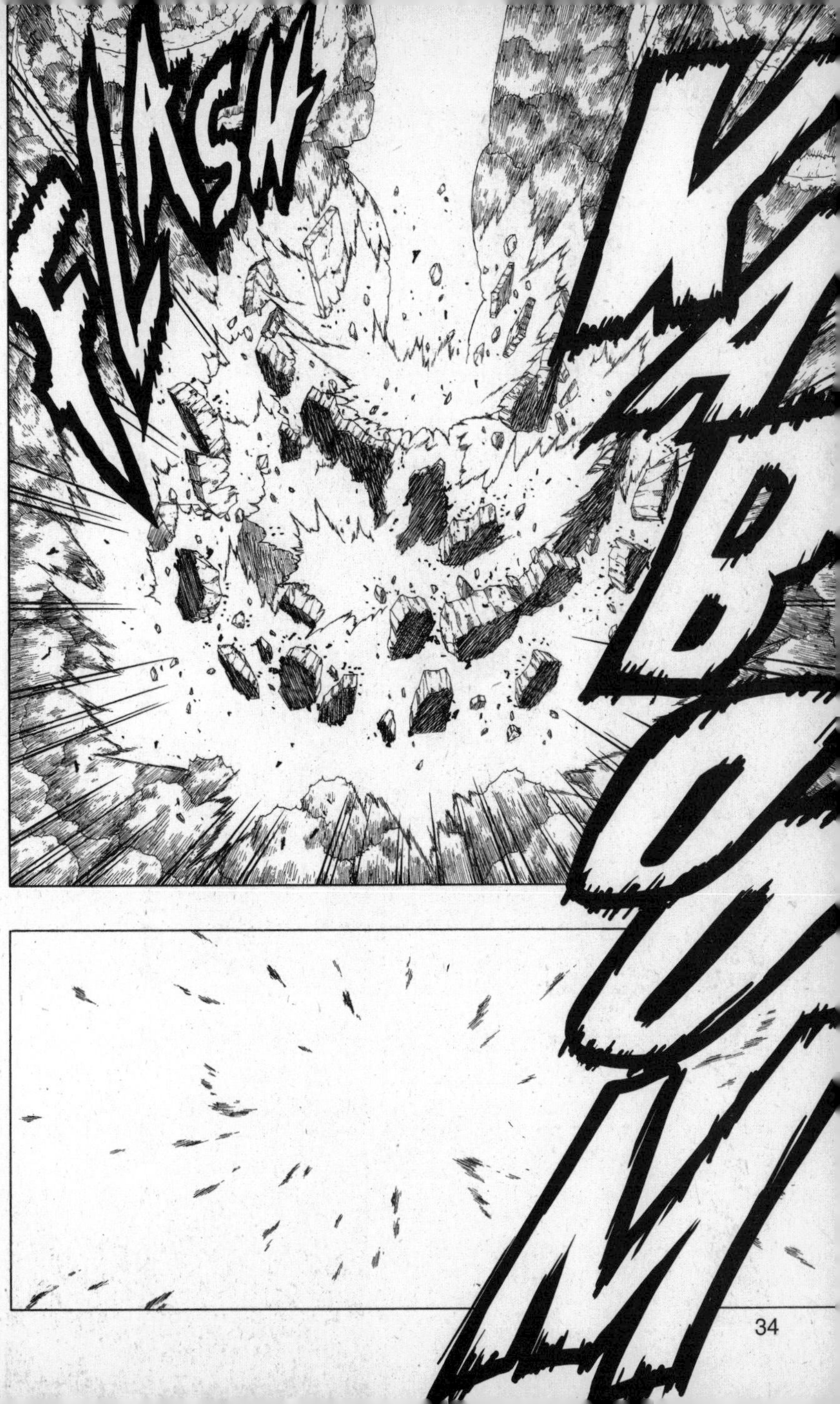
KABOOM
SLASH

READ THIS WAY

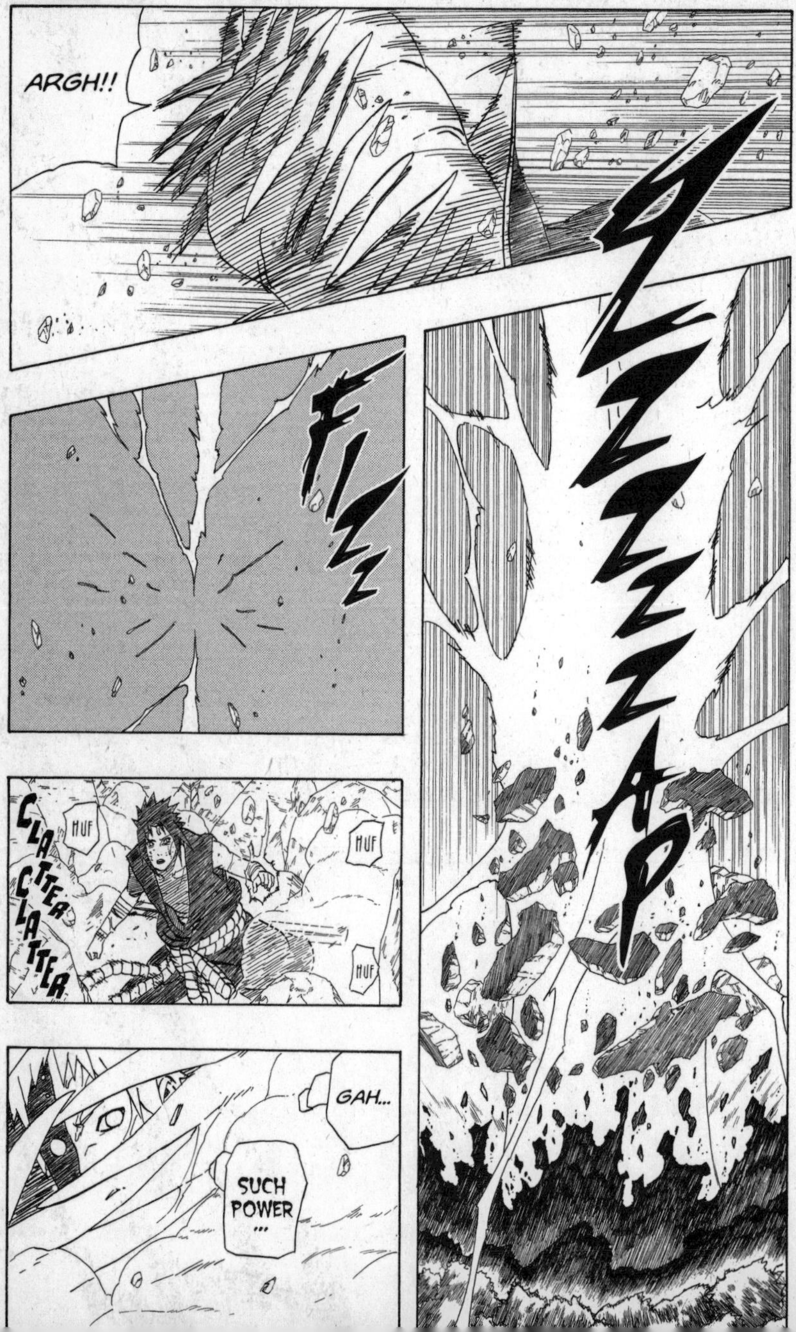

ARGH!!
FIZZZ
HUF
HUF
HUF
CLATTER CLATTER
GAH...
SUCH POWER...

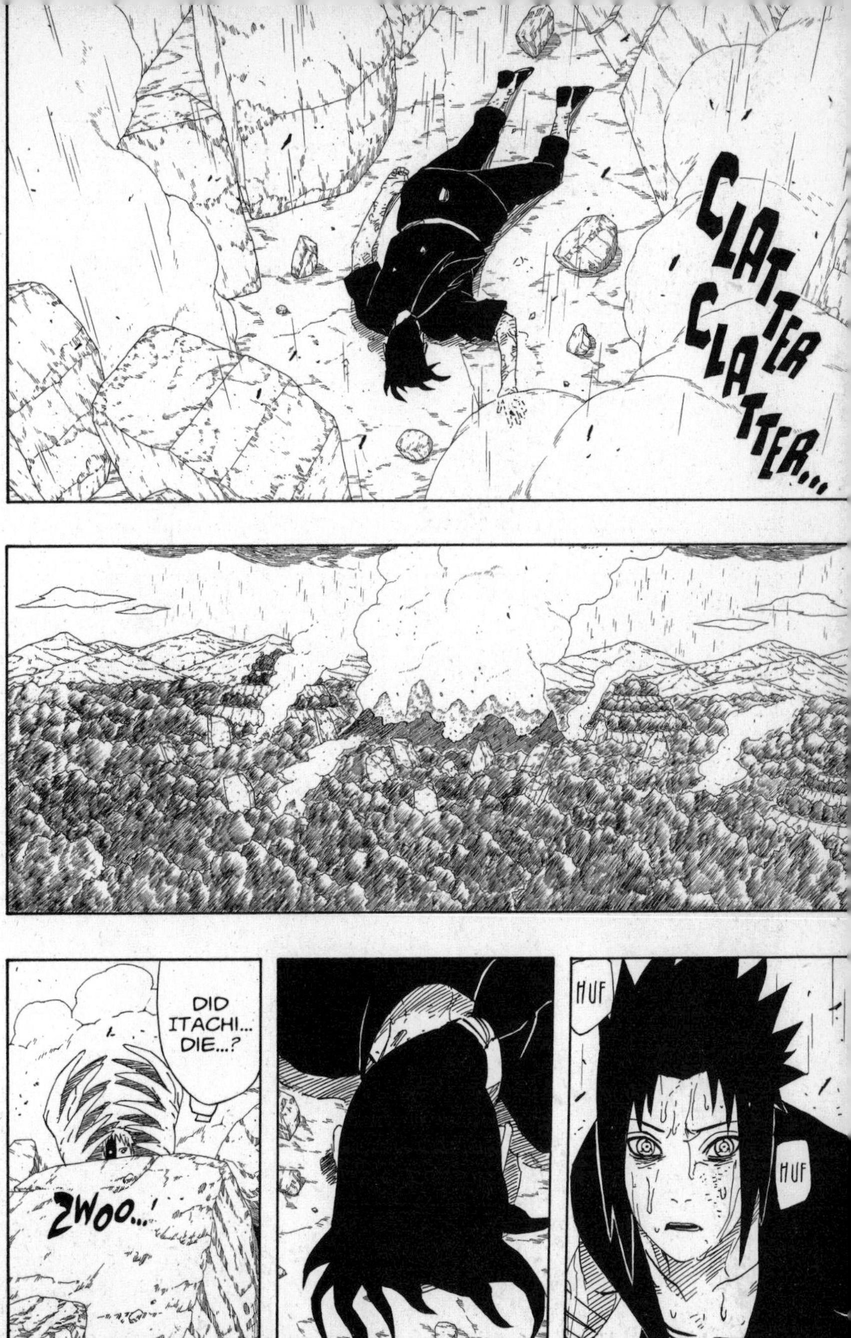
CLATTER CLATTER...
HUF
HUF
DID ITACHI... DIE...?
ZWOO...!

READ THIS WAY

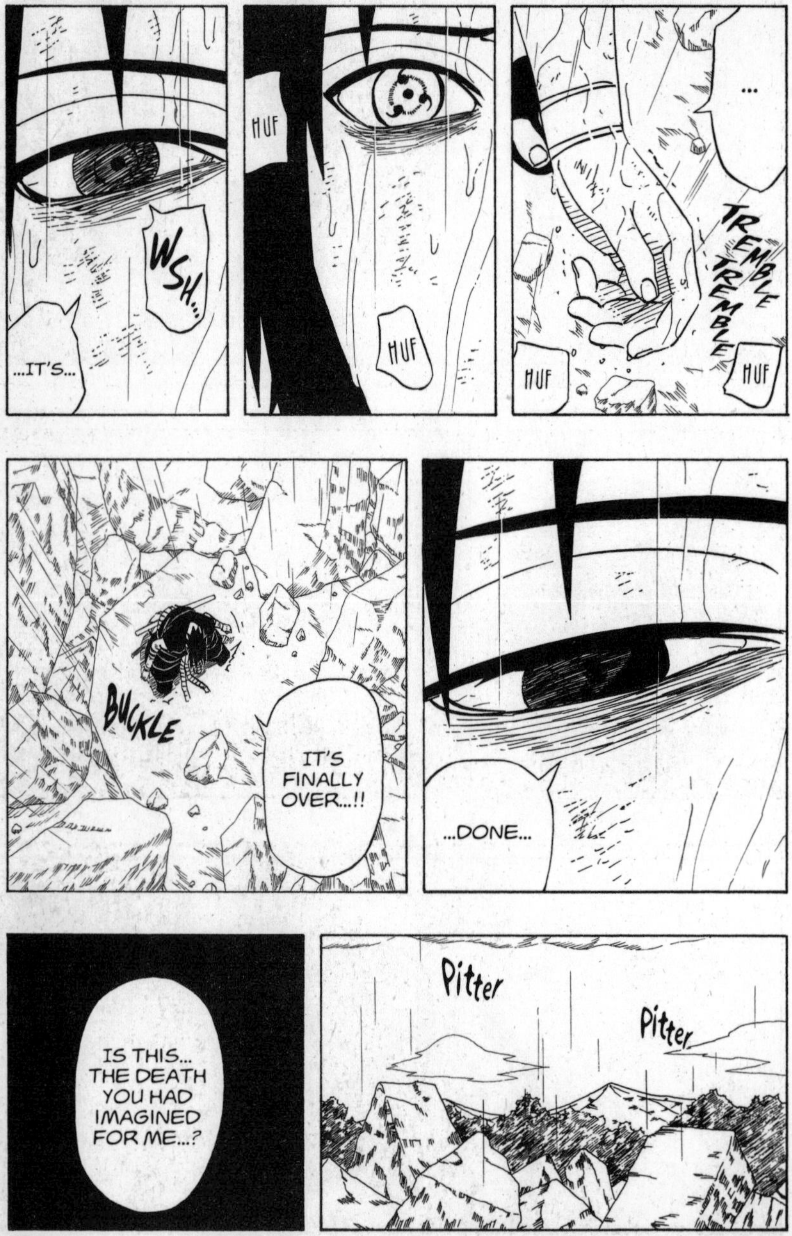
...
TREMBLE TREMBLE
HUF
HUF
HUF
HUF
WSH...
...IT'S...
...DONE...
BUCKLE
IT'S FINALLY OVER...!!
Pitter
Pitter
IS THIS... THE DEATH YOU HAD IMAGINED FOR ME...?

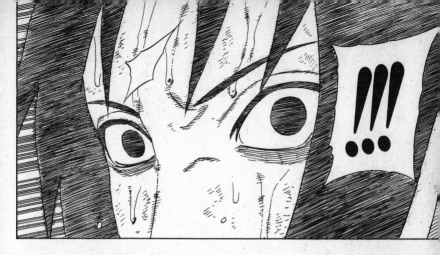

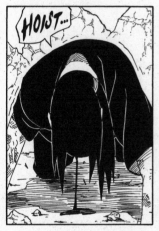

HOIST...

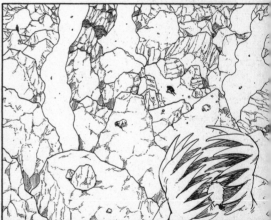

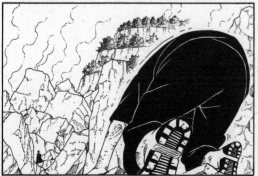

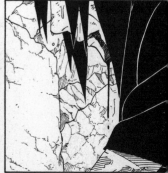

38

READ THIS WAY

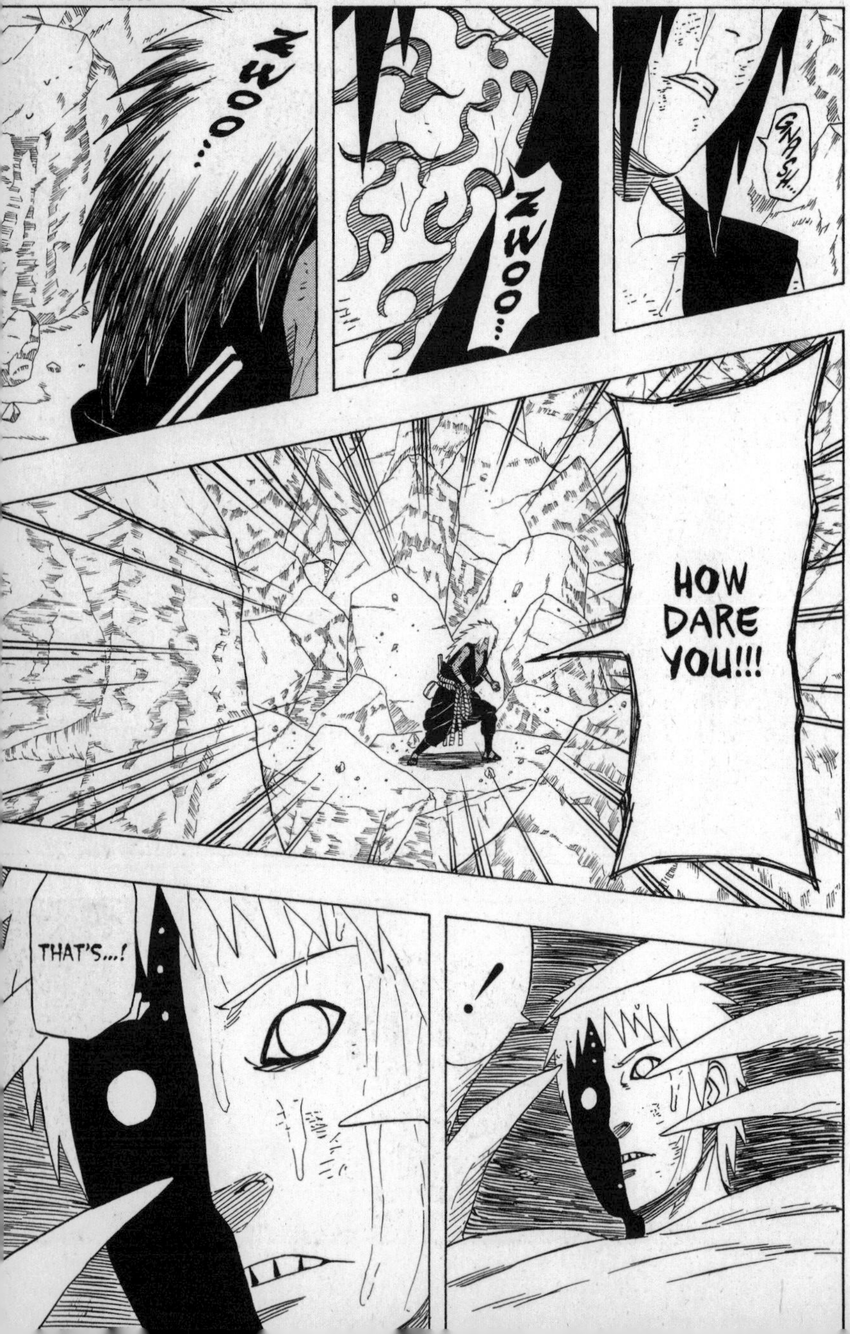
GNASH...
ZWOO...
ZWOO...
HOW DARE YOU!!!
!
THAT'S...!

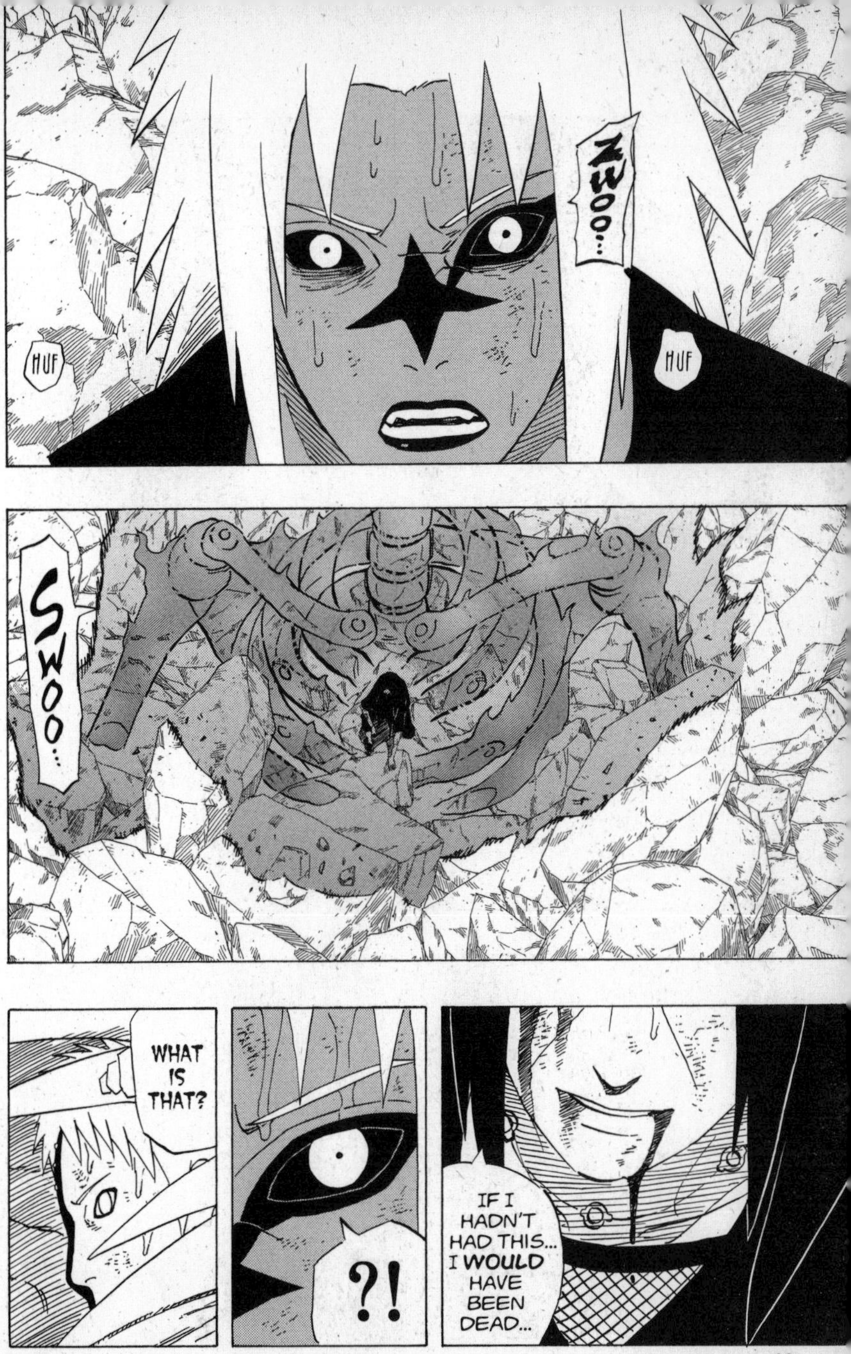
ZWOO...
HUF
HUF
SWOO...
IF I HADN'T HAD THIS... I WOULD HAVE BEEN DEAD...
?!
WHAT IS THAT?

READ THIS WAY

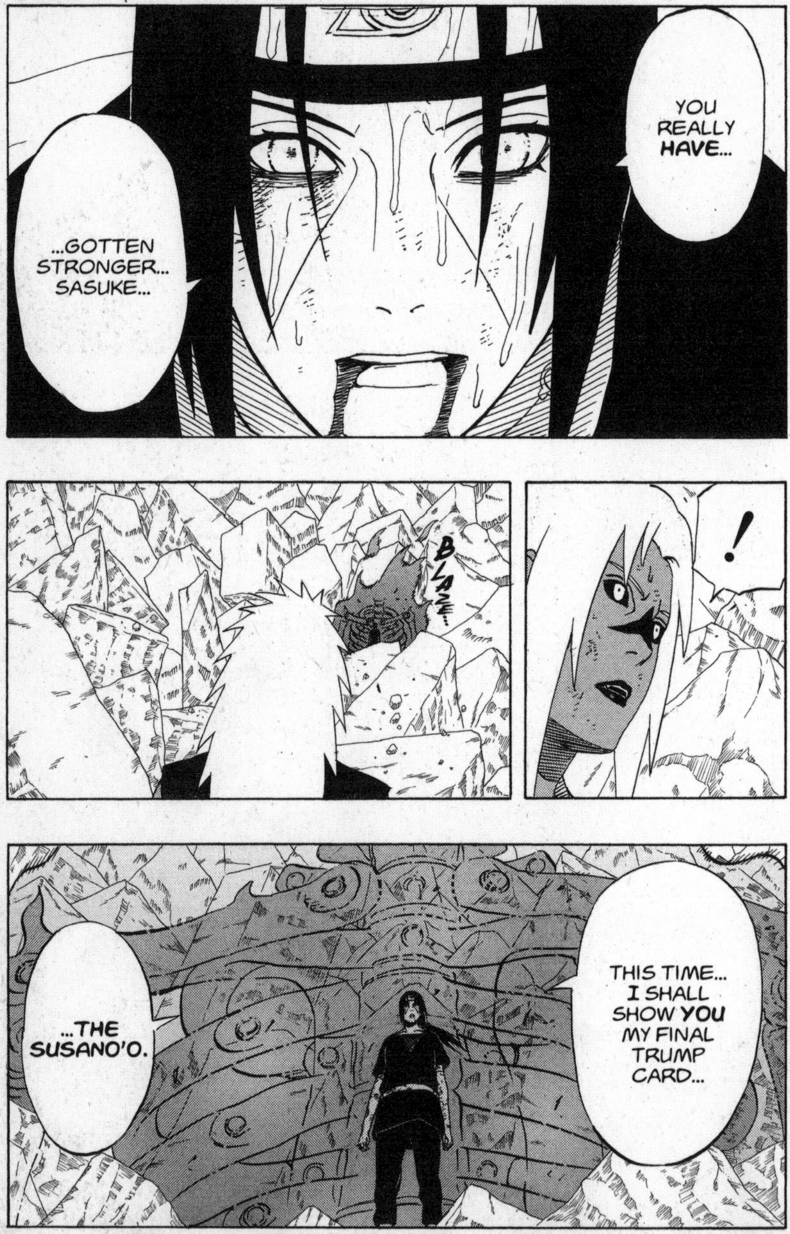
YOU REALLY HAVE...
...GOTTEN STRONGER... SASUKE...
!
BLAZE...
THIS TIME... I SHALL SHOW YOU MY FINAL TRUMP CARD...
...THE SUSANO'O.

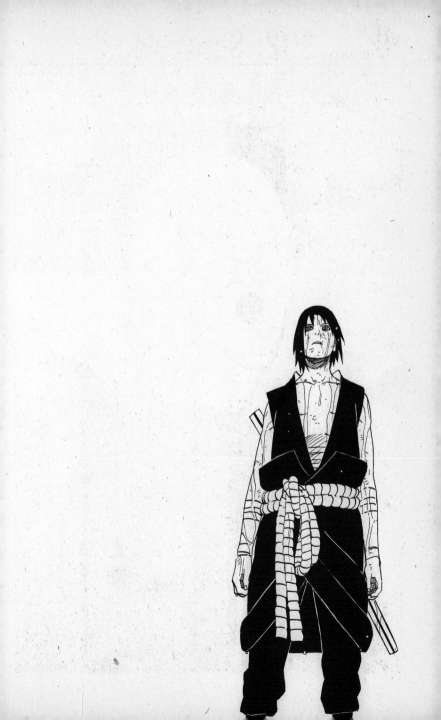

Number 392: Susano'o...!!

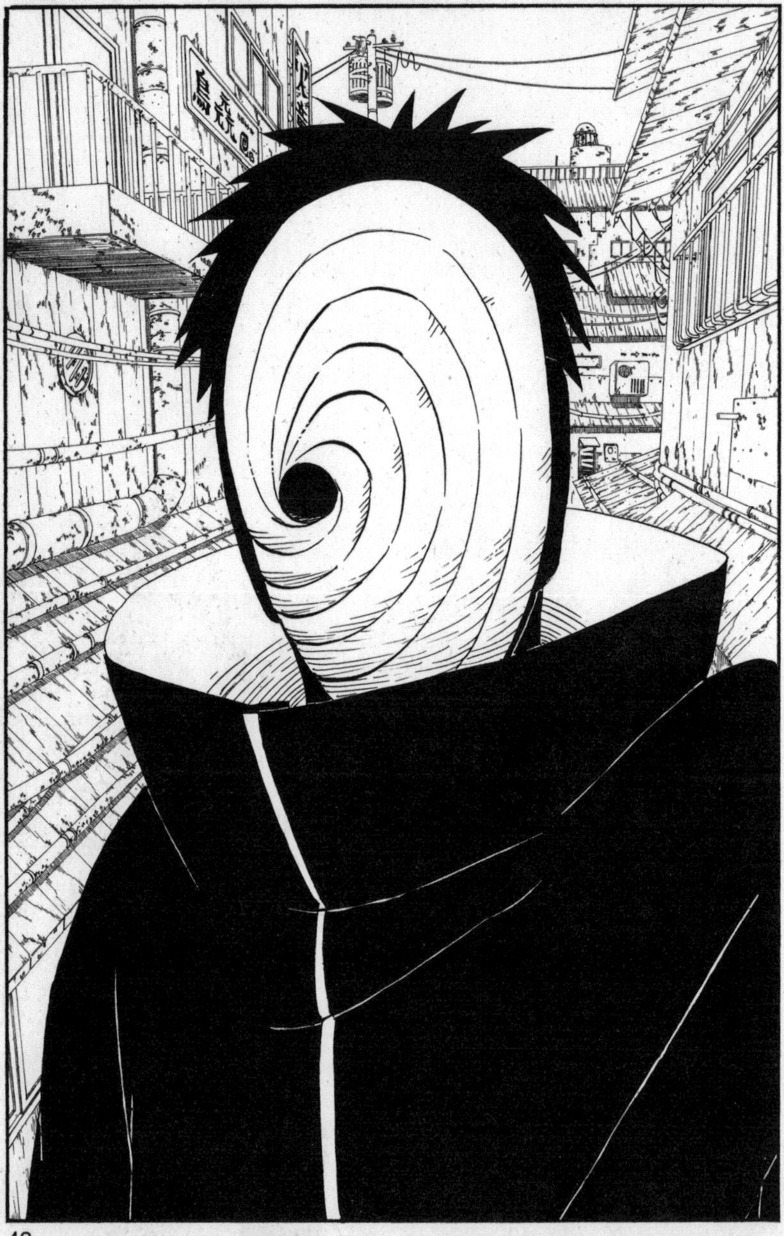

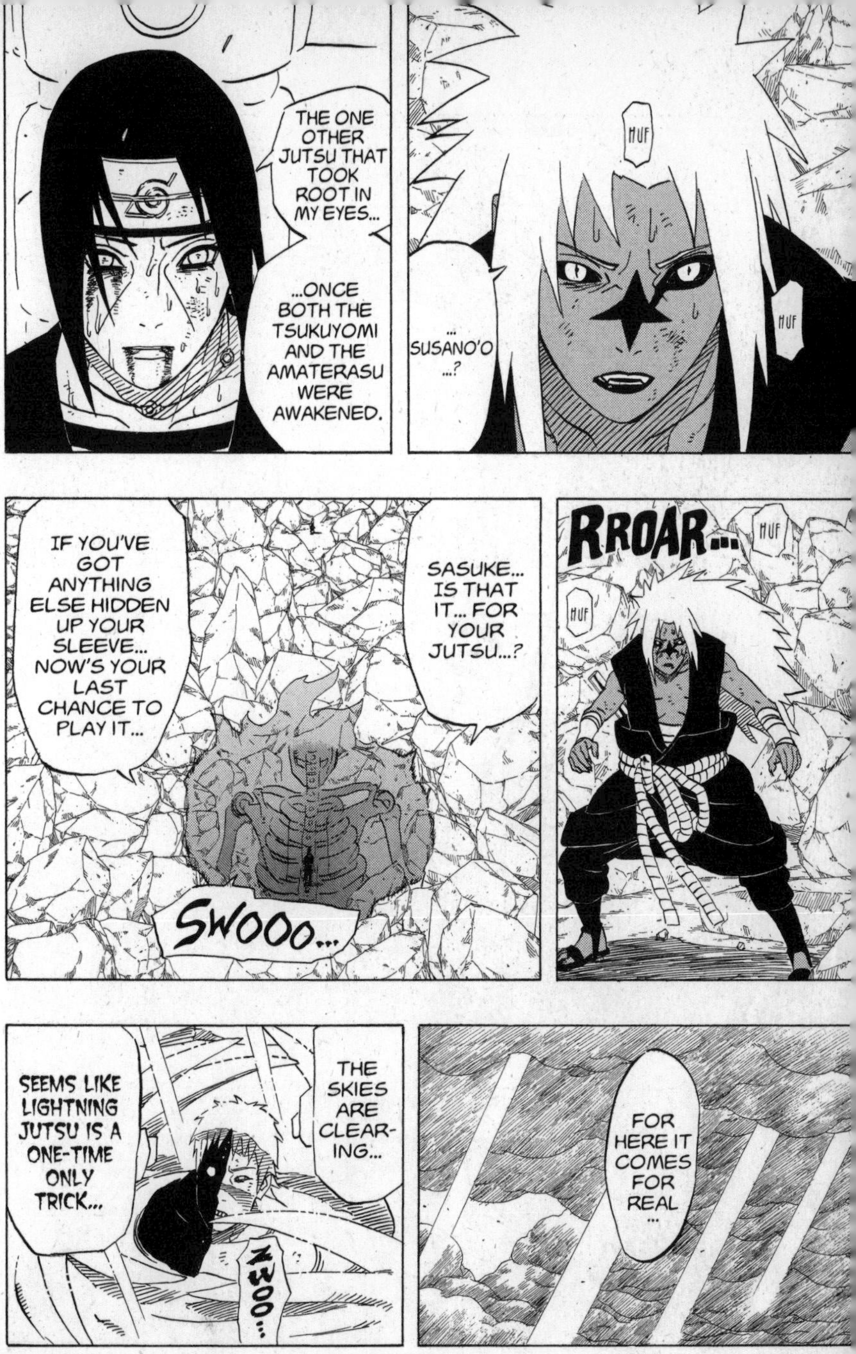
HUF
HUF
...SUSANO'O...?
THE ONE OTHER JUTSU THAT TOOK ROOT IN MY EYES...
...ONCE BOTH THE TSUKUYOMI AND THE AMATERASU WERE AWAKENED.
RROAR...
HUF
HUF
SASUKE... IS THAT IT... FOR YOUR JUTSU...?
IF YOU'VE GOT ANYTHING ELSE HIDDEN UP YOUR SLEEVE... NOW'S YOUR LAST CHANCE TO PLAY IT...
SWOOO...
FOR HERE IT COMES FOR REAL...
THE SKIES ARE CLEAR-ING...
SEEMS LIKE LIGHTNING JUTSU IS A ONE-TIME ONLY TRICK...
ZWOOO...

READ THIS WAY

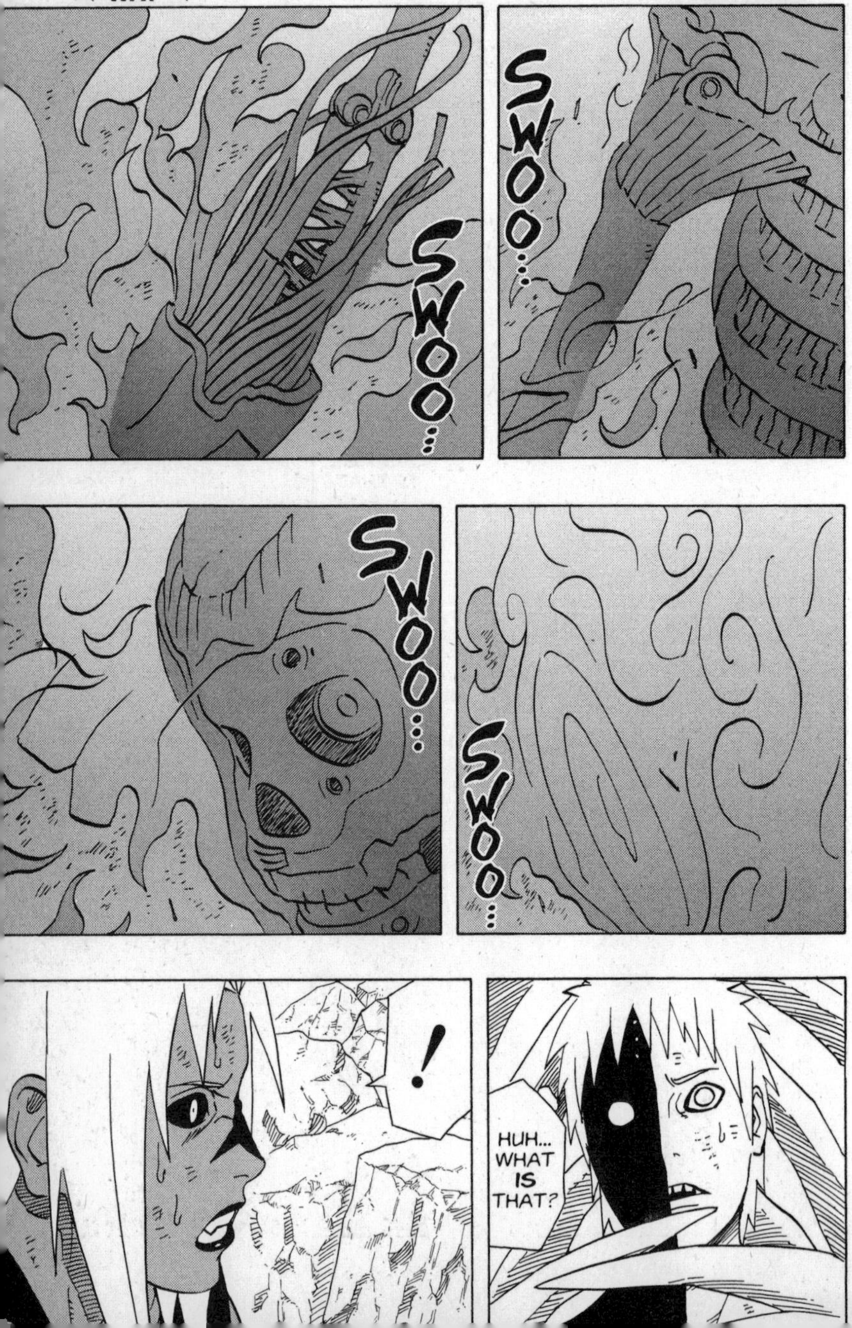
SWOOO...
SWOOO...
SWOO...
SWOOO...
HUH... WHAT IS THAT?
!

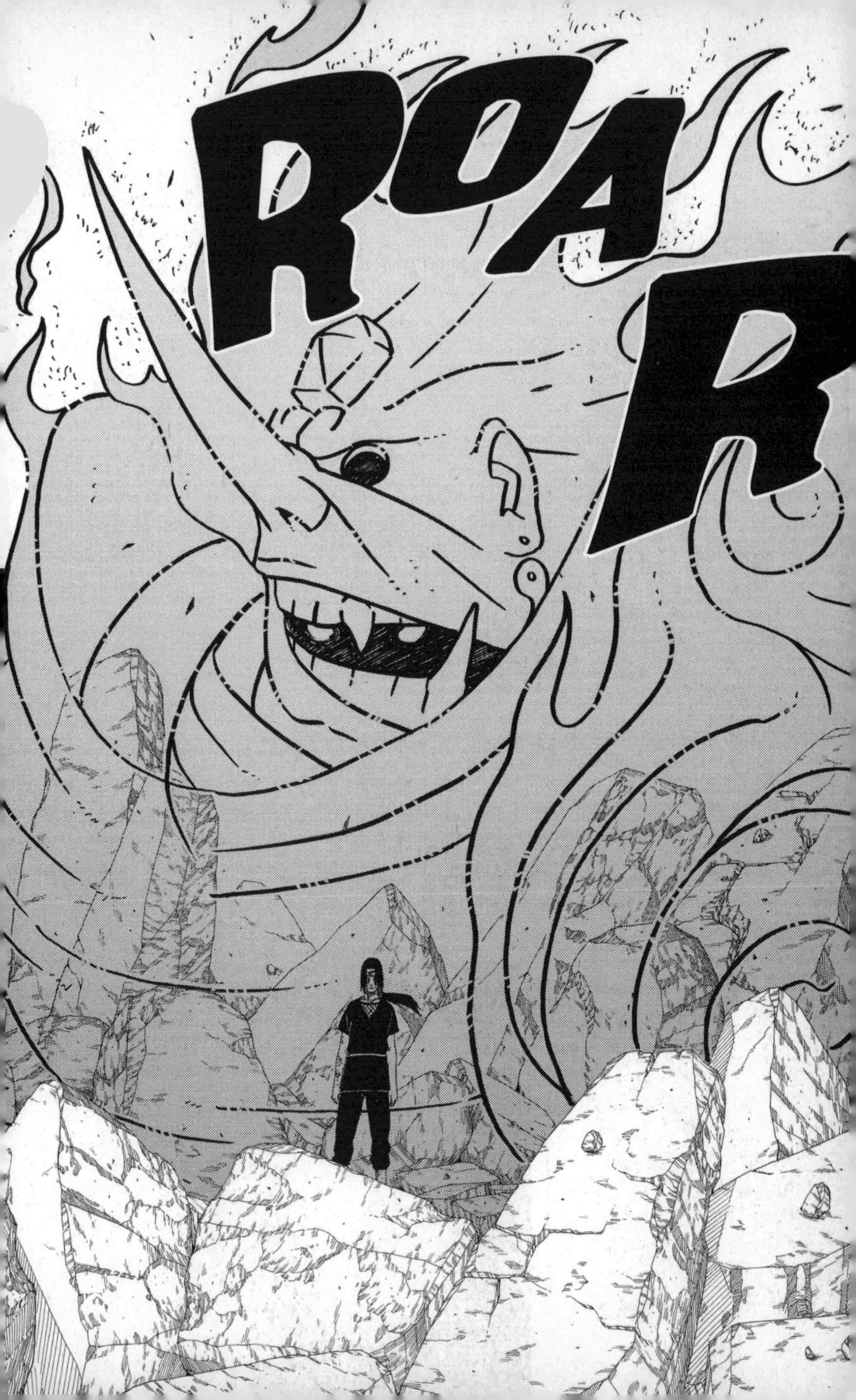
ROAR

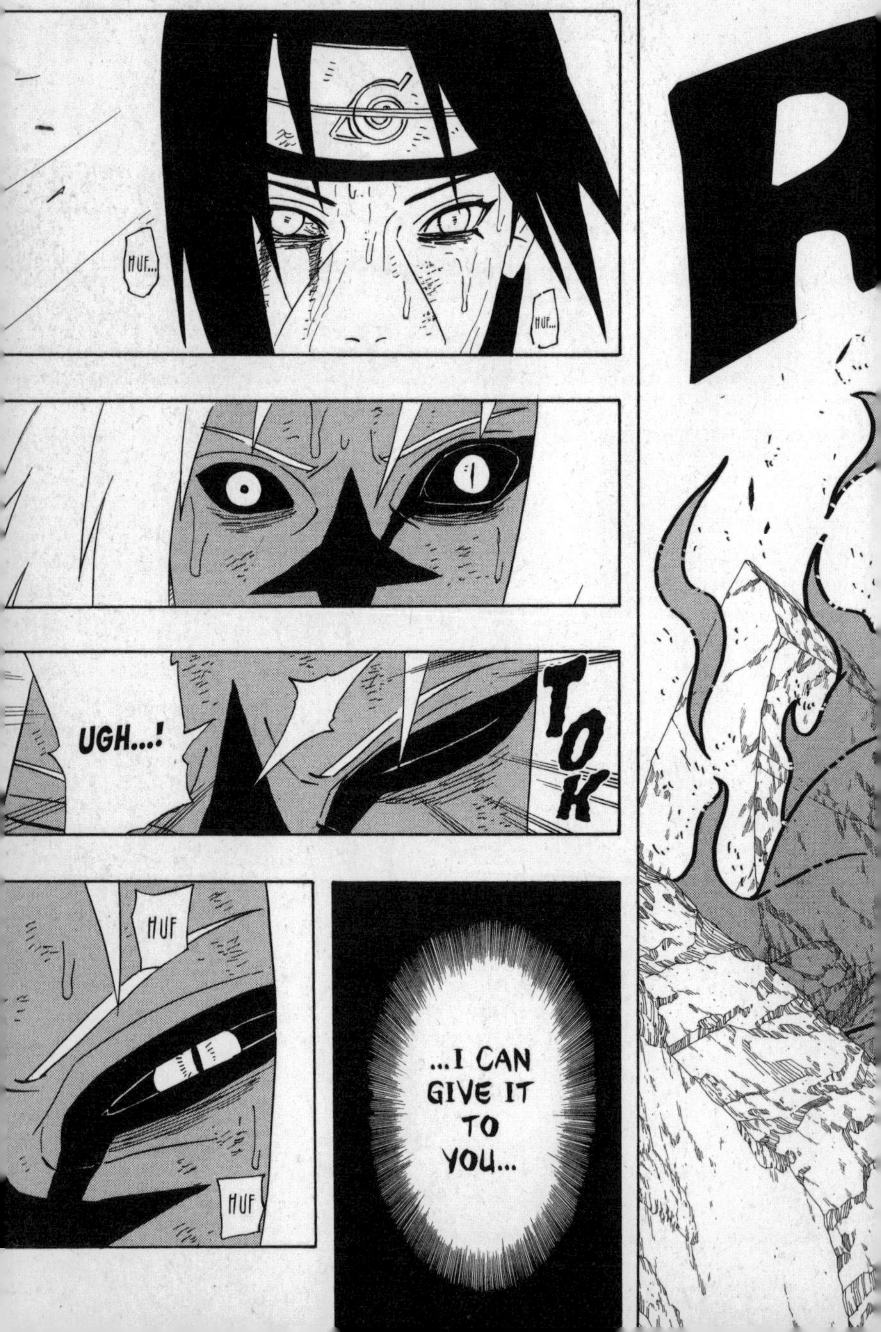
HUF...
HUF...
TOK
UGH...!
...I CAN GIVE IT TO YOU...
HUF
HUF

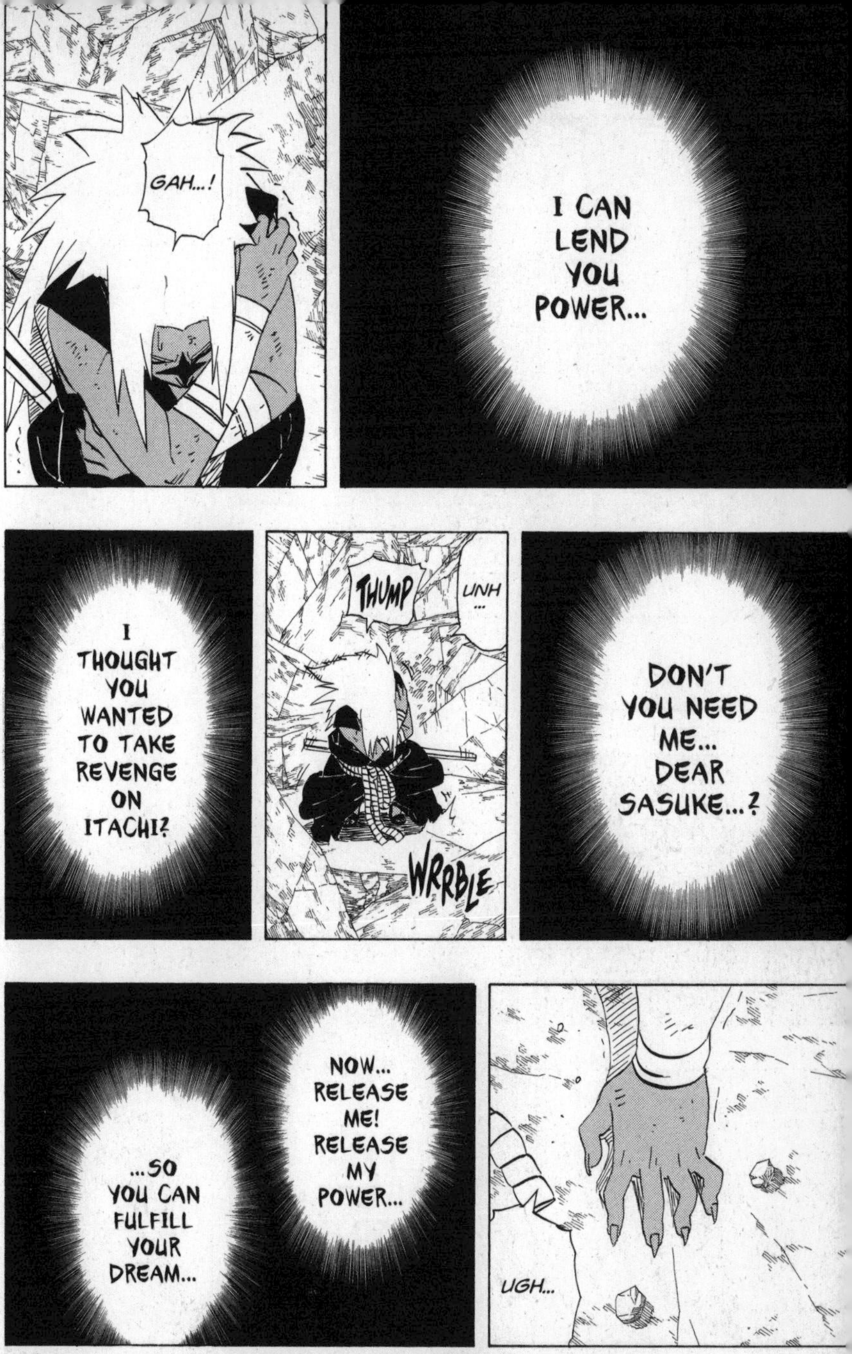
I CAN LEND YOU POWER...
GAH...!
DON'T YOU NEED ME... DEAR SASUKE...?
UNH...
THUMP
WRRBLE
I THOUGHT YOU WANTED TO TAKE REVENGE ON ITACHI?
UGH...
NOW... RELEASE ME! RELEASE MY POWER...
...SO YOU CAN FULFILL YOUR DREAM...

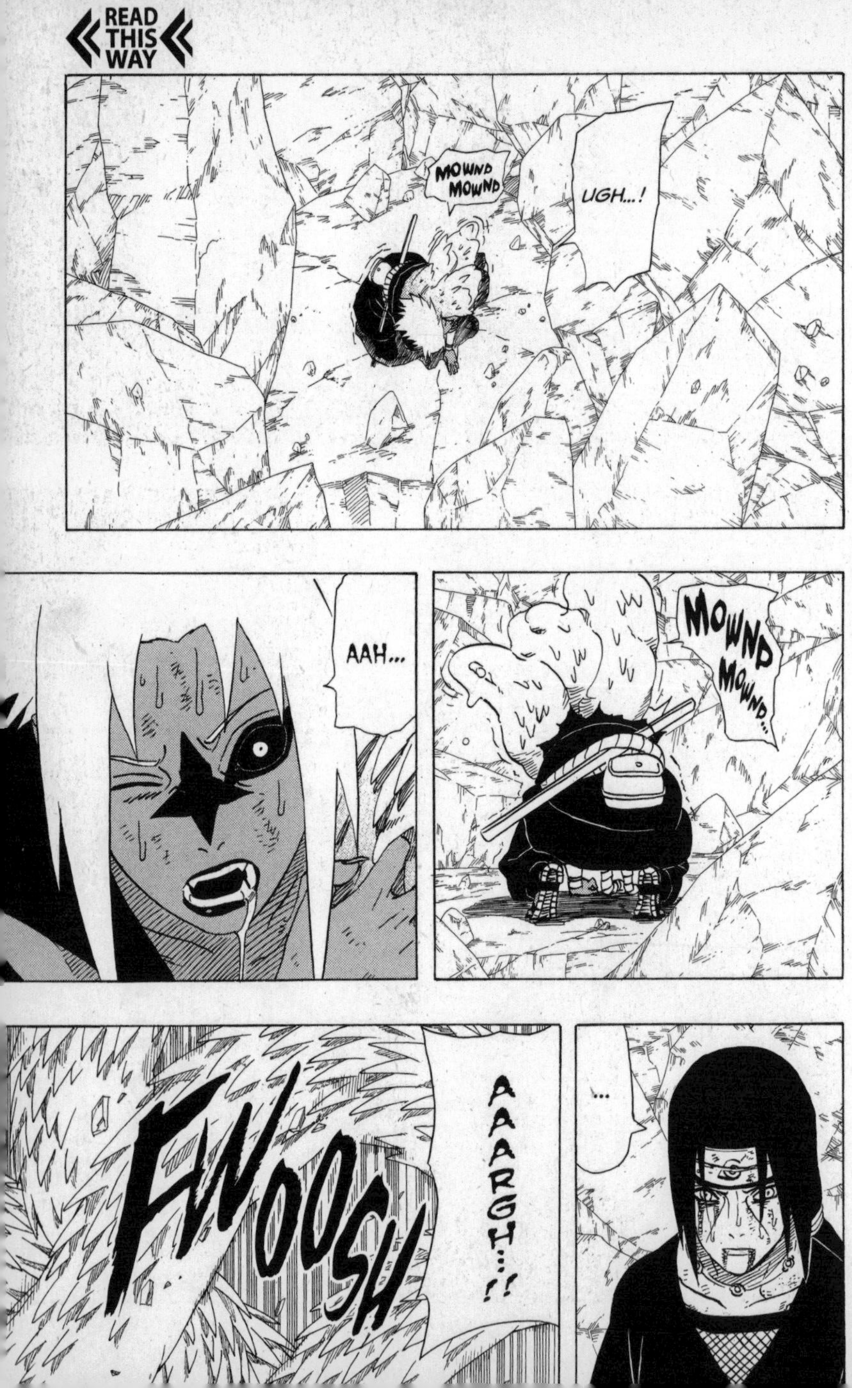
READ THIS WAY
UGH...!
MOWND MOWND
MOWND MOWND...
AAH...
...
AAARGH...!!
FWOOSH

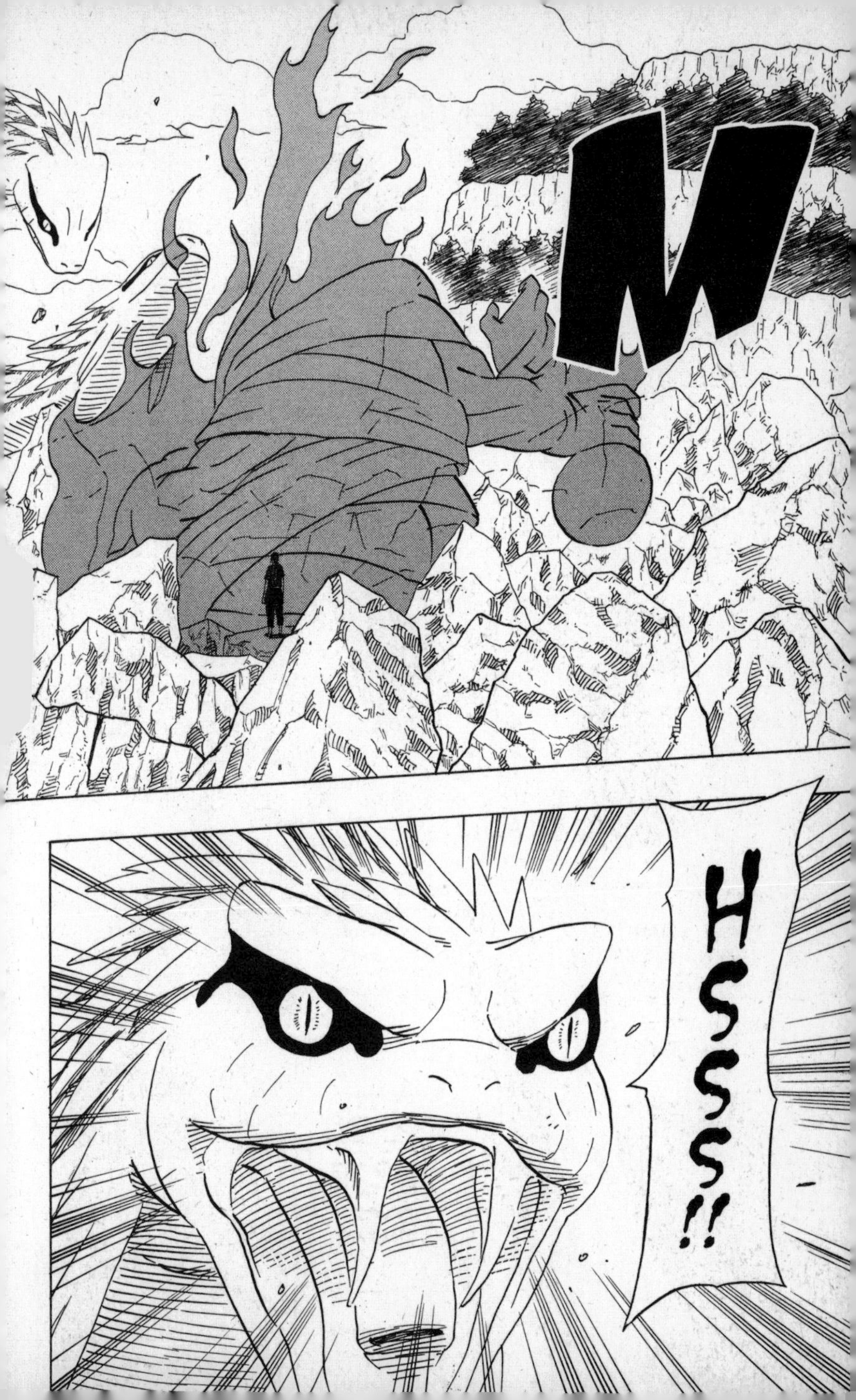
M
HSSS!!

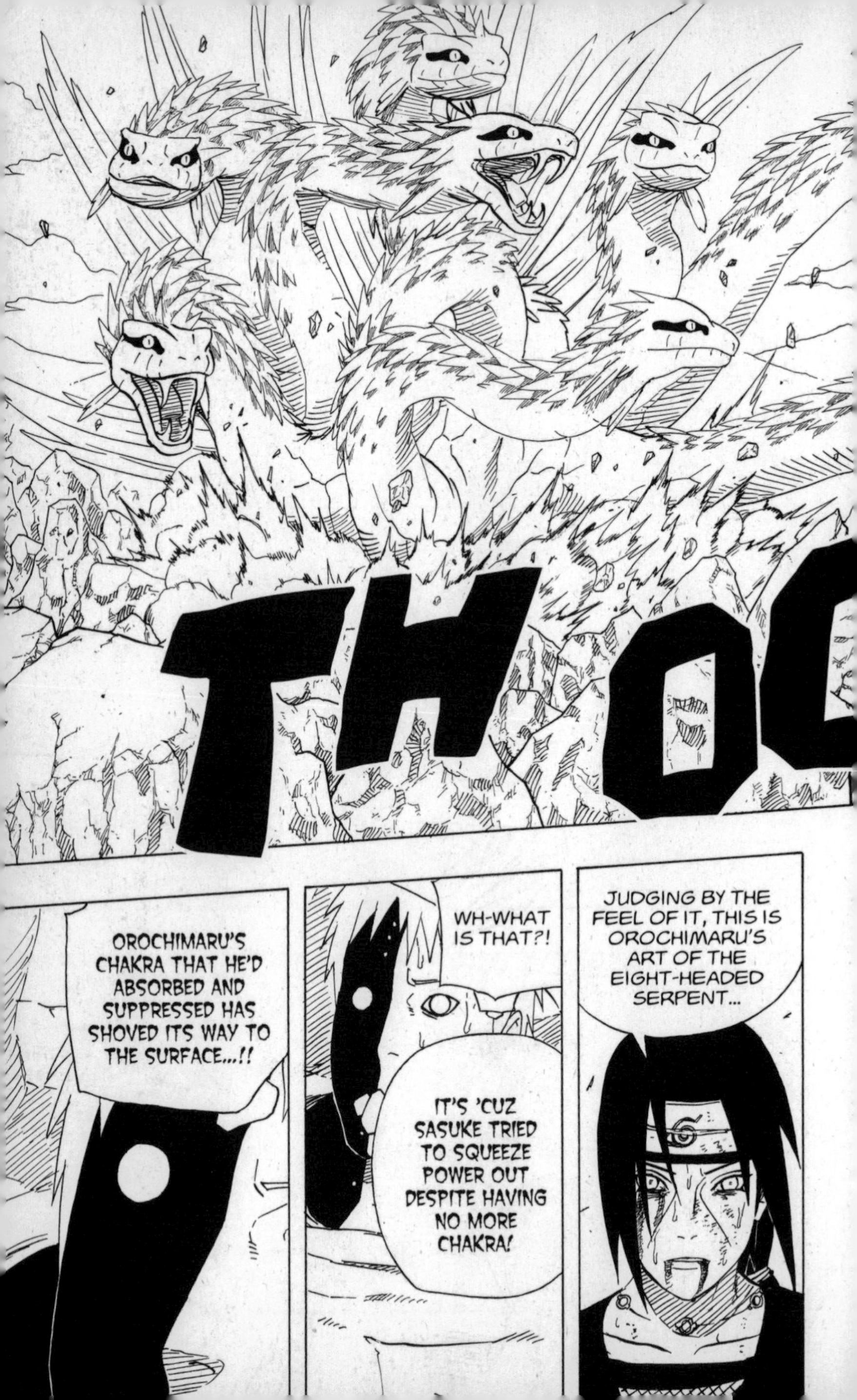
THO
JUDGING BY THE FEEL OF IT, THIS IS OROCHIMARU'S ART OF THE EIGHT-HEADED SERPENT...
WH-WHAT IS THAT?!
IT'S 'CUZ SASUKE TRIED TO SQUEEZE POWER OUT DESPITE HAVING NO MORE CHAKRA!
OROCHIMARU'S CHAKRA THAT HE'D ABSORBED AND SUPPRESSED HAS SHOVED ITS WAY TO THE SURFACE...!!

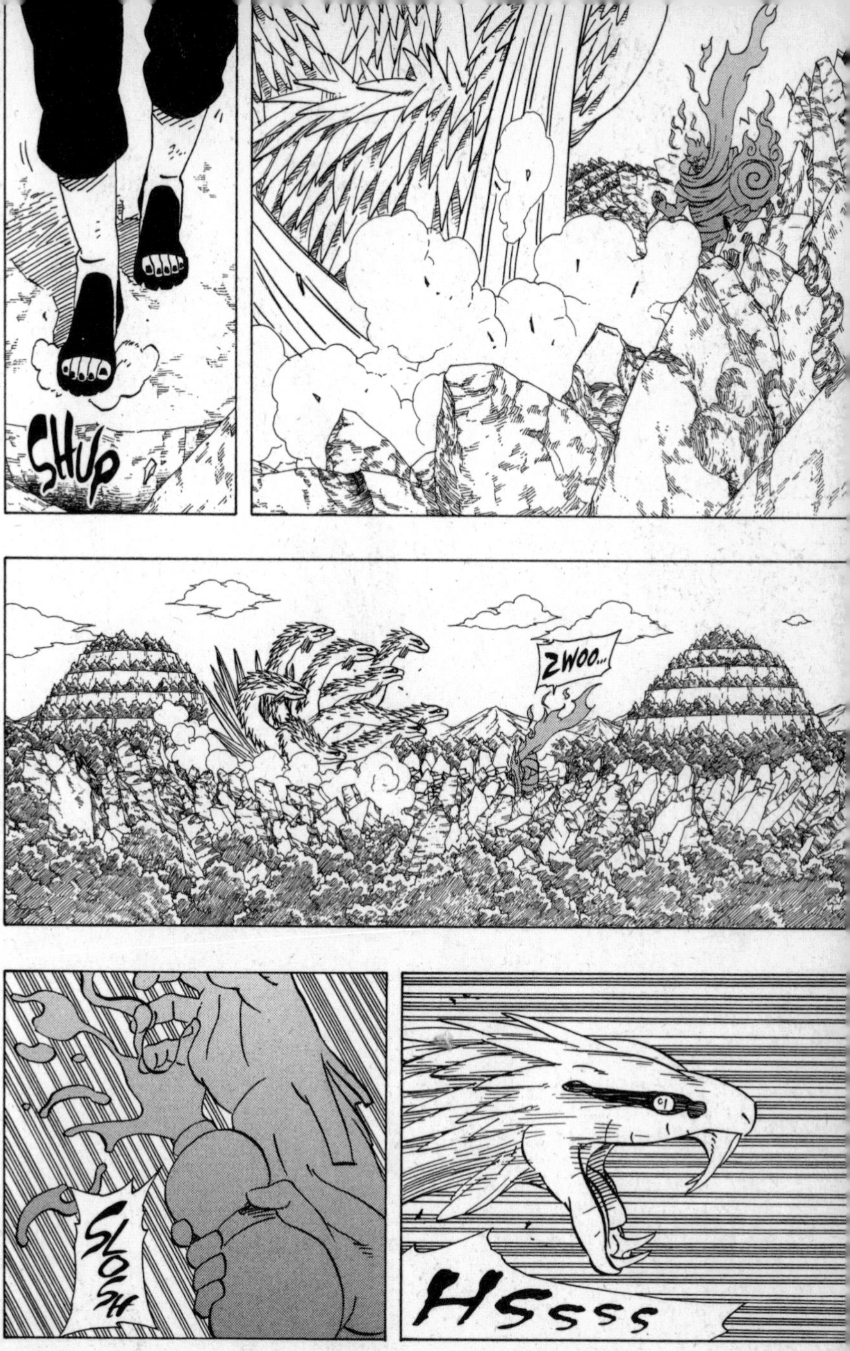
SHUP
ZWOO...
HSSSS
SLOSH

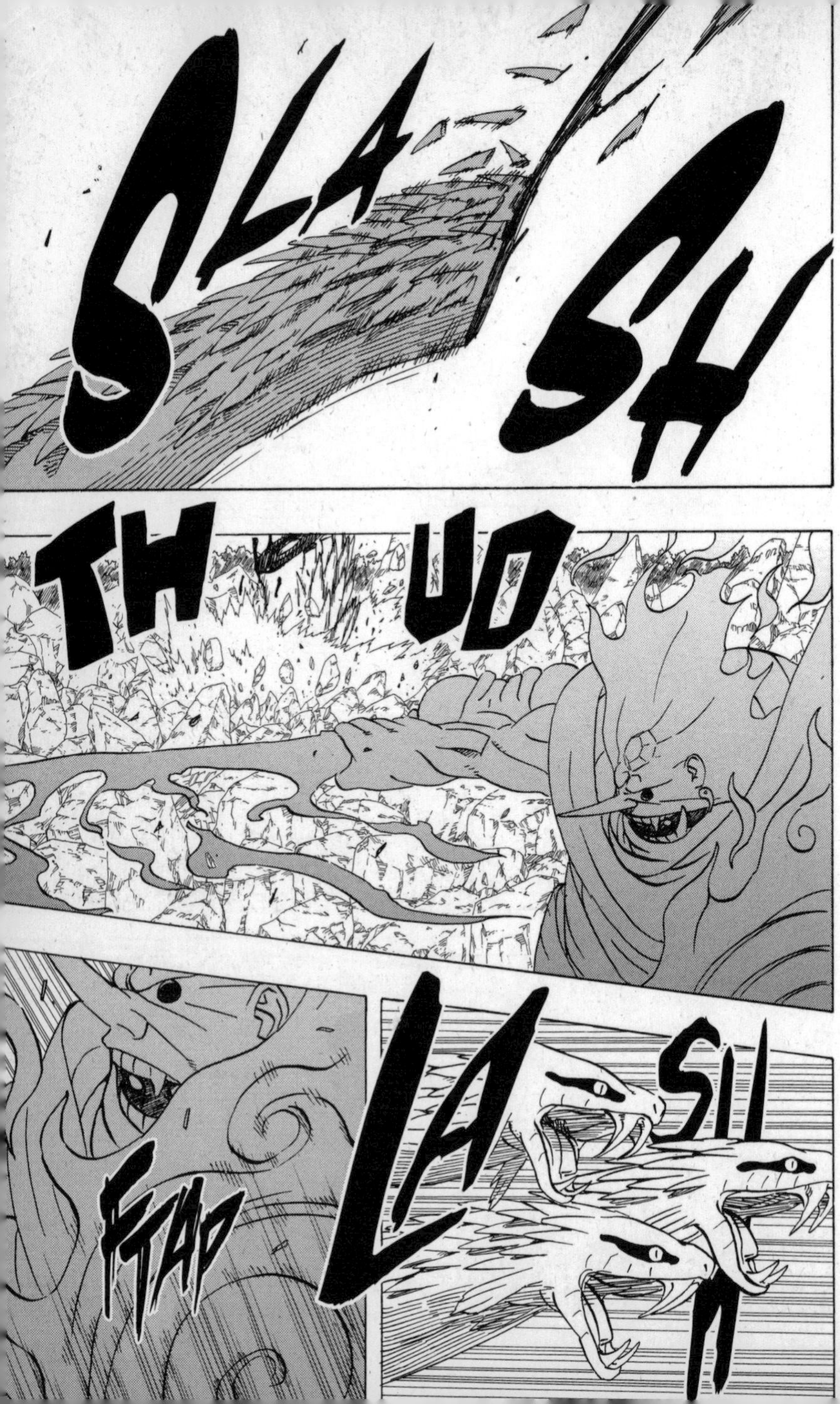
SLAASH
THUD

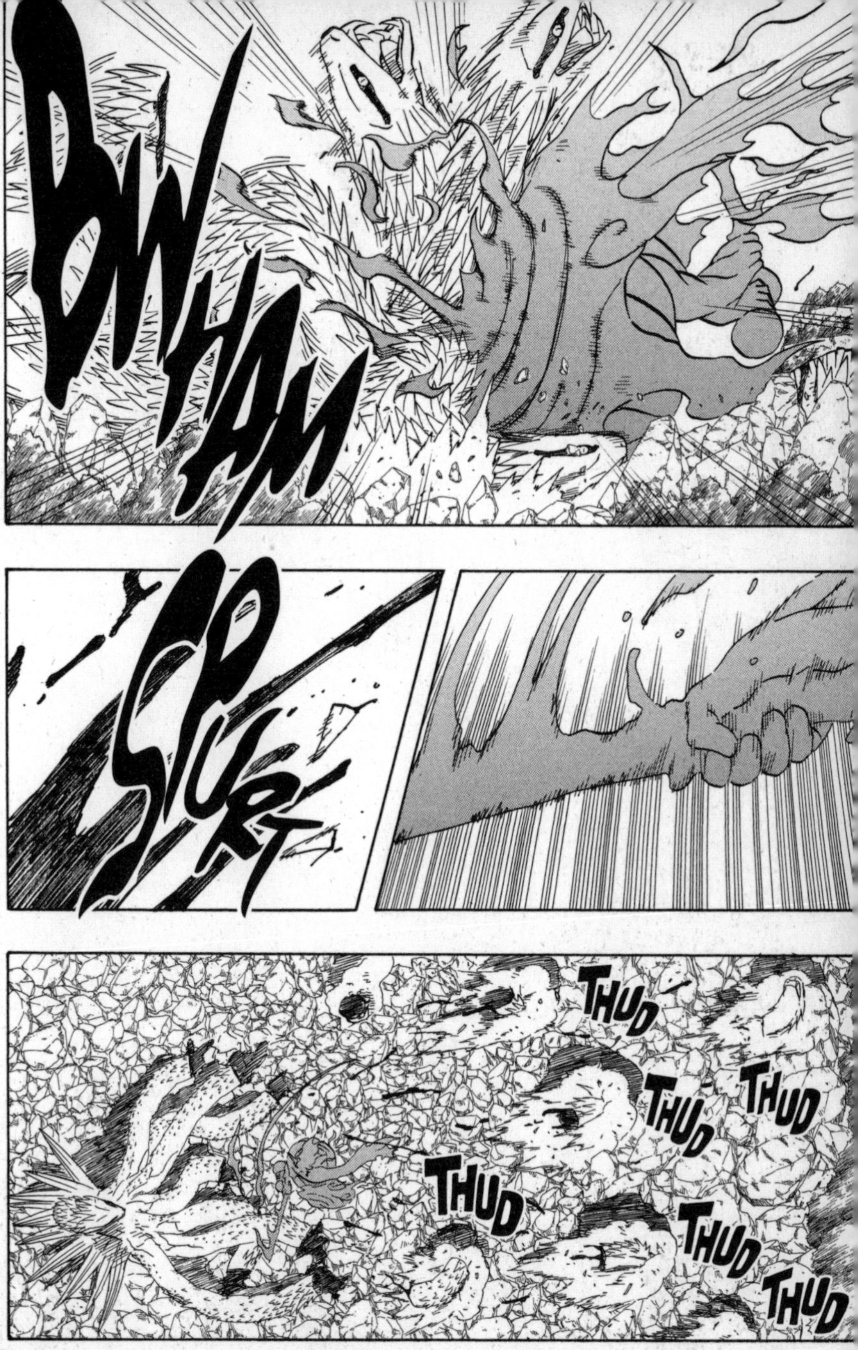
BWHAM
SPURT
THUD
THUD THUD
THUD
THUD
THUD

READ THIS WAY

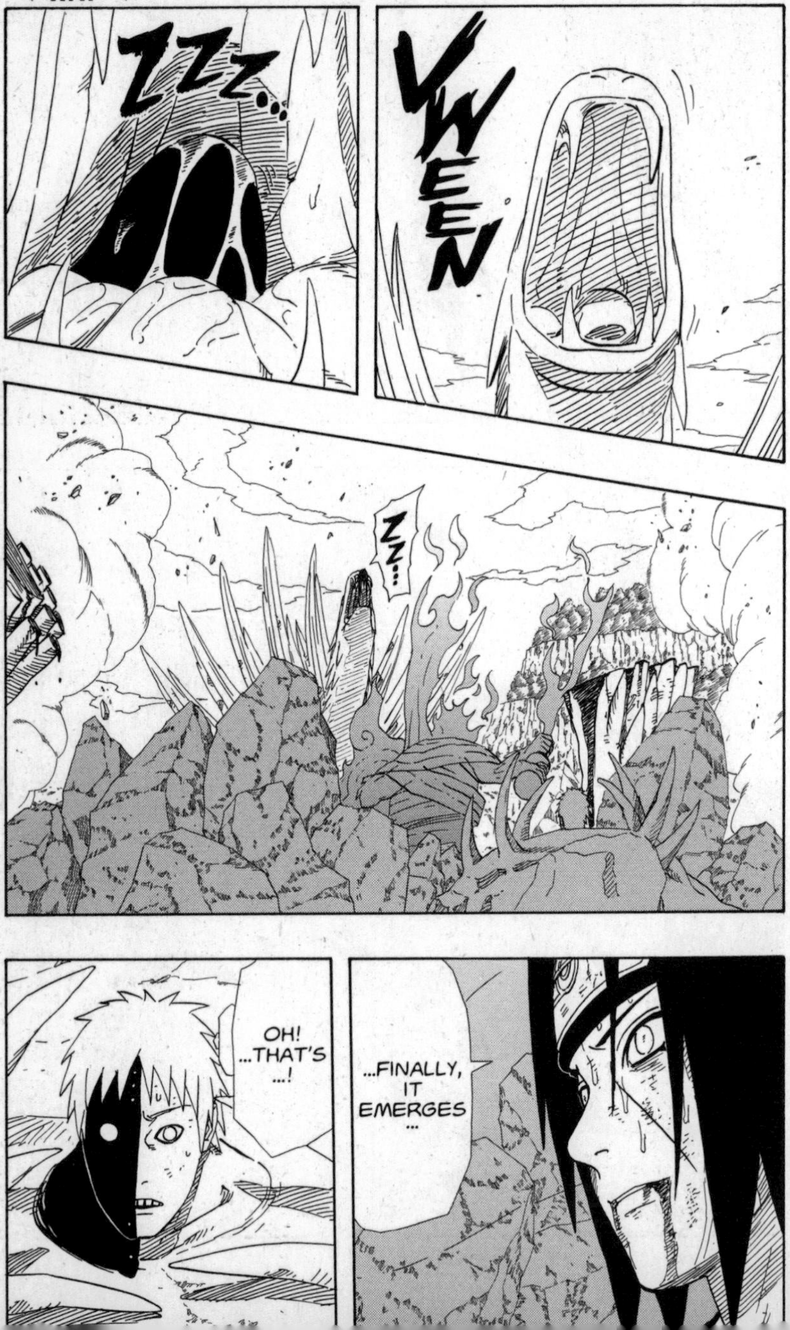
VWEEN
ZZZ...
ZZ...
...FINALLY, IT EMERGES ...
OH! ...THAT'S ...!

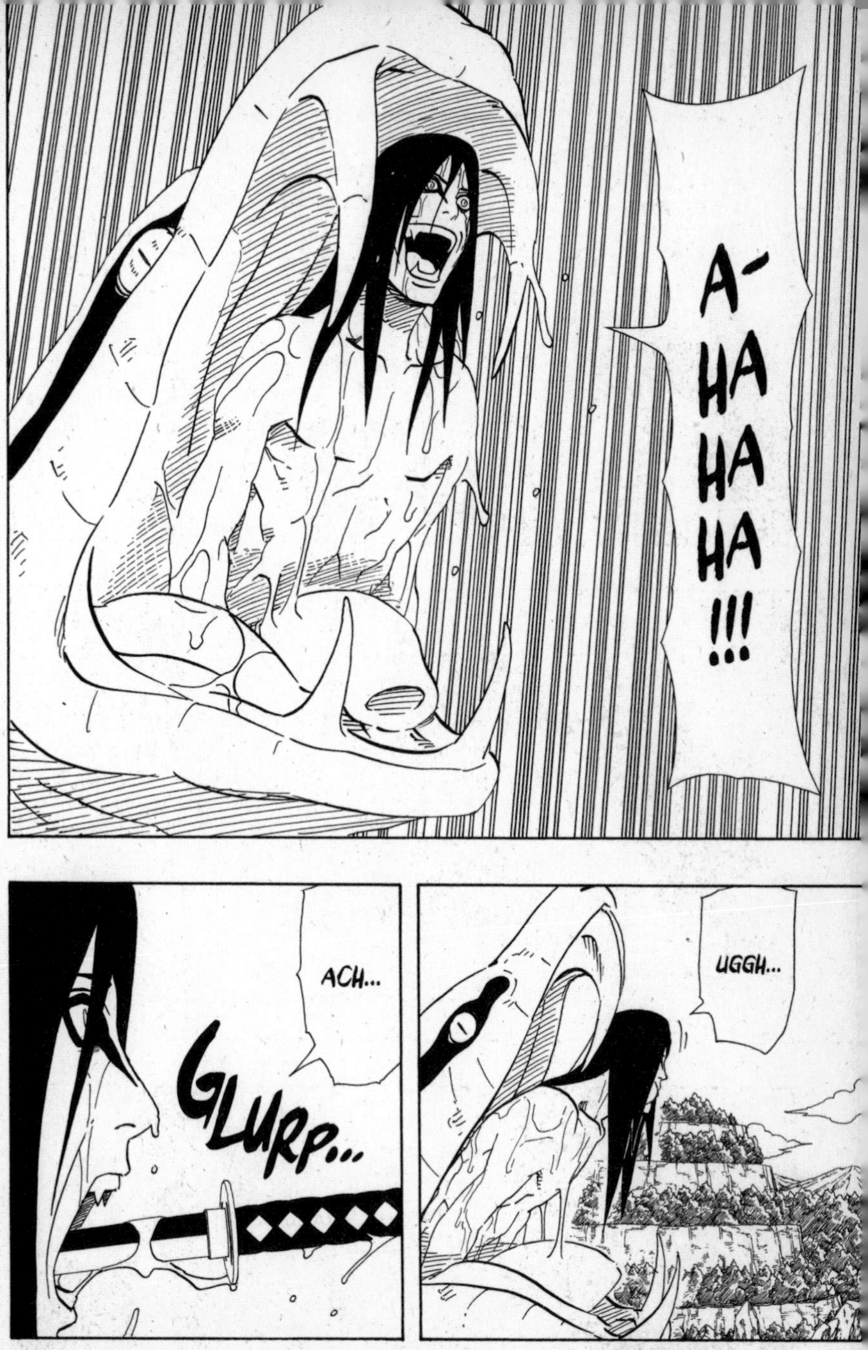
A-HAHAHAHA!!!
UGGH...
ACH...
GLURP...

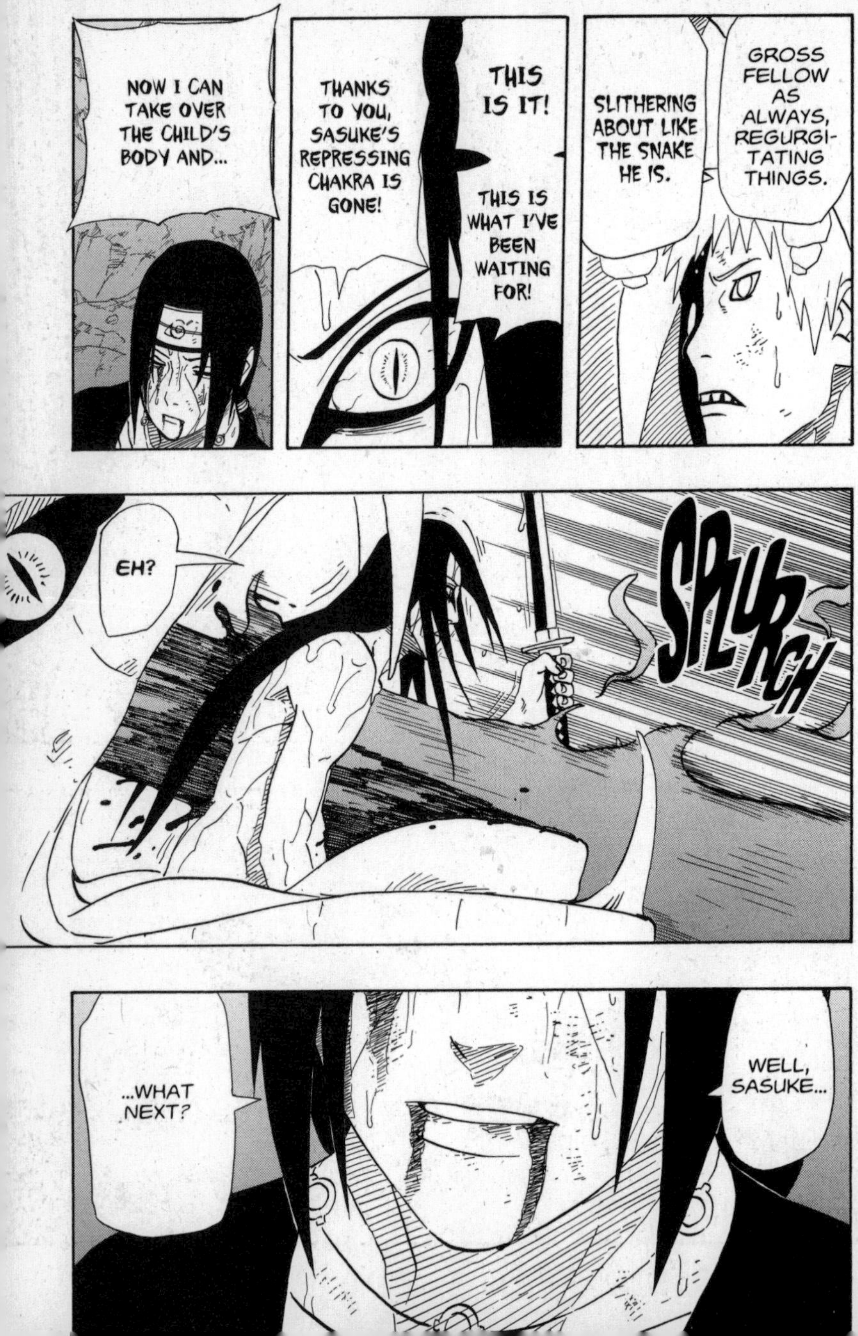
GROSS FELLOW AS ALWAYS, REGURGI-TATING THINGS.
SLITHERING ABOUT LIKE THE SNAKE HE IS.
THIS IS IT!
THIS IS WHAT I'VE BEEN WAITING FOR!
THANKS TO YOU, SASUKE'S REPRESSING CHAKRA IS GONE!
NOW I CAN TAKE OVER THE CHILD'S BODY AND...
SPLURCH
EH?
WELL, SASUKE...
...WHAT NEXT?

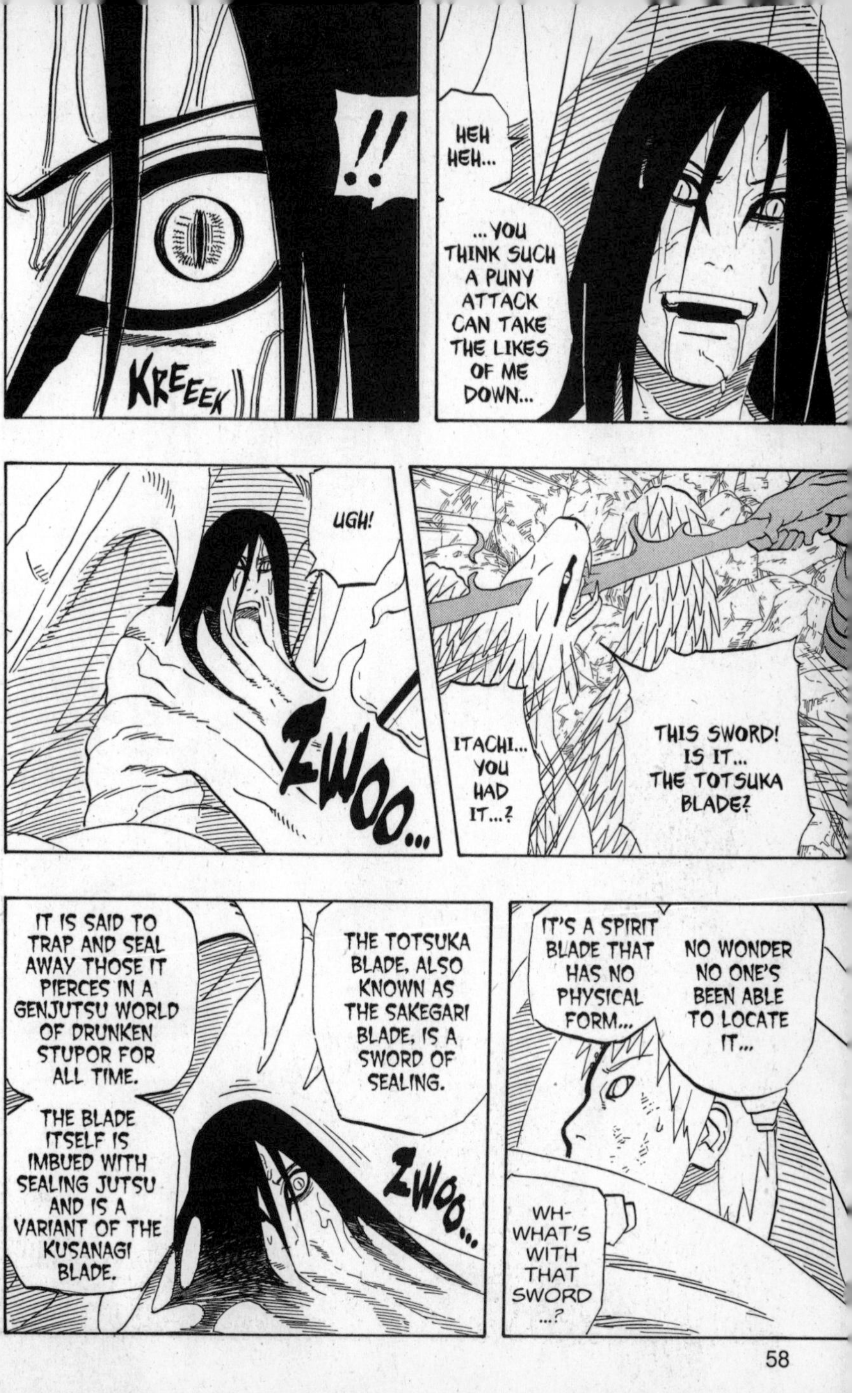
HEH HEH...
...YOU THINK SUCH A PUNY ATTACK CAN TAKE THE LIKES OF ME DOWN...
!!
KREEEK
THIS SWORD! IS IT... THE TOTSUKA BLADE?
ITACHI... YOU HAD IT...?
UGH!
ZWOO...
IT'S A SPIRIT BLADE THAT HAS NO PHYSICAL FORM...
NO WONDER NO ONE'S BEEN ABLE TO LOCATE IT...
WH-WHAT'S WITH THAT SWORD...?
THE TOTSUKA BLADE, ALSO KNOWN AS THE SAKEGARI BLADE, IS A SWORD OF SEALING.
IT IS SAID TO TRAP AND SEAL AWAY THOSE IT PIERCES IN A GENJUTSU WORLD OF DRUNKEN STUPOR FOR ALL TIME.
THE BLADE ITSELF IS IMBUED WITH SEALING JUTSU AND IS A VARIANT OF THE KUSANAGI BLADE.
ZWOO...

READ THIS WAY

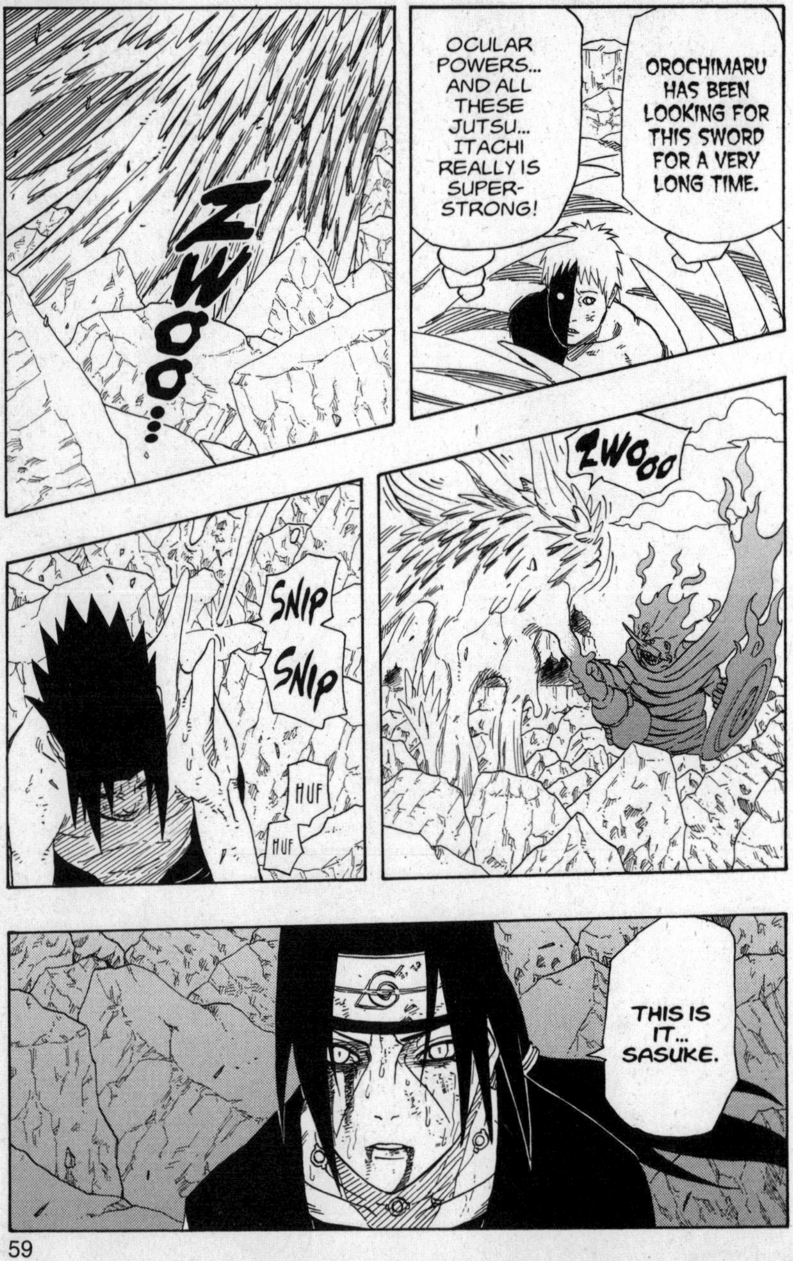
OROCHIMARU HAS BEEN LOOKING FOR THIS SWORD FOR A VERY LONG TIME.
OCULAR POWERS... AND ALL THESE JUTSU... ITACHI REALLY IS SUPER-STRONG!
ZWOOO...
ZWOOO
SNIP
SNIP
HUF
HUF
THIS IS IT... SASUKE.

MEET KISHIMOTO MASASHI'S ASSISTANTS, PART 12
ASSISTANT NO. 12: TAIRA KENJI

PROFILE

- DESPITE BEING A BRAT WHO JUST TURNED 20, HE'S SO SERIOUS HE'S NOT CUTE AT ALL.
- DOESN'T WARM UP TO ME AT ALL.
- ALWAYS ACTS COOL.
- HAS ALL SORTS OF FUNNY THOUGHTS IN HIS HEAD THAT HE NEVER SHARES.
- AMBITIOUS AND VERY STUDIOUS.
- HASN'T WON ANY AWARDS BUT DEBUTED PROMINENTLY.
- I'LL ACKNOWLEDGE THAT HE HAS A STRONG GAG SENSIBILITY.
- LOVES JOJO OVER NARUTO! ARAKI HIROHIKO-SENSEI OVER KISHIMOTO MASASHI!!
- LOVES JOJO SO MUCH, HE ONLY WARMS UP TO ME WHEN I TALK ABOUT JOJO.

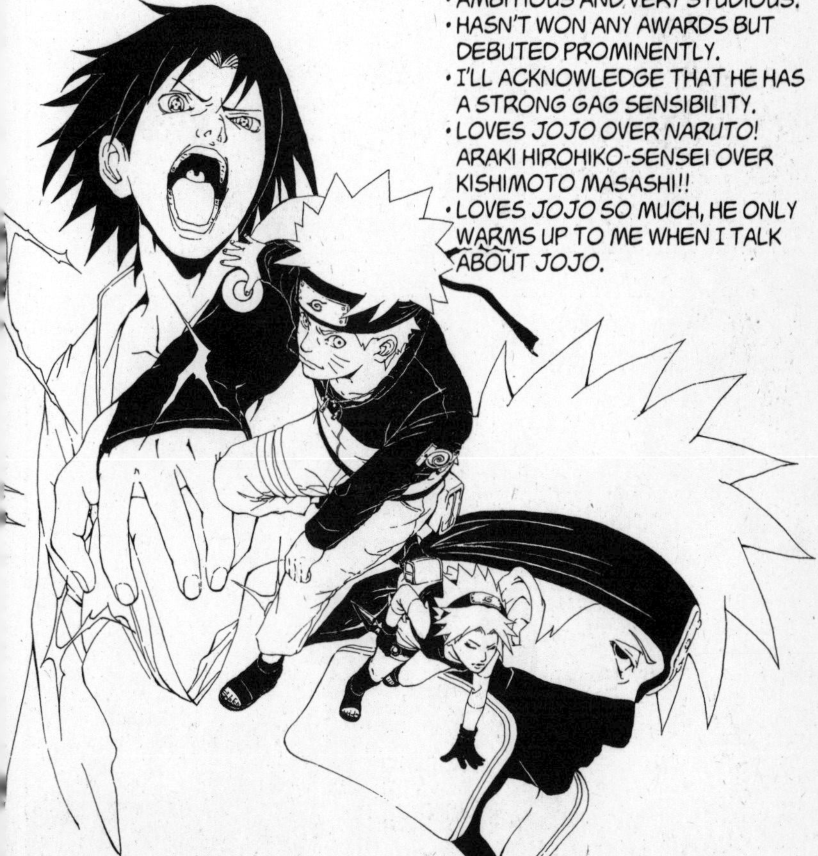

Number 393: My Eyes...!!

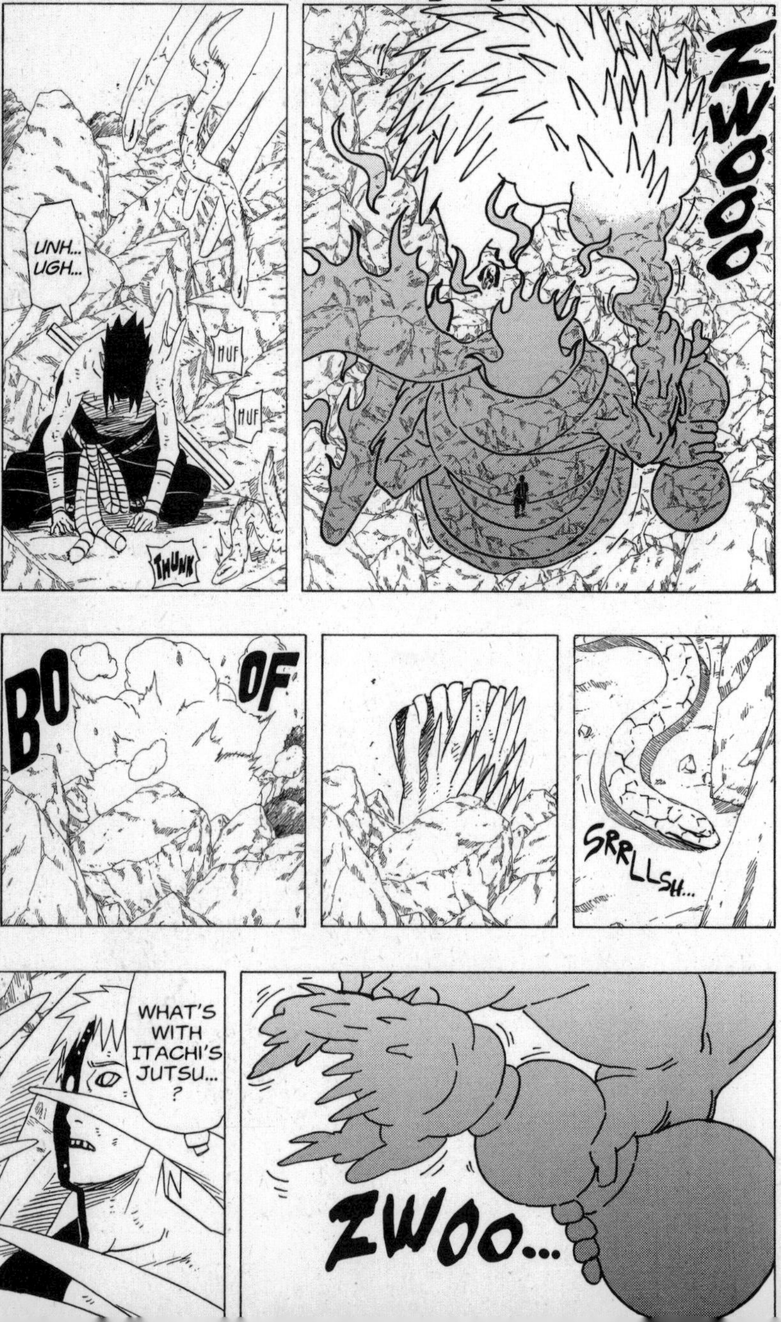
ZWOOO
UNH... UGH...
HUF
HUF
THUNK
SRRLLSH...
BOOF
ZWOO...
WHAT'S WITH ITACHI'S JUTSU...?

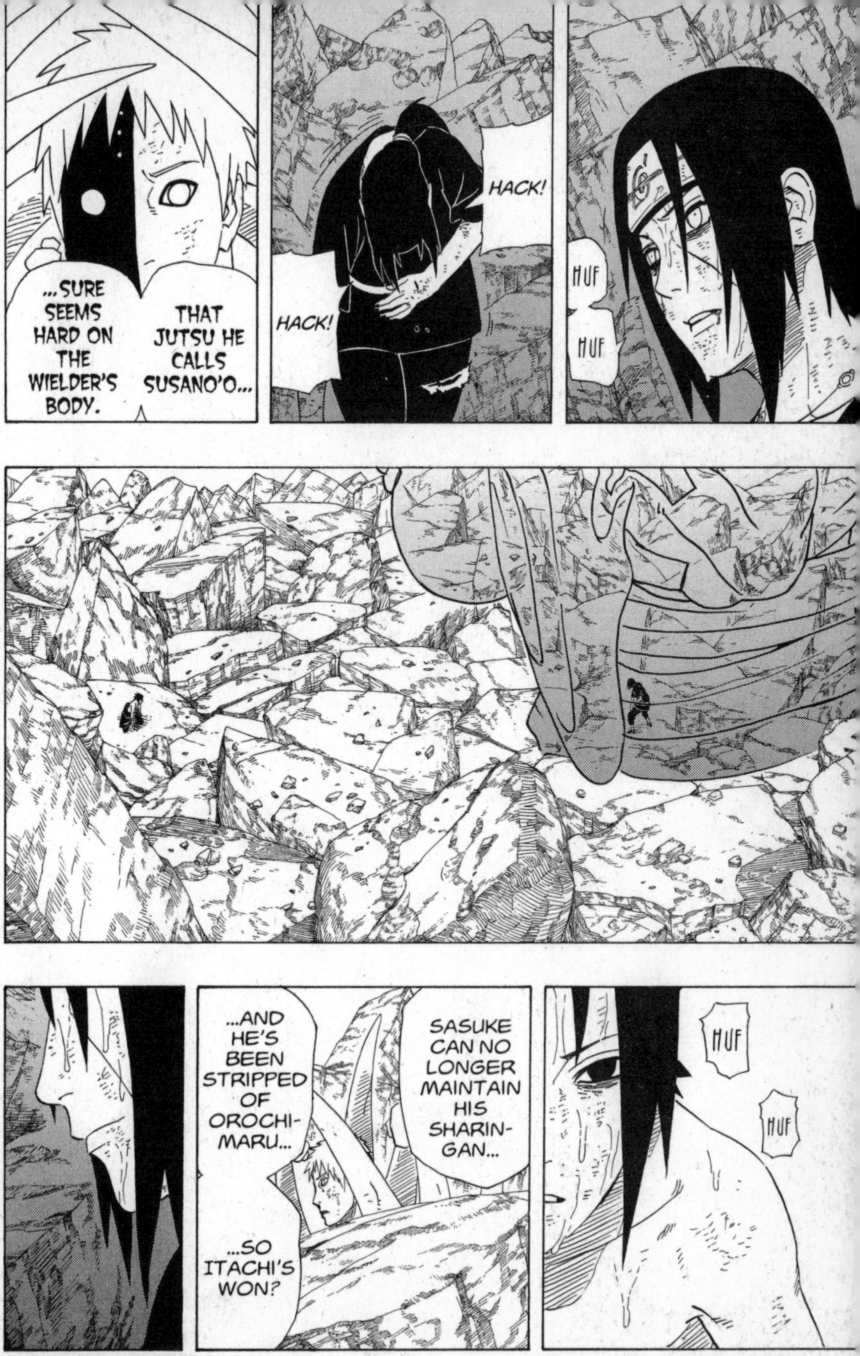
HUF
HUF
HACK!
HACK!
THAT JUTSU HE CALLS SUSANO'O...
...SURE SEEMS HARD ON THE WIELDER'S BODY.
HUF
HUF
SASUKE CAN NO LONGER MAINTAIN HIS SHARINGAN...
...AND HE'S BEEN STRIPPED OF OROCHIMARU...
...SO ITACHI'S WON?

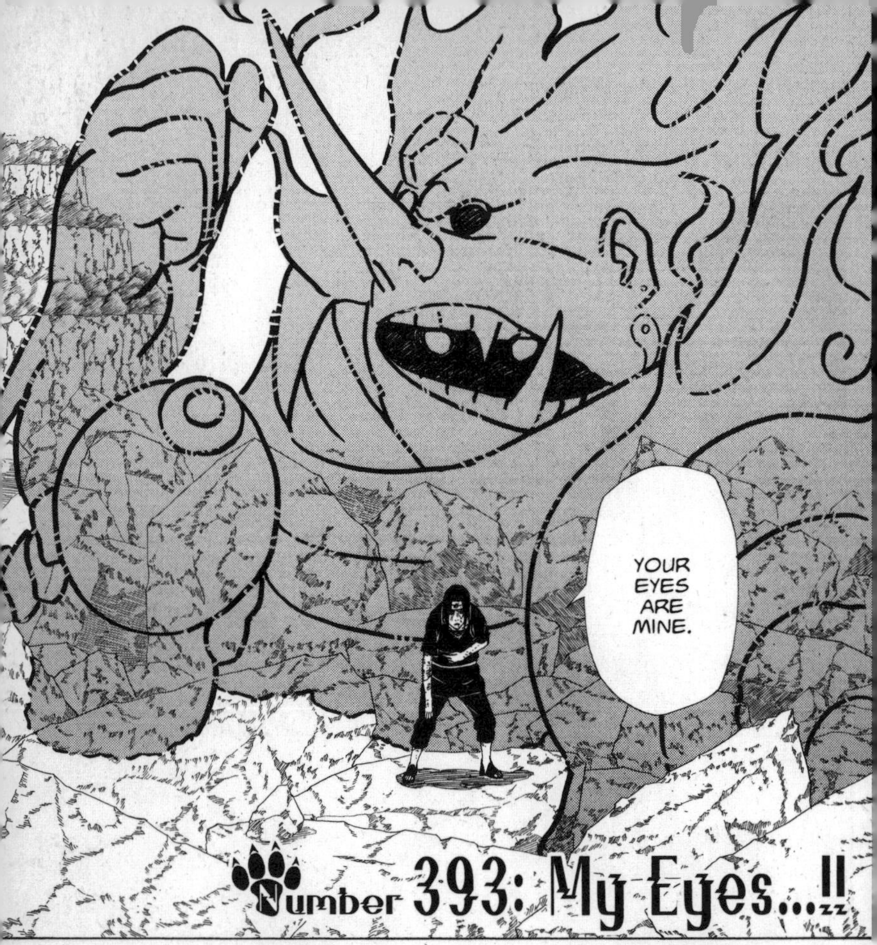
YOUR EYES ARE MINE.
Number 393: My Eyes...!!

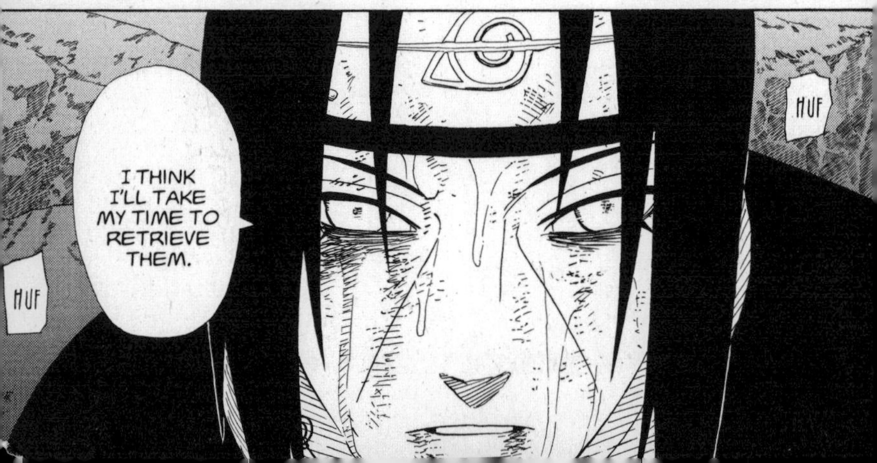
HUF
I THINK I'LL TAKE MY TIME TO RETRIEVE THEM.
HUF

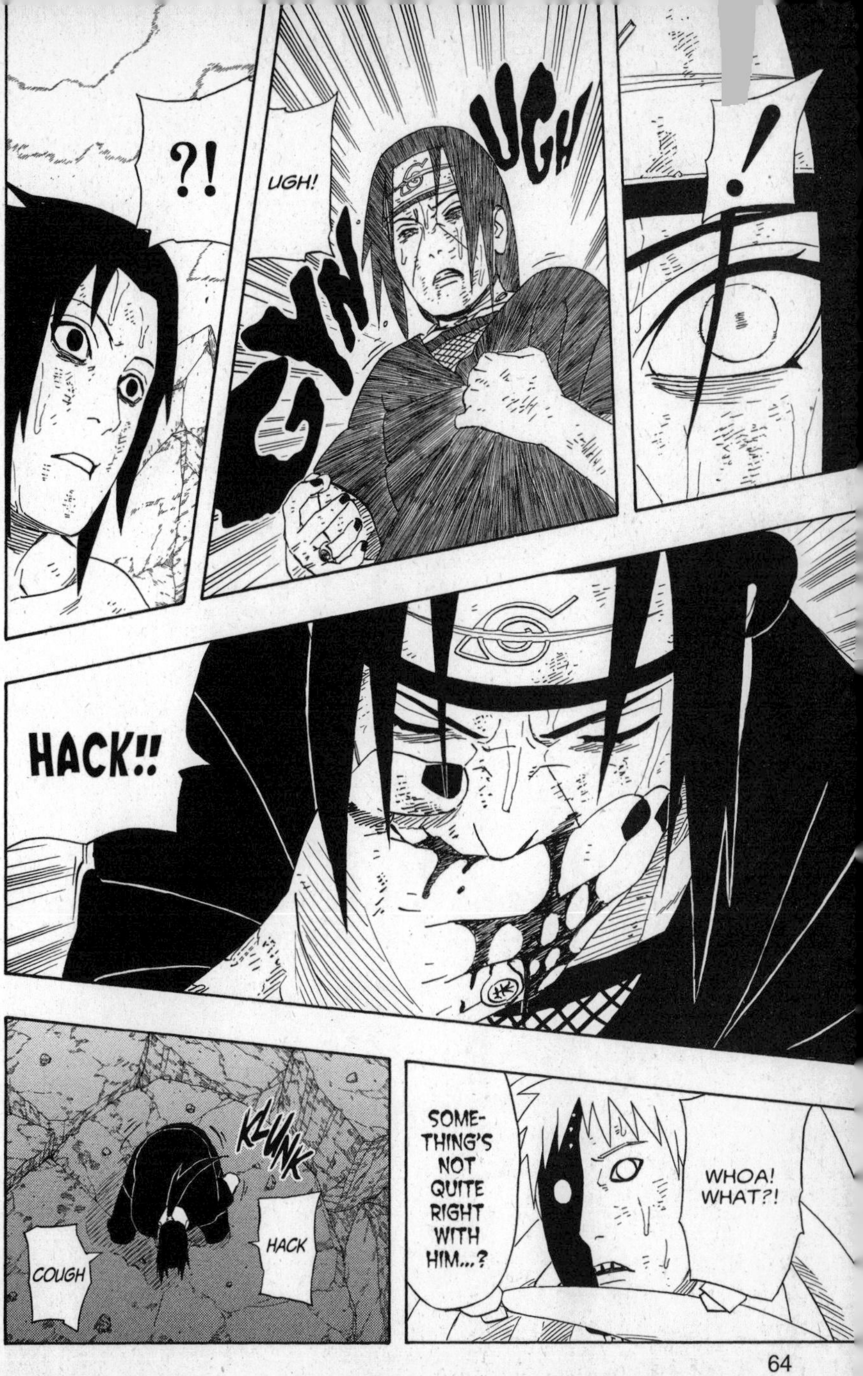
!
UGH
UGH!
?!
HACK!!
WHOA! WHAT?!
SOME-THING'S NOT QUITE RIGHT WITH HIM...?
KLUNK
HACK
COUGH

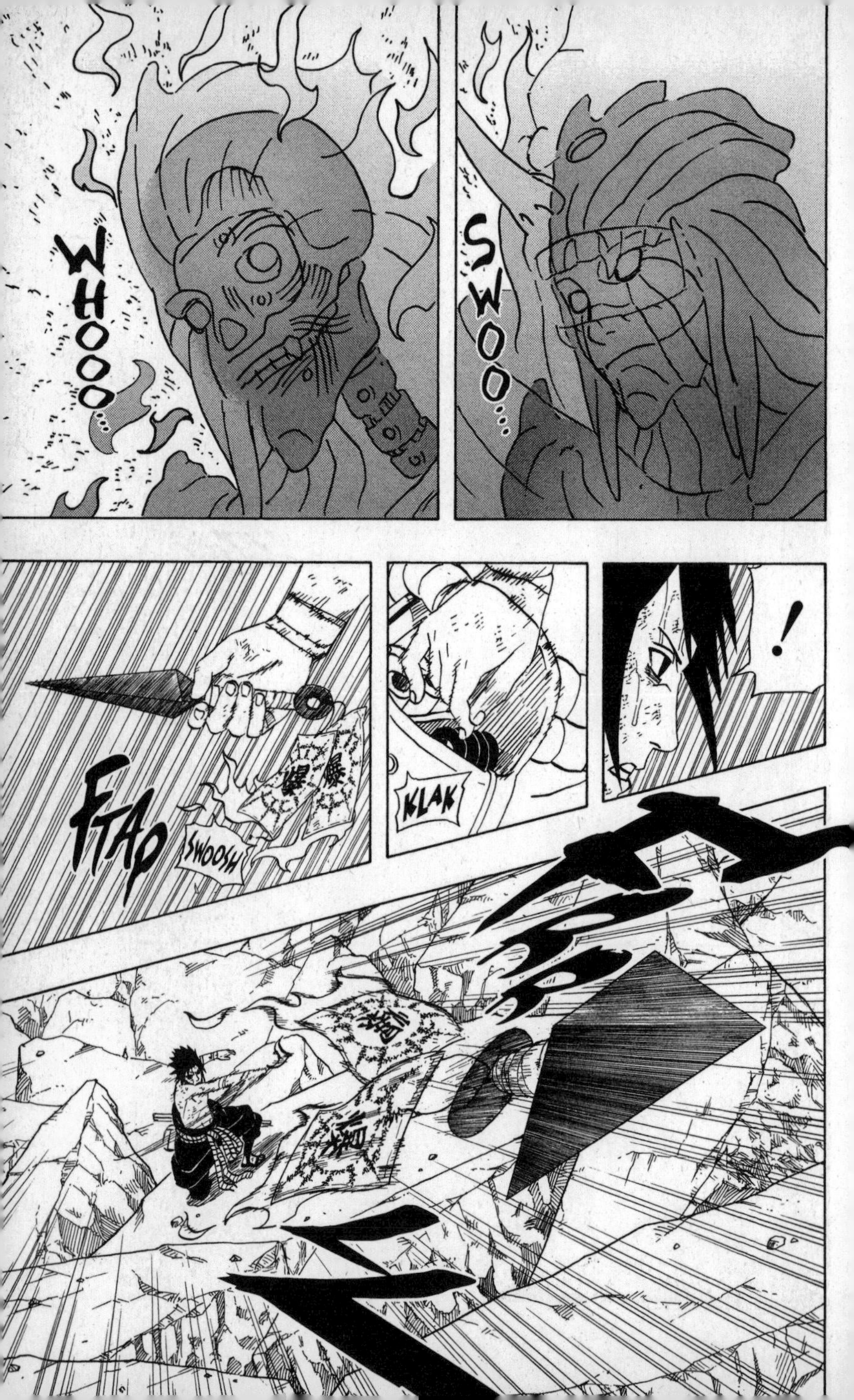
SWOOO...
WHOOO...
!
KLAK
FTAP
SWOOSH

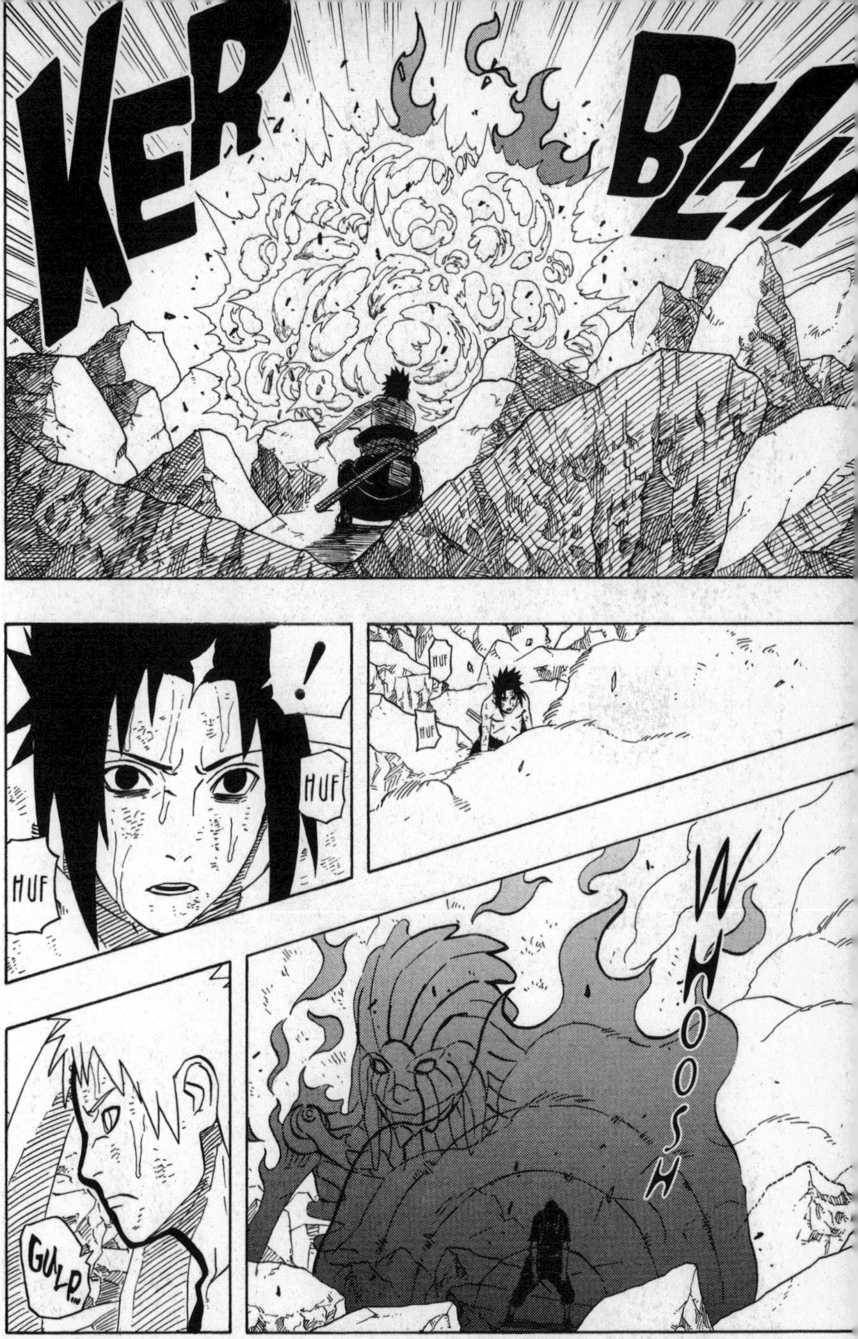
KER BLAM
HUF
HUF
!
HUF
HUF
WHOOSH
GULP...

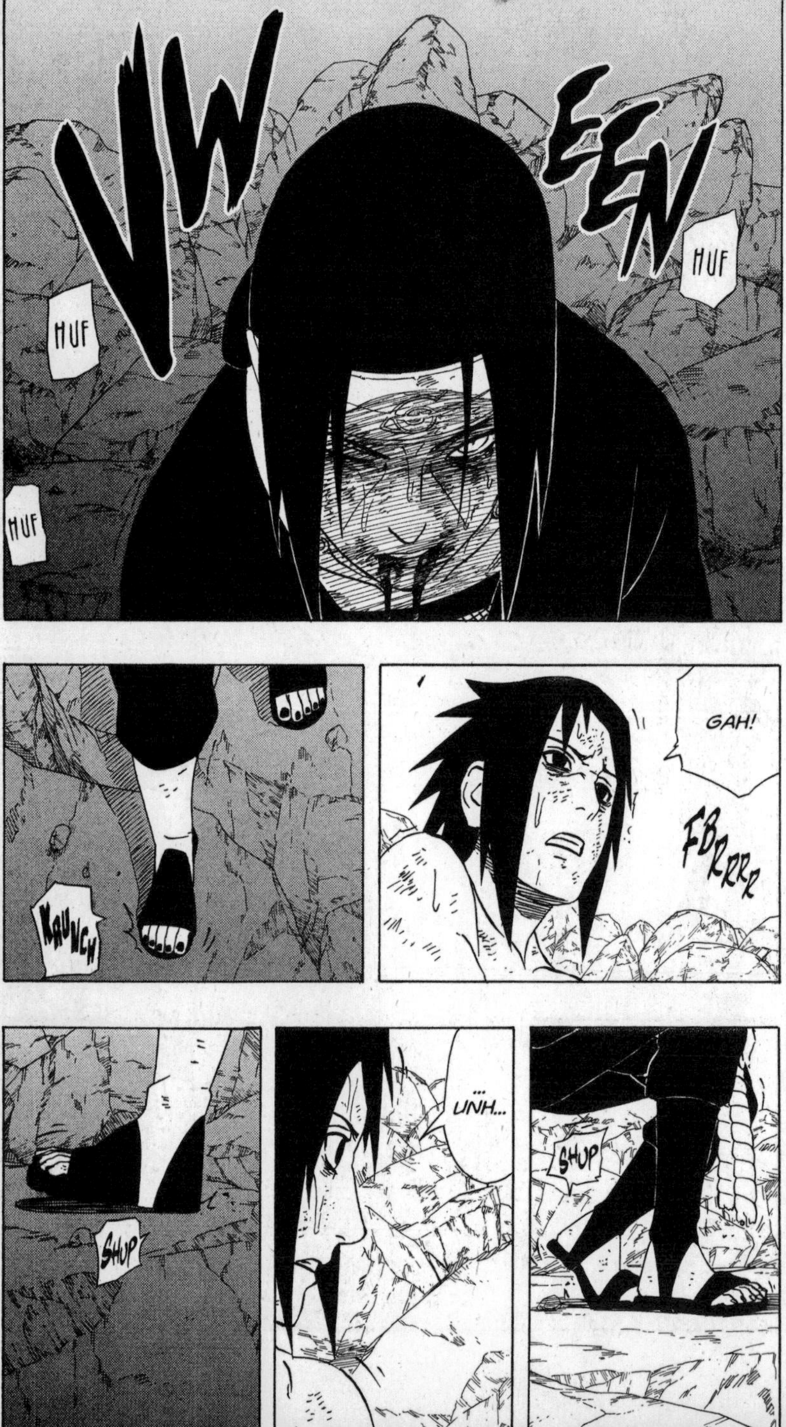

VWEEN
HUF
HUF
HUF
GAH!
FBRRRR
KRUNCH
SHUP
... UNH...
SHUP

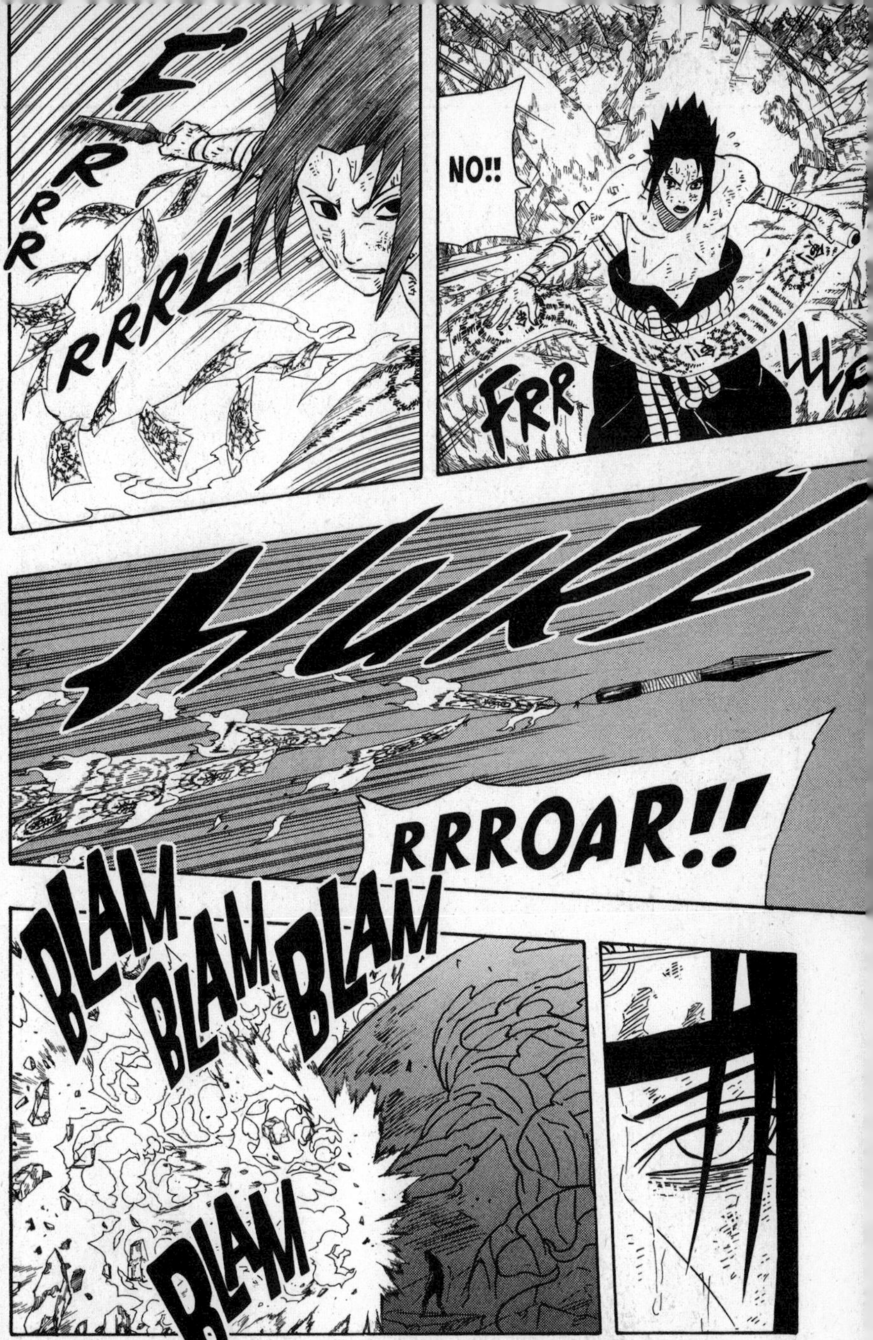
NO!!
FRR
RRRRL
RRROAR!!
BLAM
BLAM
BLAM
BLAM

READ THIS WAY

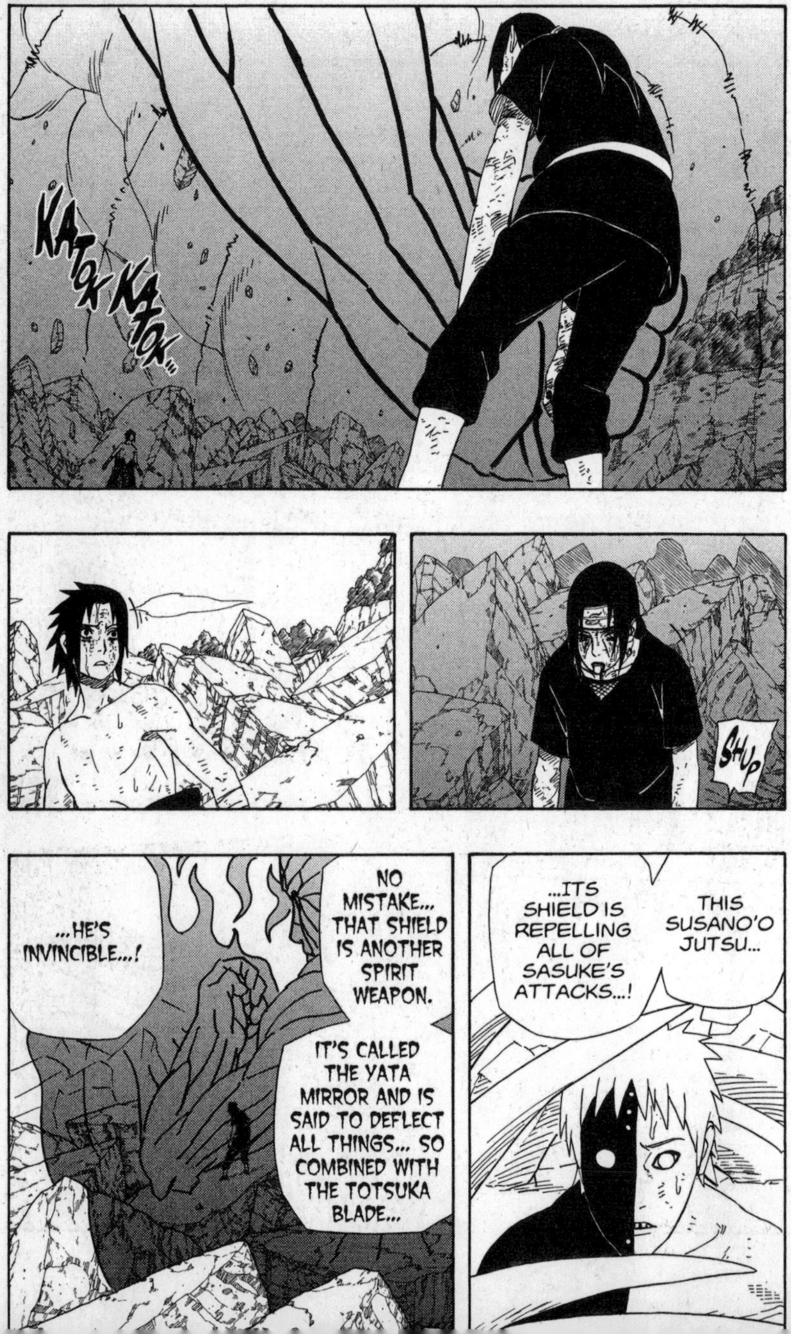
KATOK KATOK...
SHUP
THIS SUSANO'O JUTSU...
...ITS SHIELD IS REPELLING ALL OF SASUKE'S ATTACKS...!
NO MISTAKE... THAT SHIELD IS ANOTHER SPIRIT WEAPON.
IT'S CALLED THE YATA MIRROR AND IS SAID TO DEFLECT ALL THINGS... SO COMBINED WITH THE TOTSUKA BLADE...
...HE'S INVINCIBLE...!

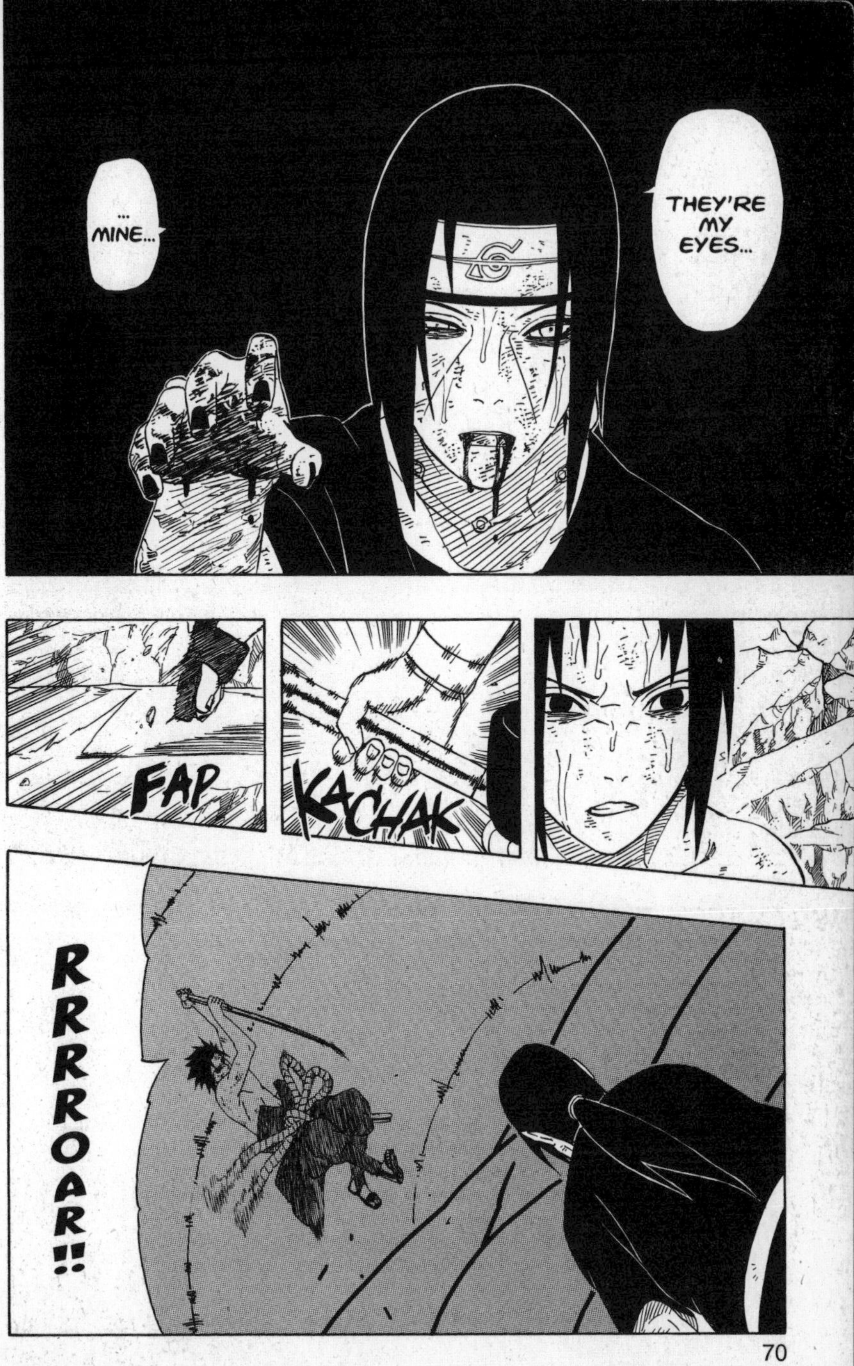
THEY'RE MY EYES...
... MINE...
KACHAK
FAP
RRRROAR!!

READ THIS WAY

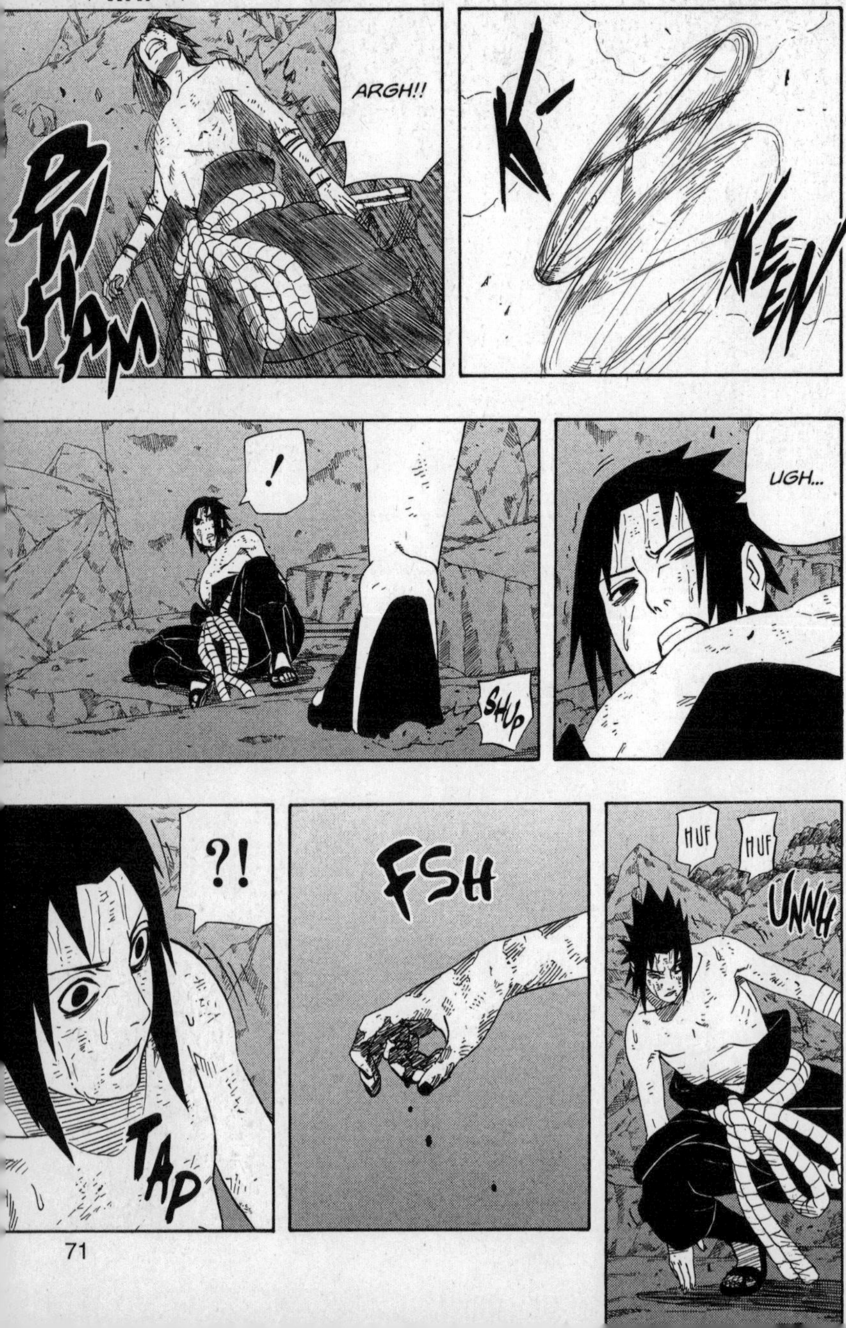
K-KEEN
ARGH!!
BWHAM
UGH...
!
SHUP
HUF
HUF
UNNH
FSH
?!
TAP

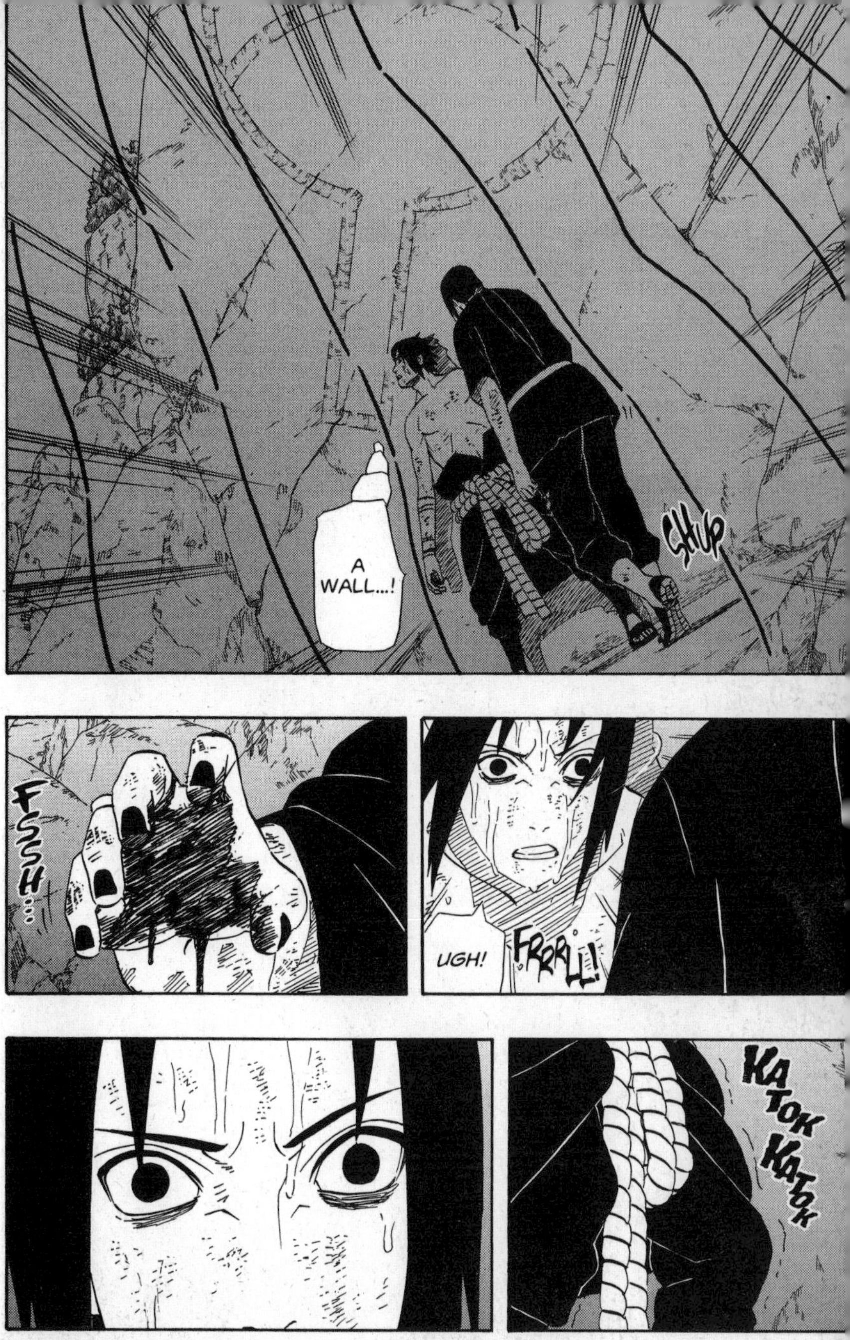
SHUP
A WALL...!
UGH!
FRRRLL!
FSSH...
KATOK KATOK

READ THIS WAY

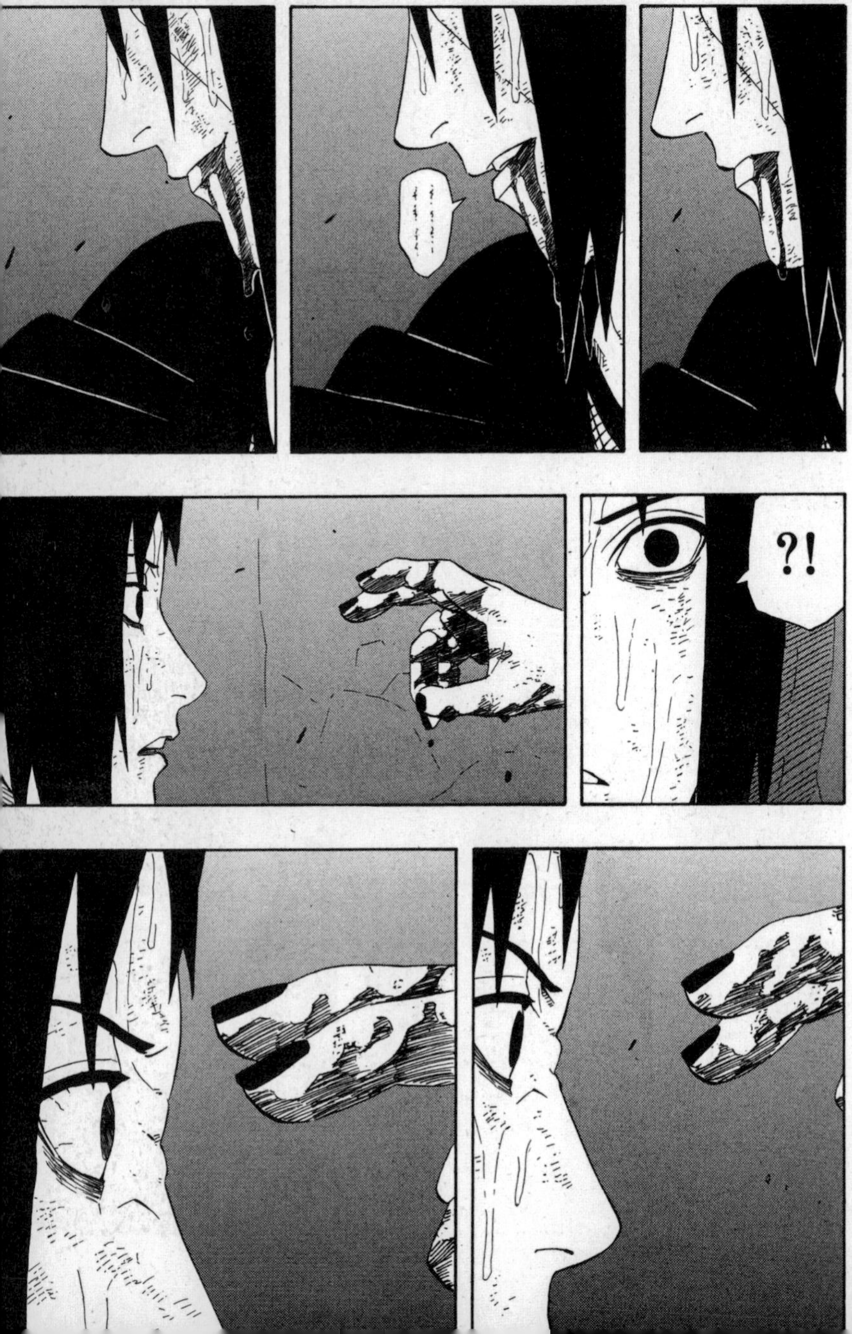
......
?!

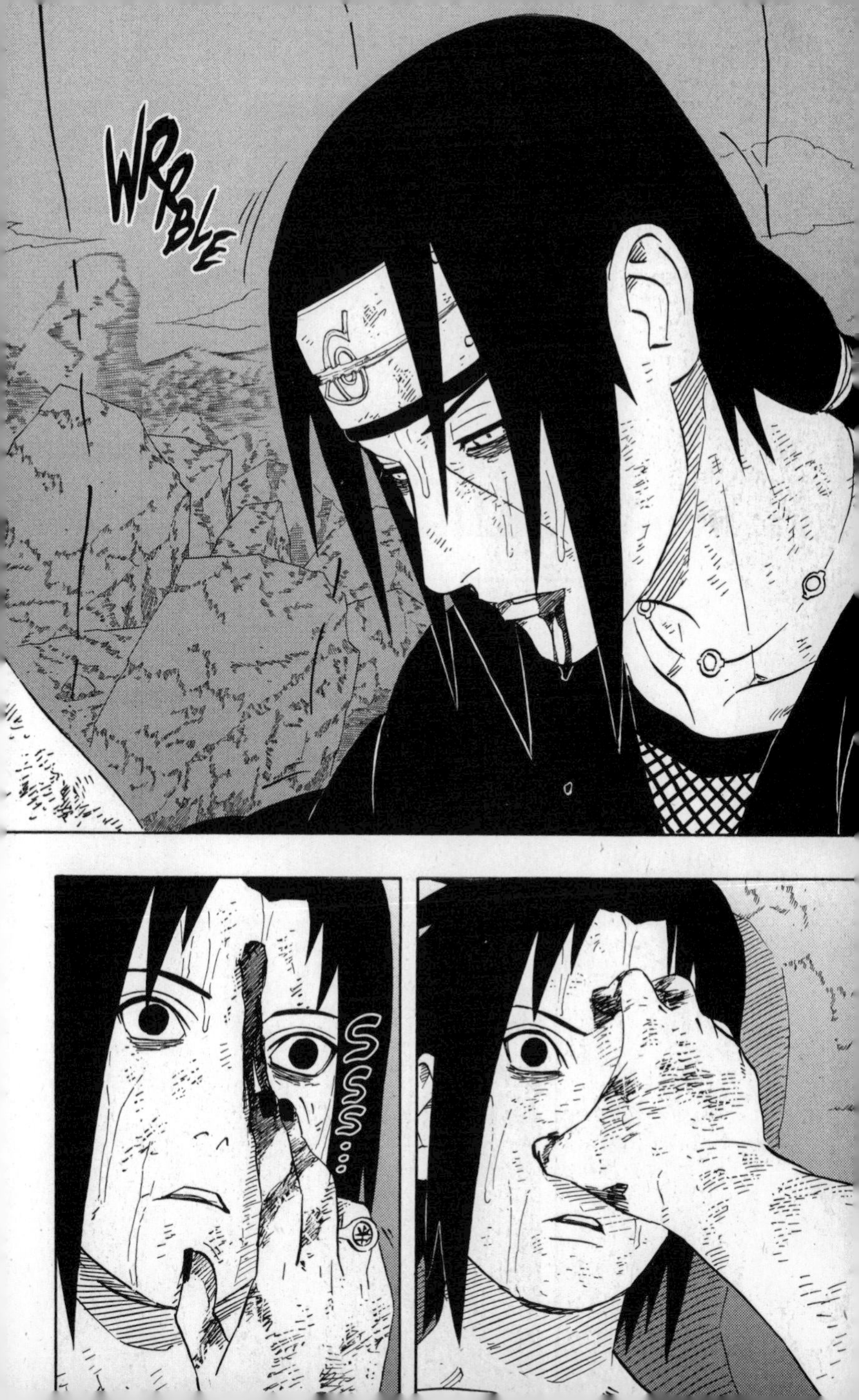
WRBBLE
SSSS...

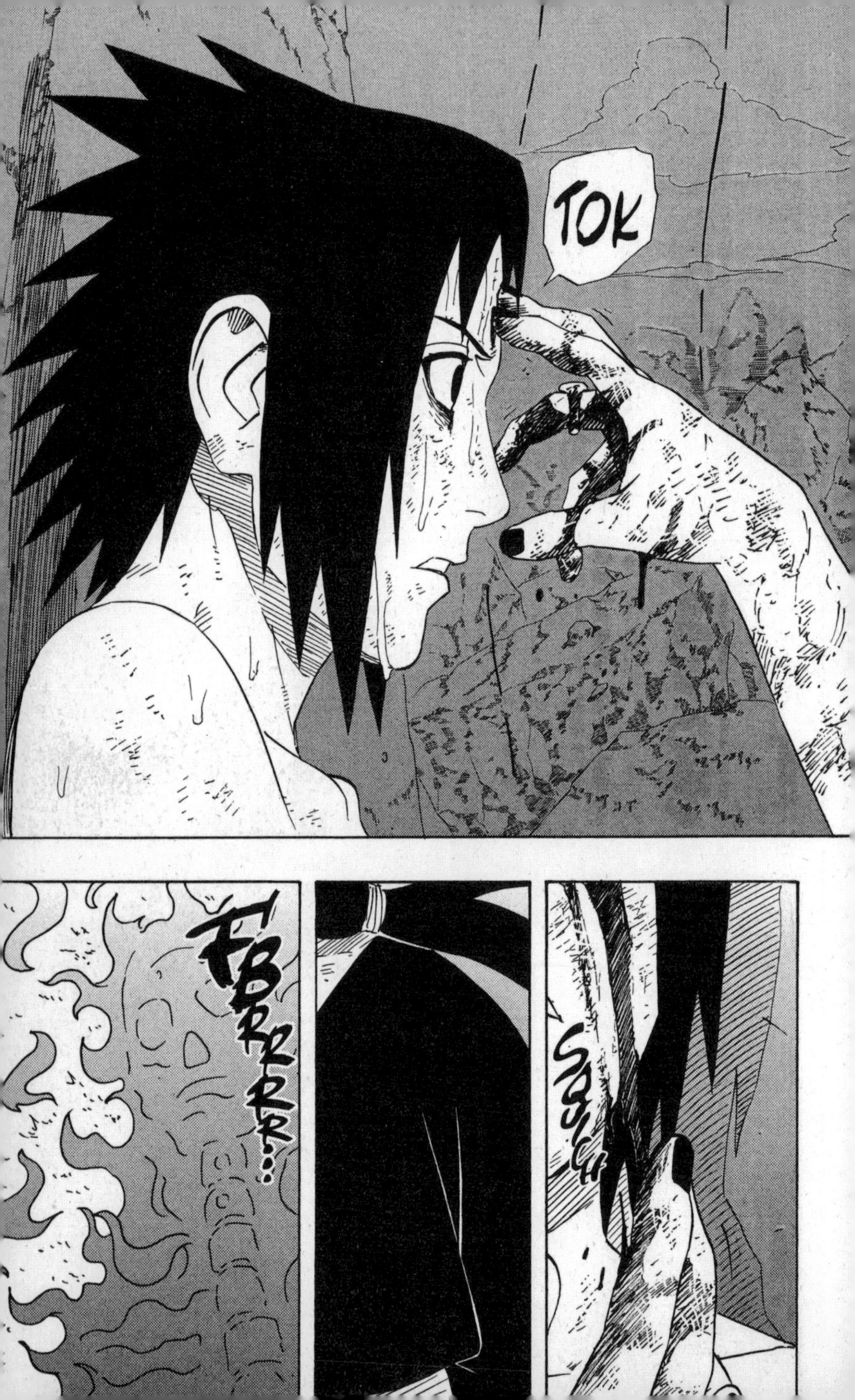
TOK
SQUCH
FBRRRRR...

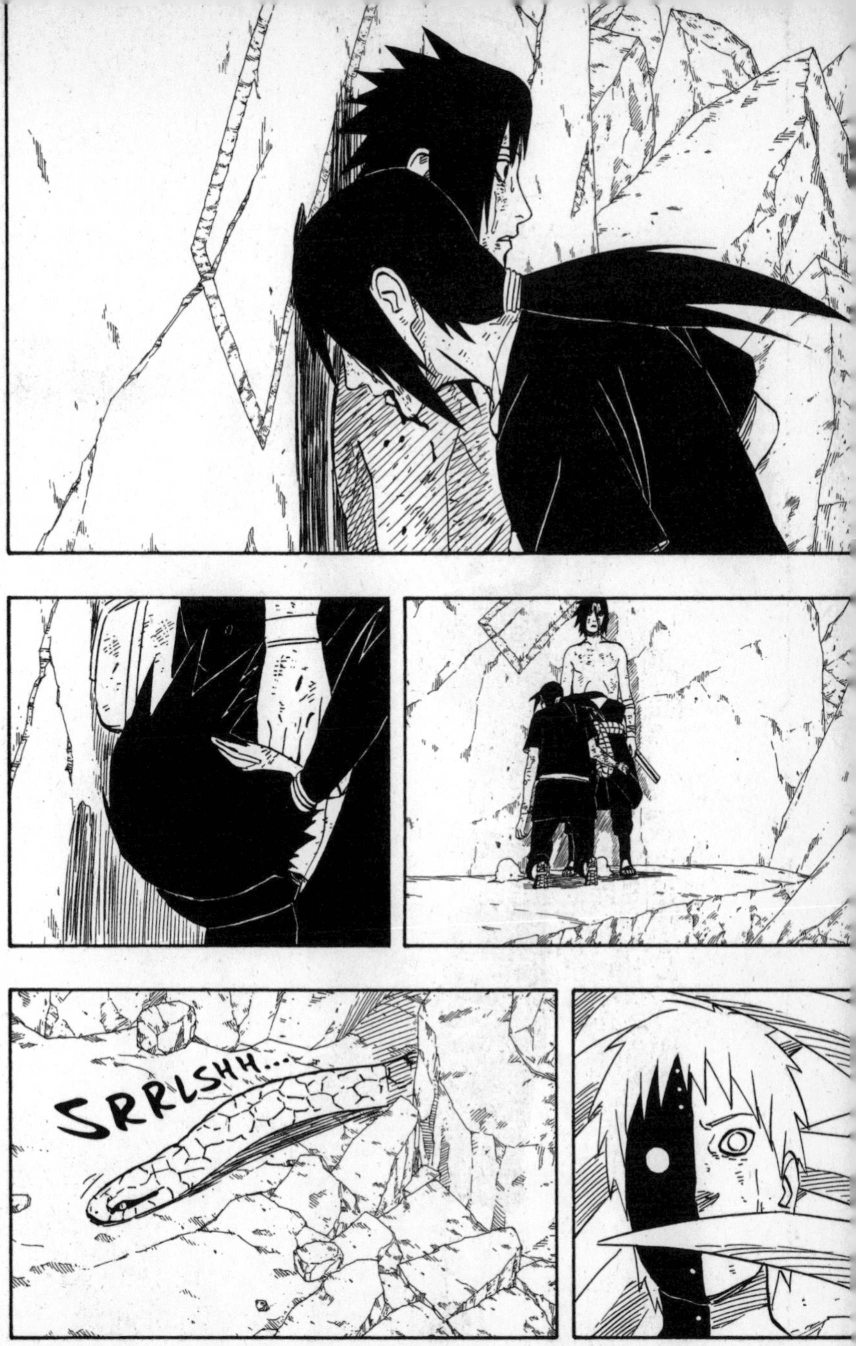
SRRLSHH...

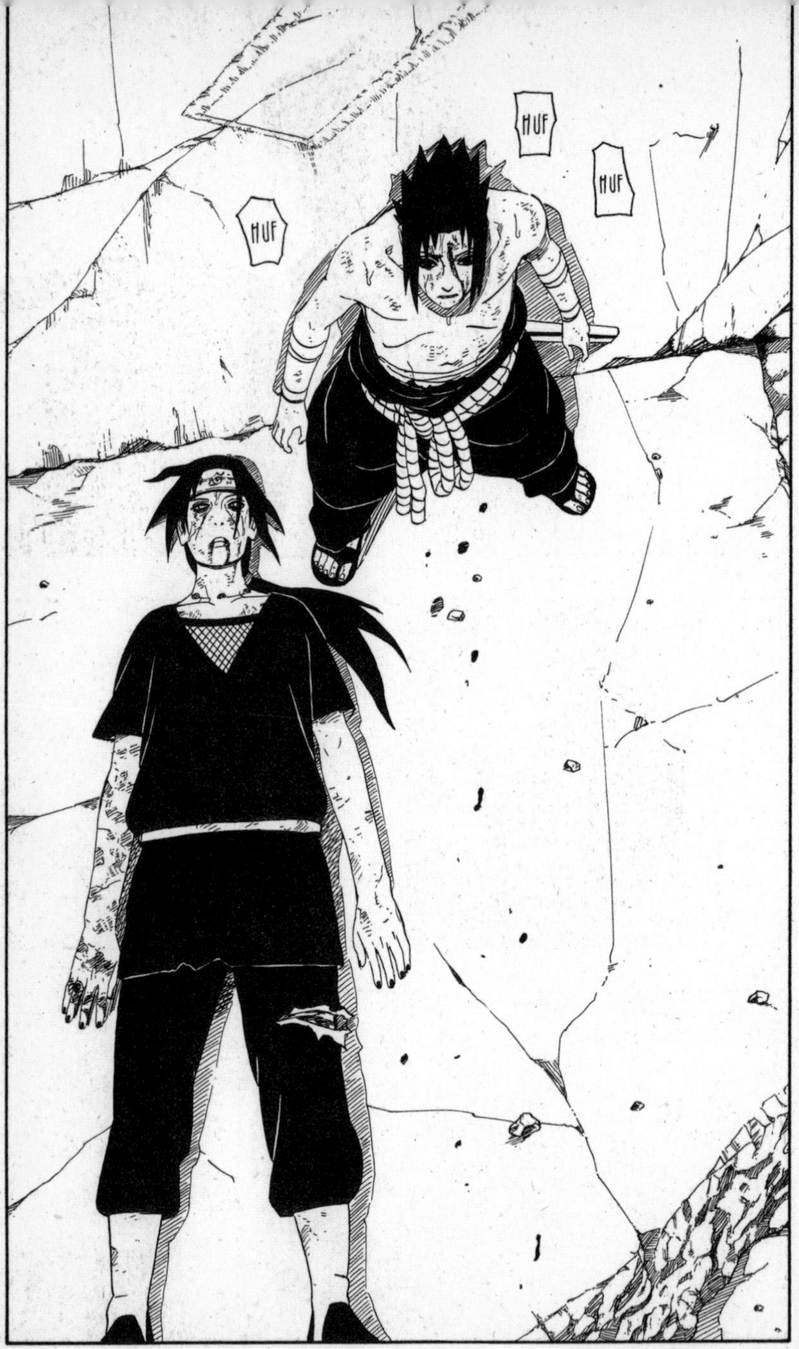
HUF
HUF
HUF

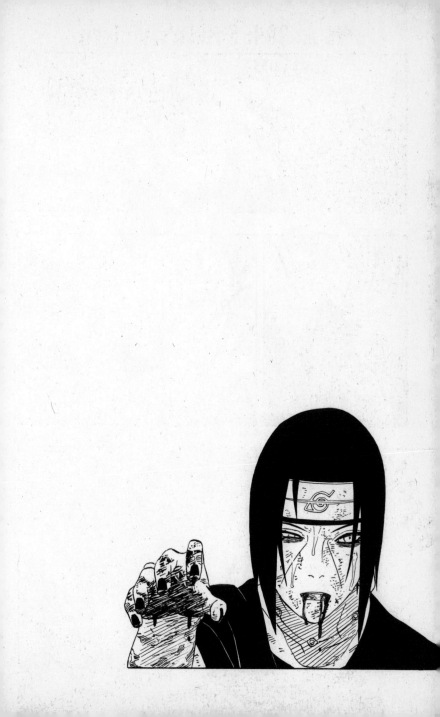

Number 394: Sasuke's Victory

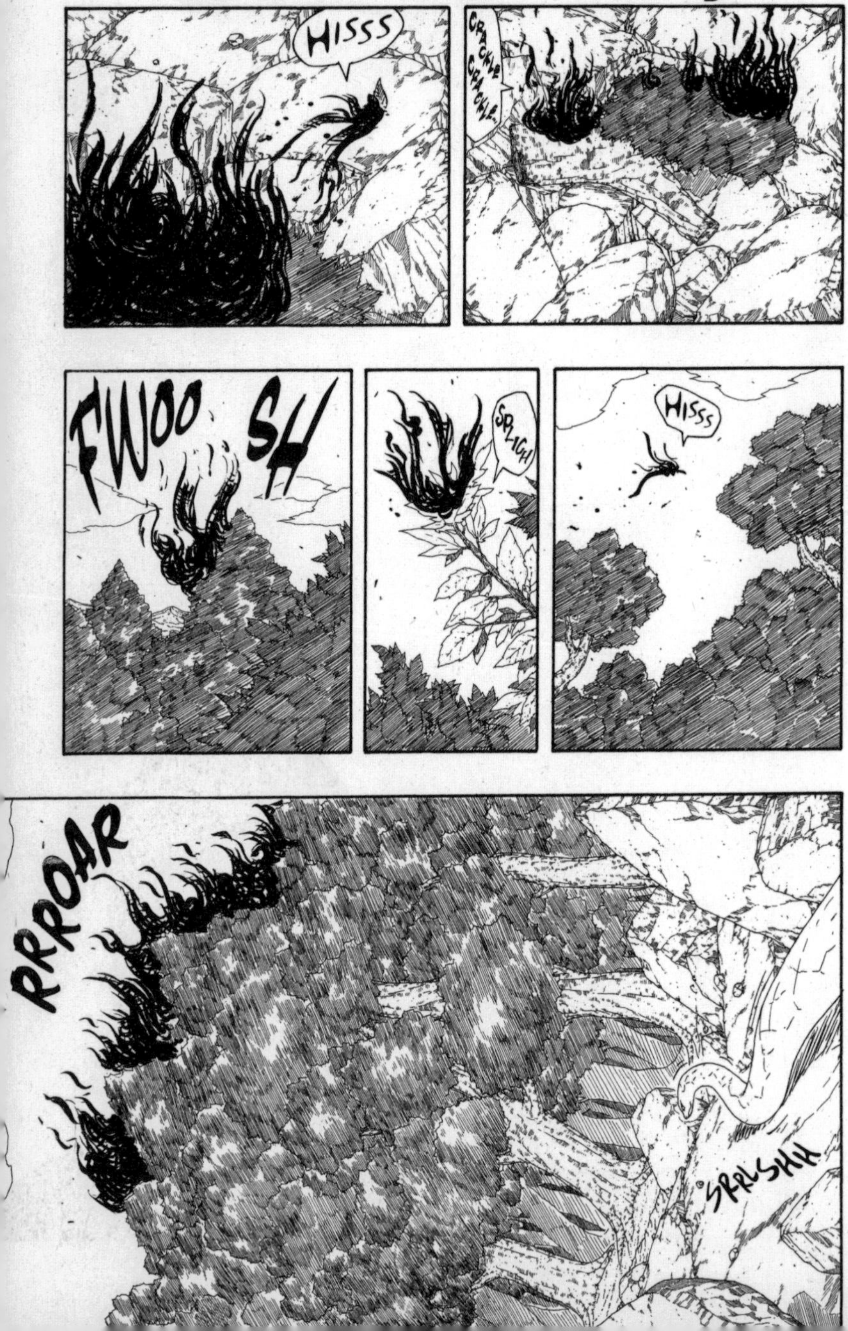

CRACKLE CRACKLE CRACKLE...
HISSS
HISSS
SPLICH
FWOOSH
SRLSHH
PRROAR

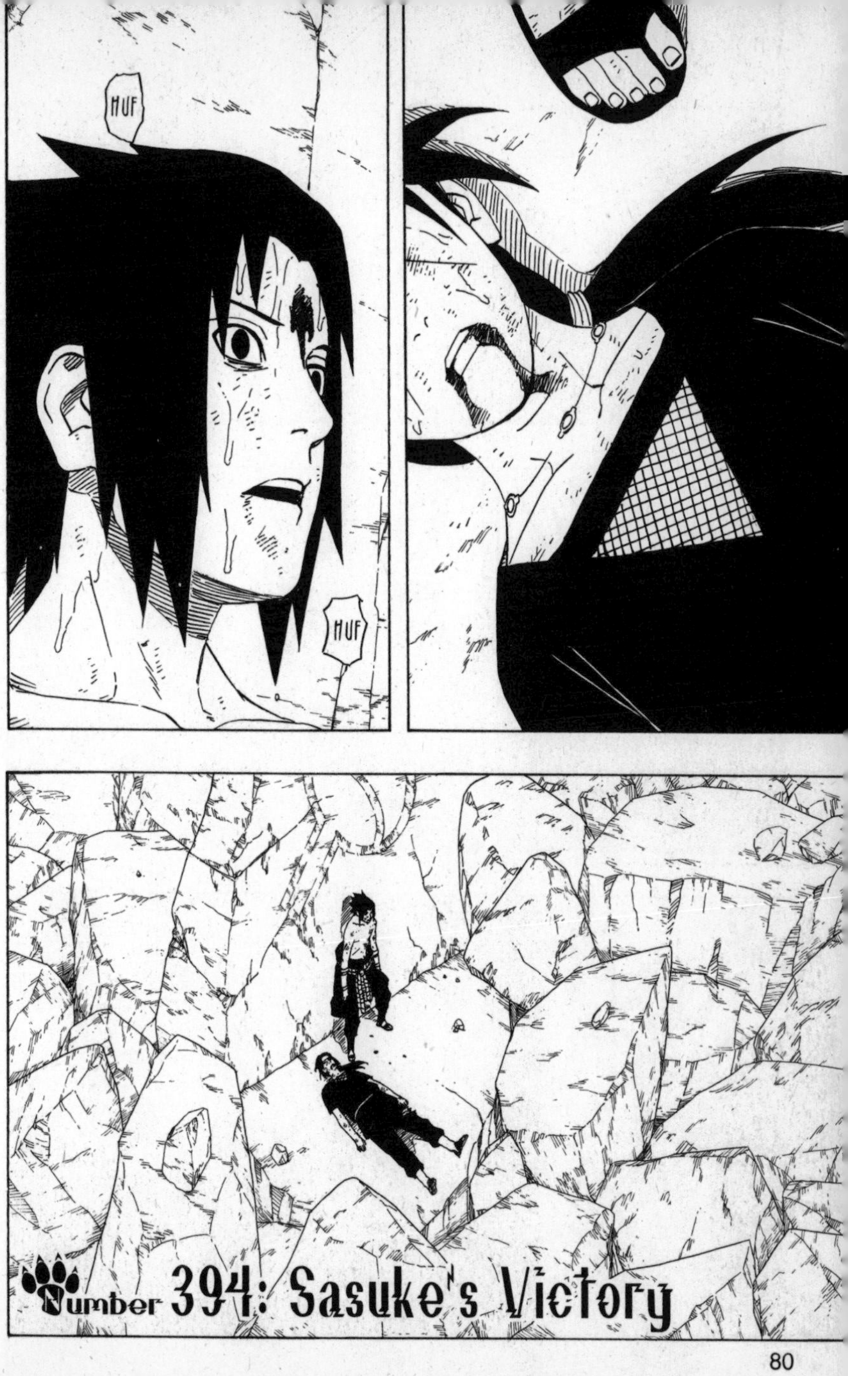
HUF
HUF
Number 394: Sasuke's Victory

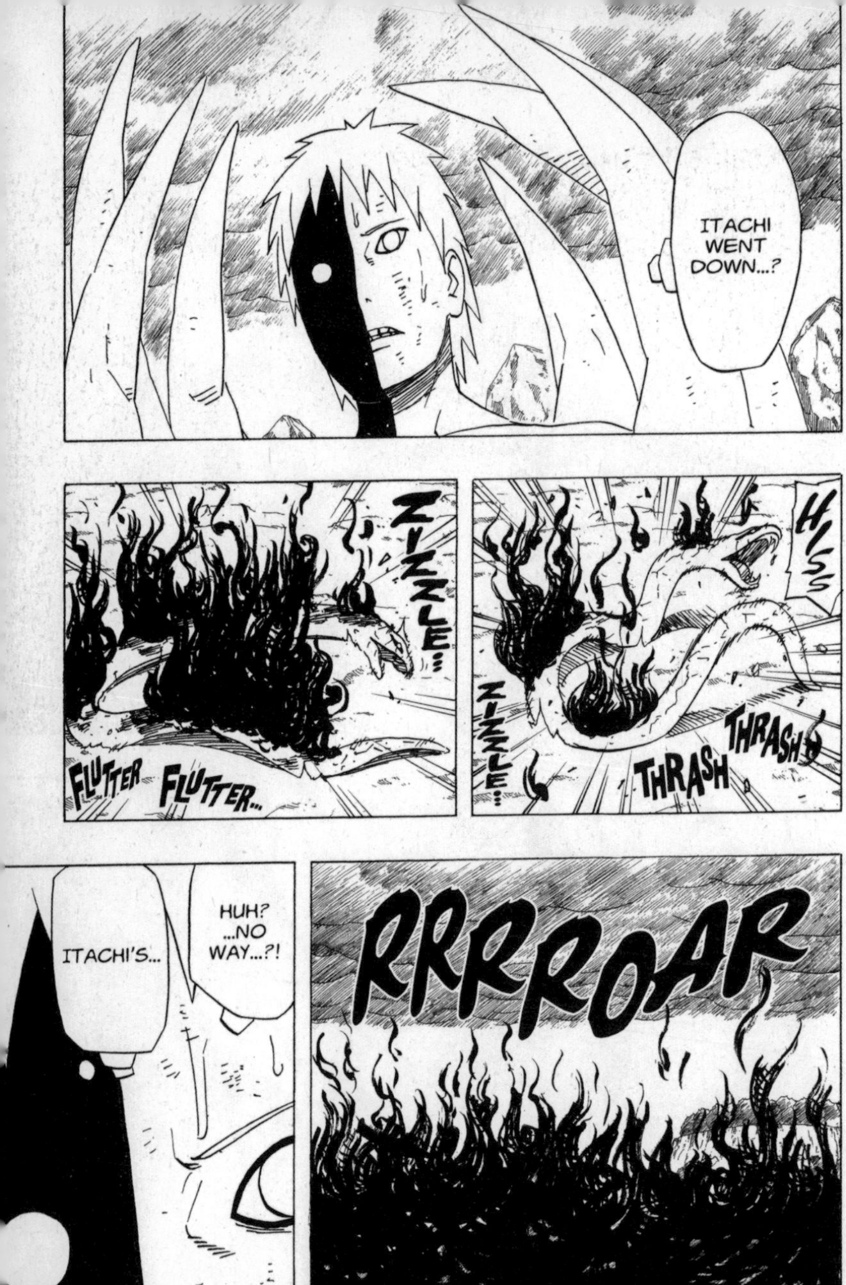
ITACHI WENT DOWN...?
HISS
ZIZZLE...
THRASH THRASH
ZIZZLE...
FLUTTER FLUTTER...
RRRROAR
HUH? ...NO WAY...?!
ITACHI'S...

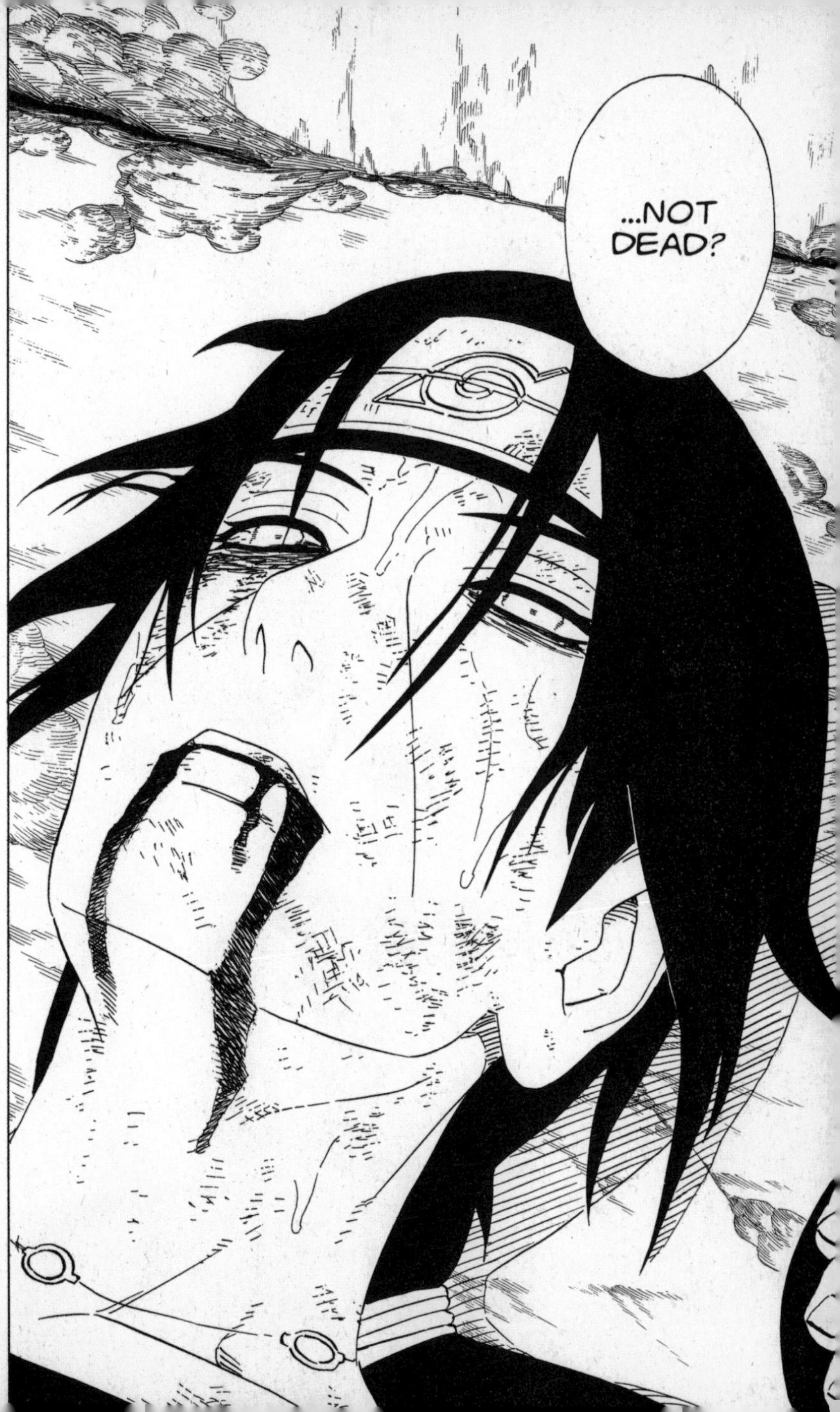
...NOT
DEAD?

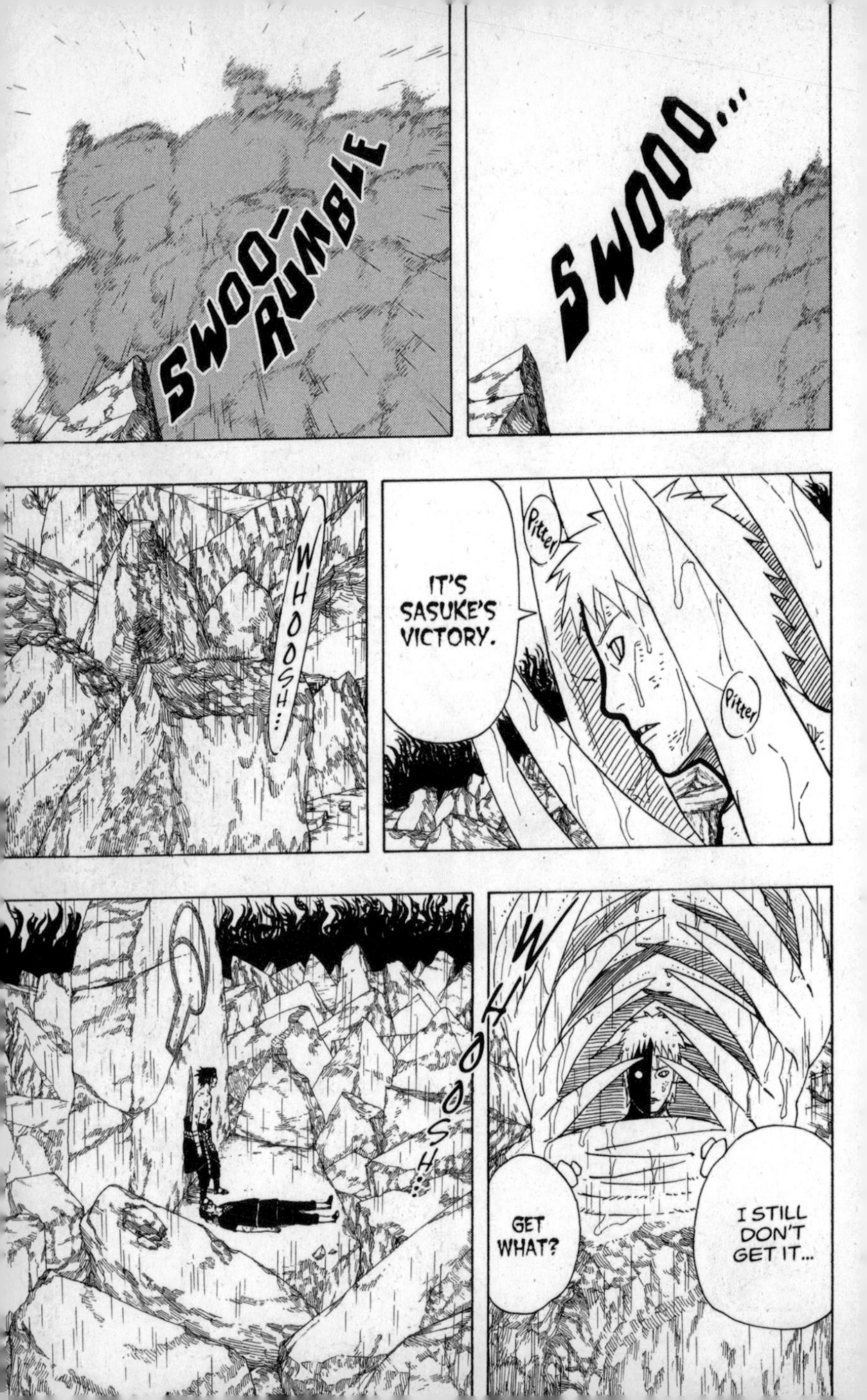
SWOO...
SWOO-RUMBLE
Pitter
IT'S SASUKE'S VICTORY.
Pitter
WHOOOSH...
I STILL DON'T GET IT...
GET WHAT?
WHOOOSH...

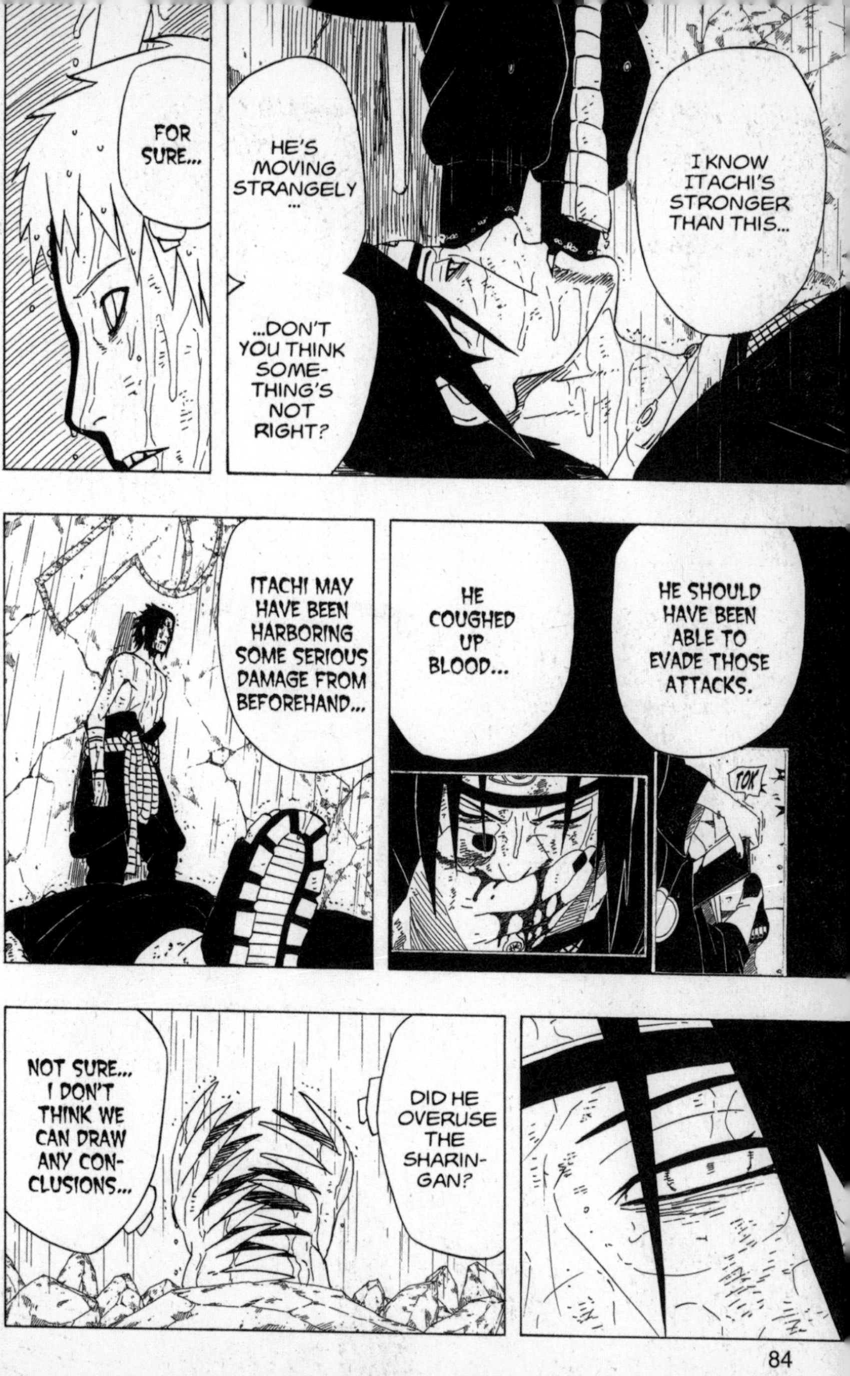
I KNOW ITACHI'S STRONGER THAN THIS...
HE'S MOVING STRANGELY...
...DON'T YOU THINK SOME-THING'S NOT RIGHT?
FOR SURE...
HE SHOULD HAVE BEEN ABLE TO EVADE THOSE ATTACKS.
HE COUGHED UP BLOOD...
TOK
ITACHI MAY HAVE BEEN HARBORING SOME SERIOUS DAMAGE FROM BEFOREHAND...
DID HE OVERUSE THE SHARIN-GAN?
NOT SURE... I DON'T THINK WE CAN DRAW ANY CON-CLUSIONS...

READ THIS WAY

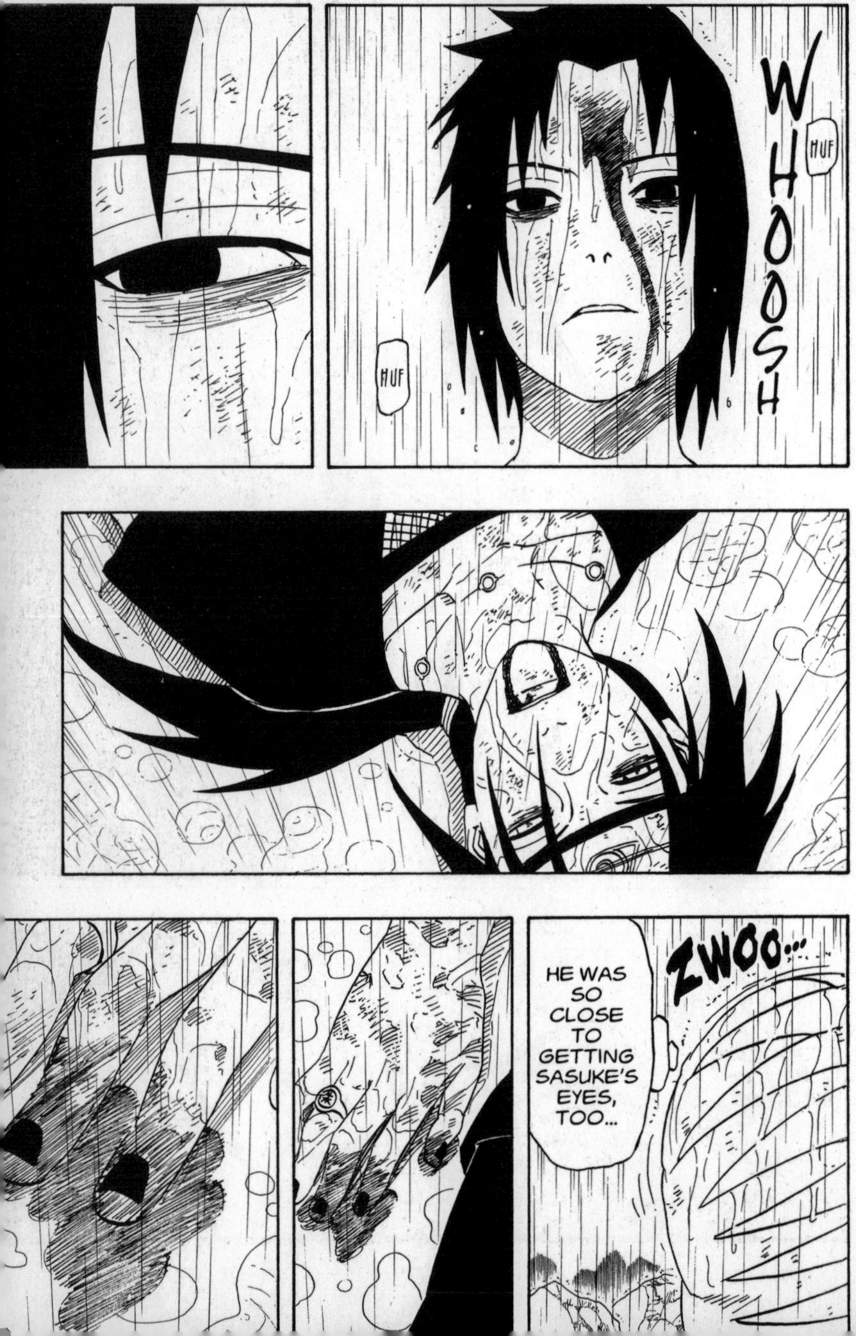
WHOOSH
HUF
HUF
ZWOO...
HE WAS SO CLOSE TO GETTING SASUKE'S EYES, TOO...

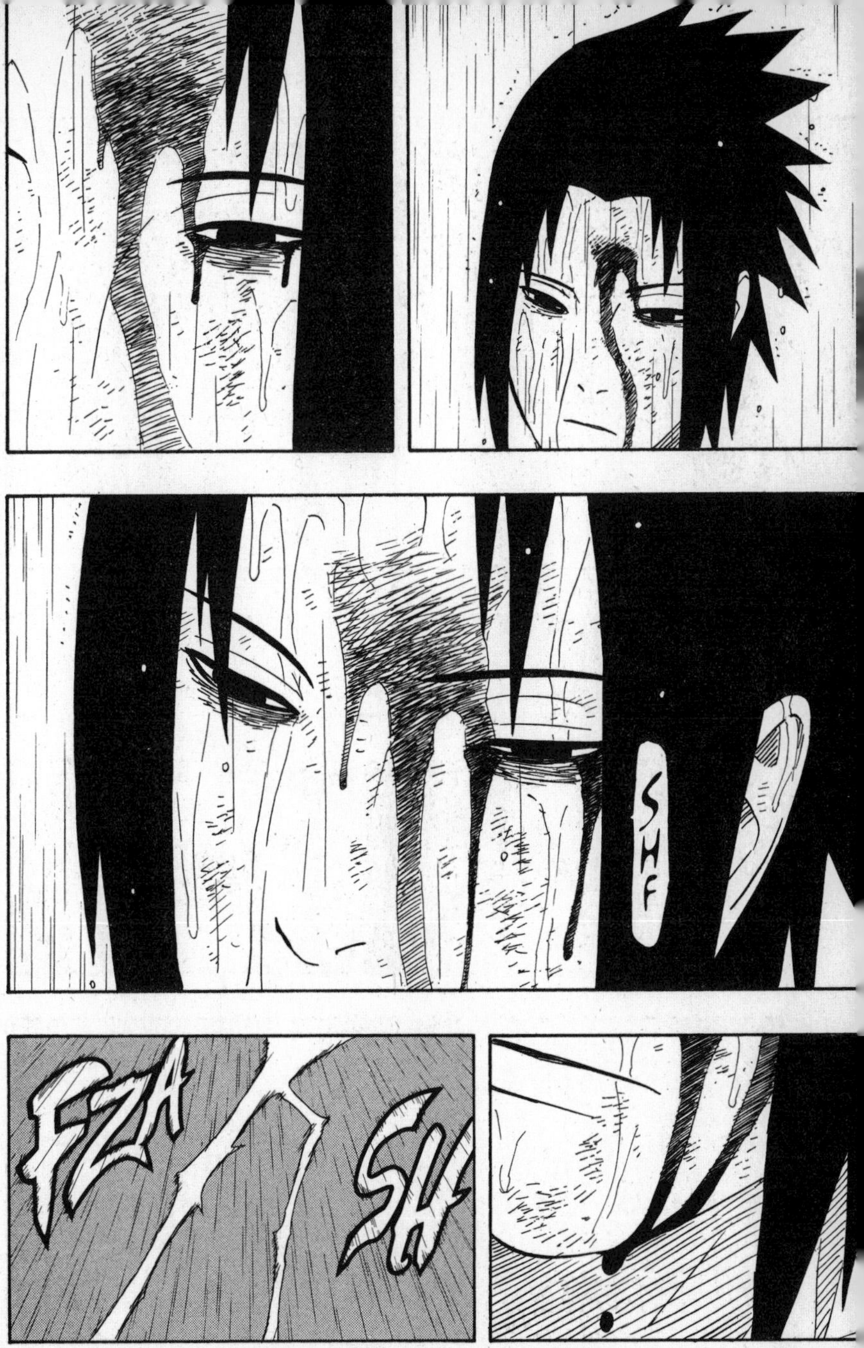
SHF
SH
FZA

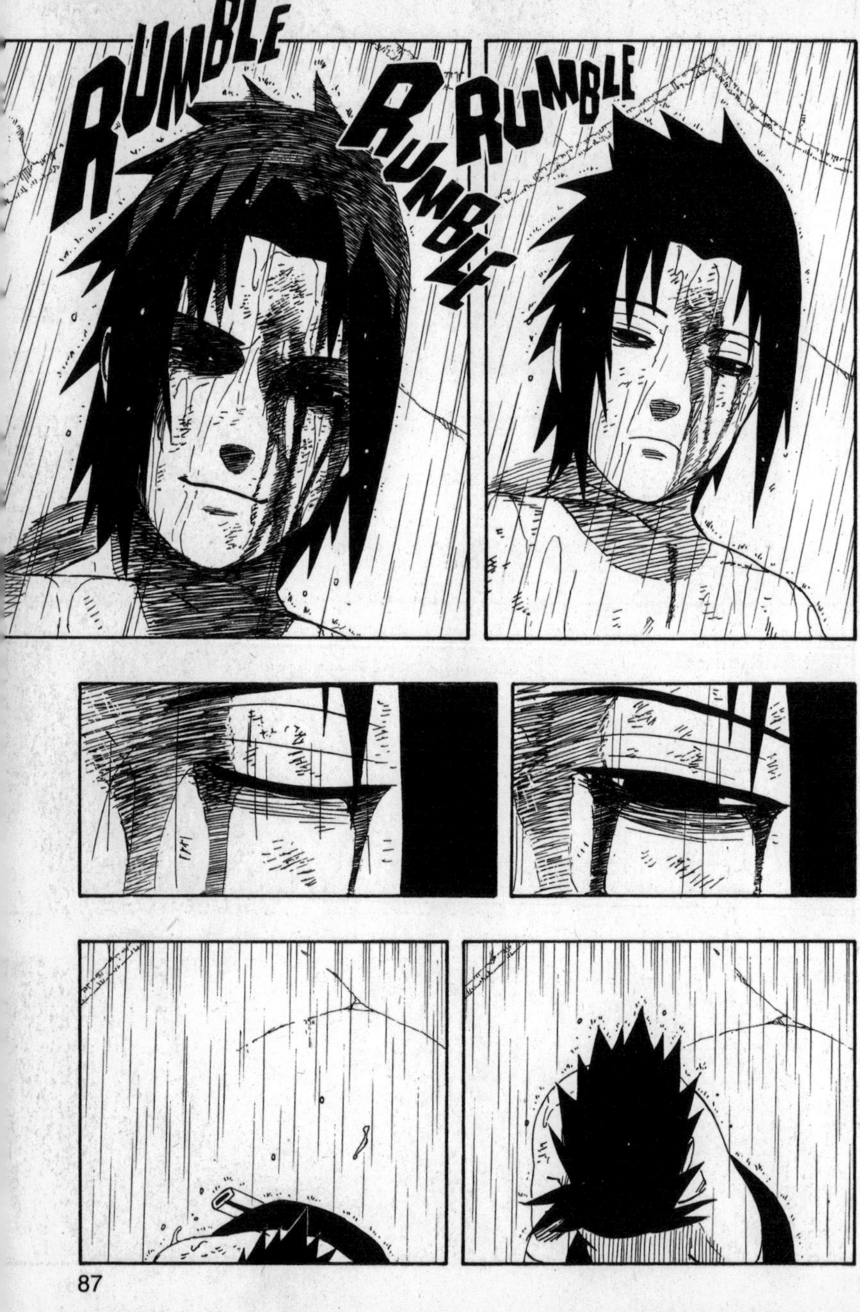
RUMBLE
RUMBLE
RUMBLE

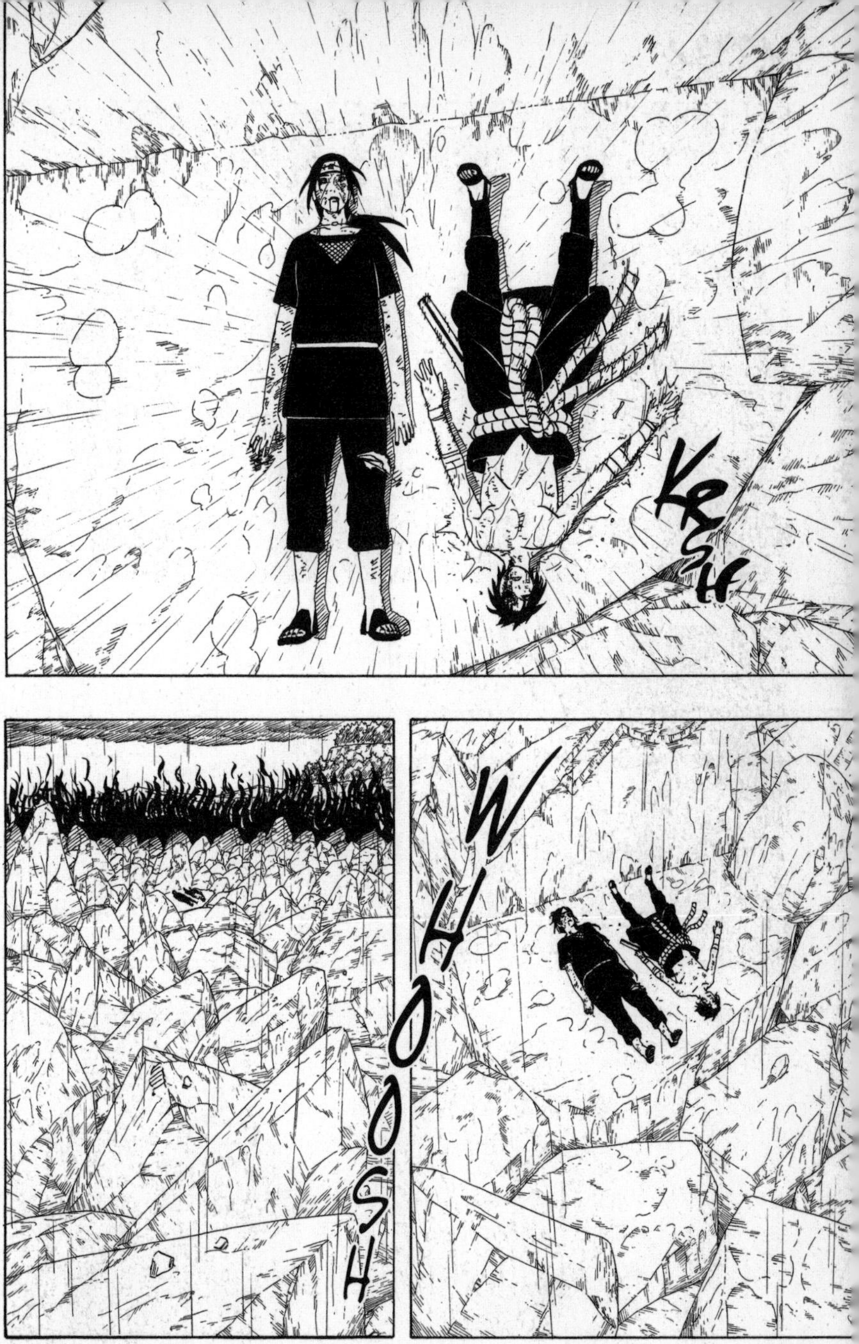
KRSH
WHOOSH

READ THIS WAY

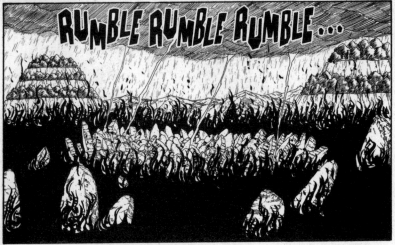

RUMBLE RUMBLE RUMBLE...

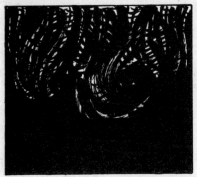

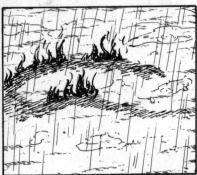

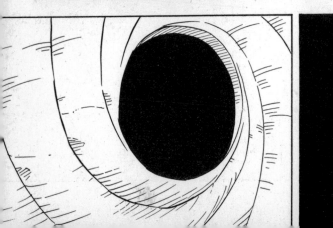

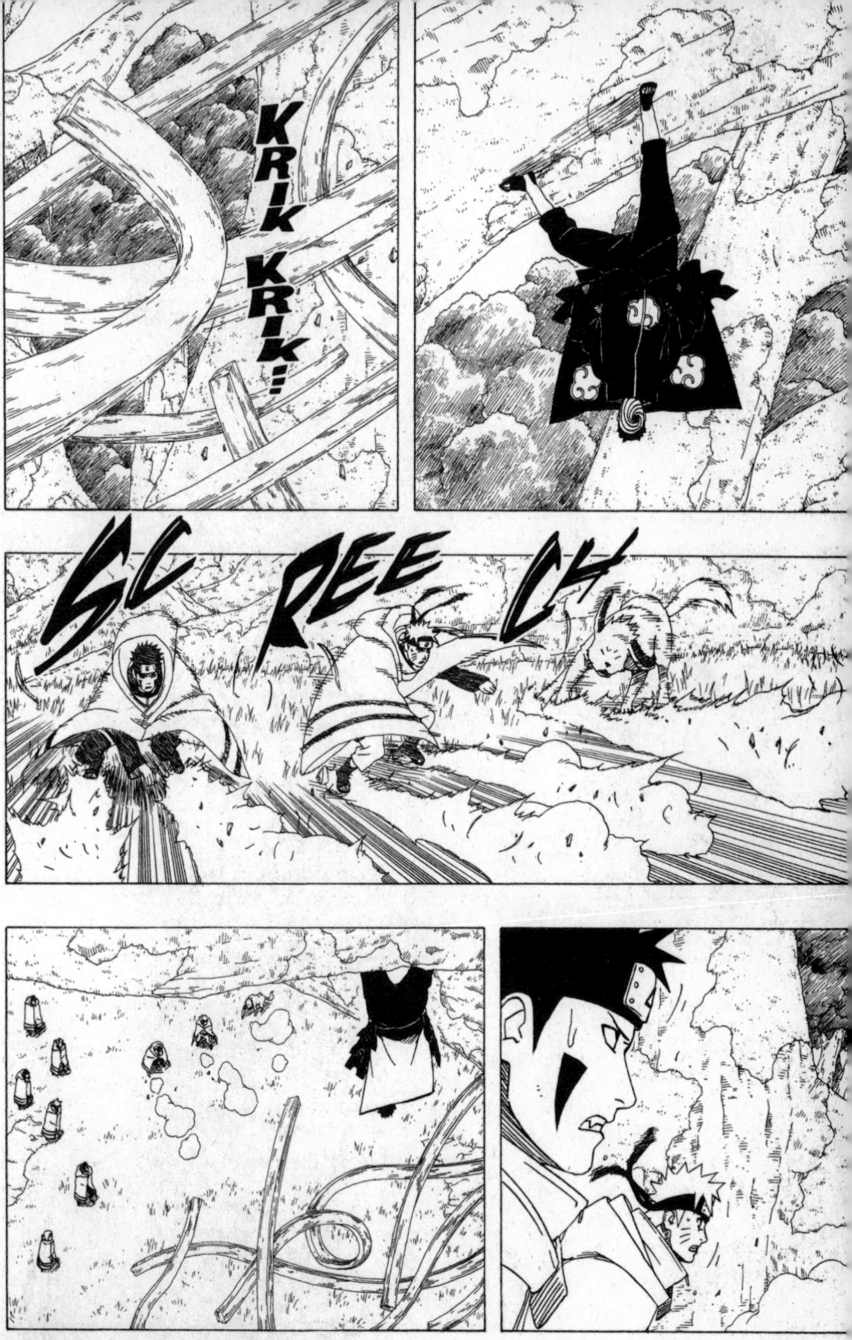
KRIK KRIK!!
SCREECH

READ THIS WAY

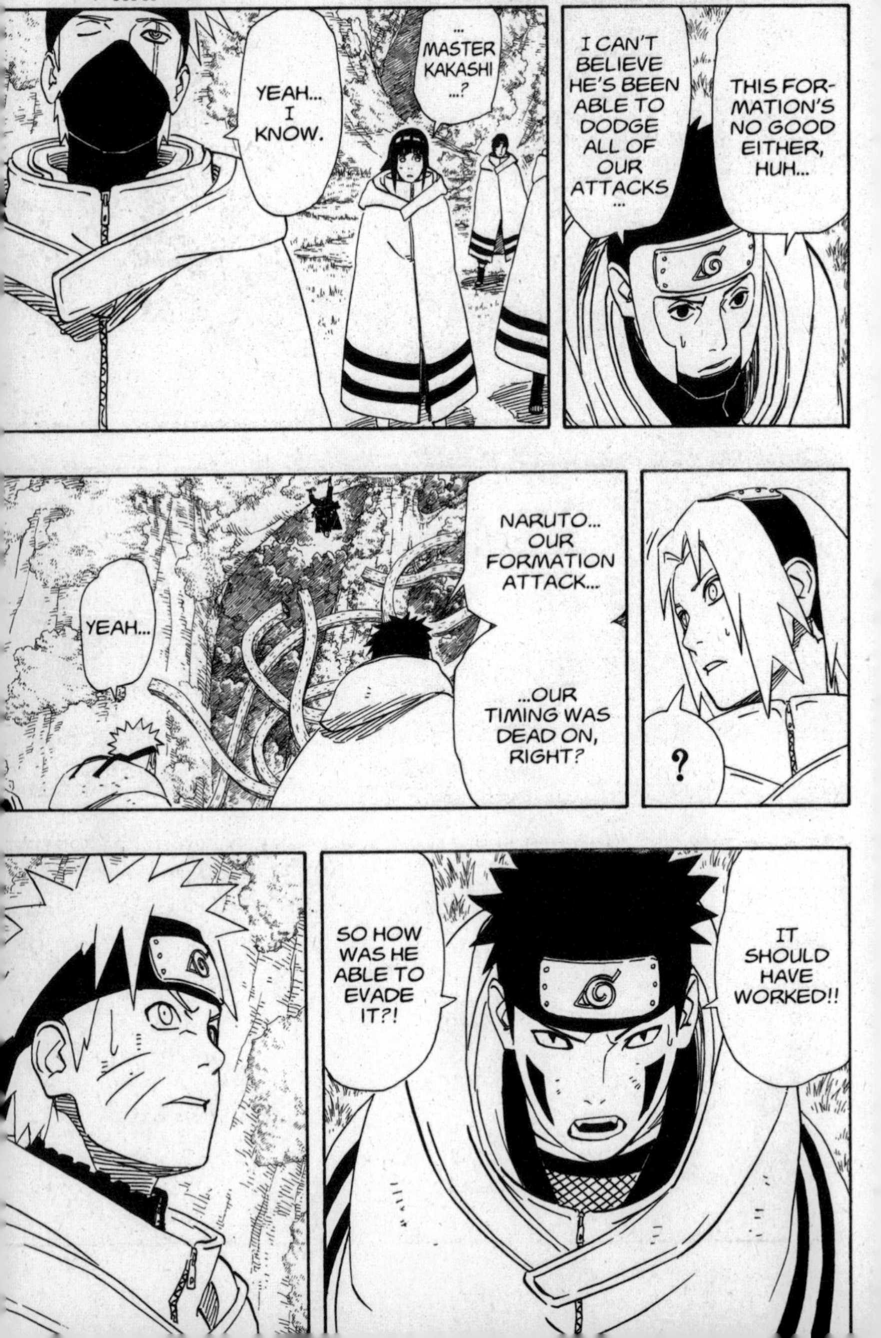
THIS FORMATION'S NO GOOD EITHER, HUH...
I CAN'T BELIEVE HE'S BEEN ABLE TO DODGE ALL OF OUR ATTACKS...
...MASTER KAKASHI...?
YEAH... I KNOW.
?
NARUTO... OUR FORMATION ATTACK...
...OUR TIMING WAS DEAD ON, RIGHT?
YEAH...
IT SHOULD HAVE WORKED!!
SO HOW WAS HE ABLE TO EVADE IT?!

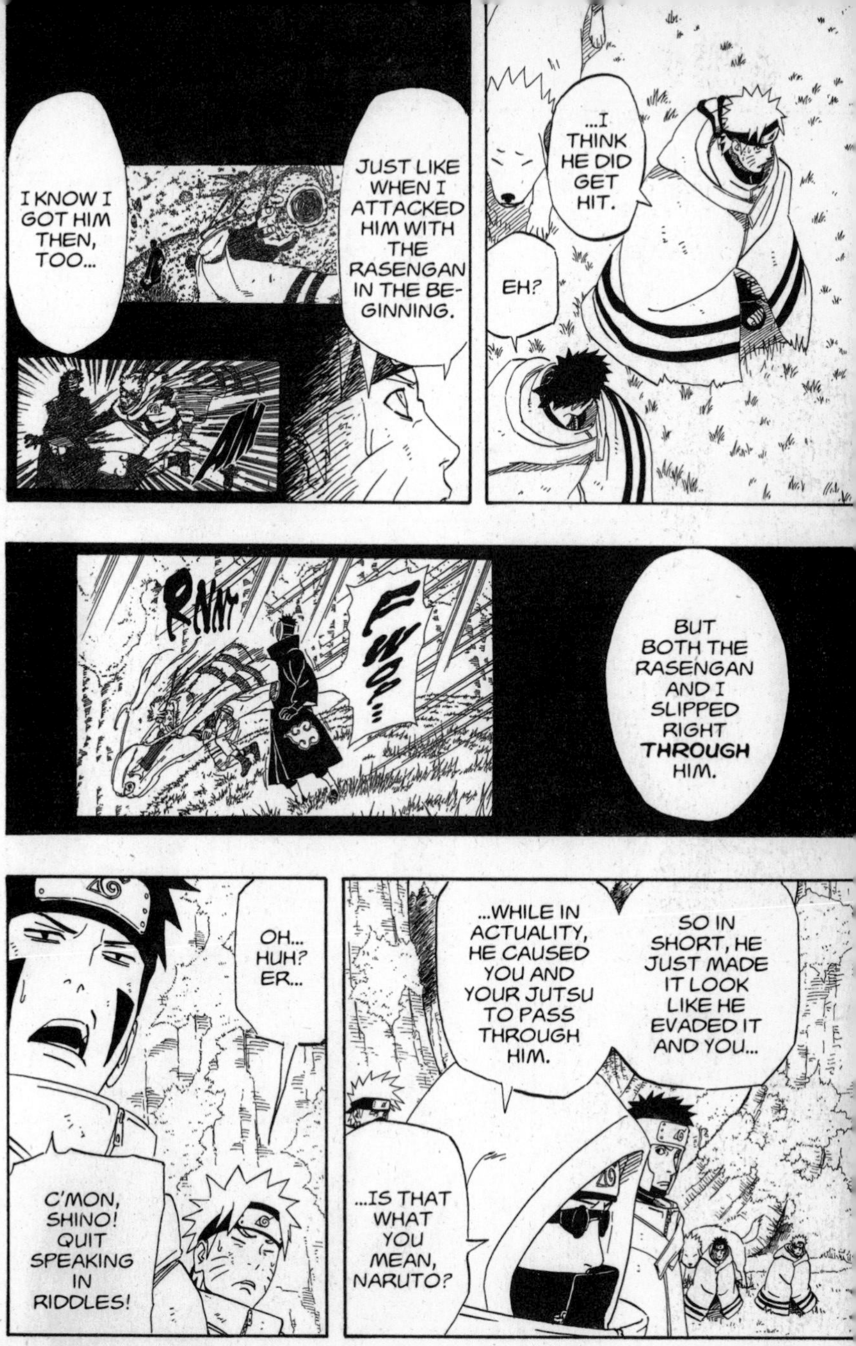
...I THINK HE DID GET HIT.
EH?
JUST LIKE WHEN I ATTACKED HIM WITH THE RASENGAN IN THE BEGINNING.
I KNOW I GOT HIM THEN, TOO...
BUT BOTH THE RASENGAN AND I SLIPPED RIGHT **THROUGH** HIM.
FWOO...
RNNT
SO IN SHORT, HE JUST MADE IT LOOK LIKE HE EVADED IT AND YOU...
...WHILE IN ACTUALITY, HE CAUSED YOU AND YOUR JUTSU TO PASS THROUGH HIM.
...IS THAT WHAT YOU MEAN, NARUTO?
OH... HUH? ER...
C'MON, SHINO! QUIT SPEAKING IN RIDDLES!

READ THIS WAY

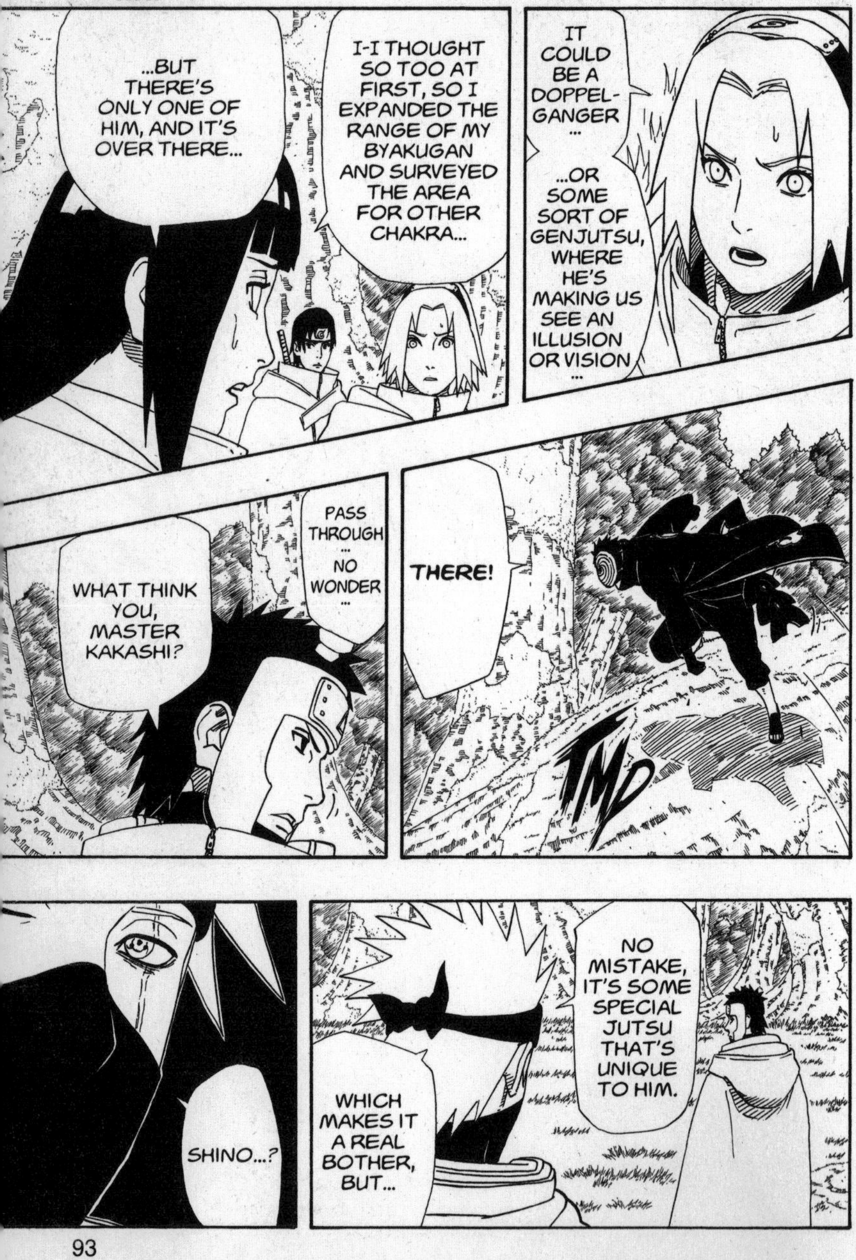

IT COULD BE A DOPPEL-GANGER...
...OR SOME SORT OF GENJUTSU, WHERE HE'S MAKING US SEE AN ILLUSION OR VISION...
I-I THOUGHT SO TOO AT FIRST, SO I EXPANDED THE RANGE OF MY BYAKUGAN AND SURVEYED THE AREA FOR OTHER CHAKRA...
...BUT THERE'S ONLY ONE OF HIM, AND IT'S OVER THERE...
THERE!
TMP
PASS THROUGH... NO WONDER...
WHAT THINK YOU, MASTER KAKASHI?
NO MISTAKE, IT'S SOME SPECIAL JUTSU THAT'S UNIQUE TO HIM.
WHICH MAKES IT A REAL BOTHER, BUT...
SHINO...?

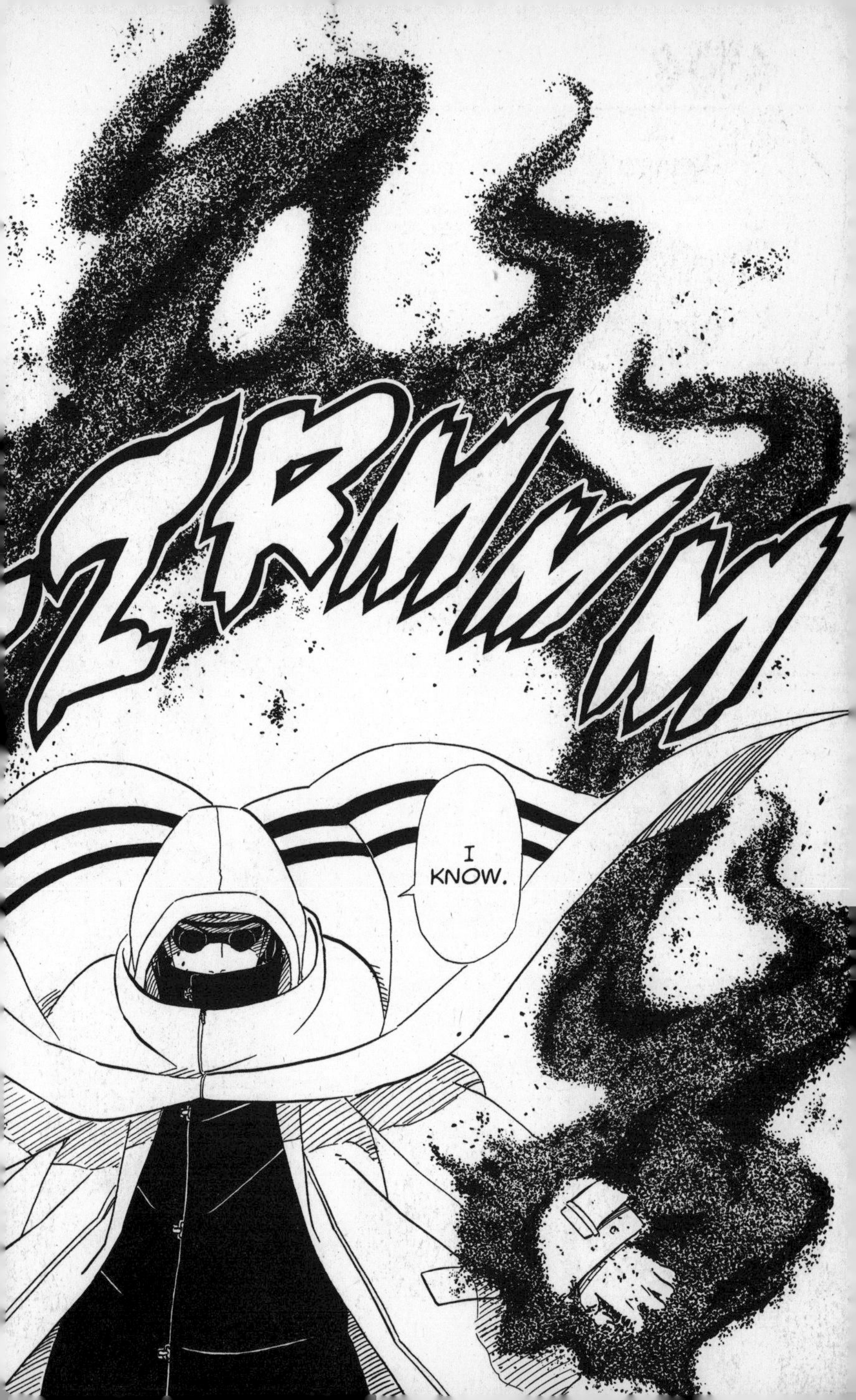
I KNOW.

READ THIS WAY

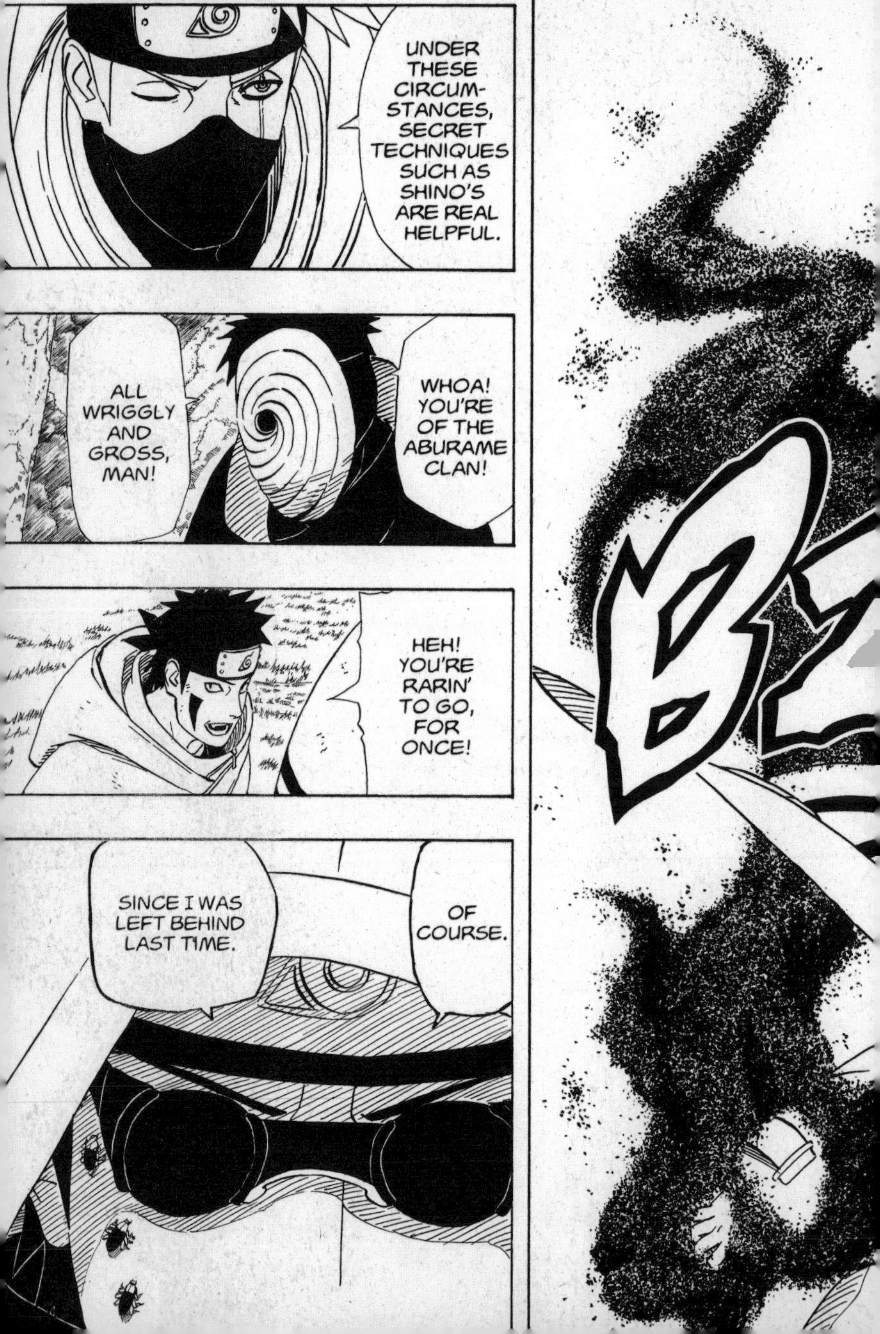
UNDER THESE CIRCUM-STANCES, SECRET TECHNIQUES SUCH AS SHINO'S ARE REAL HELPFUL.
WHOA! YOU'RE OF THE ABURAME CLAN!
ALL WRIGGLY AND GROSS, MAN!
HEH! YOU'RE RARIN' TO GO, FOR ONCE!
OF COURSE.
SINCE I WAS LEFT BEHIND LAST TIME.

NARUTO

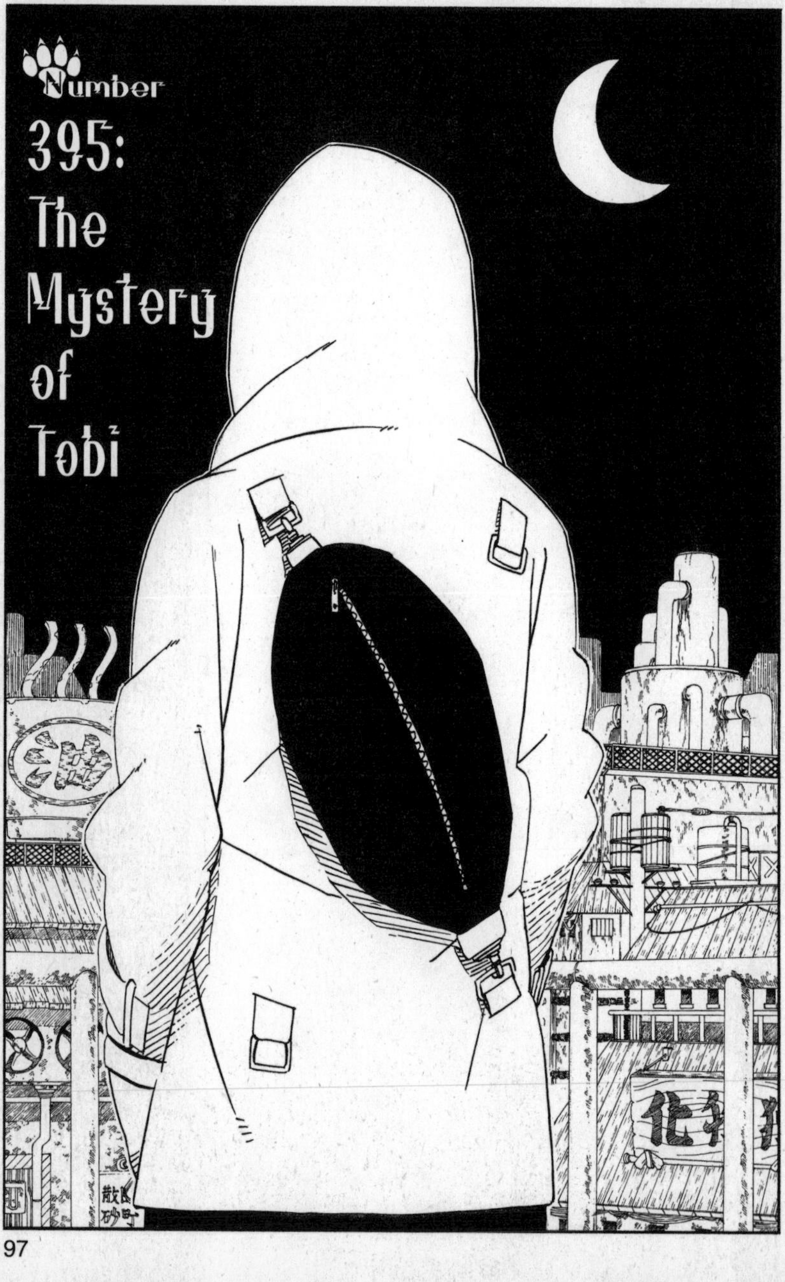
Number
395:
The Mystery of Tobi

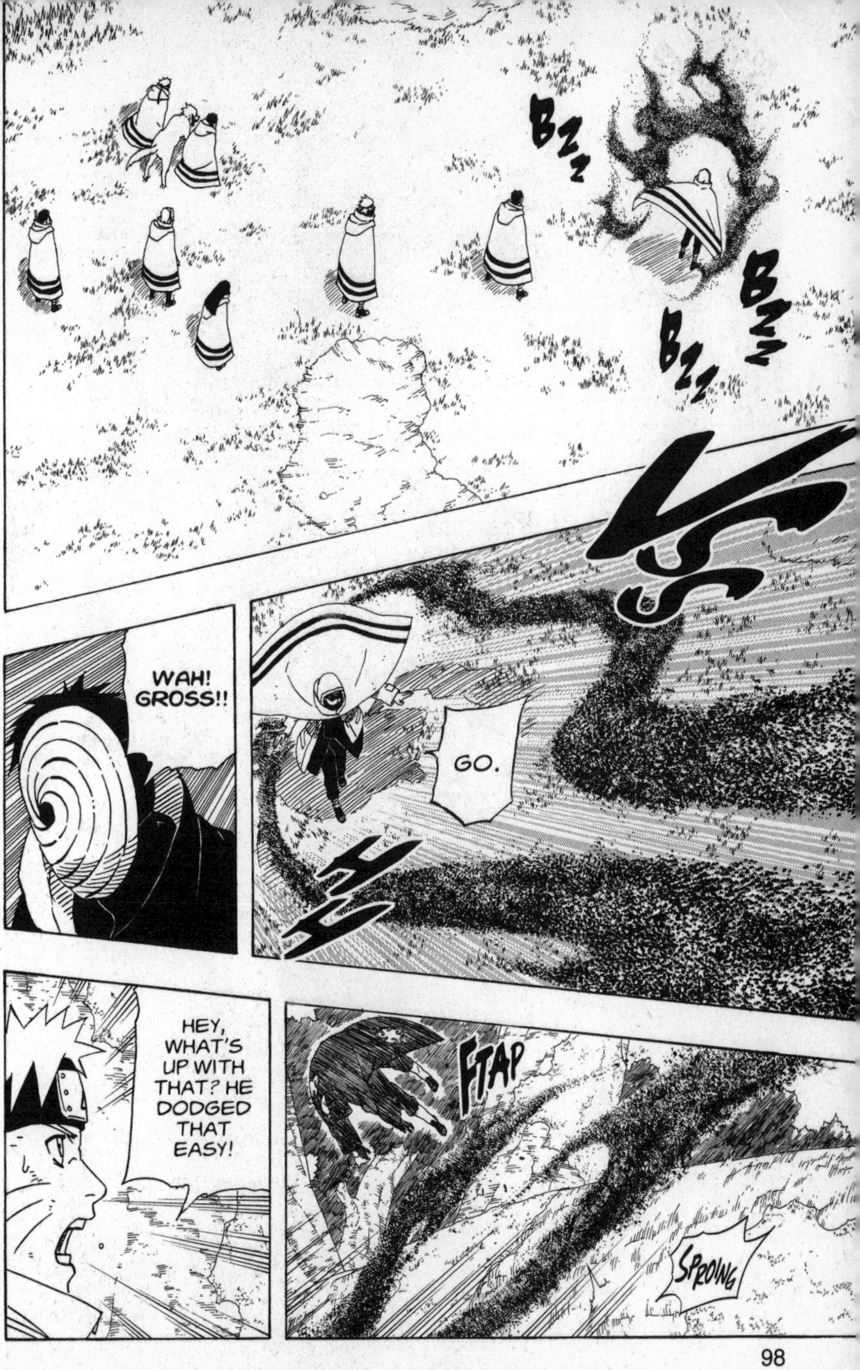
BZZ
BZZ
BZZ
GO.
WAH! GROSS!!
FTAP
SPROING
HEY, WHAT'S UP WITH THAT? HE DODGED THAT EASY!

READ THIS WAY

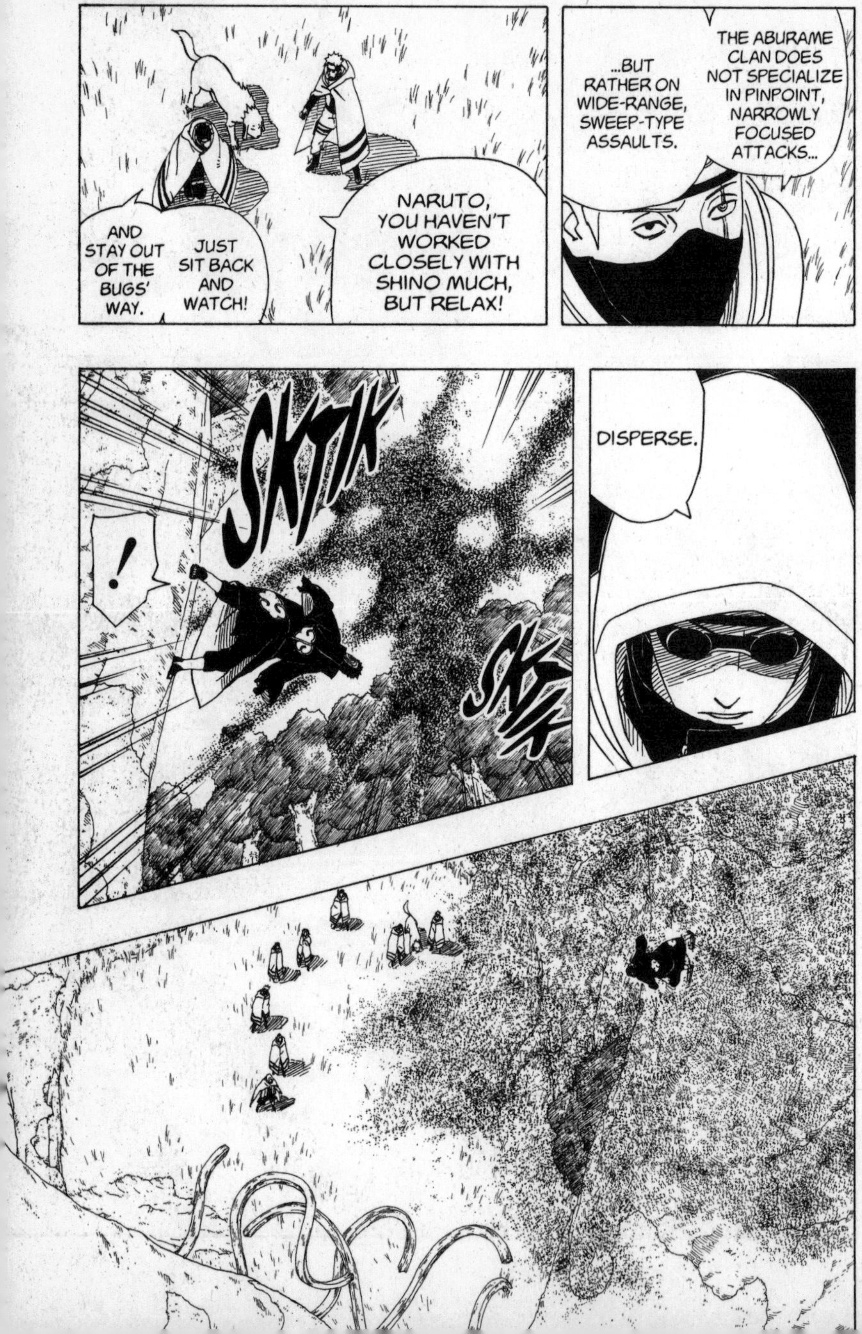
THE ABURAME CLAN DOES NOT SPECIALIZE IN PINPOINT, NARROWLY FOCUSED ATTACKS...
...BUT RATHER ON WIDE-RANGE, SWEEP-TYPE ASSAULTS.
NARUTO, YOU HAVEN'T WORKED CLOSELY WITH SHINO MUCH, BUT RELAX!
JUST SIT BACK AND WATCH!
AND STAY OUT OF THE BUGS' WAY.
DISPERSE.
SKTIK
!
SKTIK

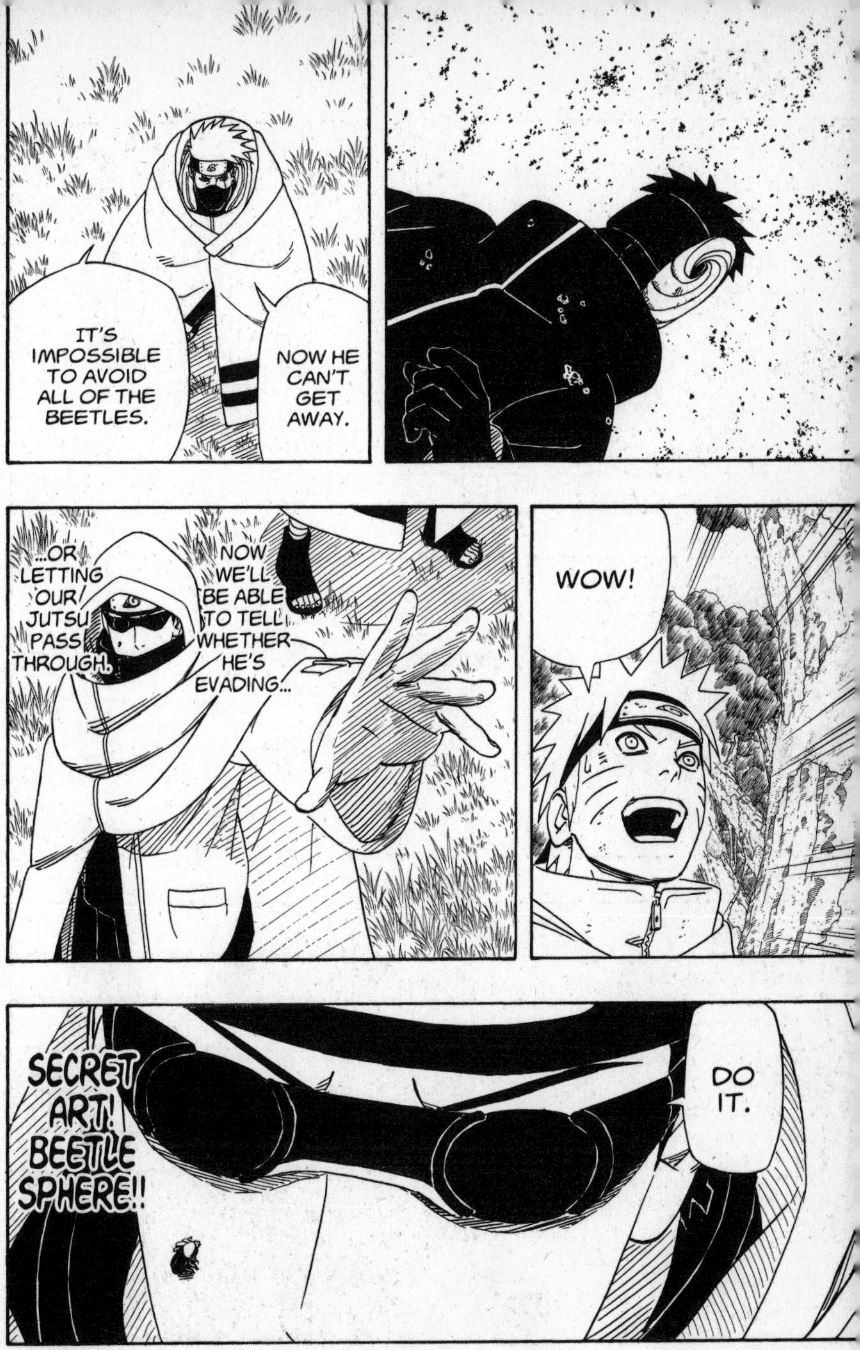
NOW HE CAN'T GET AWAY.
IT'S IMPOSSIBLE TO AVOID ALL OF THE BEETLES.
WOW!
NOW WE'LL BE ABLE TO TELL WHETHER HE'S EVADING...
...OR LETTING OUR JUTSU PASS THROUGH.
DO IT.
SECRET ART! BEETLE SPHERE!!

READ THIS WAY

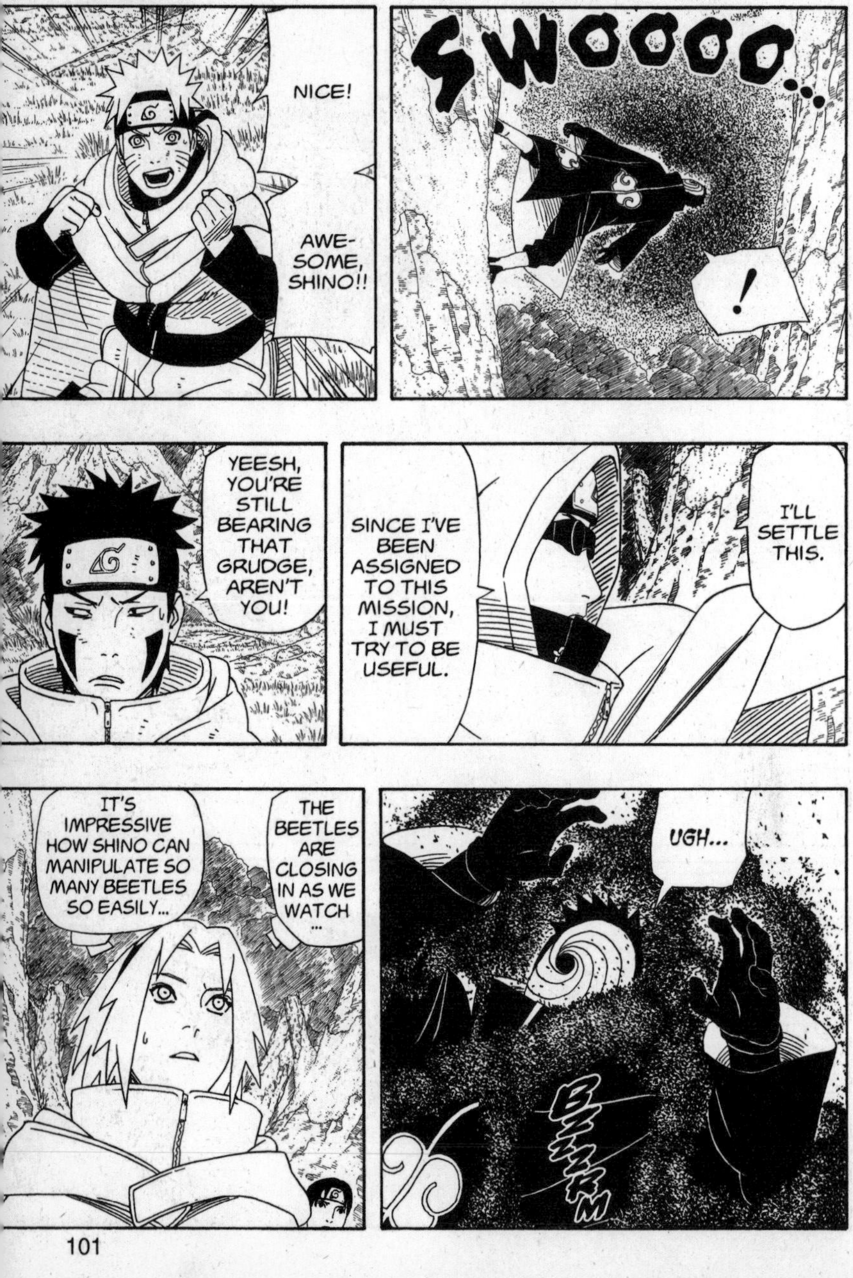
SWOOOO...
!
NICE!
AWESOME, SHINO!!
I'LL SETTLE THIS.
SINCE I'VE BEEN ASSIGNED TO THIS MISSION, I MUST TRY TO BE USEFUL.
YEESH, YOU'RE STILL BEARING THAT GRUDGE, AREN'T YOU!
UGH...
BZZZM
THE BEETLES ARE CLOSING IN AS WE WATCH...
IT'S IMPRESSIVE HOW SHINO CAN MANIPULATE SO MANY BEETLES SO EASILY...

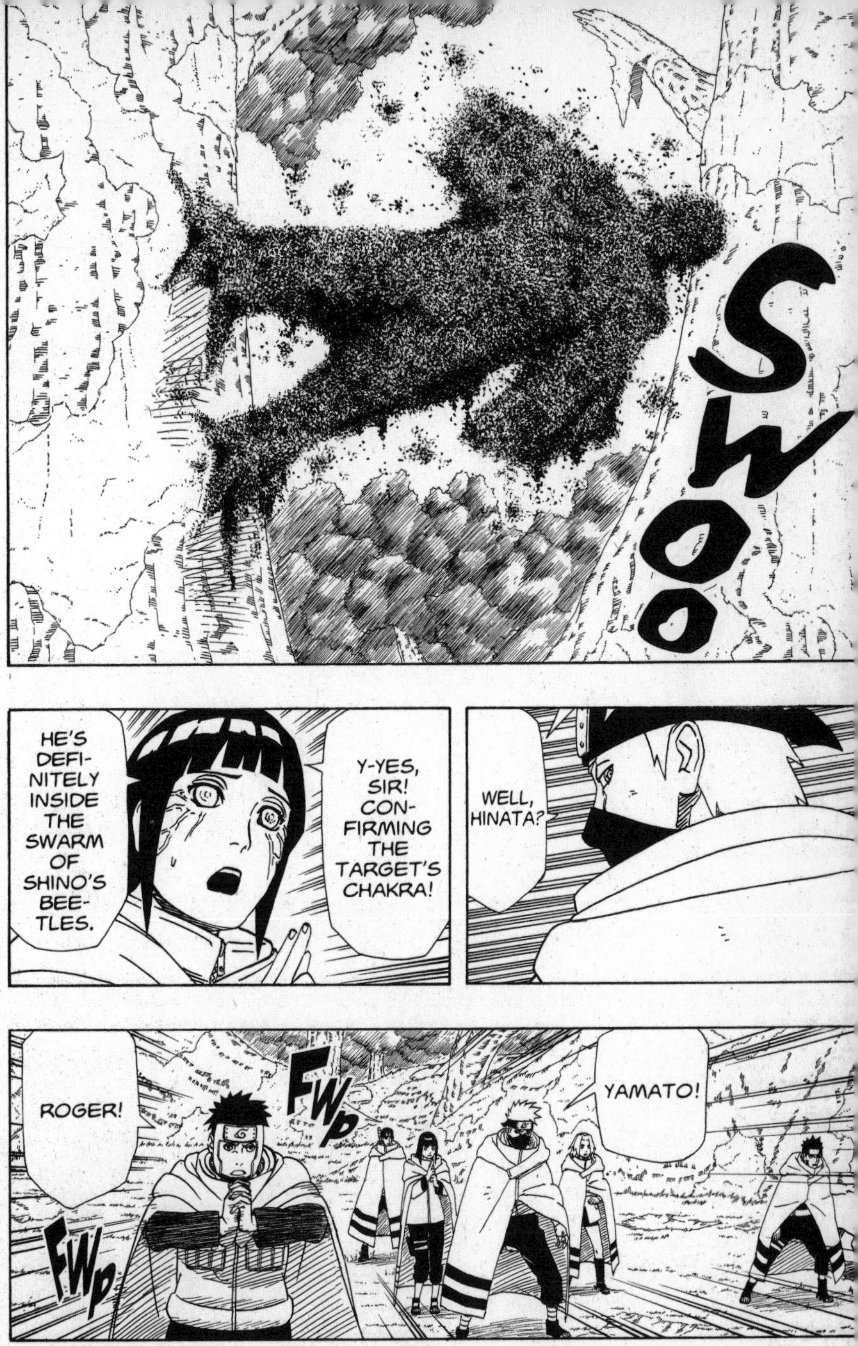
SWOOO
WELL, HINATA?
Y-YES, SIR! CON-FIRMING THE TARGET'S CHAKRA!
HE'S DEFI-NITELY INSIDE THE SWARM OF SHINO'S BEE-TLES.
YAMATO!
FWP
ROGER!
FWP

READ THIS WAY

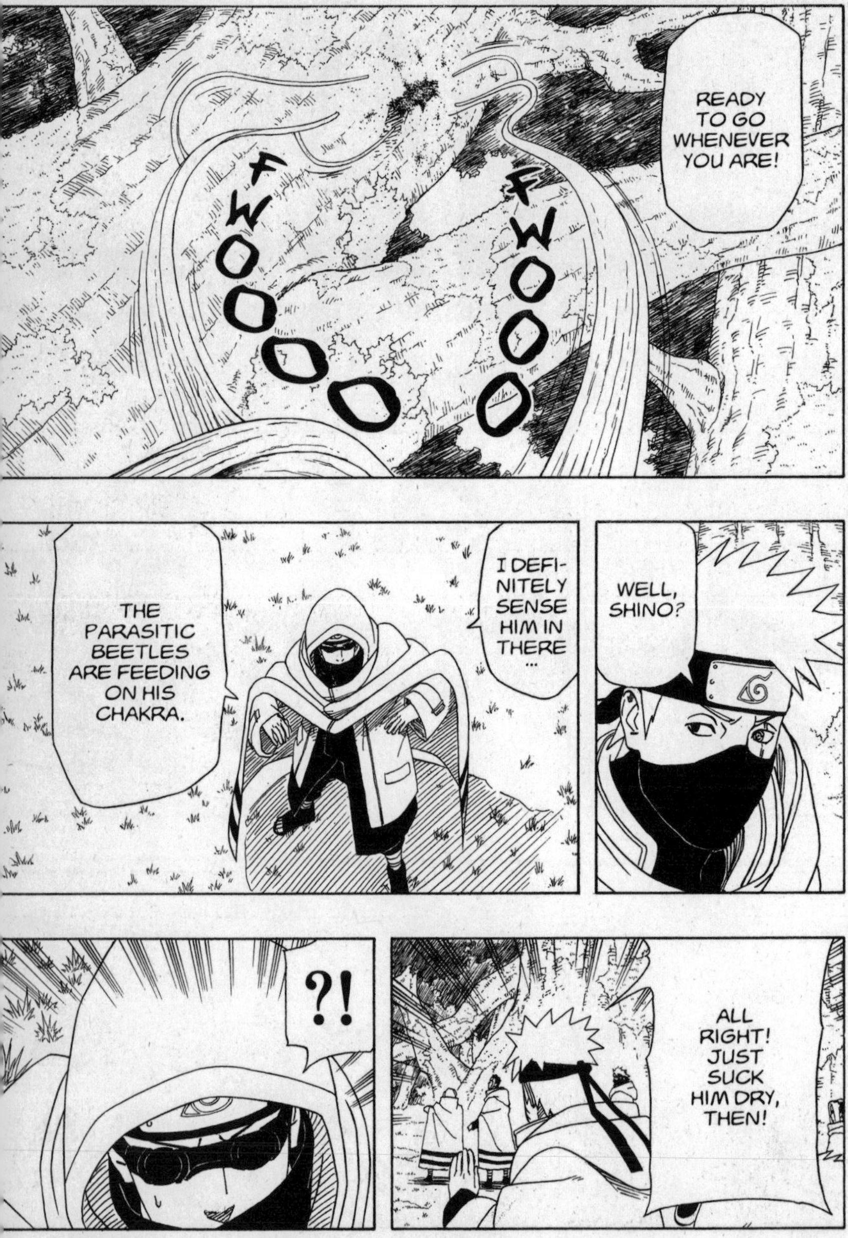
READY TO GO WHENEVER YOU ARE!
FWOOOO
FWOOOO
WELL, SHINO?
I DEFINITELY SENSE HIM IN THERE ...
THE PARASITIC BEETLES ARE FEEDING ON HIS CHAKRA.
ALL RIGHT! JUST SUCK HIM DRY, THEN!
?!

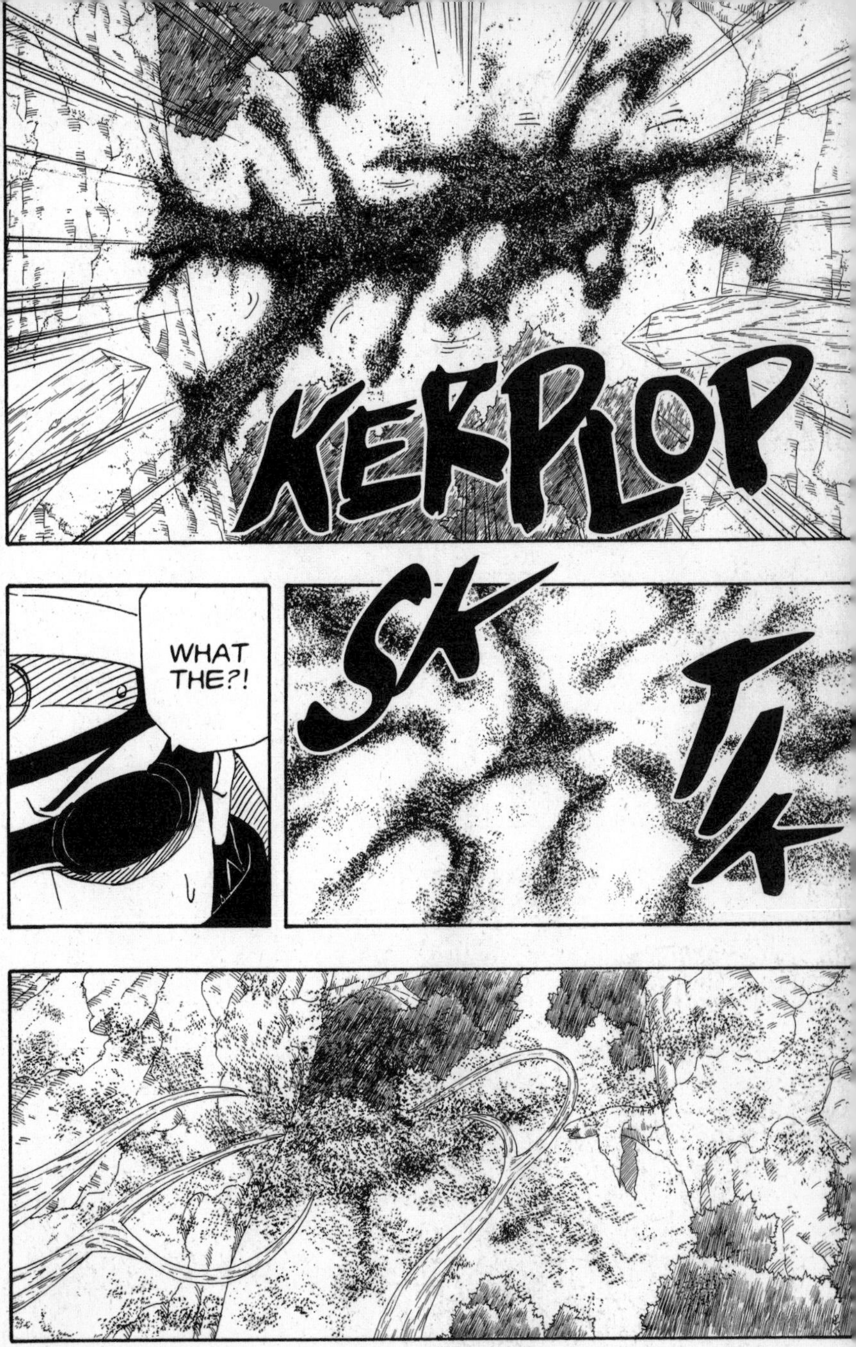
KERPLOP
SK
TIK
WHAT THE?!

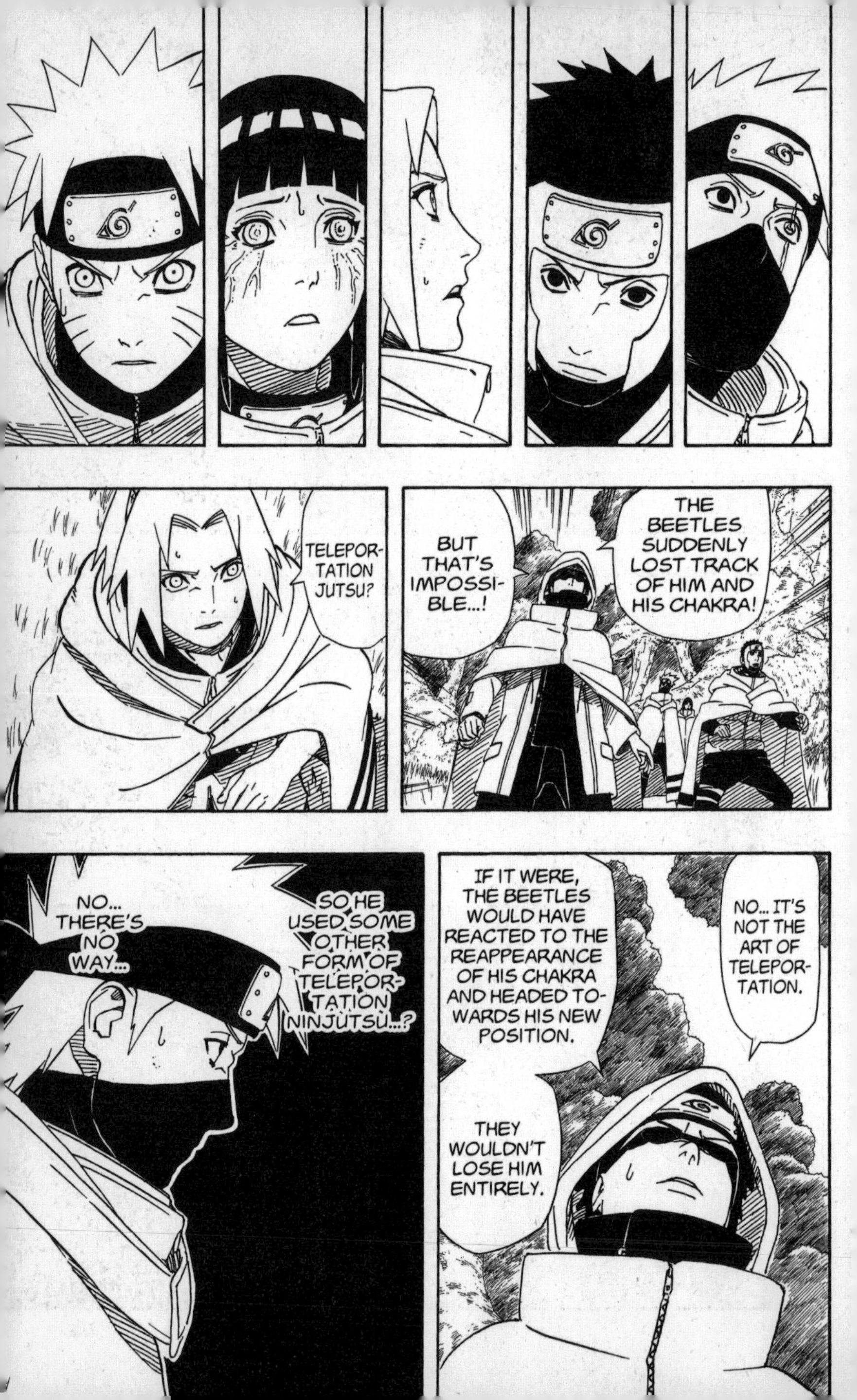
THE BEETLES SUDDENLY LOST TRACK OF HIM AND HIS CHAKRA!
BUT THAT'S IMPOSSIBLE...!
TELEPORTATION JUTSU?
NO... IT'S NOT THE ART OF TELEPORTATION.
IF IT WERE, THE BEETLES WOULD HAVE REACTED TO THE REAPPEARANCE OF HIS CHAKRA AND HEADED TOWARDS HIS NEW POSITION.
THEY WOULDN'T LOSE HIM ENTIRELY.
SO HE USED SOME OTHER FORM OF TELEPORTATION NINJUTSU...?
NO... THERE'S NO WAY...

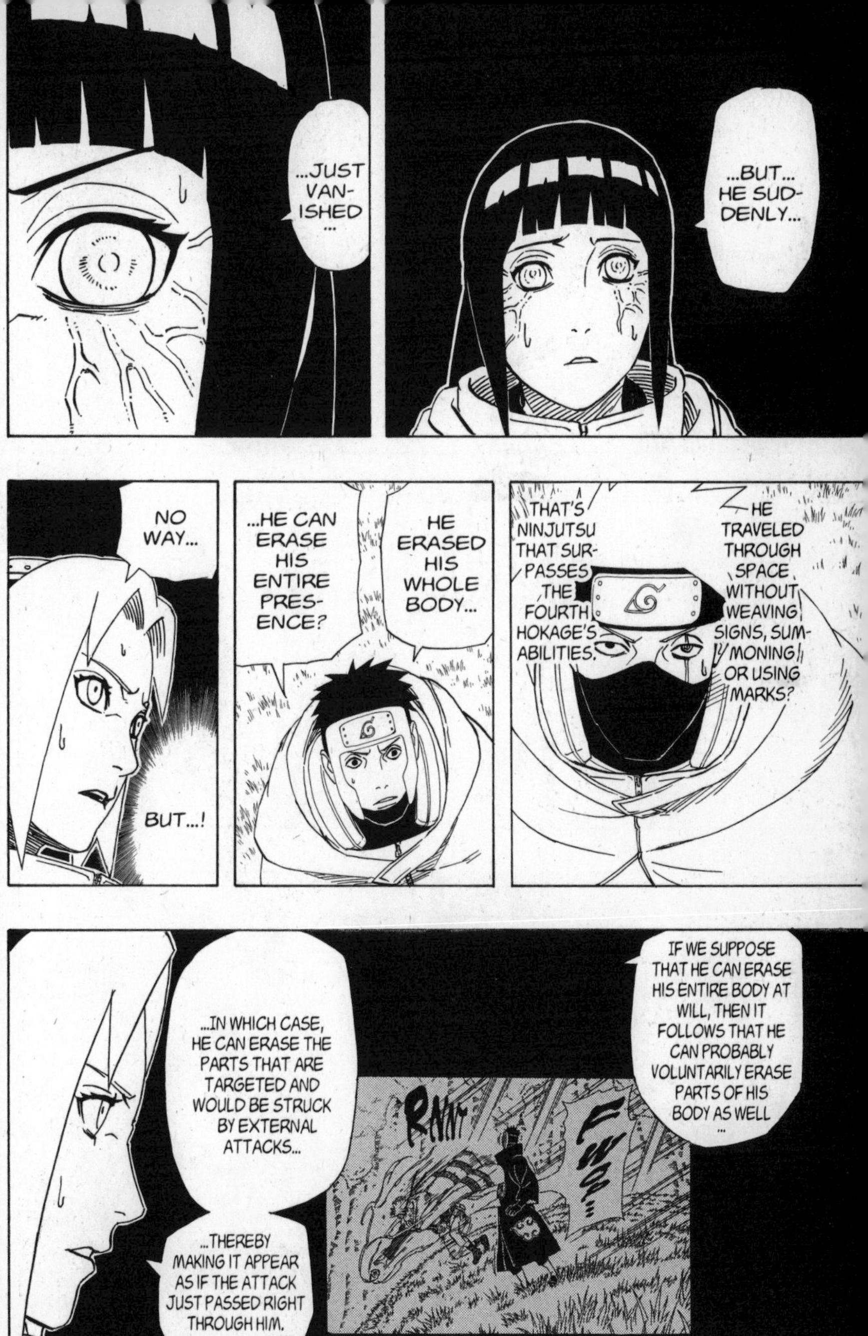

...BUT... HE SUDDENLY...
...JUST VANISHED...
HE TRAVELED THROUGH SPACE WITHOUT WEAVING SIGNS, SUMMONING OR USING MARKS?
THAT'S NINJUTSU THAT SURPASSES THE FOURTH HOKAGE'S ABILITIES.
HE ERASED HIS WHOLE BODY...
...HE CAN ERASE HIS ENTIRE PRESENCE?
NO WAY...
BUT...!
IF WE SUPPOSE THAT HE CAN ERASE HIS ENTIRE BODY AT WILL, THEN IT FOLLOWS THAT HE CAN PROBABLY VOLUNTARILY ERASE PARTS OF HIS BODY AS WELL...
...IN WHICH CASE, HE CAN ERASE THE PARTS THAT ARE TARGETED AND WOULD BE STRUCK BY EXTERNAL ATTACKS...
RNNT
...THEREBY MAKING IT APPEAR AS IF THE ATTACK JUST PASSED RIGHT THROUGH HIM.

READ THIS WAY

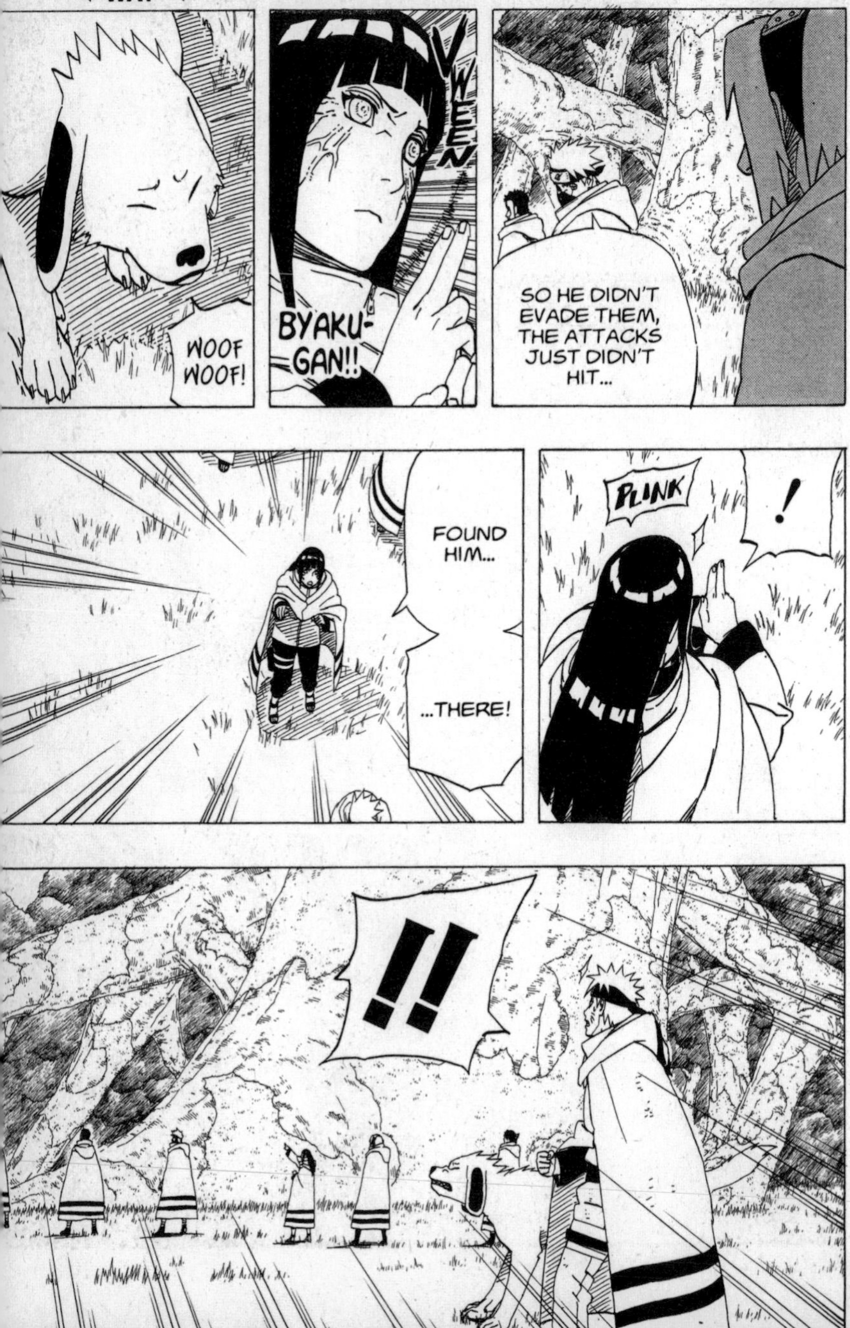
SO HE DIDN'T EVADE THEM, THE ATTACKS JUST DIDN'T HIT...
VWEEN
BYAKU-GAN!!
WOOF WOOF!
PLINK
!
FOUND HIM...
...THERE!
!!

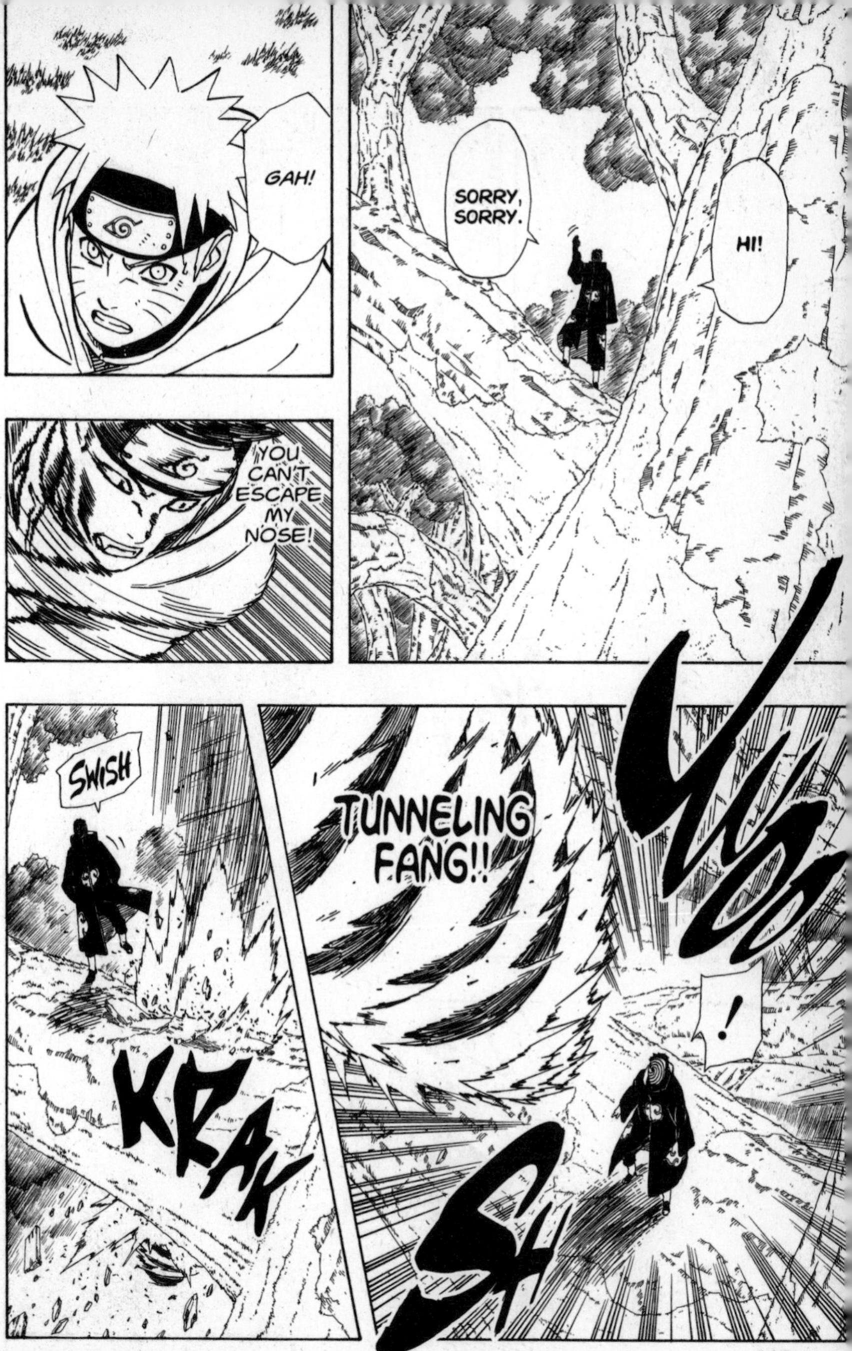
HI!
SORRY, SORRY.
GAH!
YOU CAN'T ESCAPE MY NOSE!
TUNNELING FANG!!
!
SWISH
KRAK

READ THIS WAY

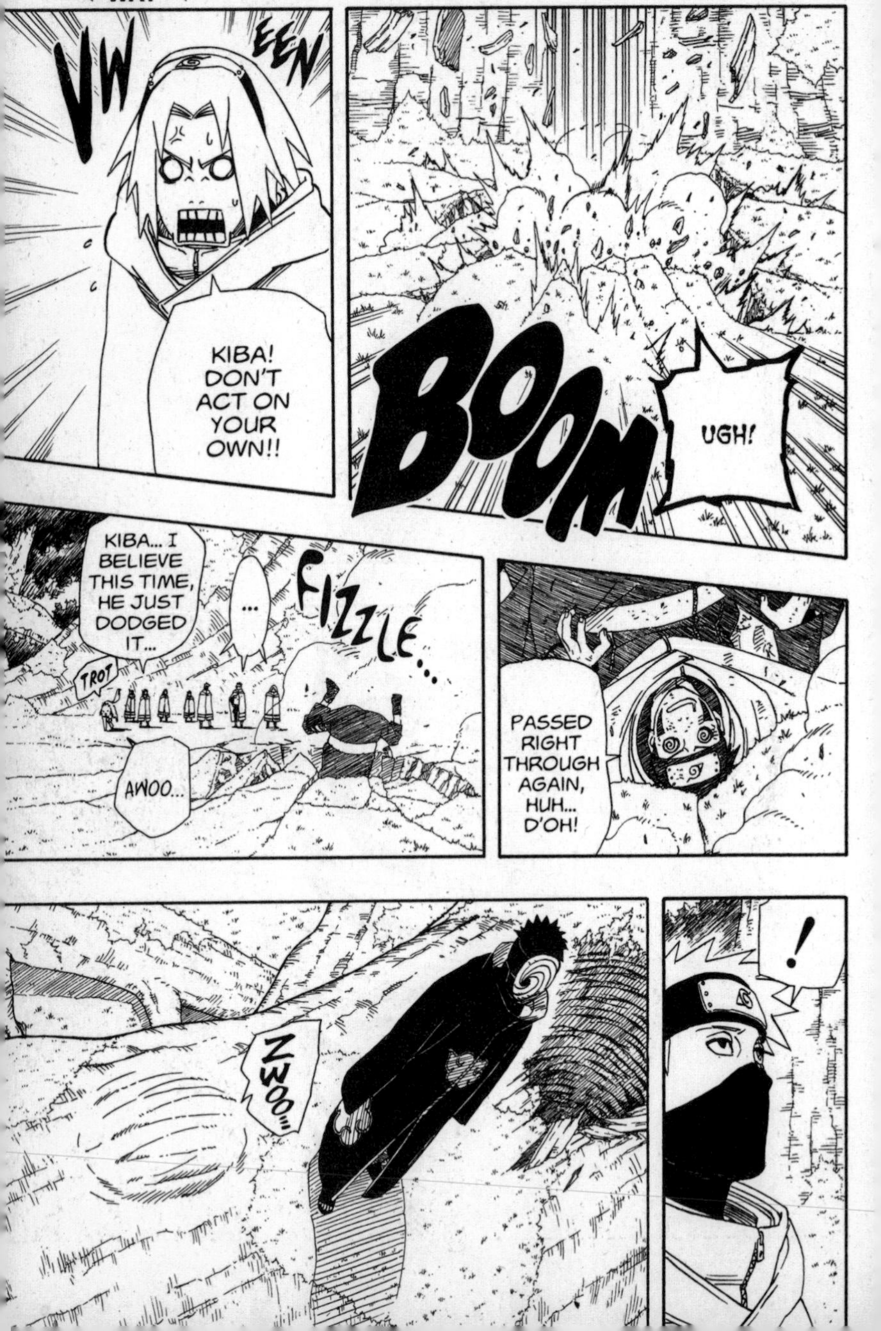
BOOM
UGH!
VWEEN
KIBA! DON'T ACT ON YOUR OWN!!
PASSED RIGHT THROUGH AGAIN, HUH... D'OH!
FIZZLE...
...
KIBA... I BELIEVE THIS TIME, HE JUST DODGED IT...
TROT
AWOO...
!
ZWOO...

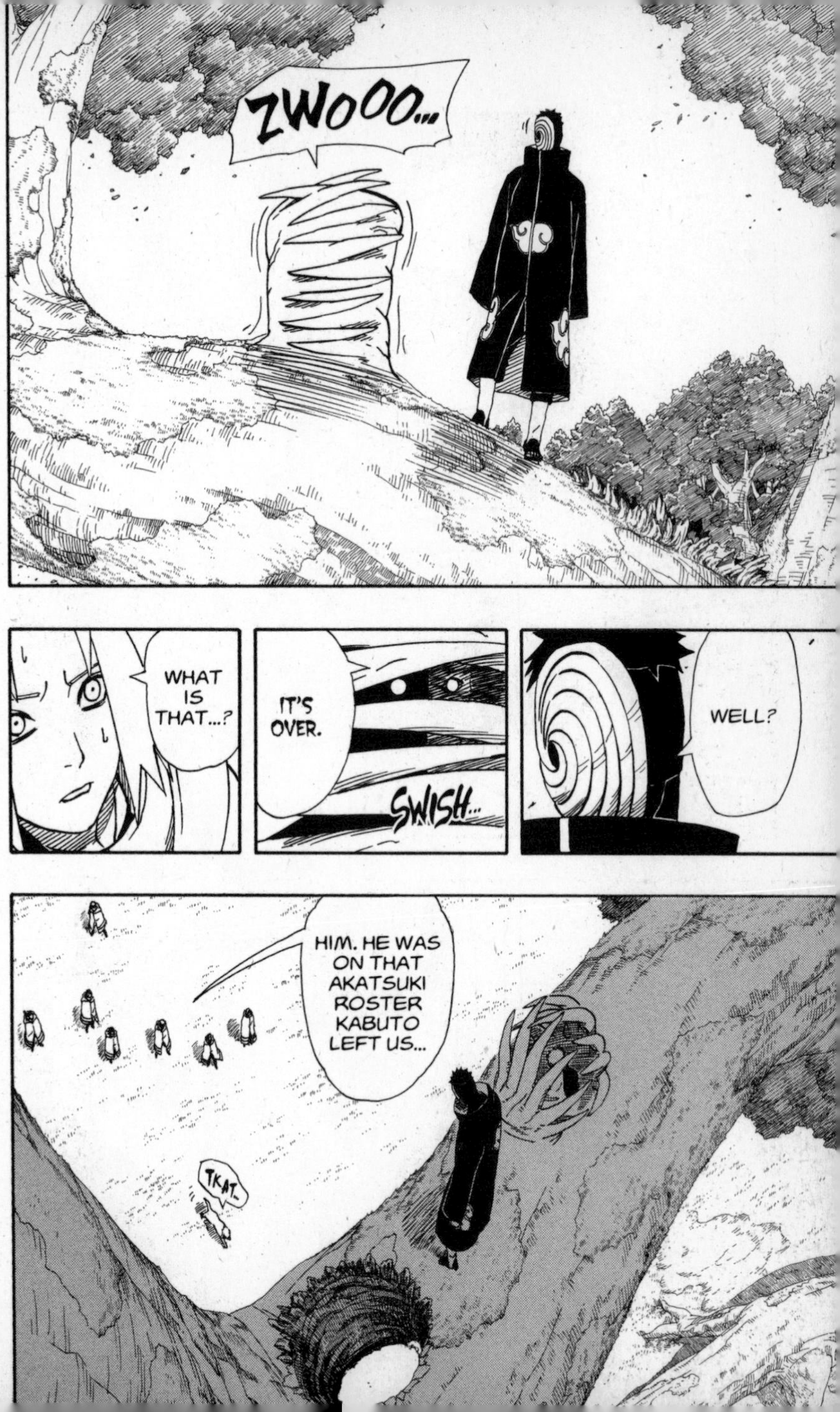
ZWOOO...
WELL?
IT'S OVER.
SWISH...
WHAT IS THAT...?
HIM. HE WAS ON THAT AKATSUKI ROSTER KABUTO LEFT US...
TKAT...

READ THIS WAY

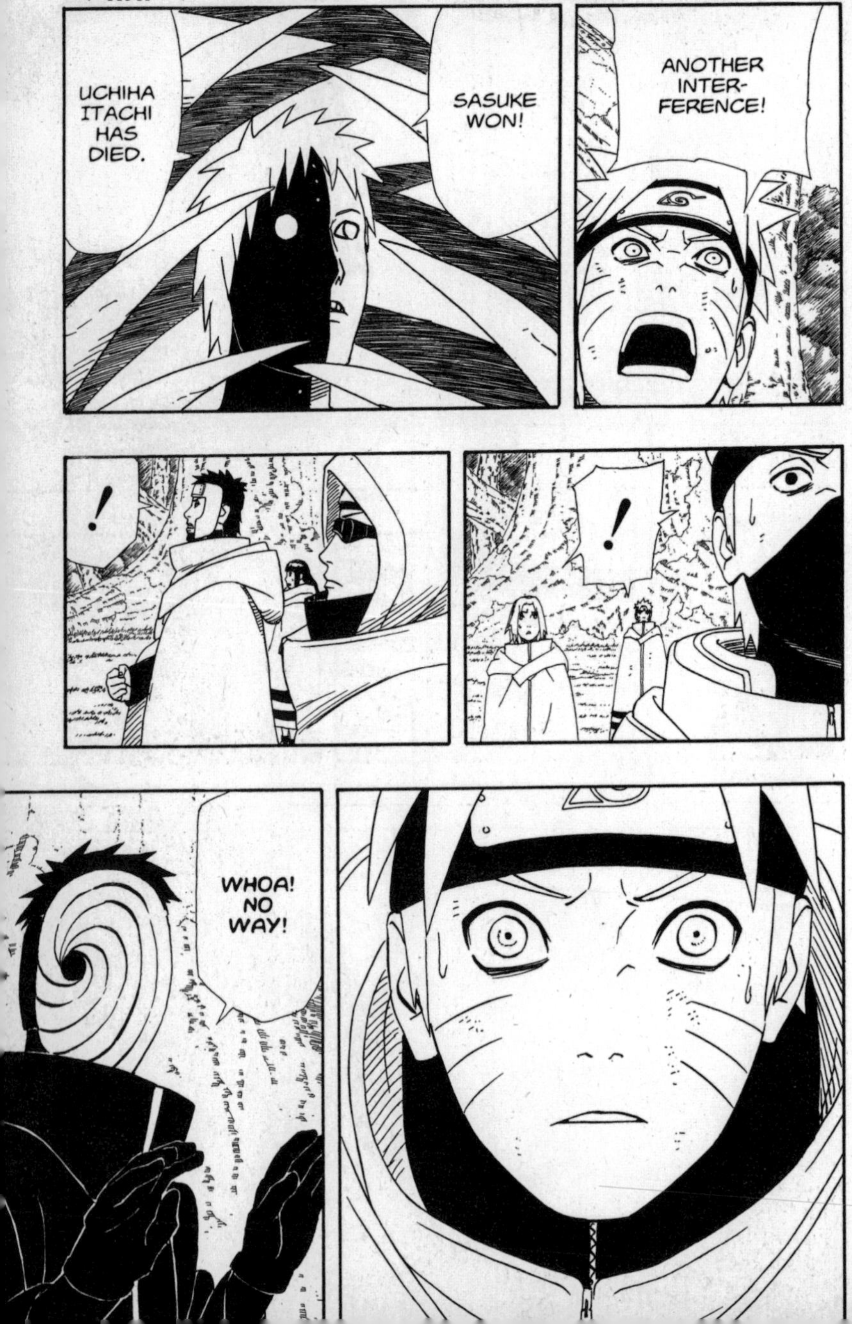
ANOTHER INTER-FERENCE!
SASUKE WON!
UCHIHA ITACHI HAS DIED.
!
!
WHOA! NO WAY!

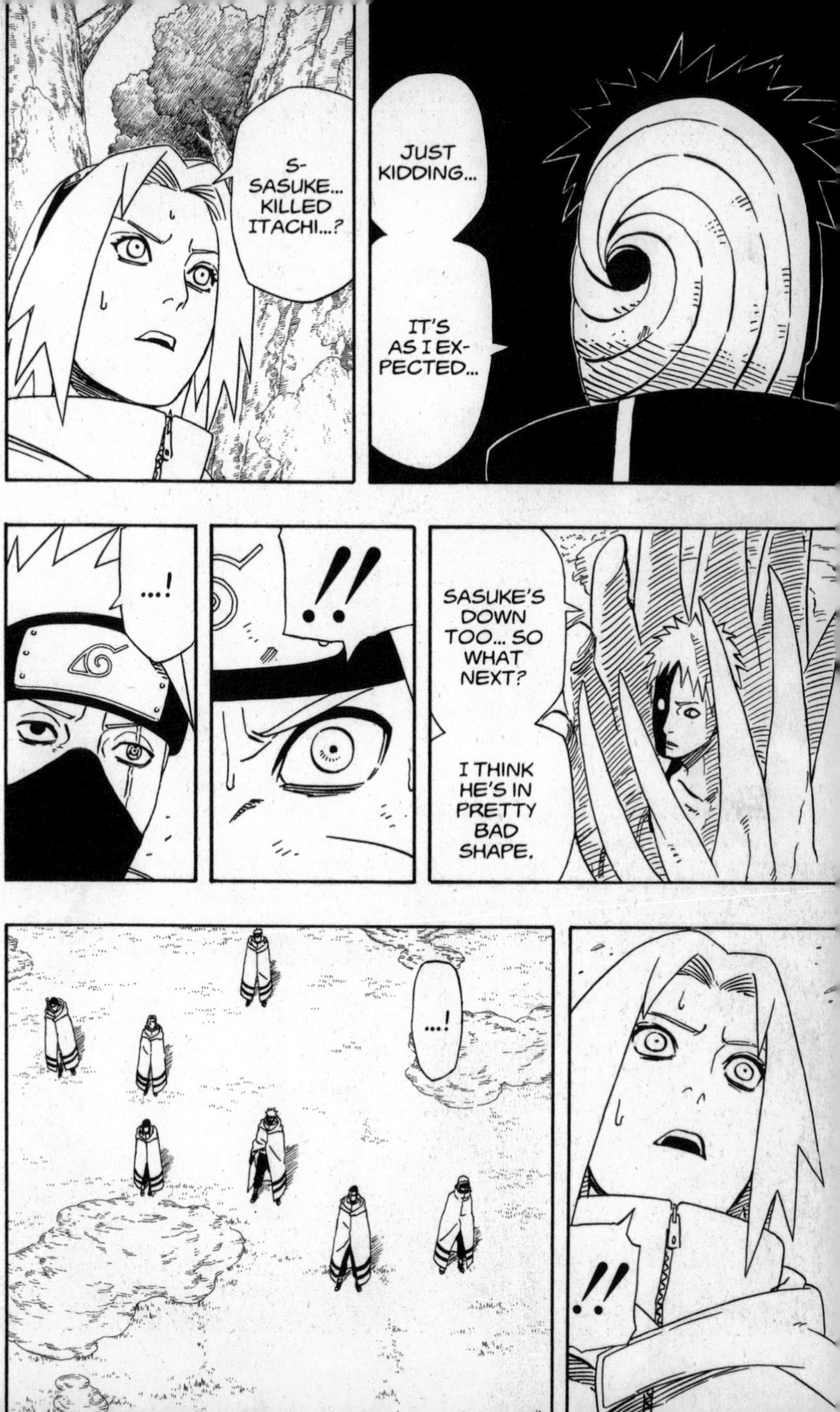
JUST KIDDING...
IT'S AS I EX-PECTED...
S- SASUKE... KILLED ITACHI...?
SASUKE'S DOWN TOO... SO WHAT NEXT?
I THINK HE'S IN PRETTY BAD SHAPE.
!!
...!
!!
...!

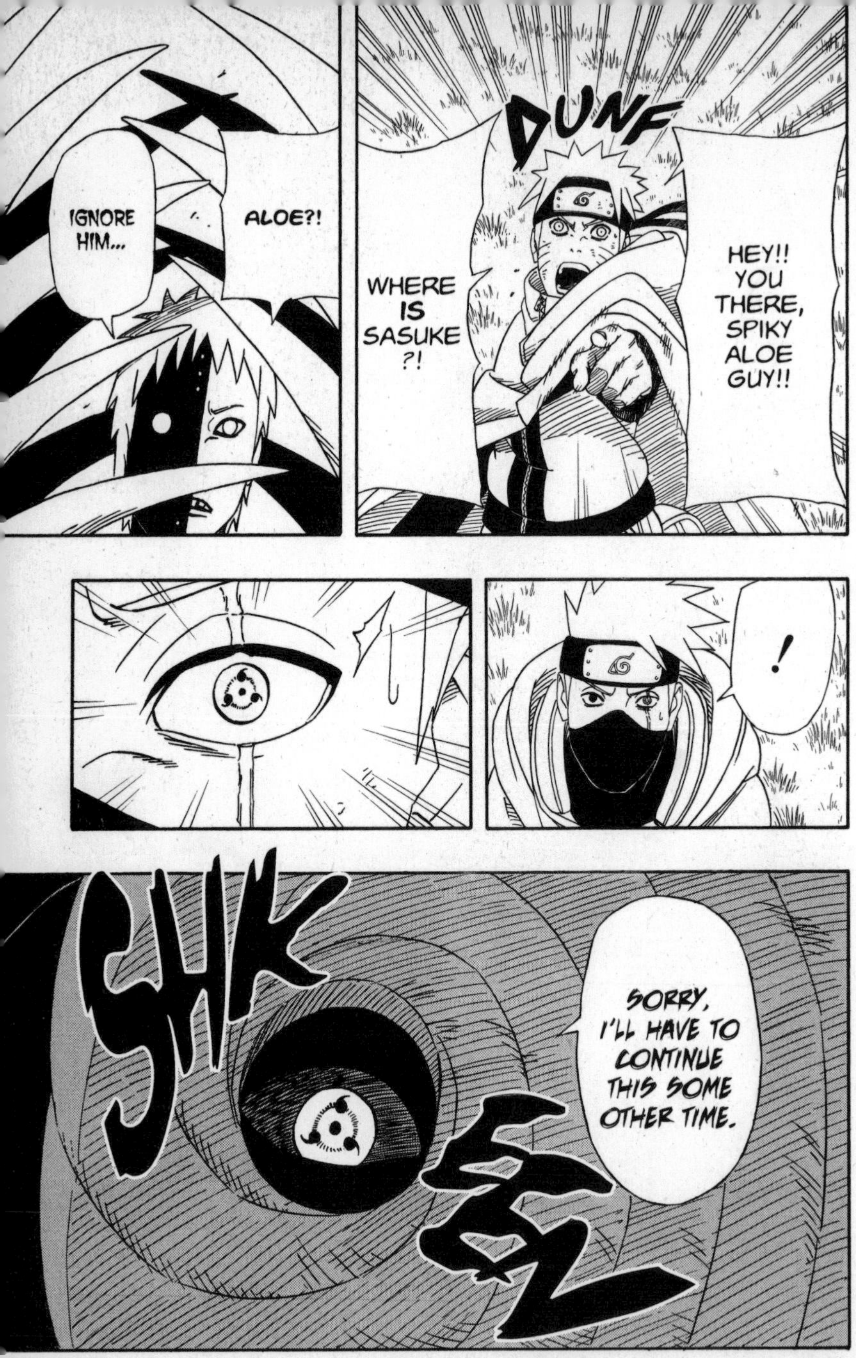
DUNF
HEY!! YOU THERE, SPIKY ALOE GUY!!
WHERE IS SASUKE?!
ALOE?!
IGNORE HIM...
!
SORRY, I'LL HAVE TO CONTINUE THIS SOME OTHER TIME.
SHK

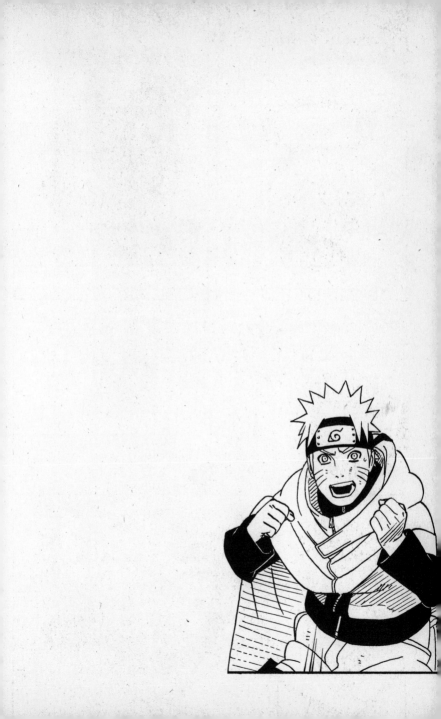

Number 396: Self-Intro

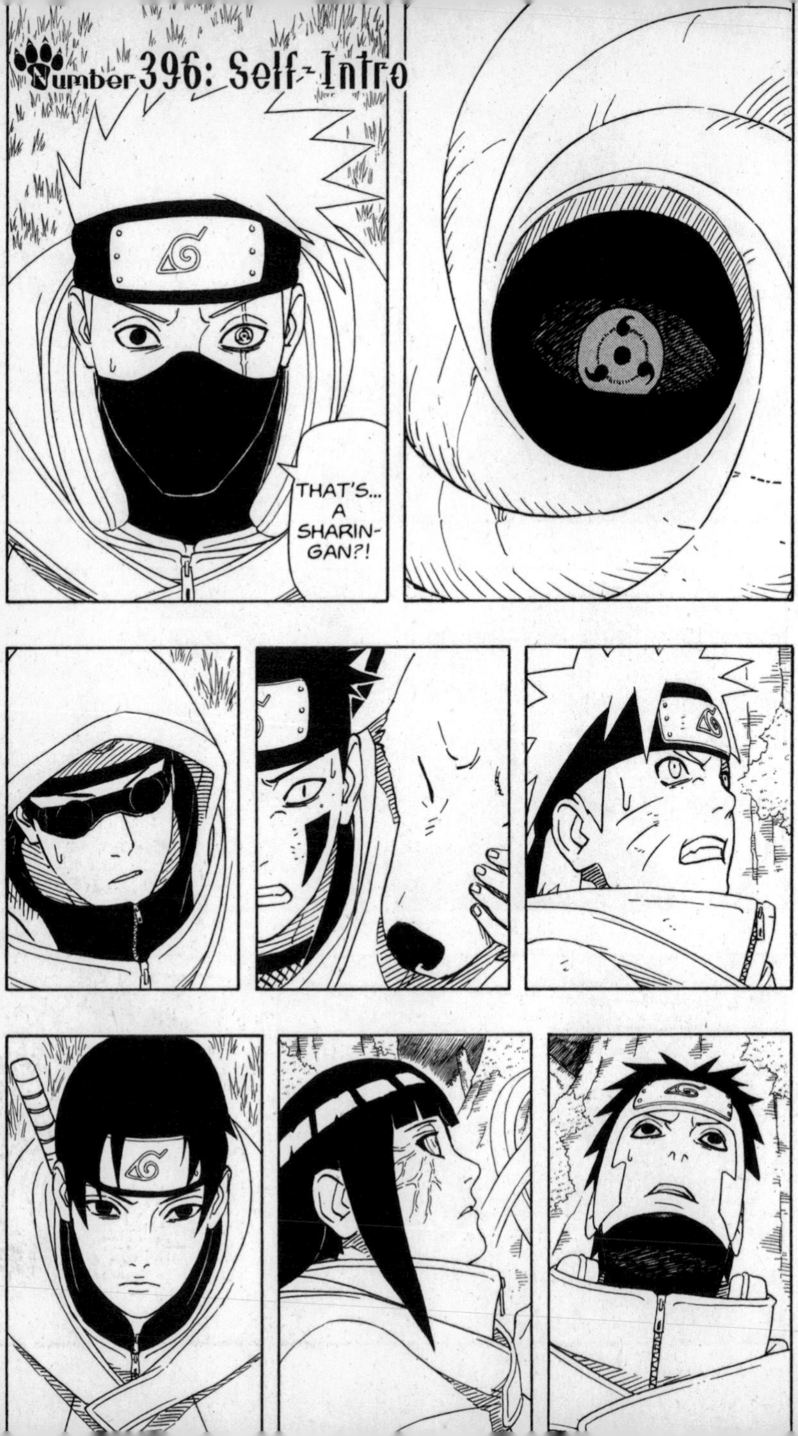
THAT'S... A SHARIN-GAN?!

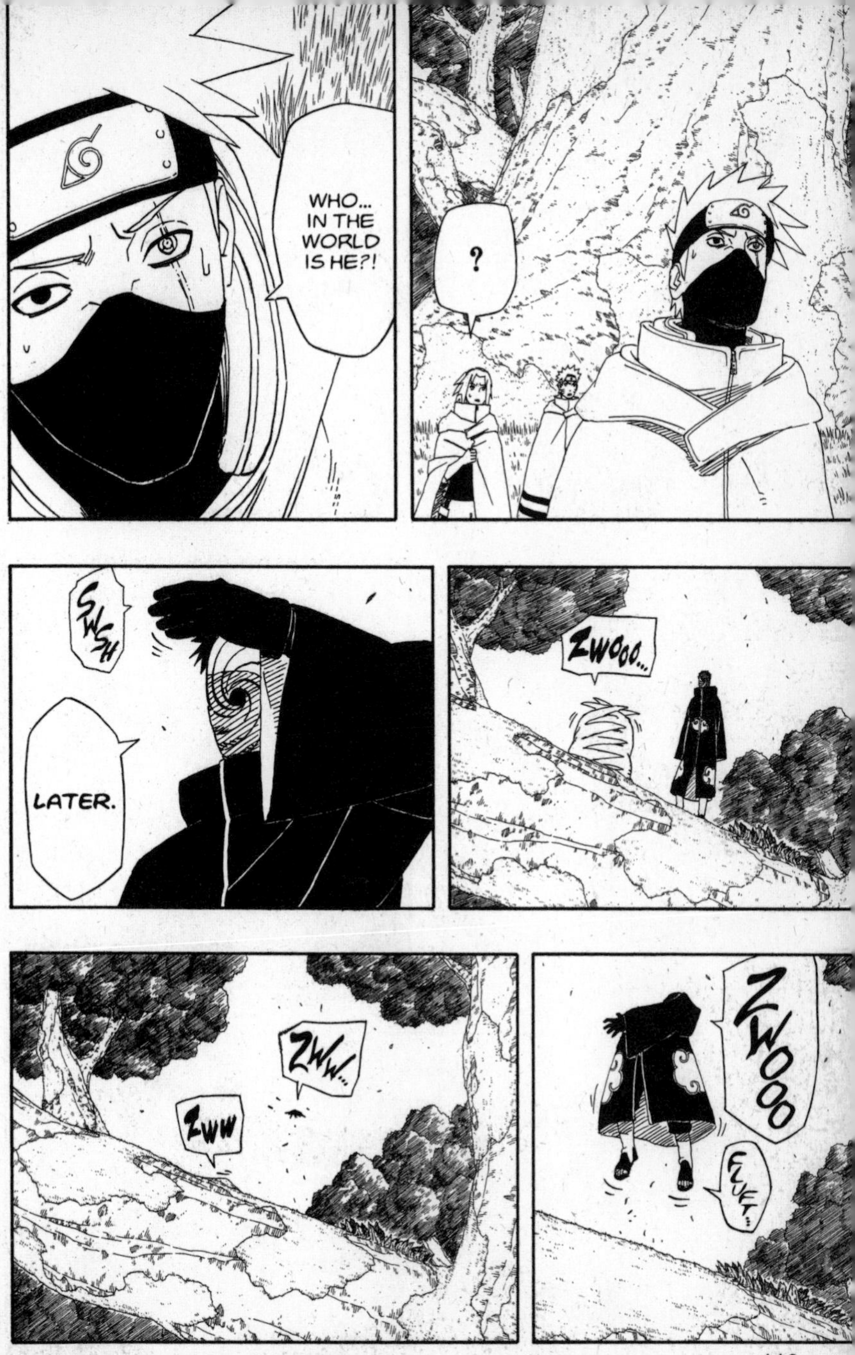
?
WHO... IN THE WORLD IS HE?!
ZWOOO...
SWSH
LATER.
ZWOOO
FLUFF...
ZWW...
ZWW

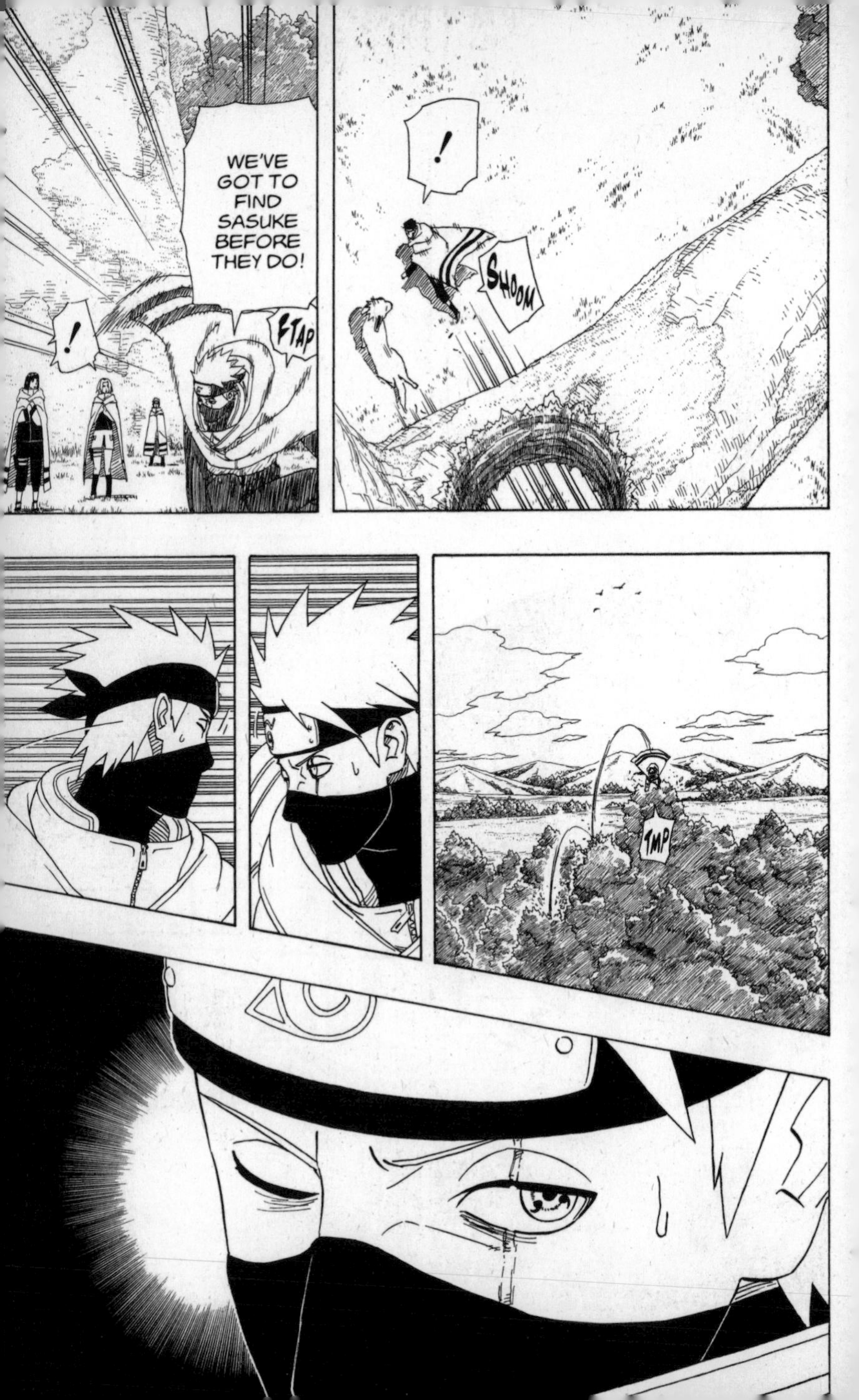
!
SHOOM
WE'VE GOT TO FIND SASUKE BEFORE THEY DO!
FTAP
!
TMP

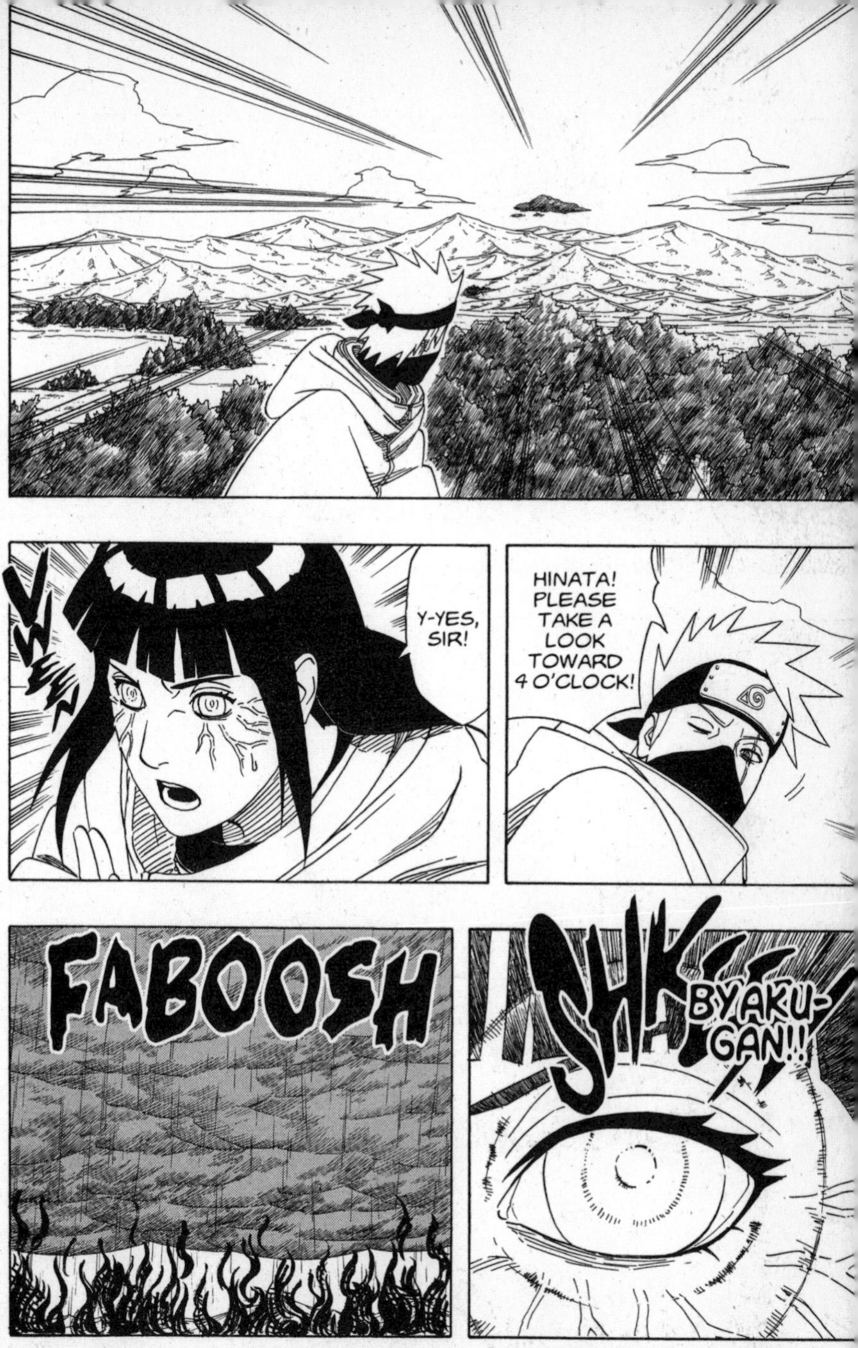
HINATA! PLEASE TAKE A LOOK TOWARD 4 O'CLOCK!
Y-YES, SIR!
SHK
BYAKU-GAN!!
FABOOSH

READ THIS WAY

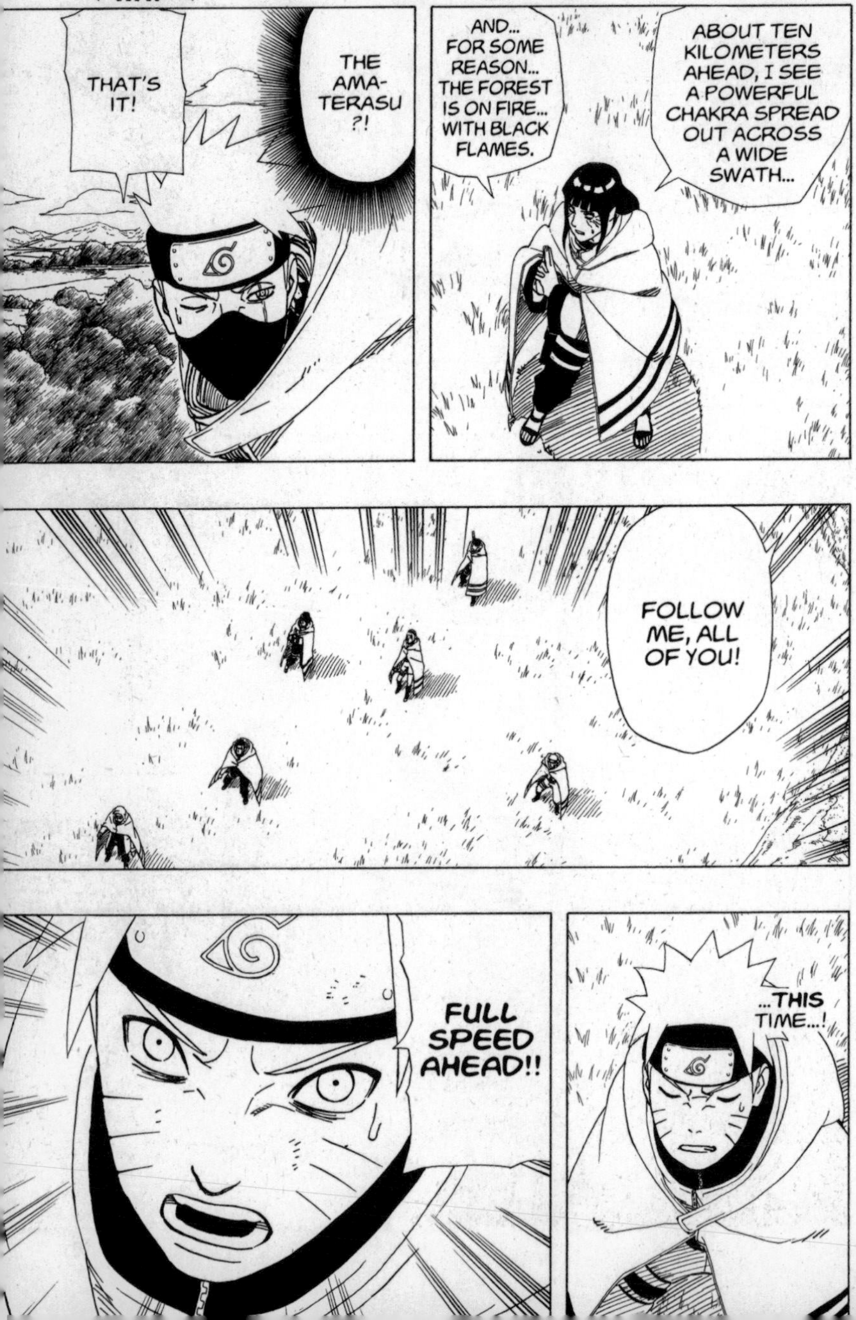
ABOUT TEN KILOMETERS AHEAD, I SEE A POWERFUL CHAKRA SPREAD OUT ACROSS A WIDE SWATH...
AND... FOR SOME REASON... THE FOREST IS ON FIRE... WITH BLACK FLAMES.
THE AMA-TERASU ?!
THAT'S IT!
FOLLOW ME, ALL OF YOU!
...THIS TIME...!
FULL SPEED AHEAD!!

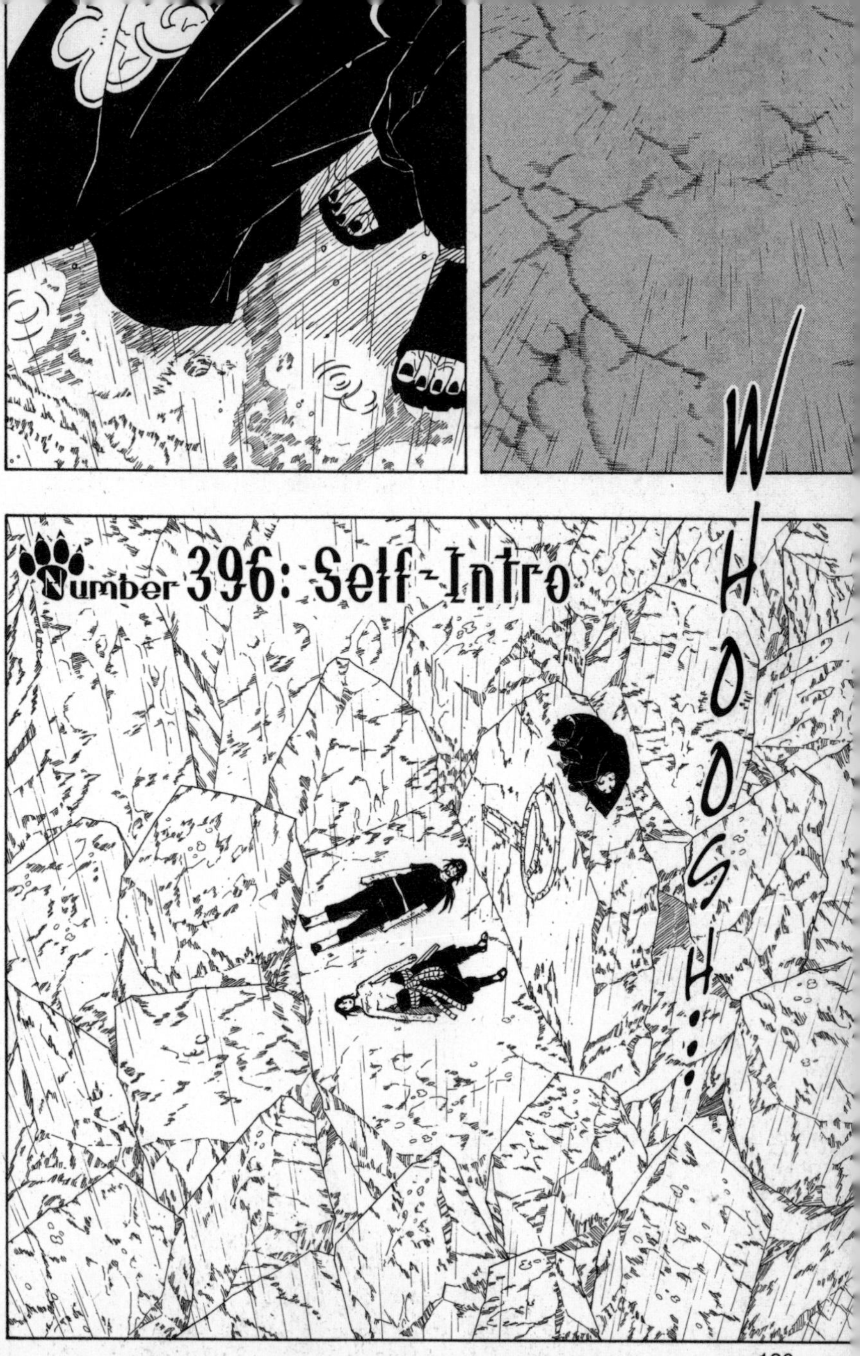
Number 396: Self-Intro
WHOOSH...

READ THIS WAY

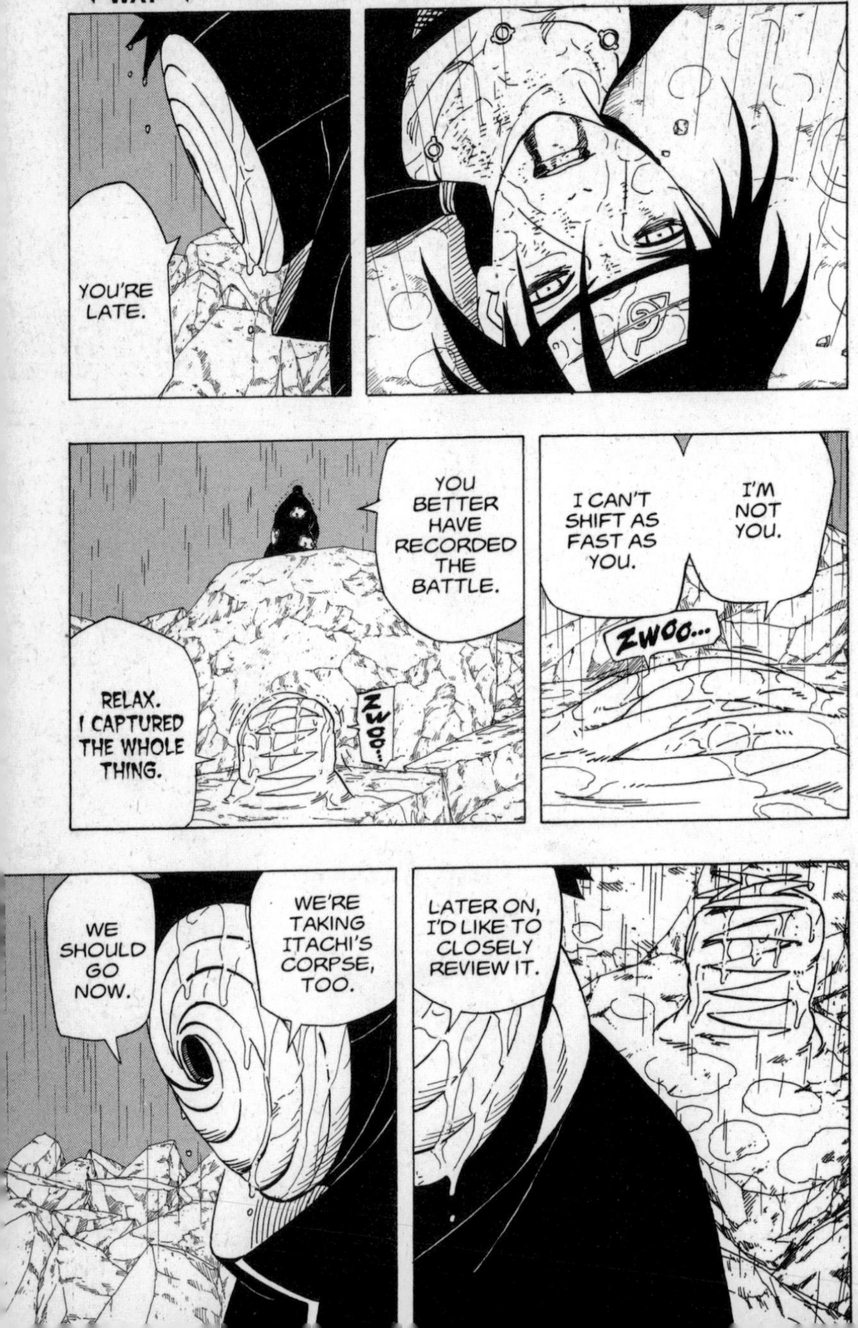
YOU'RE LATE.
I'M NOT YOU.
I CAN'T SHIFT AS FAST AS YOU.
ZWOO...
YOU BETTER HAVE RECORDED THE BATTLE.
ZWOO...
RELAX. I CAPTURED THE WHOLE THING.
LATER ON, I'D LIKE TO CLOSELY REVIEW IT.
WE'RE TAKING ITACHI'S CORPSE, TOO.
WE SHOULD GO NOW.

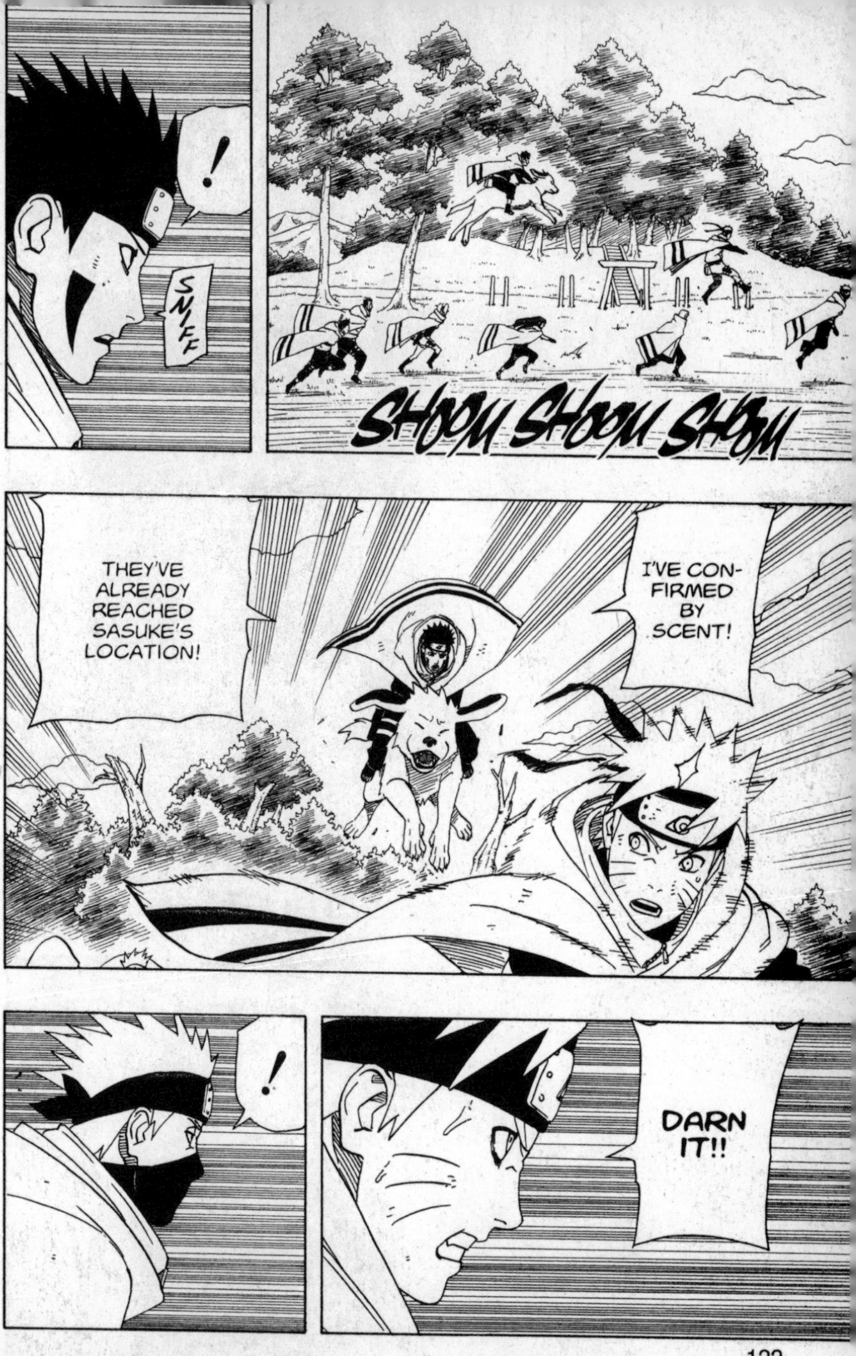
SHOOM SHOOM SHOOM
!
SNIFF
I'VE CON-
FIRMED
BY
SCENT!
THEY'VE
ALREADY
REACHED
SASUKE'S
LOCATION!
DARN
IT!!
!

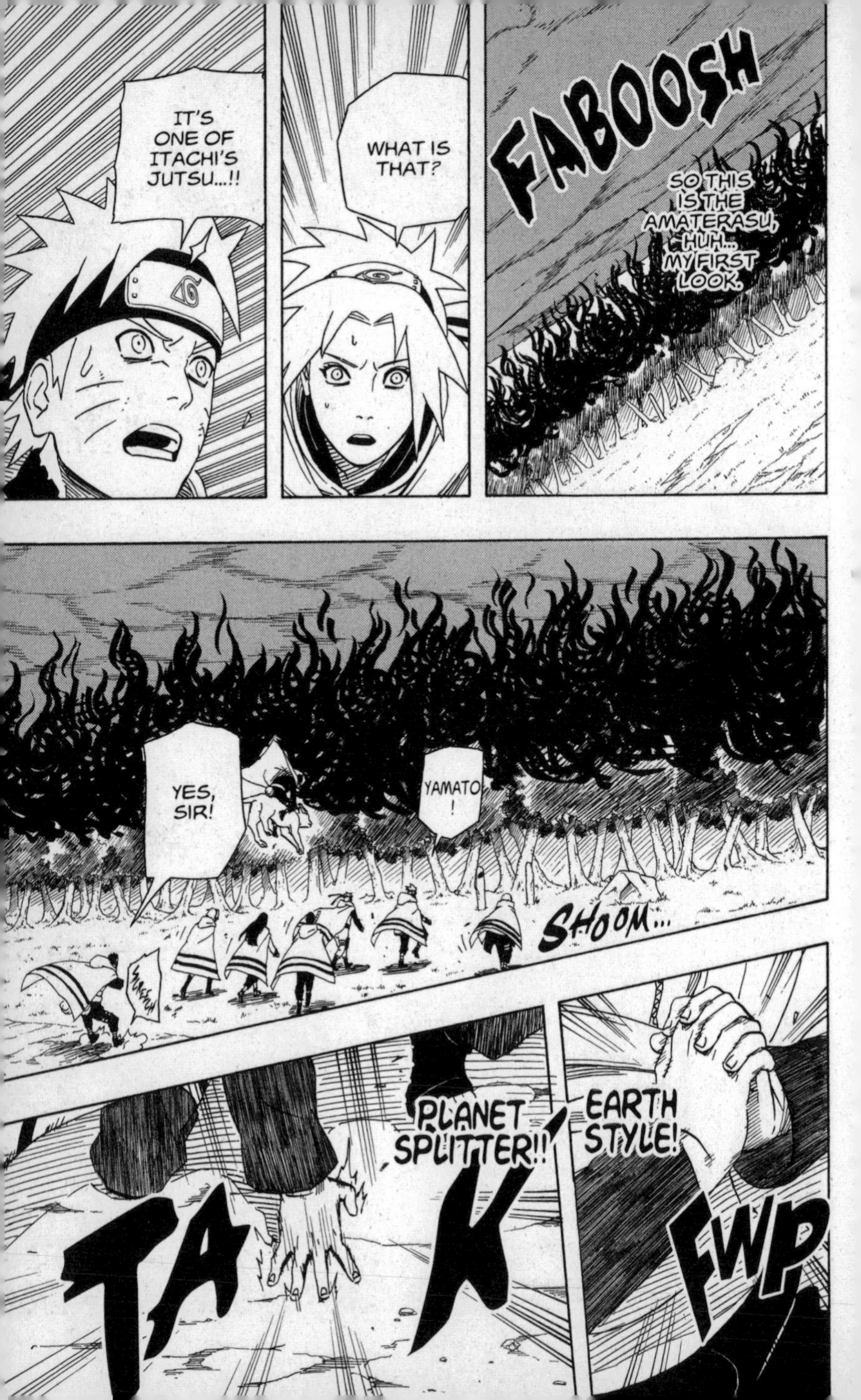
FABOOSH
SO THIS IS THE AMATERASU, HUH... MY FIRST LOOK.
WHAT IS THAT?
IT'S ONE OF ITACHI'S JUTSU...!!
SHOOM...
YAMATO!
YES, SIR!
FWP
EARTH STYLE!
PLANET SPLITTER!!
TAK

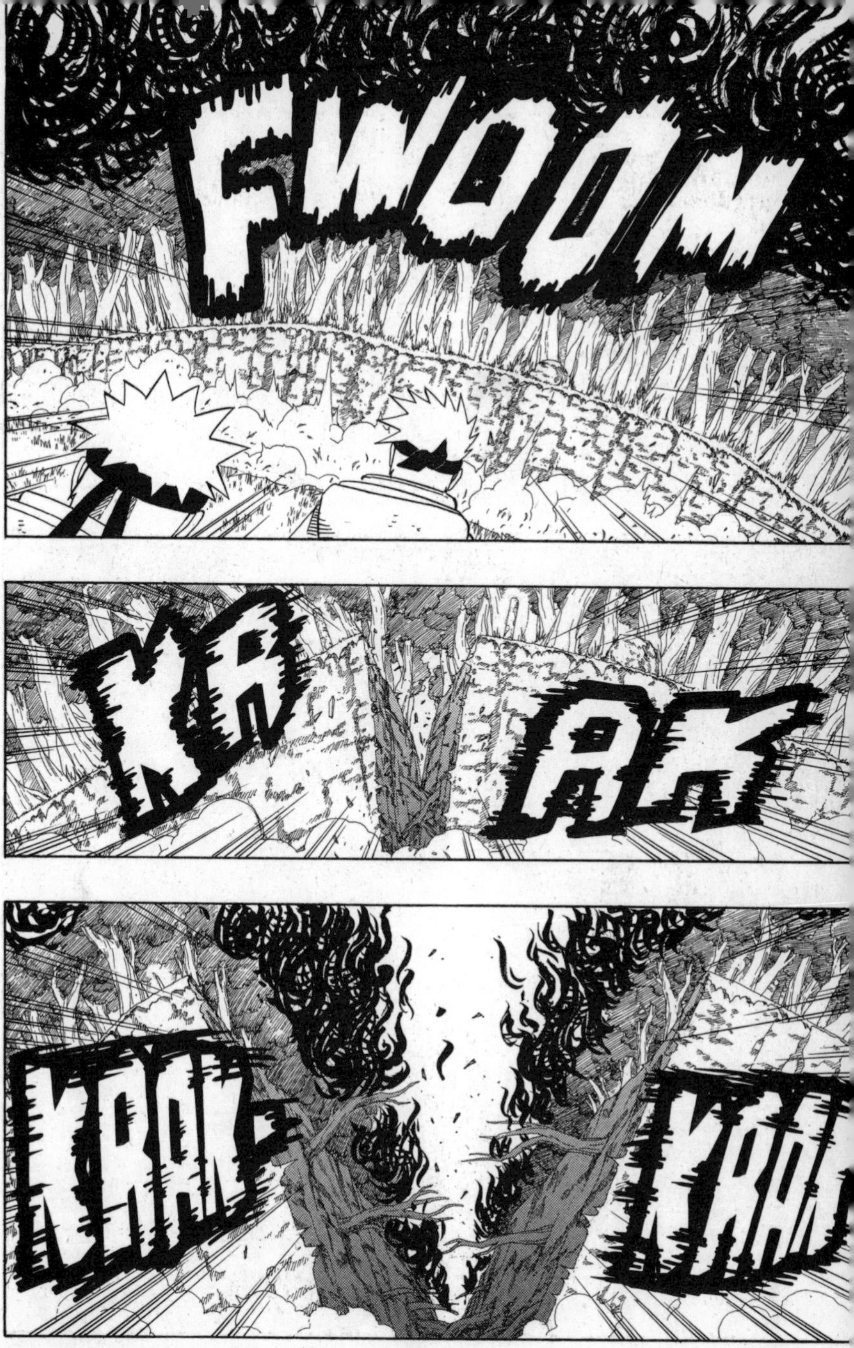
FWOOM
KRAK
KRA
KRAK

READ THIS WAY

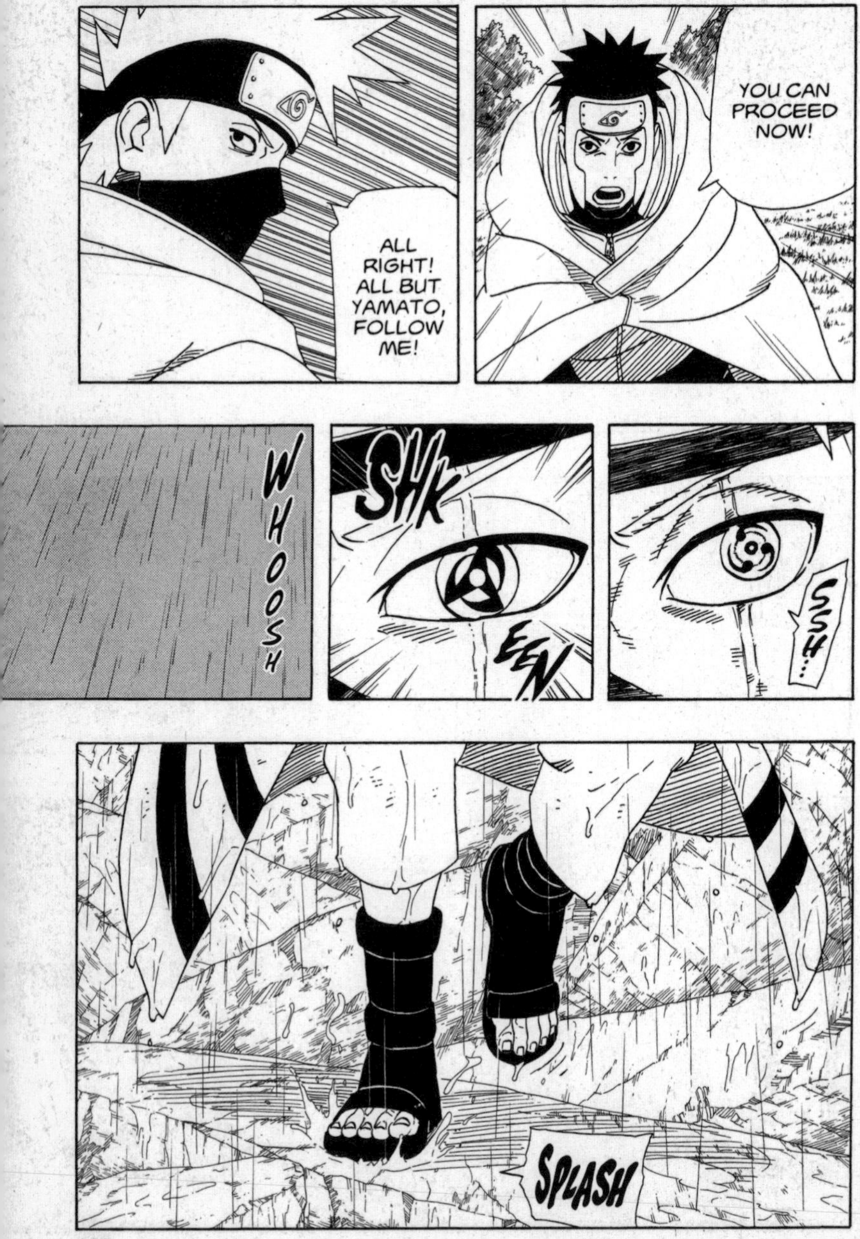
YOU CAN PROCEED NOW!
ALL RIGHT! ALL BUT YAMATO, FOLLOW ME!
SSH...
SHK
EEN
WHOOOSH
SPLASH

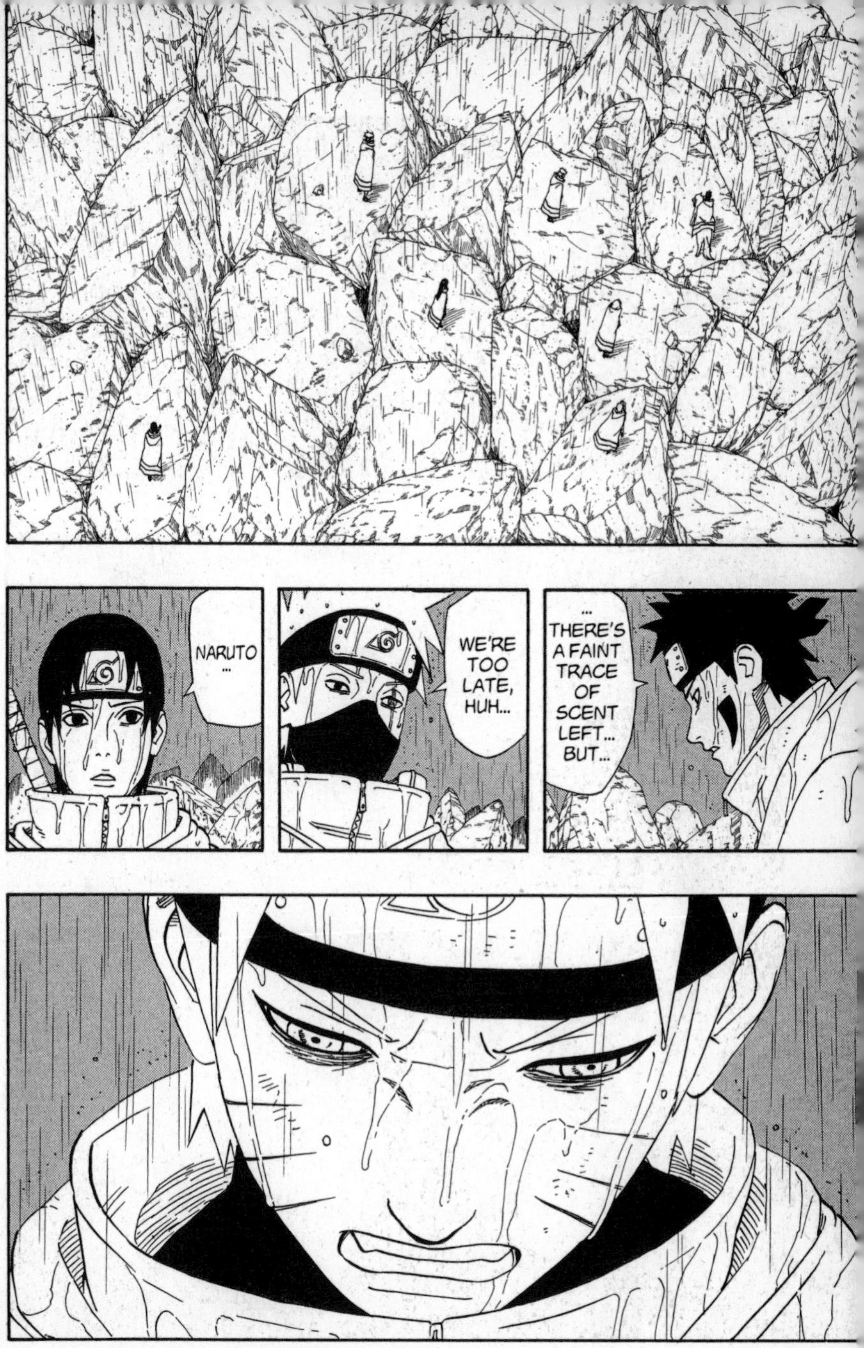
... THERE'S A FAINT TRACE OF SCENT LEFT... BUT...
WE'RE TOO LATE, HUH...
NARUTO ...

READ THIS WAY

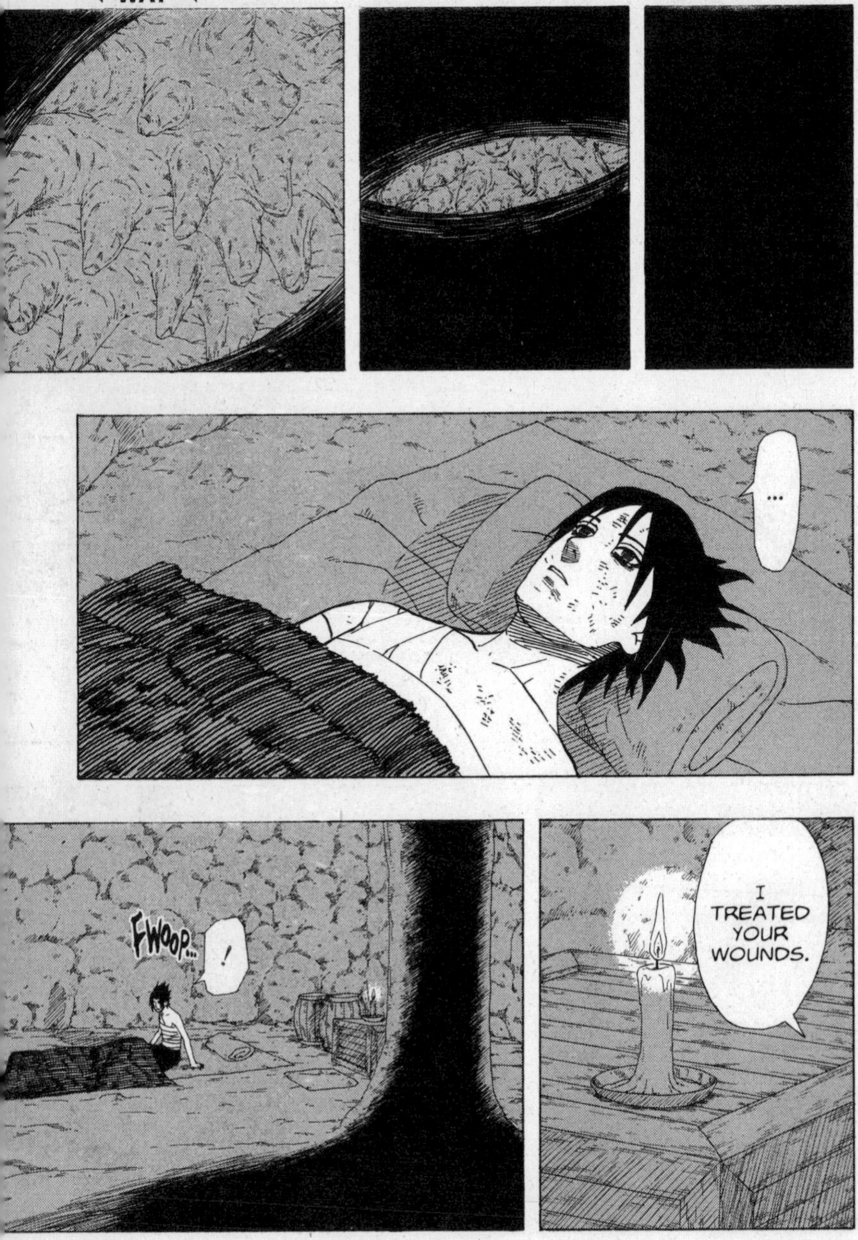
...
I TREATED YOUR WOUNDS.
!
FWOOP...

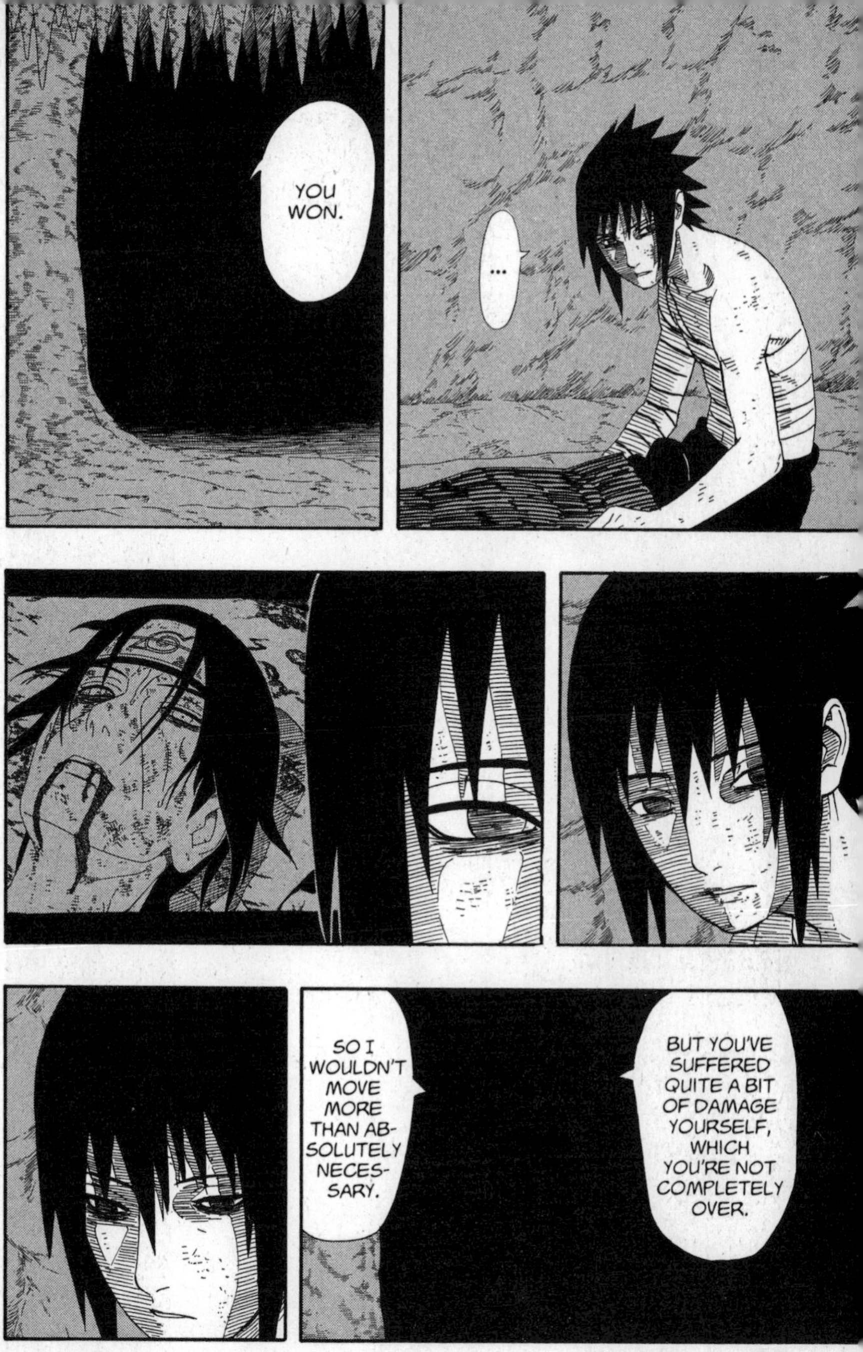
...
YOU WON.
BUT YOU'VE SUFFERED QUITE A BIT OF DAMAGE YOURSELF, WHICH YOU'RE NOT COMPLETELY OVER.
SO I WOULDN'T MOVE MORE THAN AB-SOLUTELY NECES-SARY.

READ THIS WAY

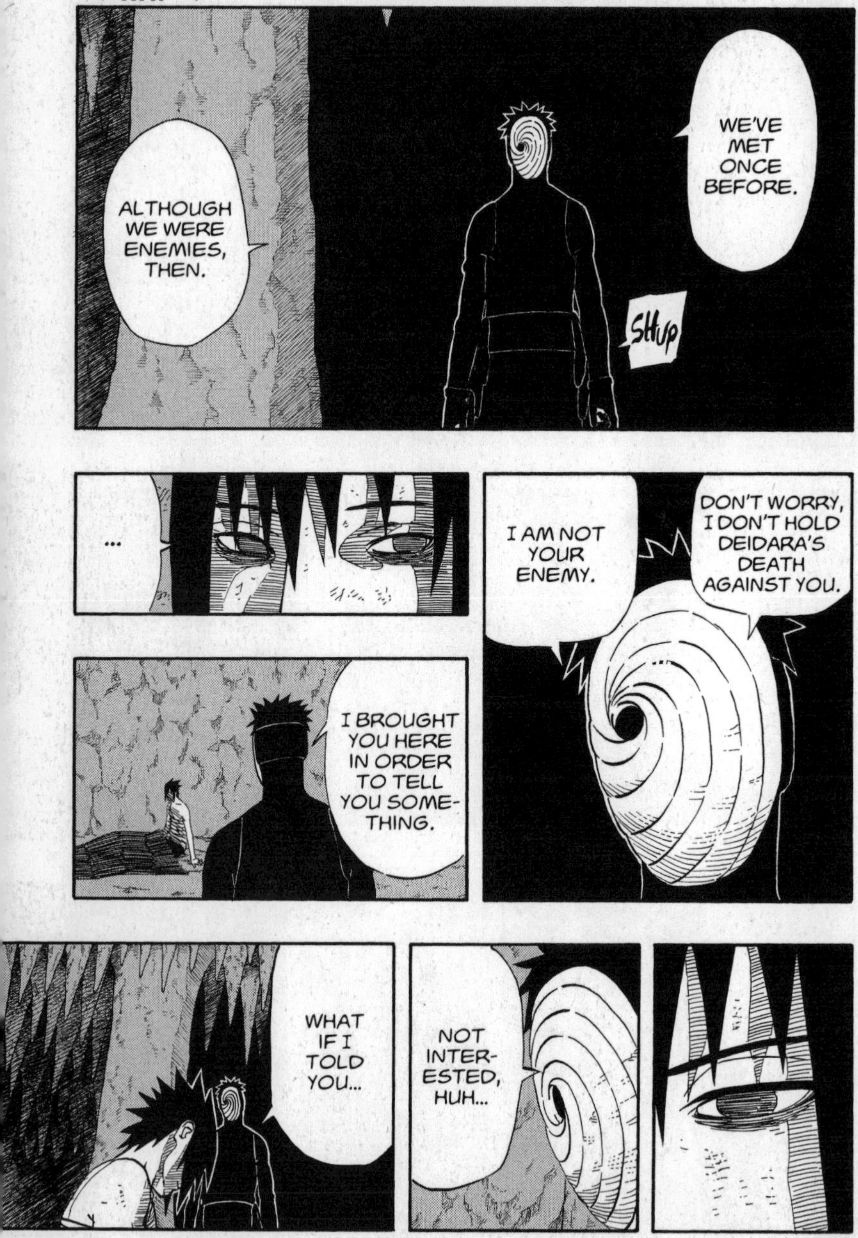
WE'VE MET ONCE BEFORE.
SHUP
ALTHOUGH WE WERE ENEMIES, THEN.
DON'T WORRY, I DON'T HOLD DEIDARA'S DEATH AGAINST YOU.
I AM NOT YOUR ENEMY.
...
I BROUGHT YOU HERE IN ORDER TO TELL YOU SOME-THING.
NOT INTER-ESTED, HUH...
WHAT IF I TOLD YOU...

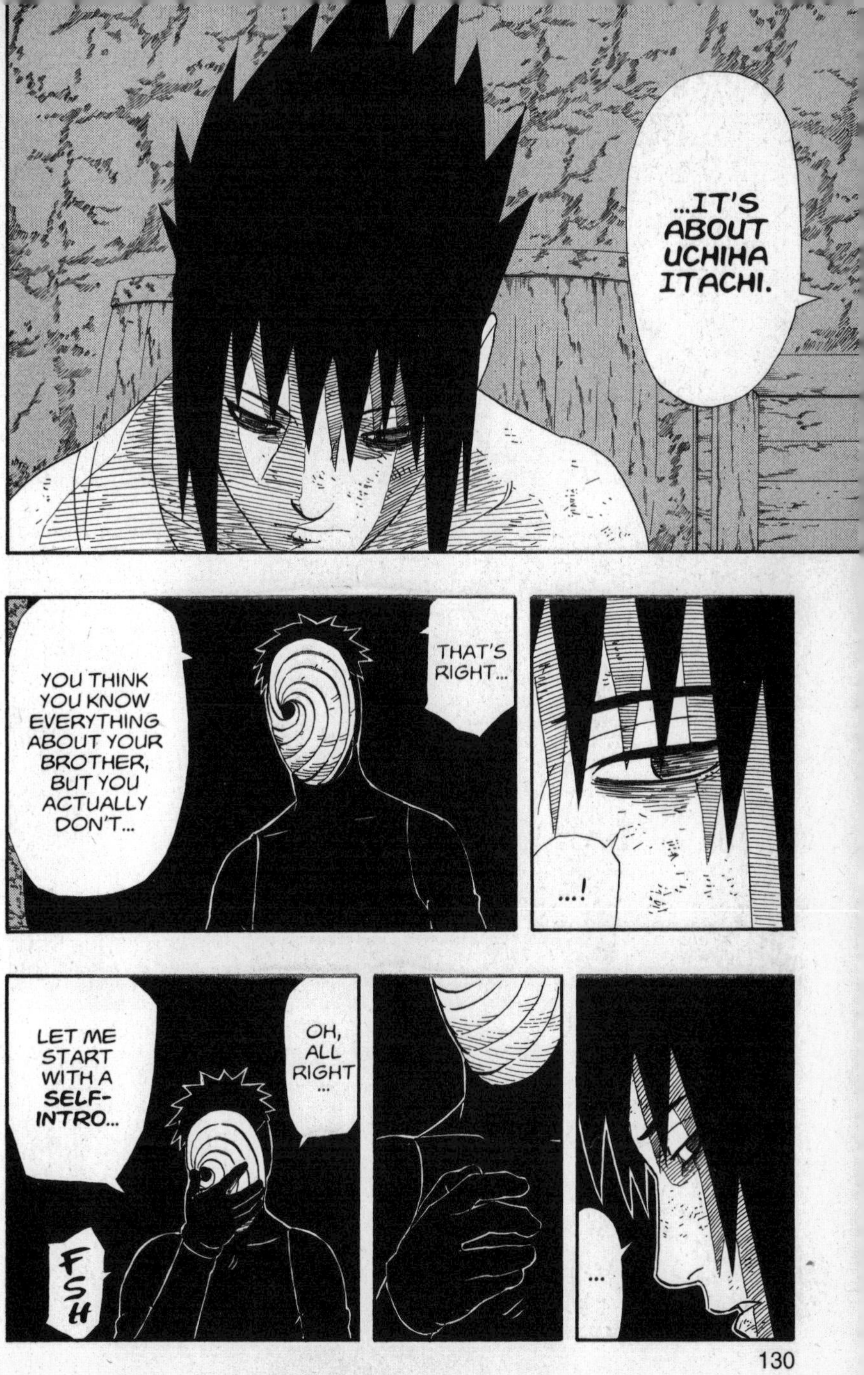
...IT'S ABOUT UCHIHA ITACHI.
...!
THAT'S RIGHT...
YOU THINK YOU KNOW EVERYTHING ABOUT YOUR BROTHER, BUT YOU ACTUALLY DON'T...
...
OH, ALL RIGHT...
LET ME START WITH A SELF-INTRO...
FSH

READ THIS WAY

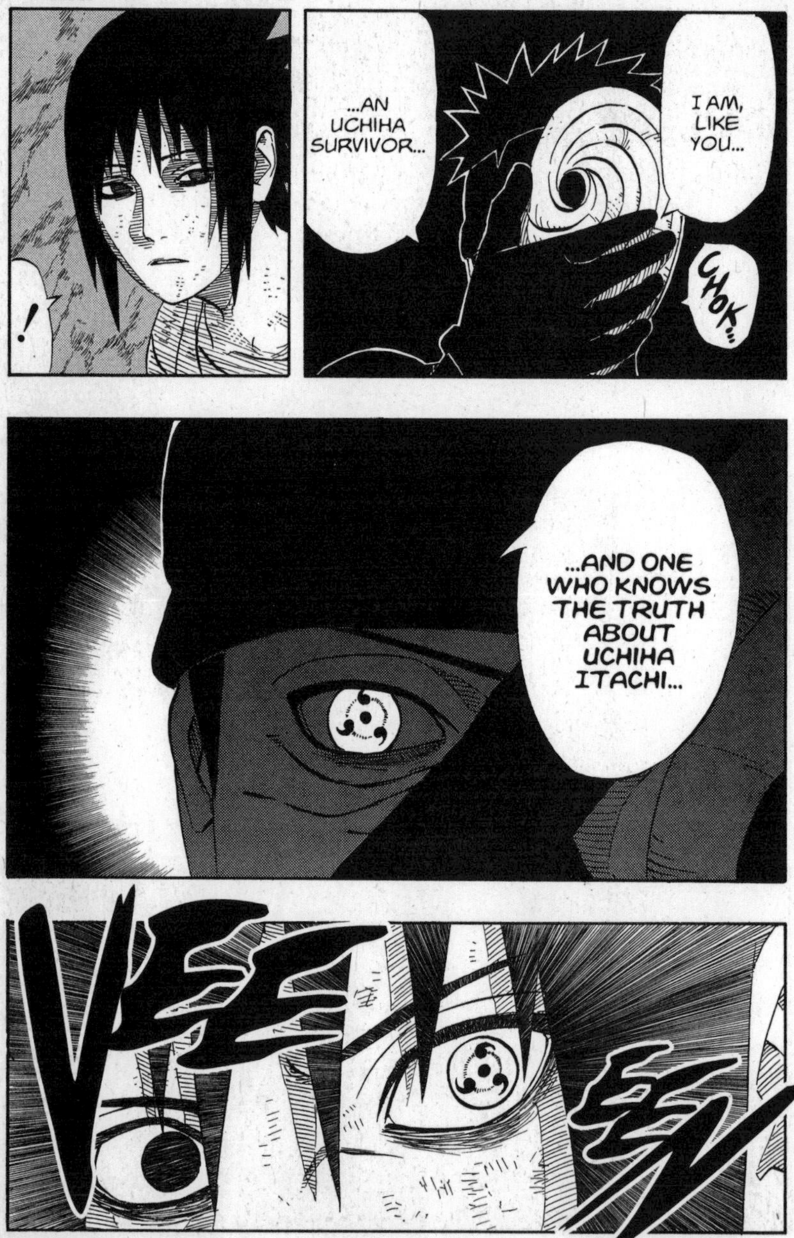
I AM, LIKE YOU...
...AN UCHIHA SURVIVOR...
CHOK...
!
...AND ONE WHO KNOWS THE TRUTH ABOUT UCHIHA ITACHI...

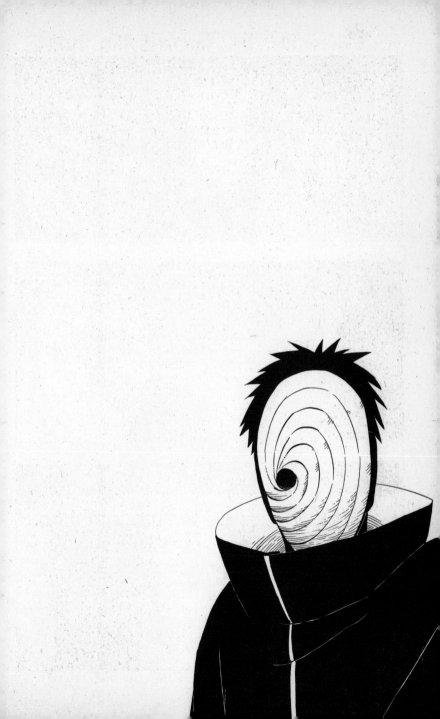

Number 397: The Man with the Truth

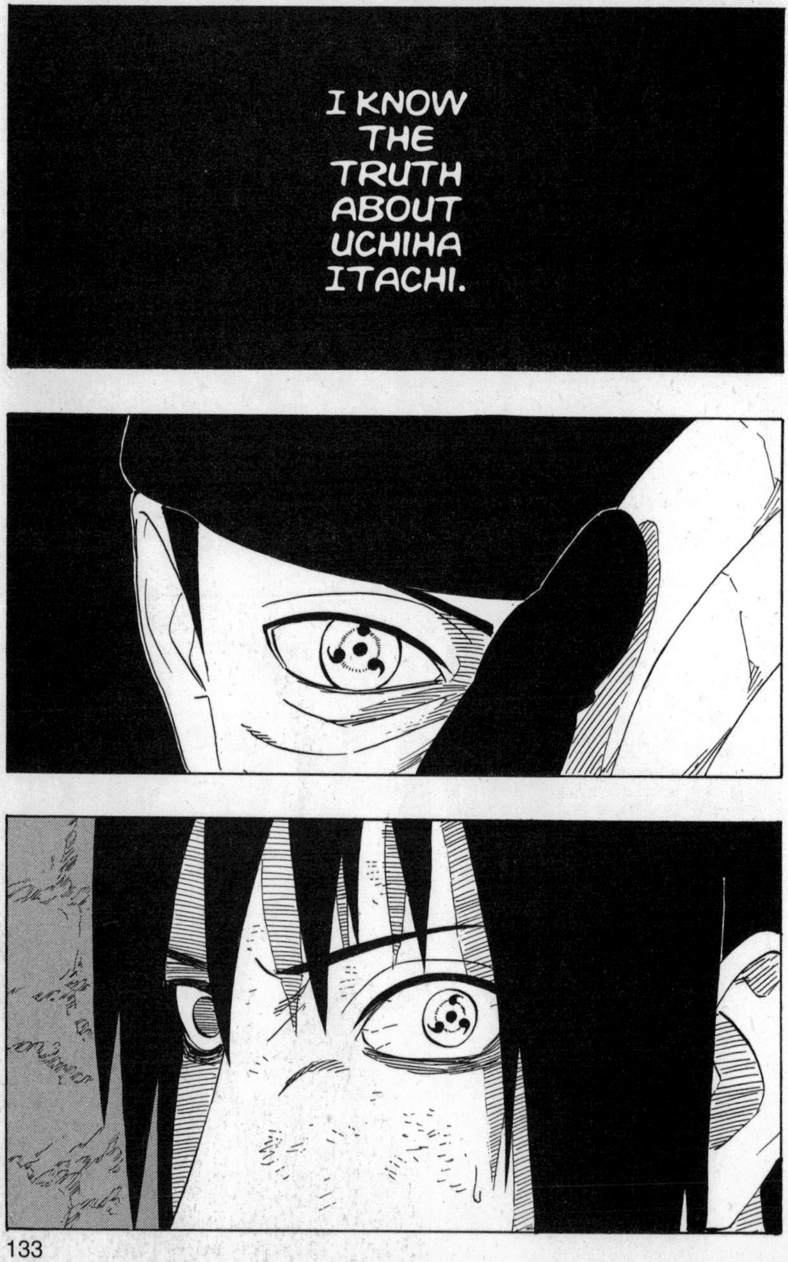
I KNOW THE TRUTH ABOUT UCHIHA ITACHI.

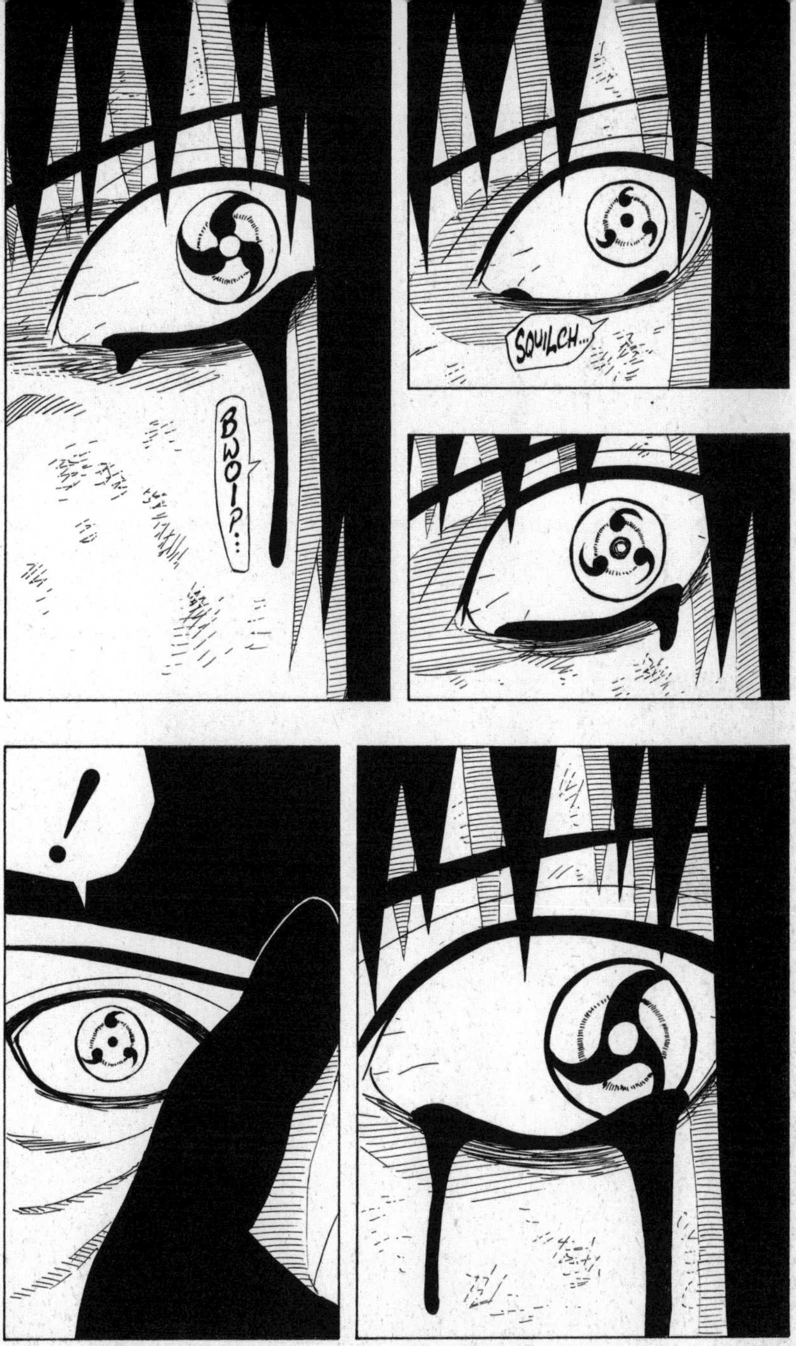
SQUILCH...
BWOIP...
!

READ THIS WAY

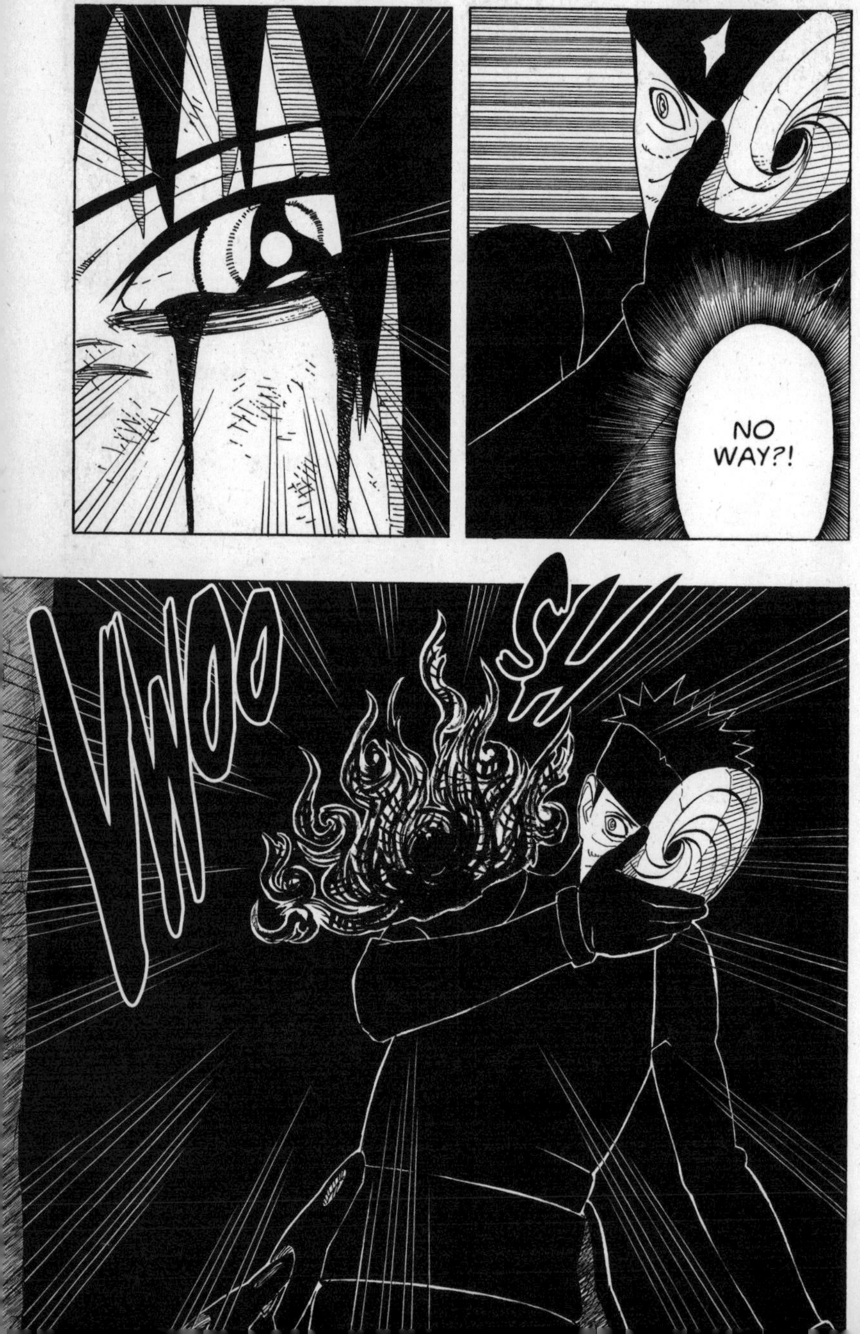
NO WAY?!
VWOOSH

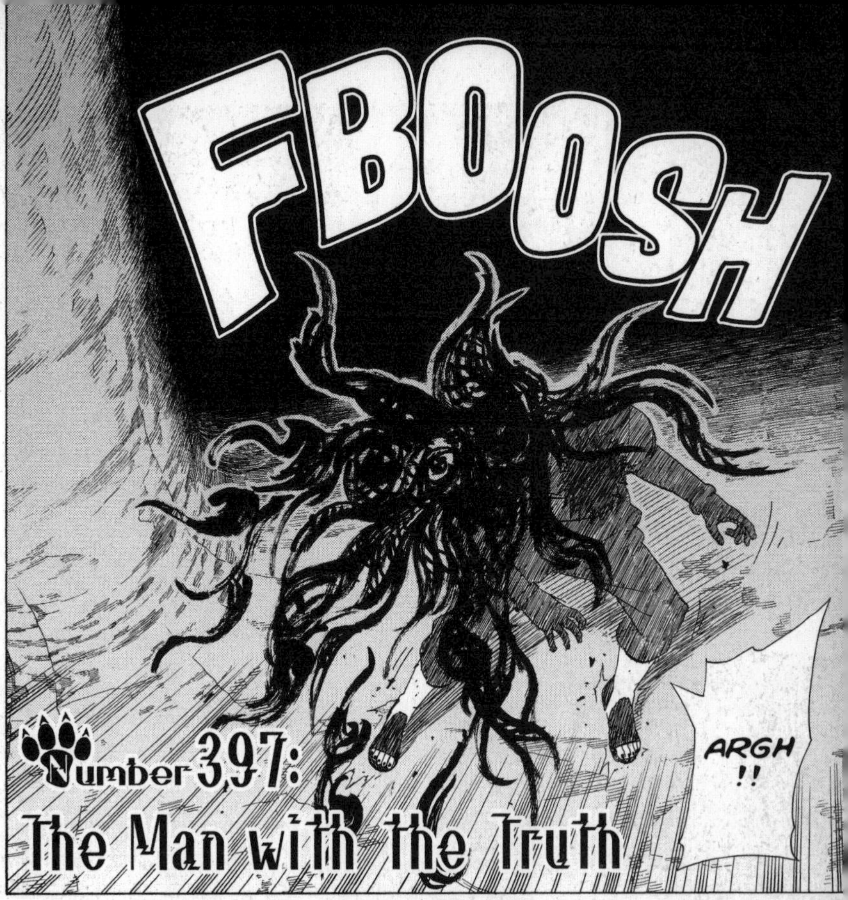
FBOOSH
Number 397:
The Man with the Truth
ARGH !!

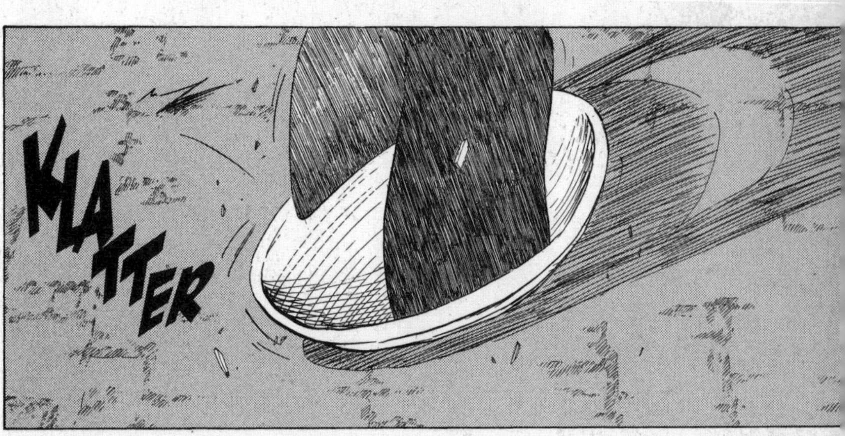
KLATTER

READ THIS WAY

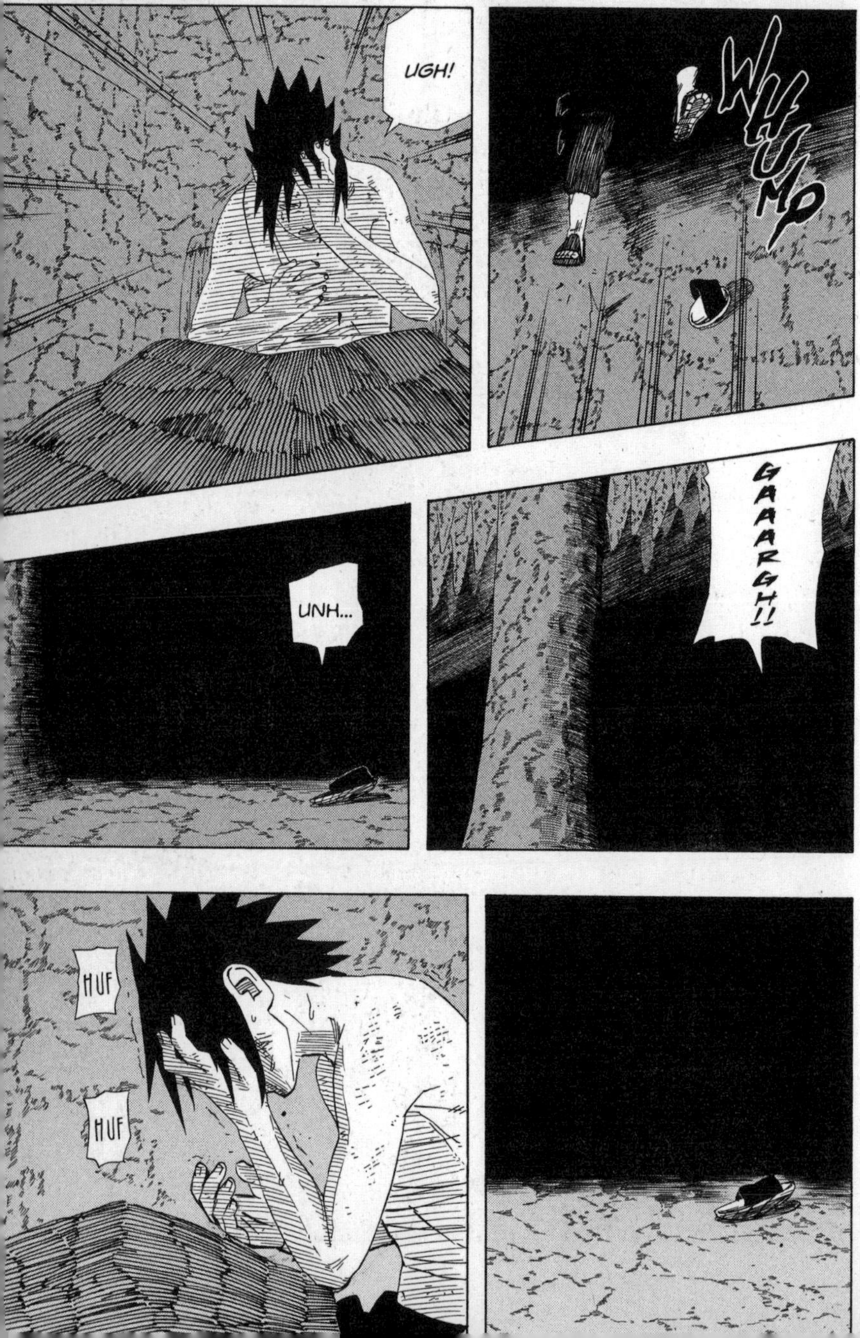
WHUMP
UGH!
GAAAARGH!!
UNH...
HUF
HUF

HUF
HUF
HUF
HUF
WSH...
HUF
HUF

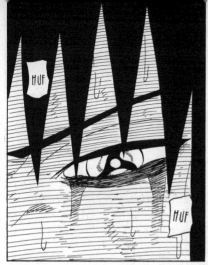

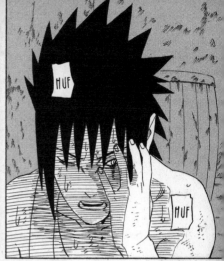

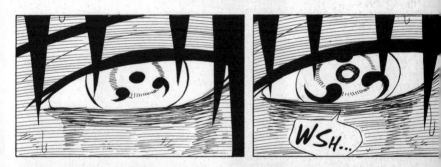

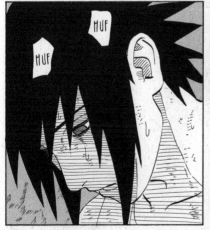

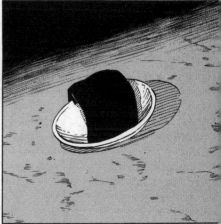

READ THIS WAY

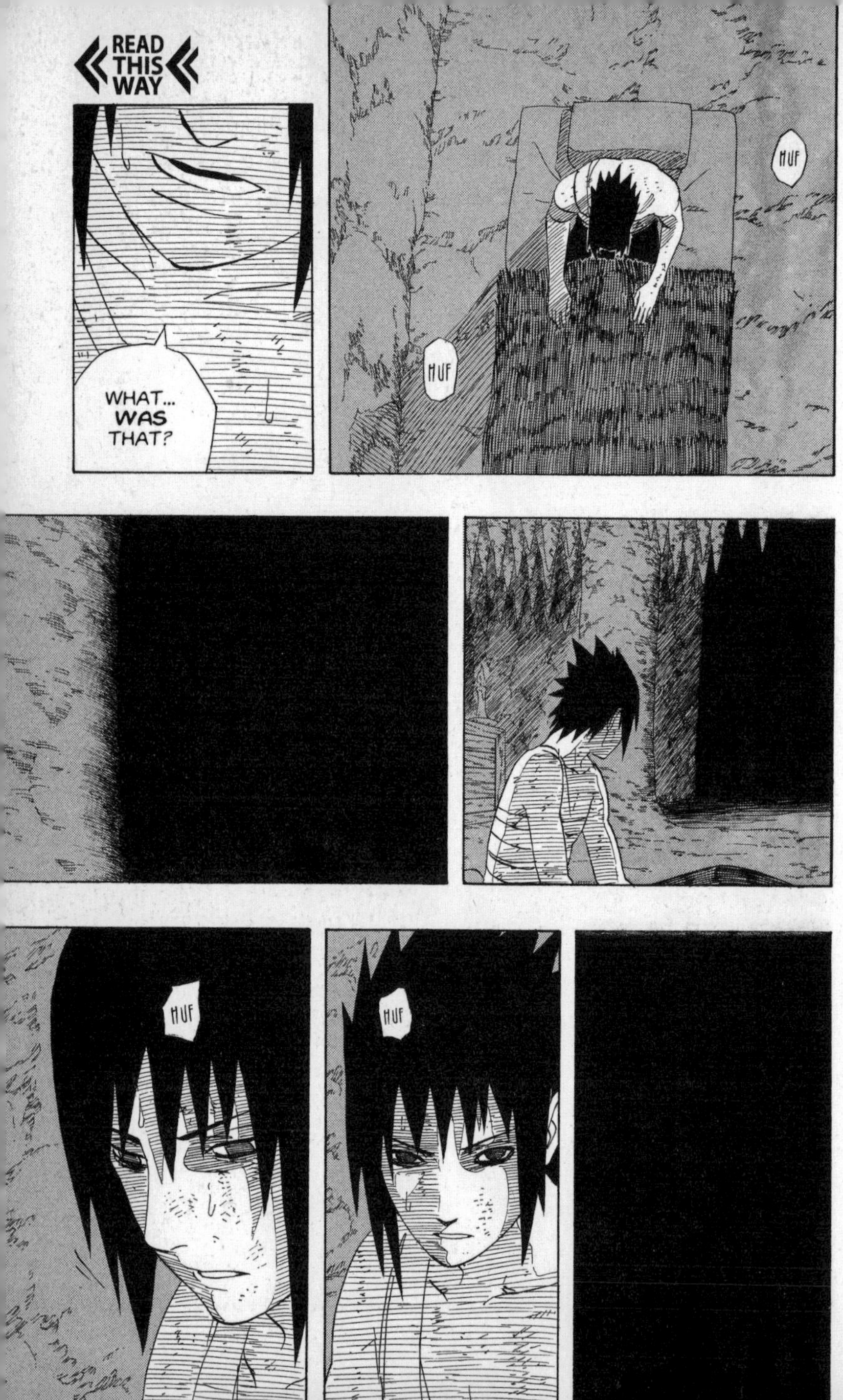

HUF
HUF
WHAT... WAS THAT?
HUF
HUF

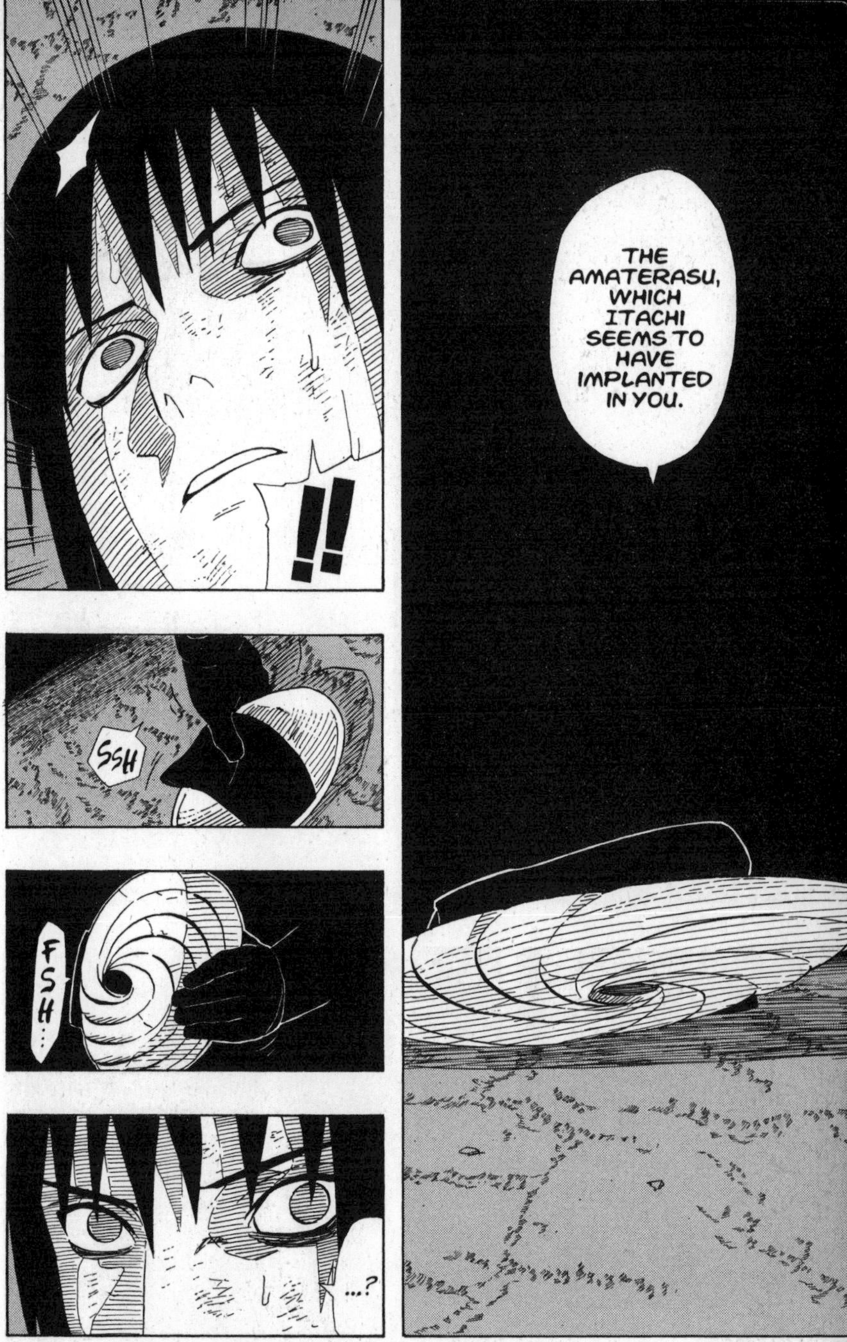
THE AMATERASU, WHICH ITACHI SEEMS TO HAVE IMPLANTED IN YOU.
!!
SSH
FSH...
...?

READ THIS WAY

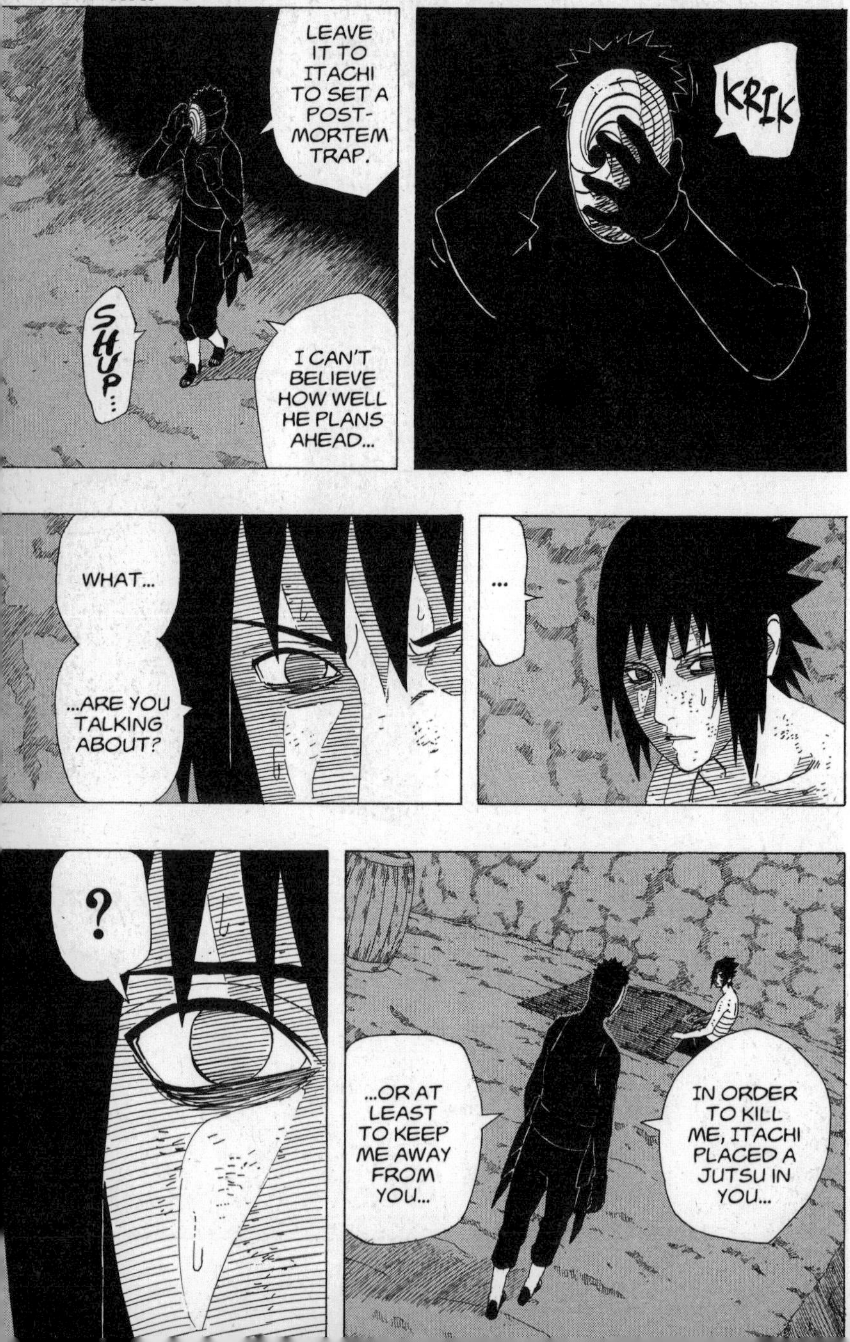
KRIK
LEAVE IT TO ITACHI TO SET A POST-MORTEM TRAP.
I CAN'T BELIEVE HOW WELL HE PLANS AHEAD...
SHUP...
...
WHAT...
...ARE YOU TALKING ABOUT?
IN ORDER TO KILL ME, ITACHI PLACED A JUTSU IN YOU...
...OR AT LEAST TO KEEP ME AWAY FROM YOU...
?

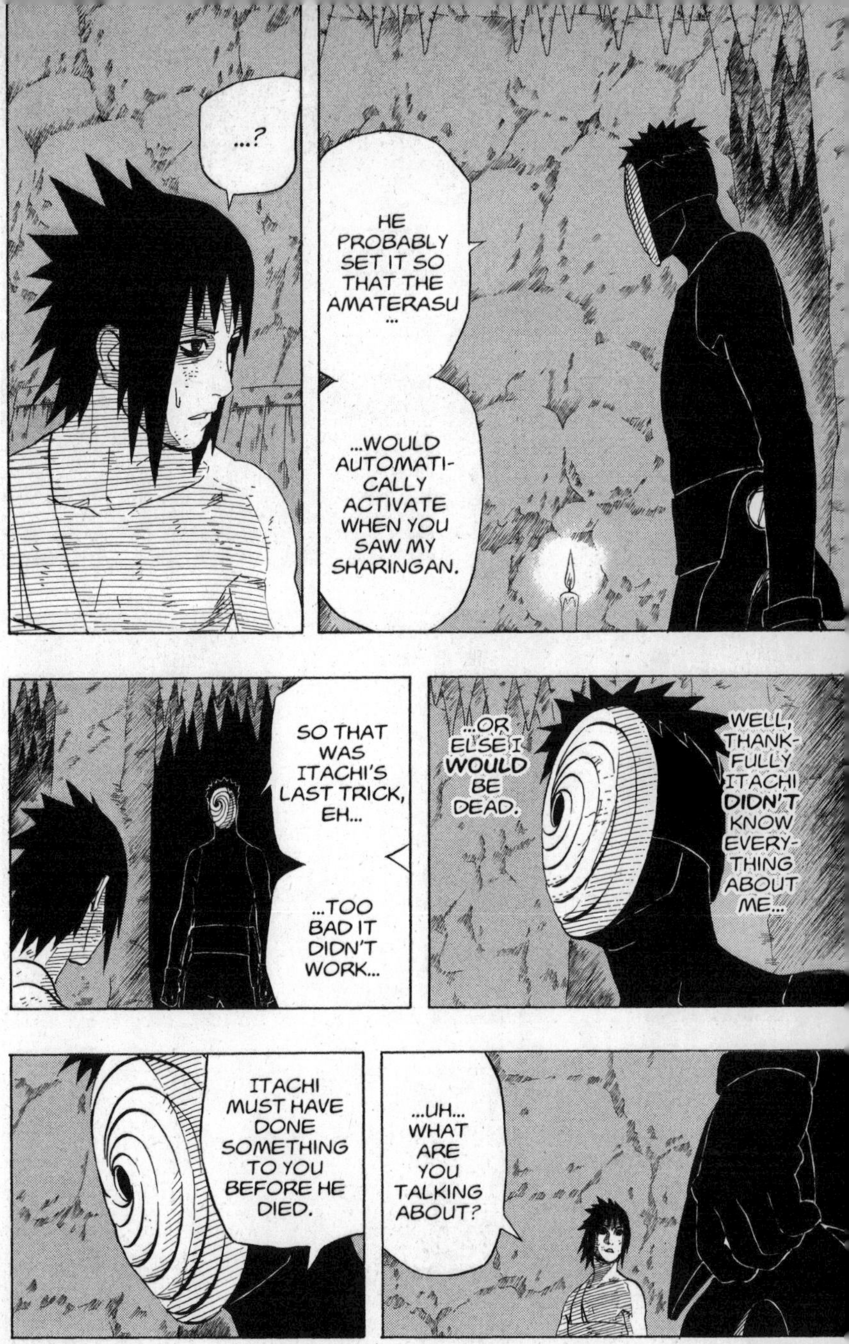
HE PROBABLY SET IT SO THAT THE AMATERASU...
...WOULD AUTOMATICALLY ACTIVATE WHEN YOU SAW MY SHARINGAN.
...?
WELL, THANKFULLY ITACHI **DIDN'T** KNOW EVERYTHING ABOUT ME...
...OR ELSE I **WOULD** BE DEAD.
SO THAT WAS ITACHI'S LAST TRICK, EH...
...TOO BAD IT DIDN'T WORK...
...UH... WHAT ARE YOU TALKING ABOUT?
ITACHI MUST HAVE DONE SOMETHING TO YOU BEFORE HE DIED.

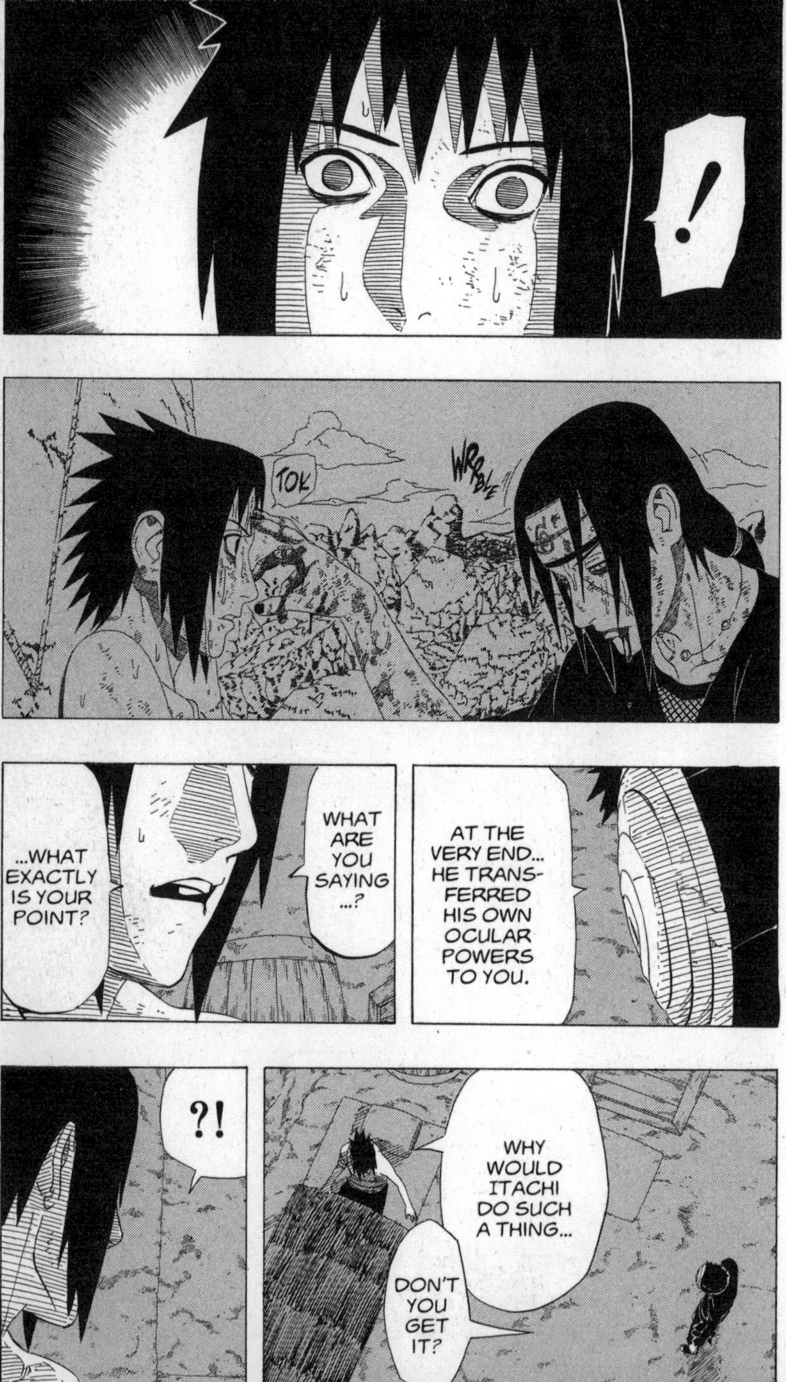
!
WRBBLE
TOK
AT THE VERY END... HE TRANS-FERRED HIS OWN OCULAR POWERS TO YOU.
WHAT ARE YOU SAYING ...?
...WHAT EXACTLY IS YOUR POINT?
WHY WOULD ITACHI DO SUCH A THING...
DON'T YOU GET IT?
?!

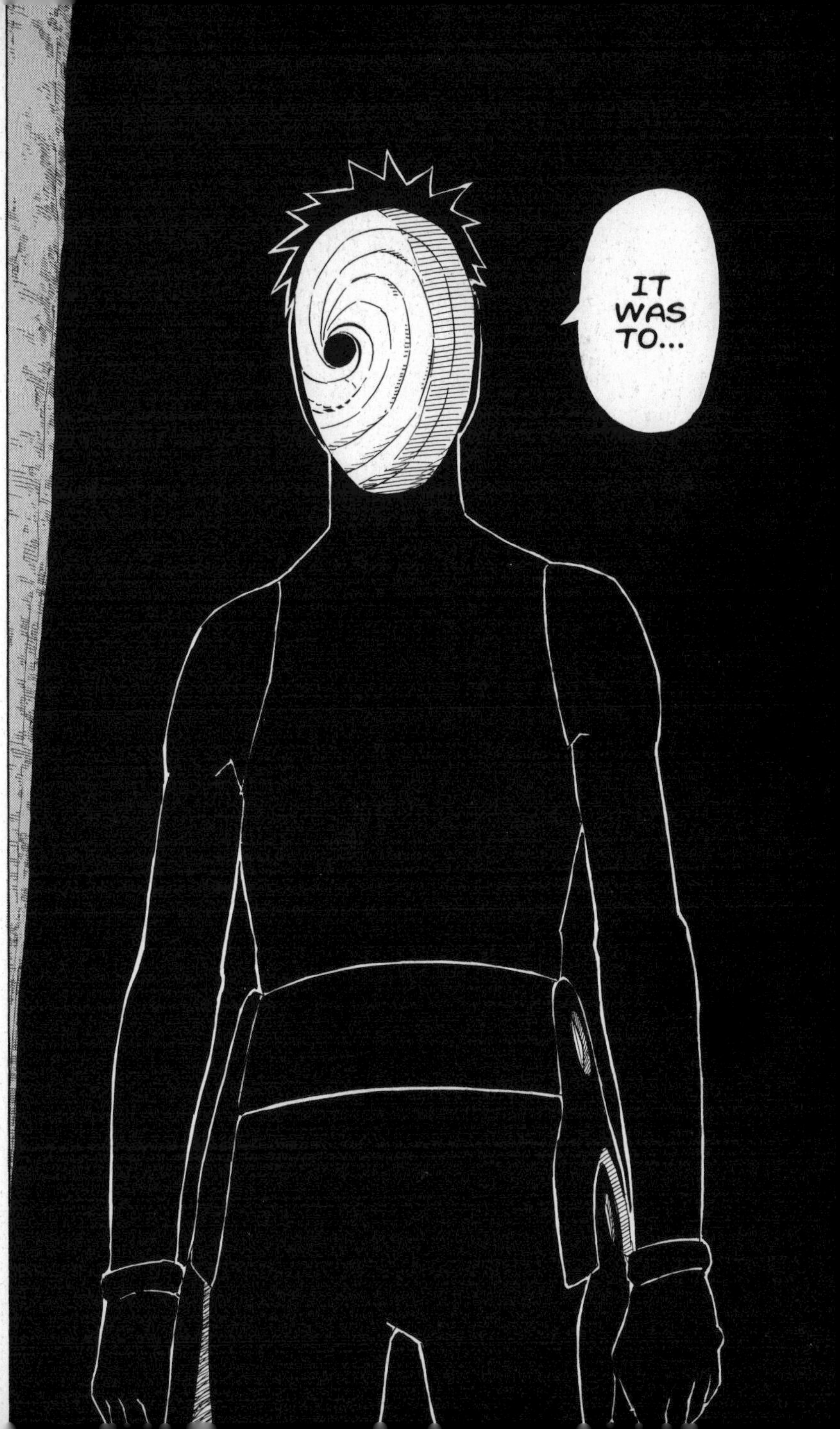
IT WAS TO...

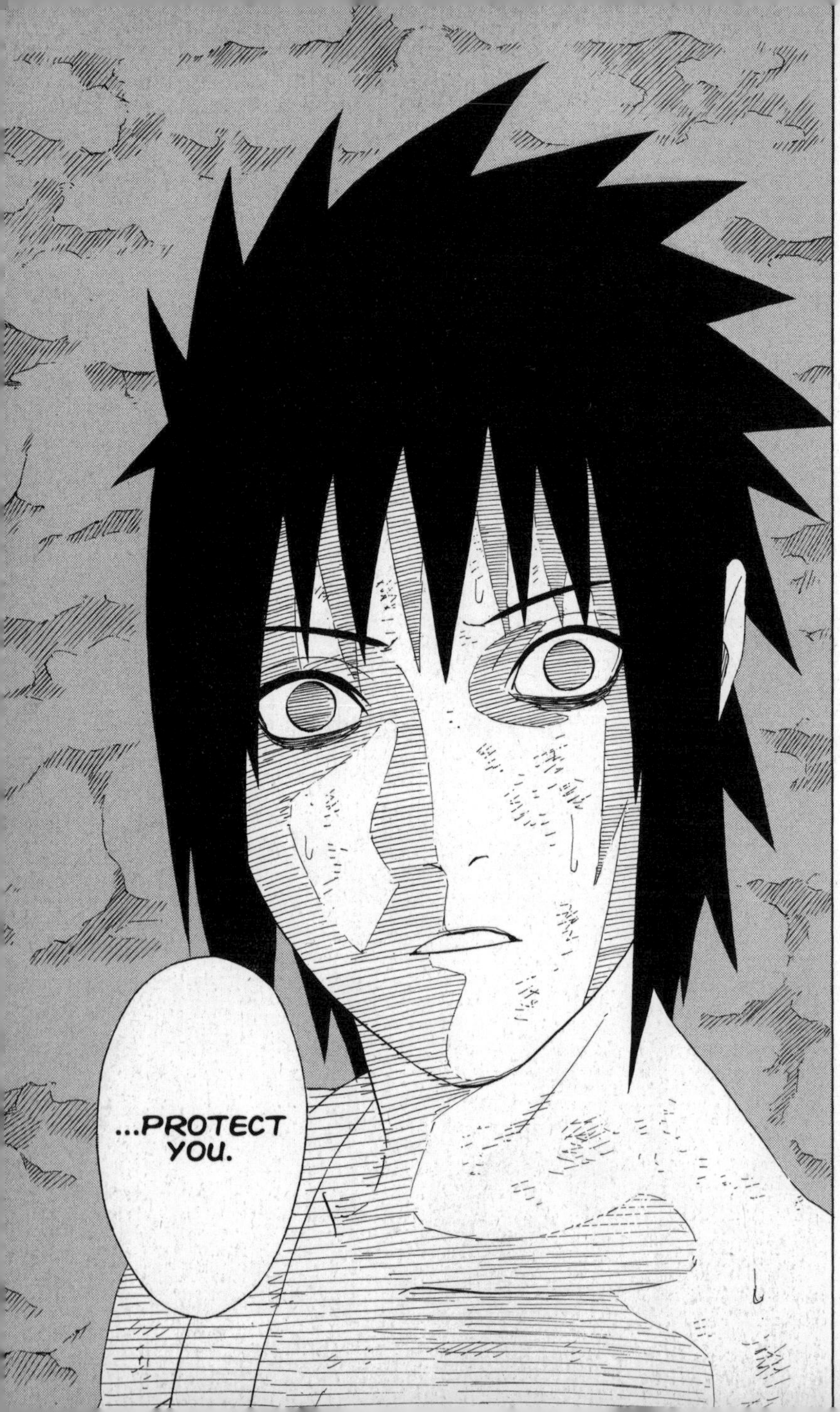
...PROTECT YOU.

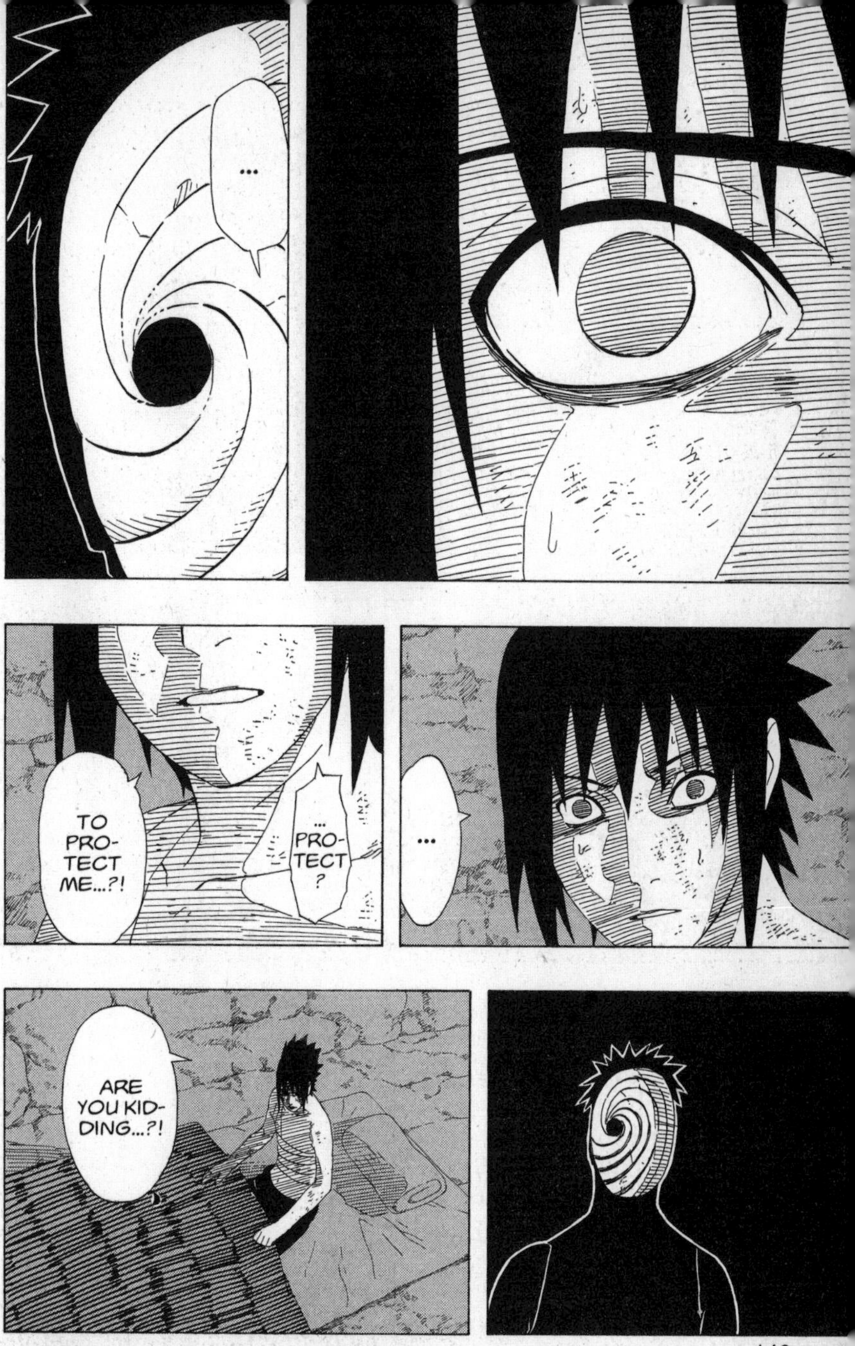
...
...
...PROTECT?
TO PROTECT ME...?!
ARE YOU KIDDING...?!

READ THIS WAY

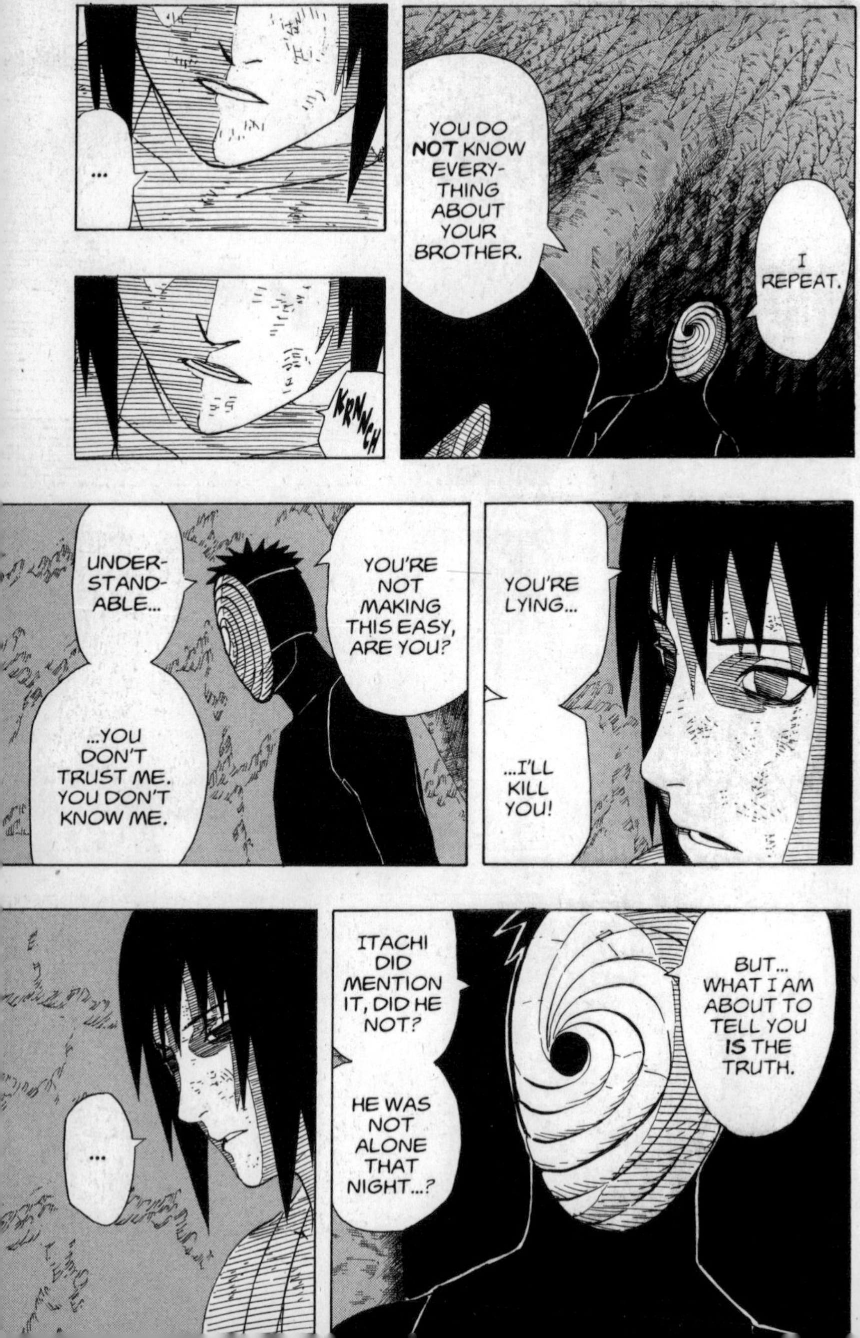
I REPEAT.
YOU DO NOT KNOW EVERYTHING ABOUT YOUR BROTHER.
...
KRNNCH
YOU'RE LYING...
...I'LL KILL YOU!
YOU'RE NOT MAKING THIS EASY, ARE YOU?
UNDERSTANDABLE...
...YOU DON'T TRUST ME. YOU DON'T KNOW ME.
BUT... WHAT I AM ABOUT TO TELL YOU IS THE TRUTH.
ITACHI DID MENTION IT, DID HE NOT?
HE WAS NOT ALONE THAT NIGHT...?
...

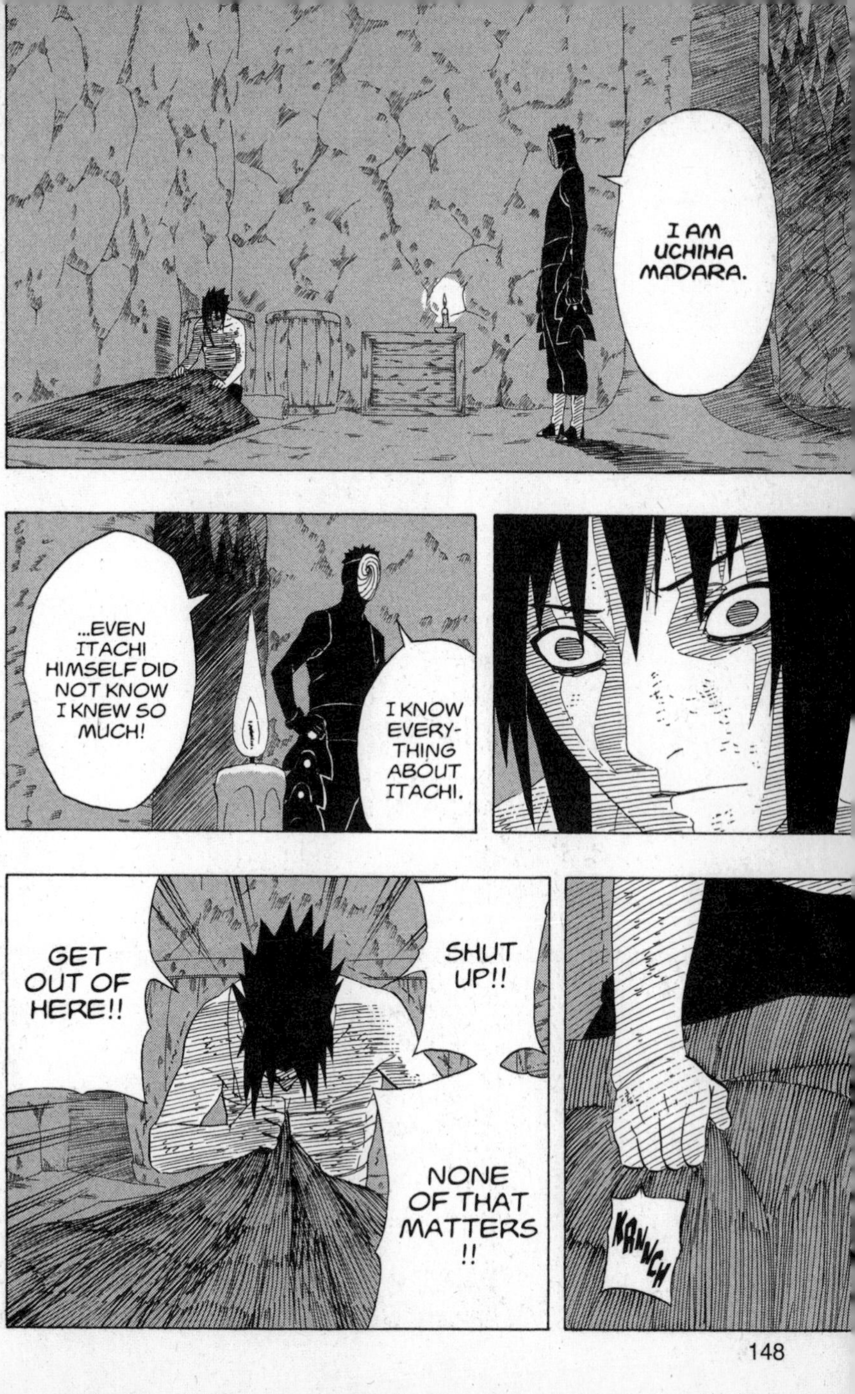
I AM UCHIHA MADARA.
I KNOW EVERYTHING ABOUT ITACHI.
...EVEN ITACHI HIMSELF DID NOT KNOW I KNEW SO MUCH!
KRNNCH
SHUT UP!!
GET OUT OF HERE!!
NONE OF THAT MATTERS!!

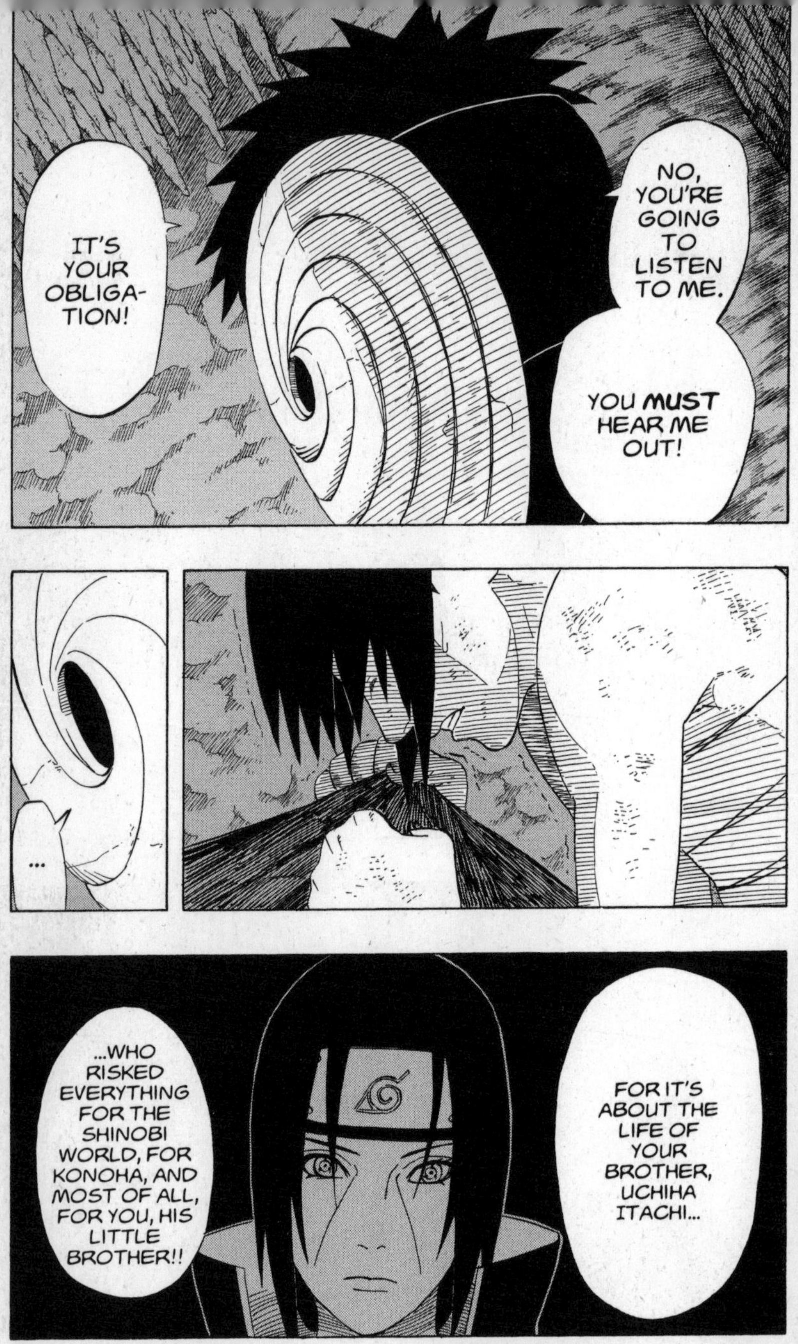
NO, YOU'RE GOING TO LISTEN TO ME.
YOU MUST HEAR ME OUT!
IT'S YOUR OBLIGATION!
...
FOR IT'S ABOUT THE LIFE OF YOUR BROTHER, UCHIHA ITACHI...
...WHO RISKED EVERYTHING FOR THE SHINOBI WORLD, FOR KONOHA, AND MOST OF ALL, FOR YOU, HIS LITTLE BROTHER!!

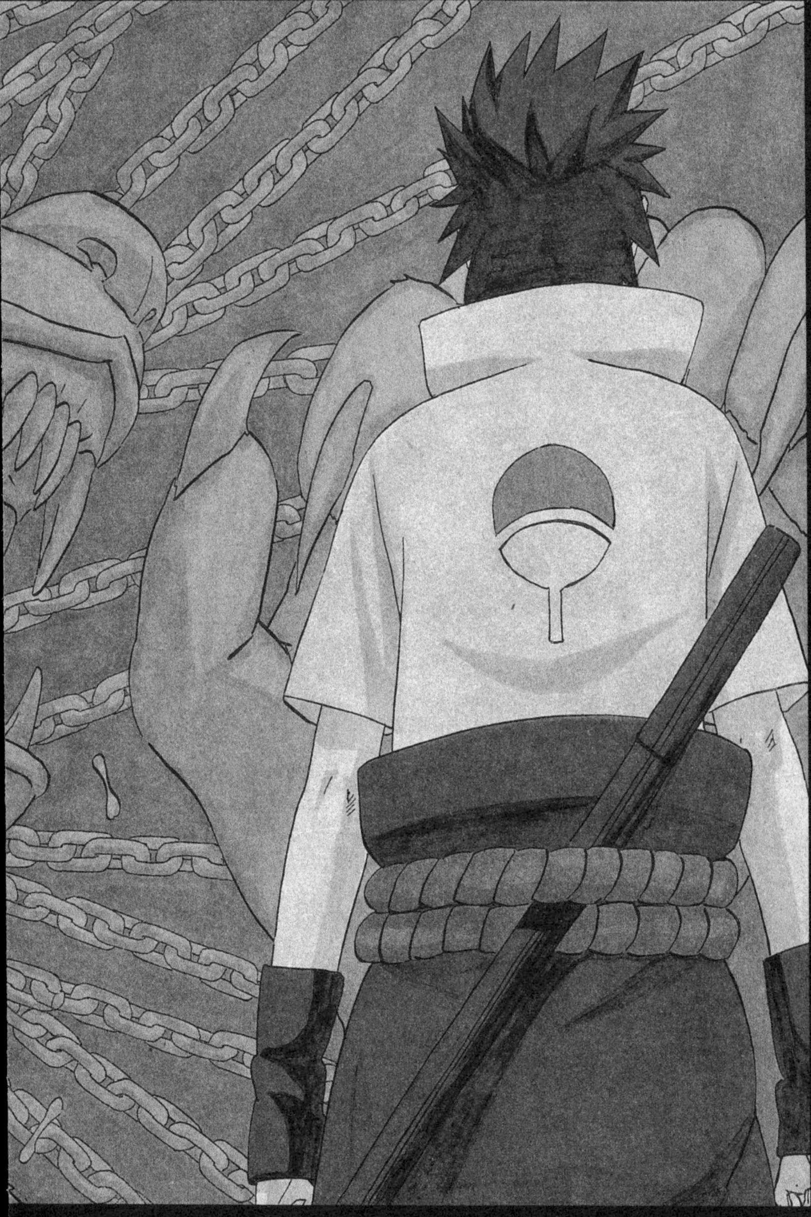

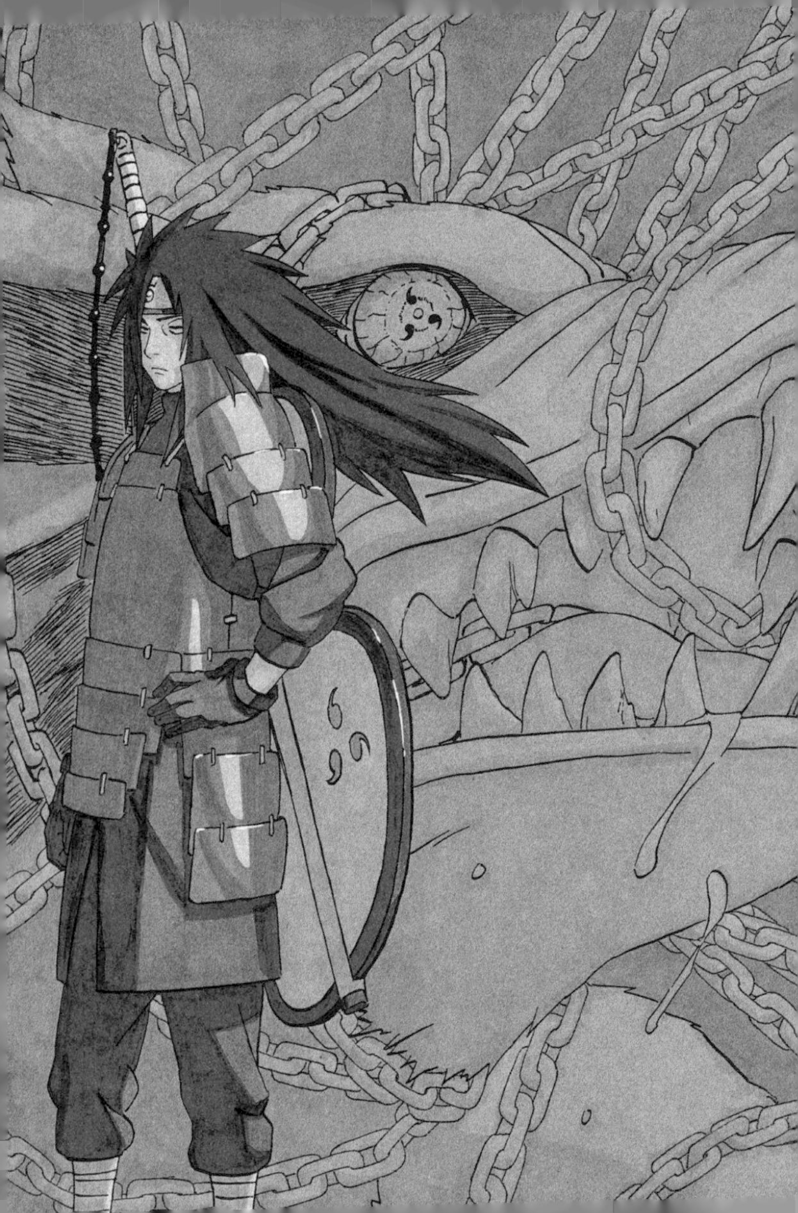

NARUTO

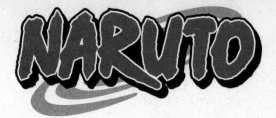

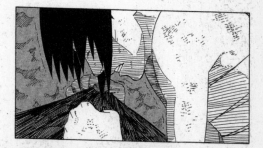

READ THIS WAY

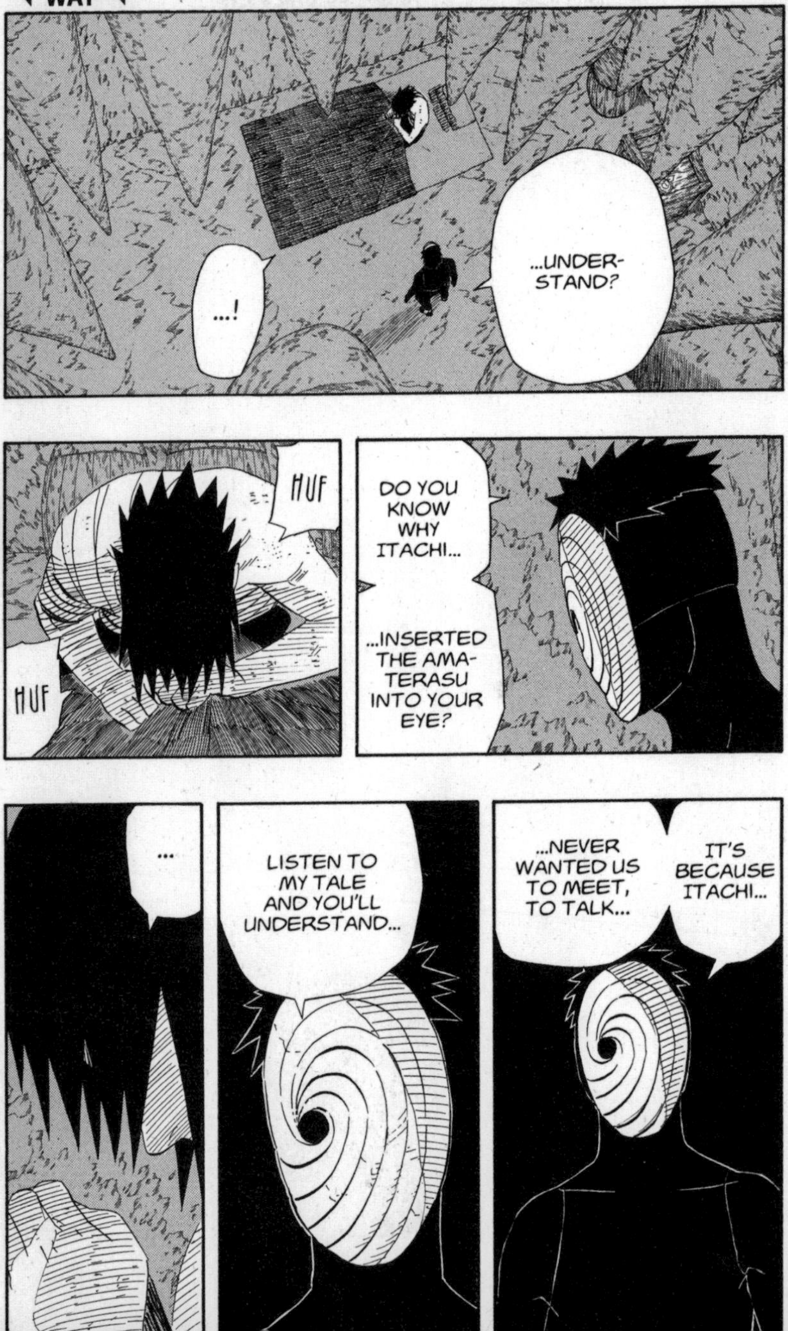
...UNDER-STAND?
...!
DO YOU KNOW WHY ITACHI...
...INSERTED THE AMA-TERASU INTO YOUR EYE?
HUF
HUF
IT'S BECAUSE ITACHI...
...NEVER WANTED US TO MEET, TO TALK...
LISTEN TO MY TALE AND YOU'LL UNDERSTAND...
...

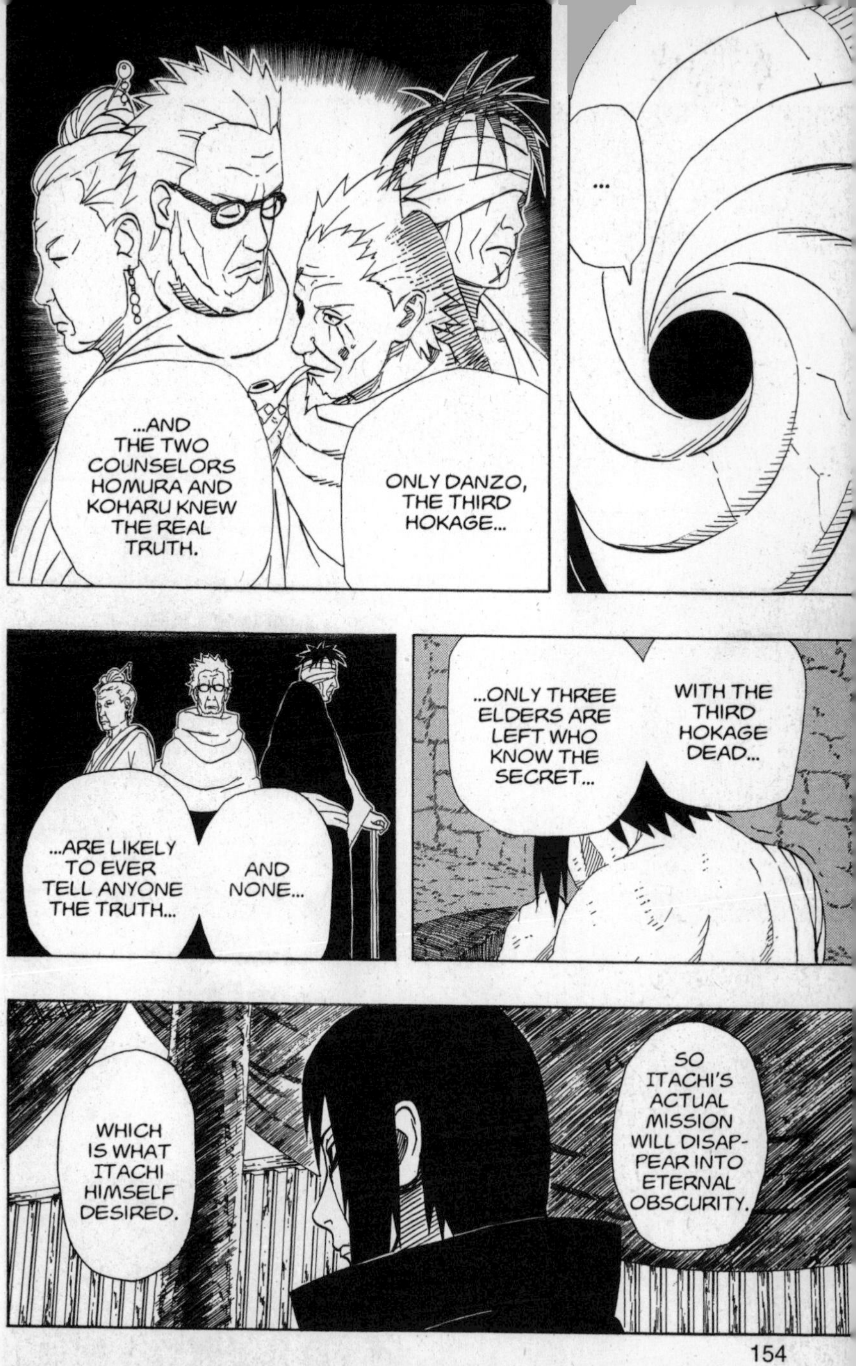
...
ONLY DANZO, THE THIRD HOKAGE...
...AND THE TWO COUNSELORS HOMURA AND KOHARU KNEW THE REAL TRUTH.
WITH THE THIRD HOKAGE DEAD...
...ONLY THREE ELDERS ARE LEFT WHO KNOW THE SECRET...
AND NONE...
...ARE LIKELY TO EVER TELL ANYONE THE TRUTH...
SO ITACHI'S ACTUAL MISSION WILL DISAPPEAR INTO ETERNAL OBSCURITY.
WHICH IS WHAT ITACHI HIMSELF DESIRED.

READ THIS WAY

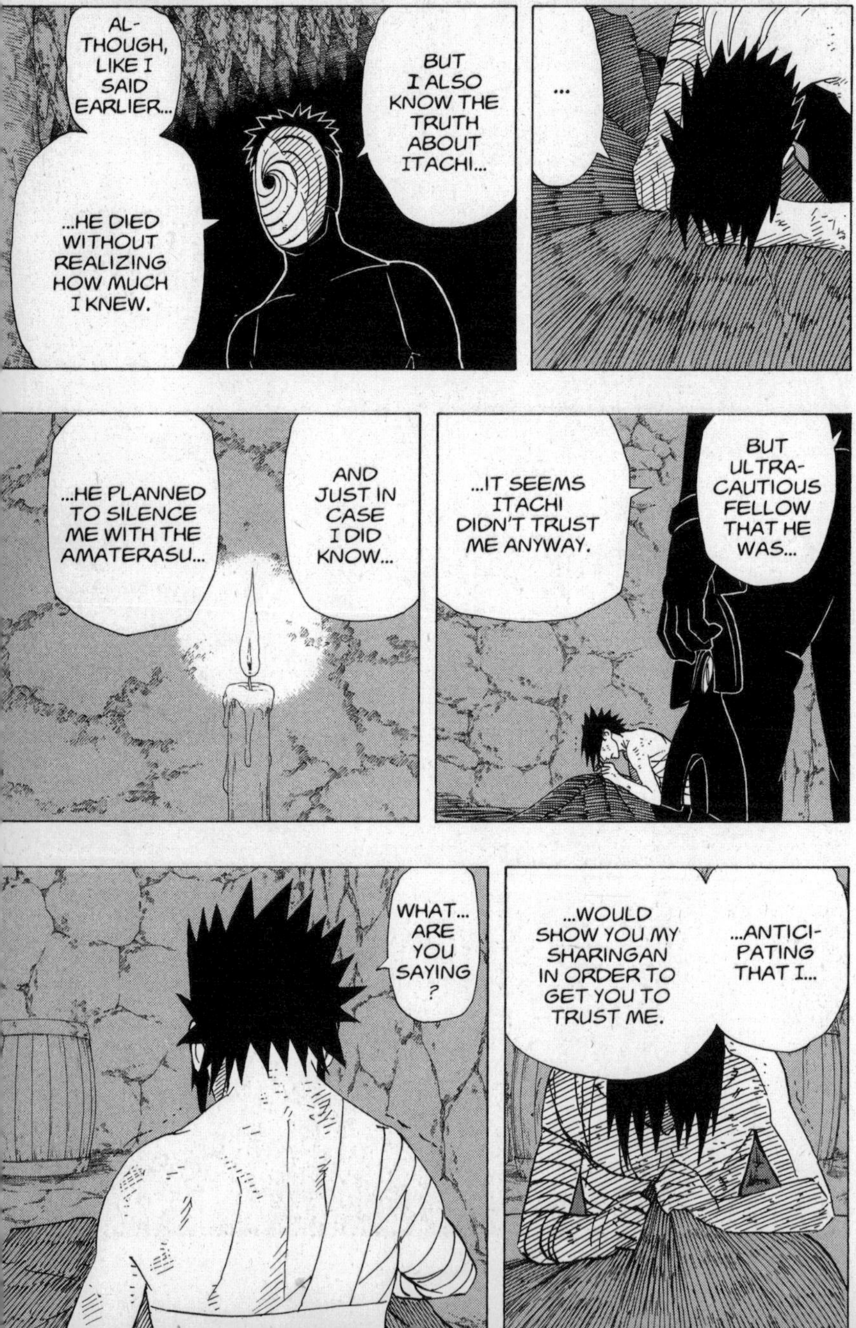
...
BUT I ALSO KNOW THE TRUTH ABOUT ITACHI...
AL-THOUGH, LIKE I SAID EARLIER...
...HE DIED WITHOUT REALIZING HOW MUCH I KNEW.
BUT ULTRA-CAUTIOUS FELLOW THAT HE WAS...
...IT SEEMS ITACHI DIDN'T TRUST ME ANYWAY.
AND JUST IN CASE I DID KNOW...
...HE PLANNED TO SILENCE ME WITH THE AMATERASU...
...ANTICI-PATING THAT I...
...WOULD SHOW YOU MY SHARINGAN IN ORDER TO GET YOU TO TRUST ME.
WHAT... ARE YOU SAYING?

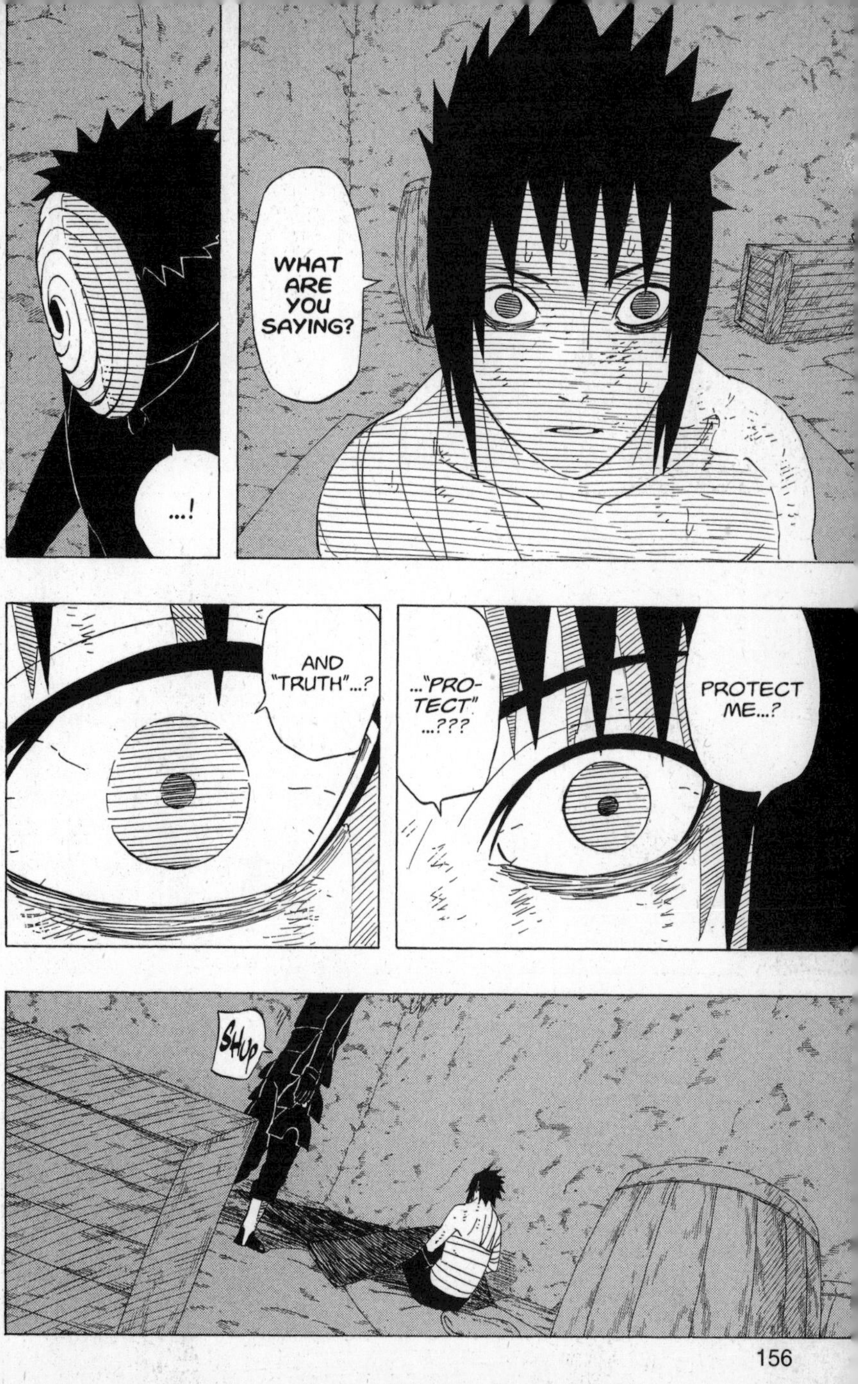
WHAT ARE YOU SAYING?
...!
PROTECT ME...?
..."PRO-TECT" ...???
AND "TRUTH"...?
SHUP

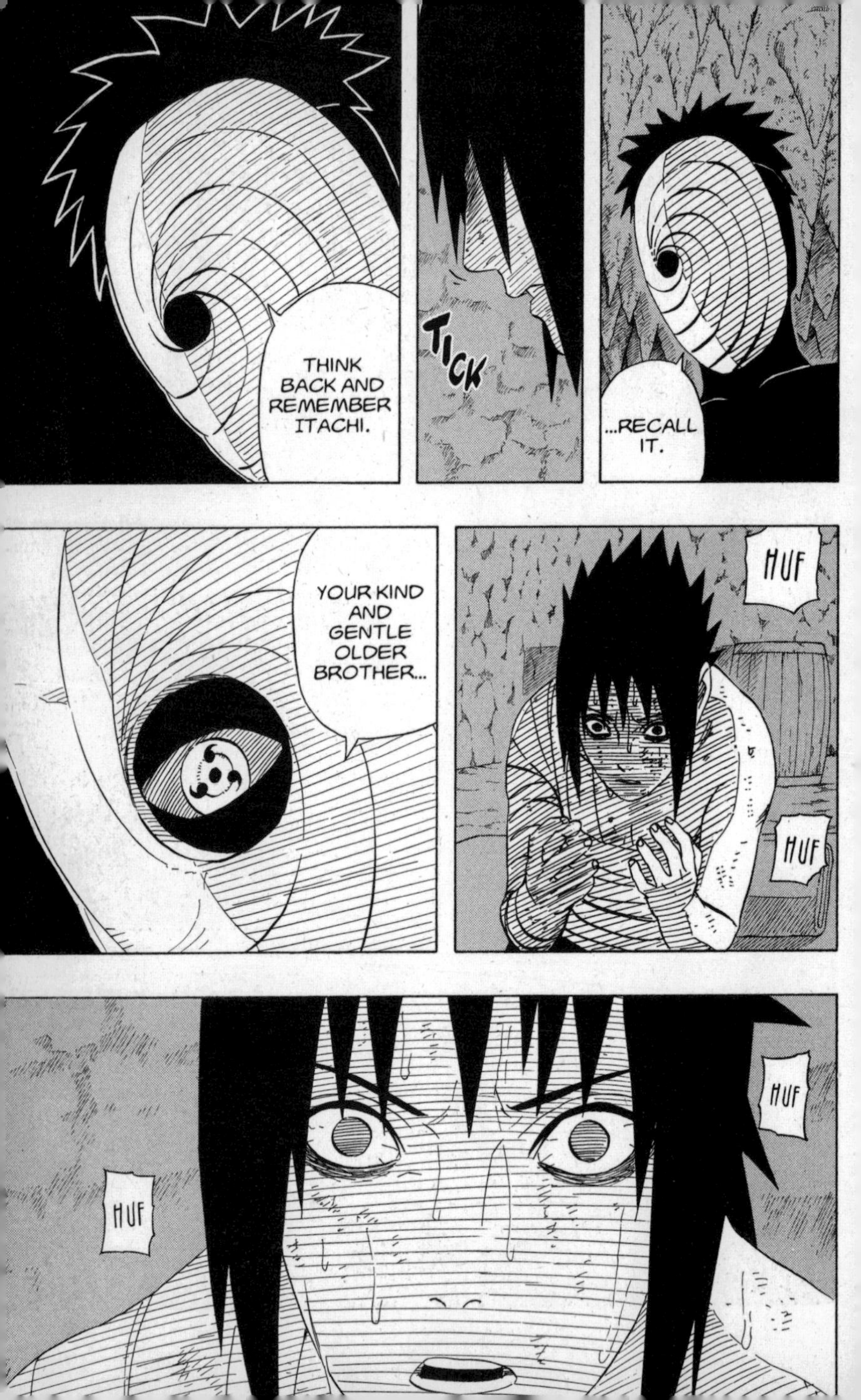
...RECALL IT.
TICK
THINK BACK AND REMEMBER ITACHI.
HUF
HUF
YOUR KIND AND GENTLE OLDER BROTHER...
HUF
HUF

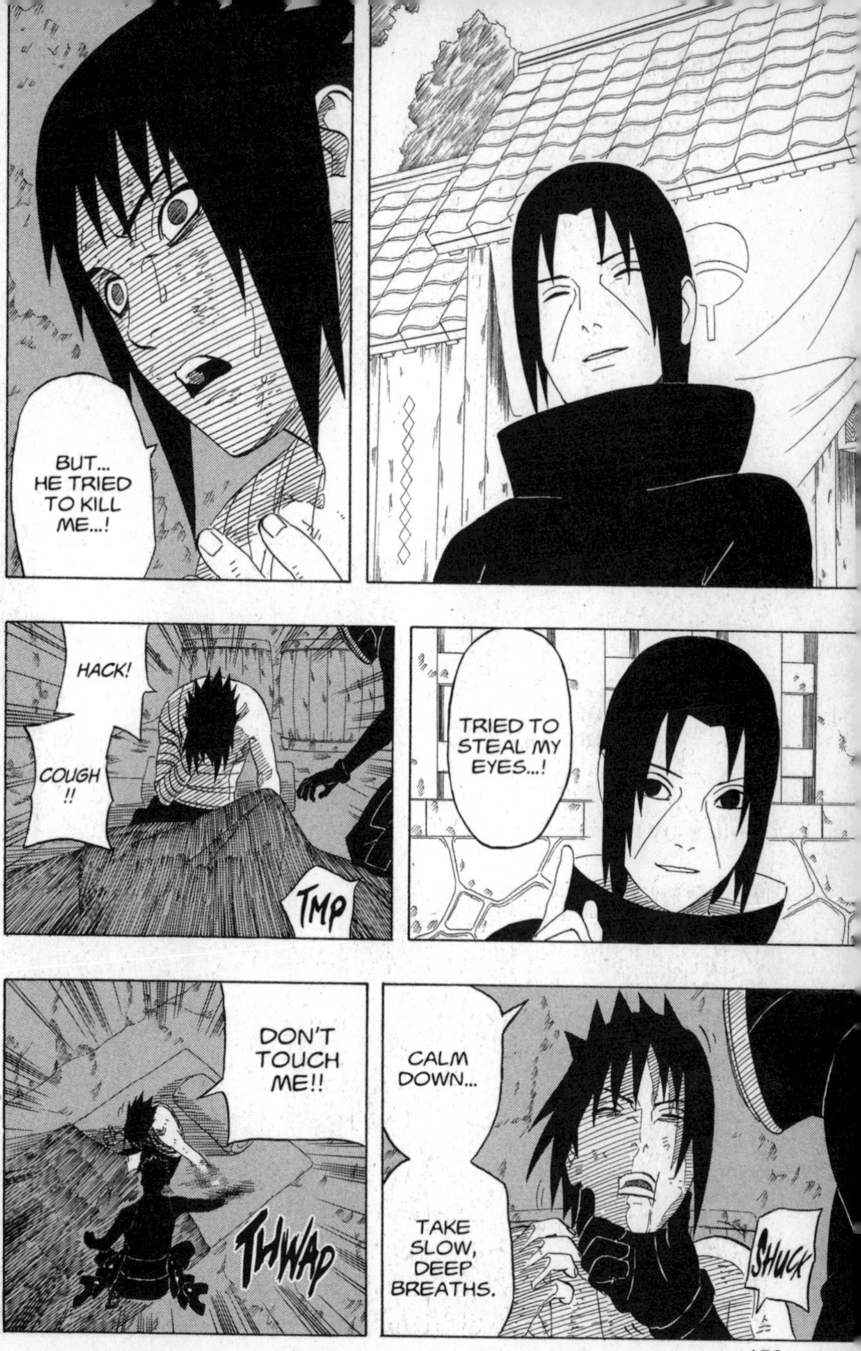
BUT... HE TRIED TO KILL ME...!
TRIED TO STEAL MY EYES...!
HACK!
COUGH!!
TMP
CALM DOWN...
TAKE SLOW, DEEP BREATHS.
SHUCK
DON'T TOUCH ME!!
THWAP

READ THIS WAY

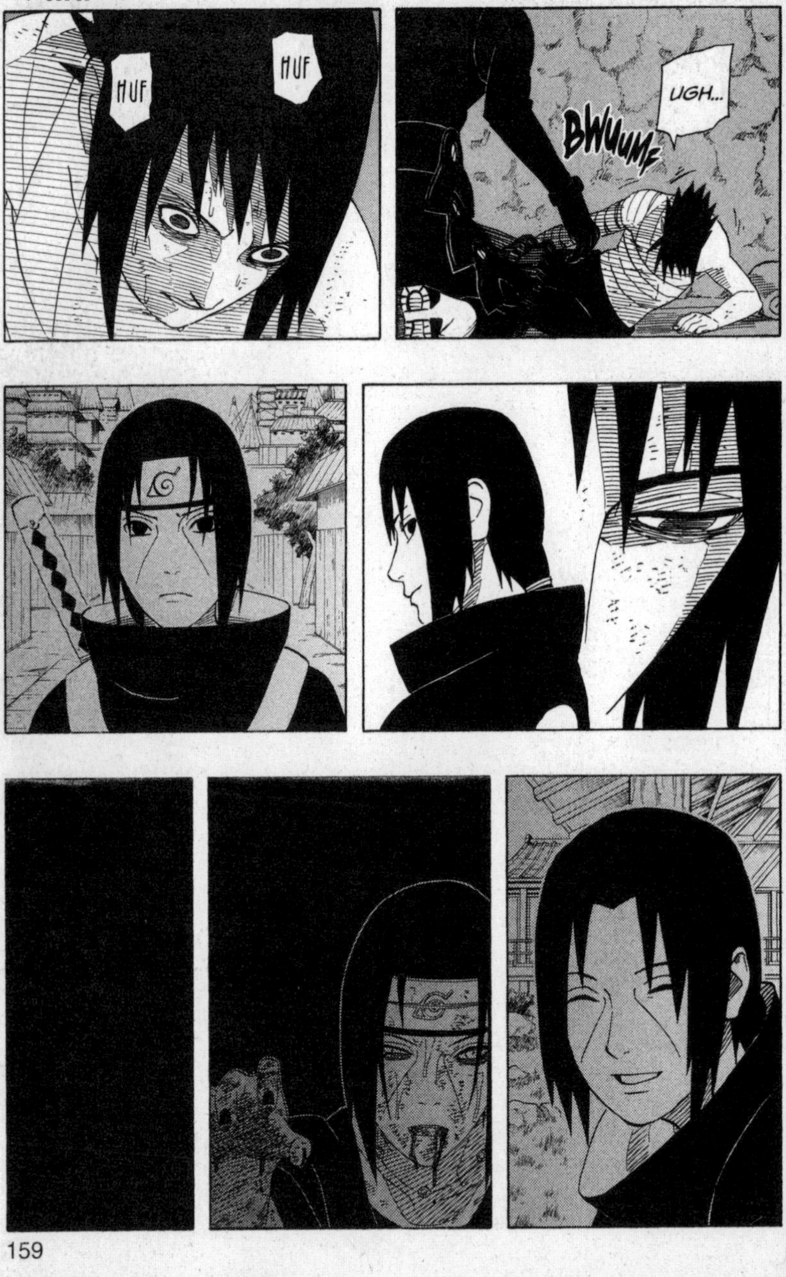
UGH...
BWUUMF
HUF
HUF

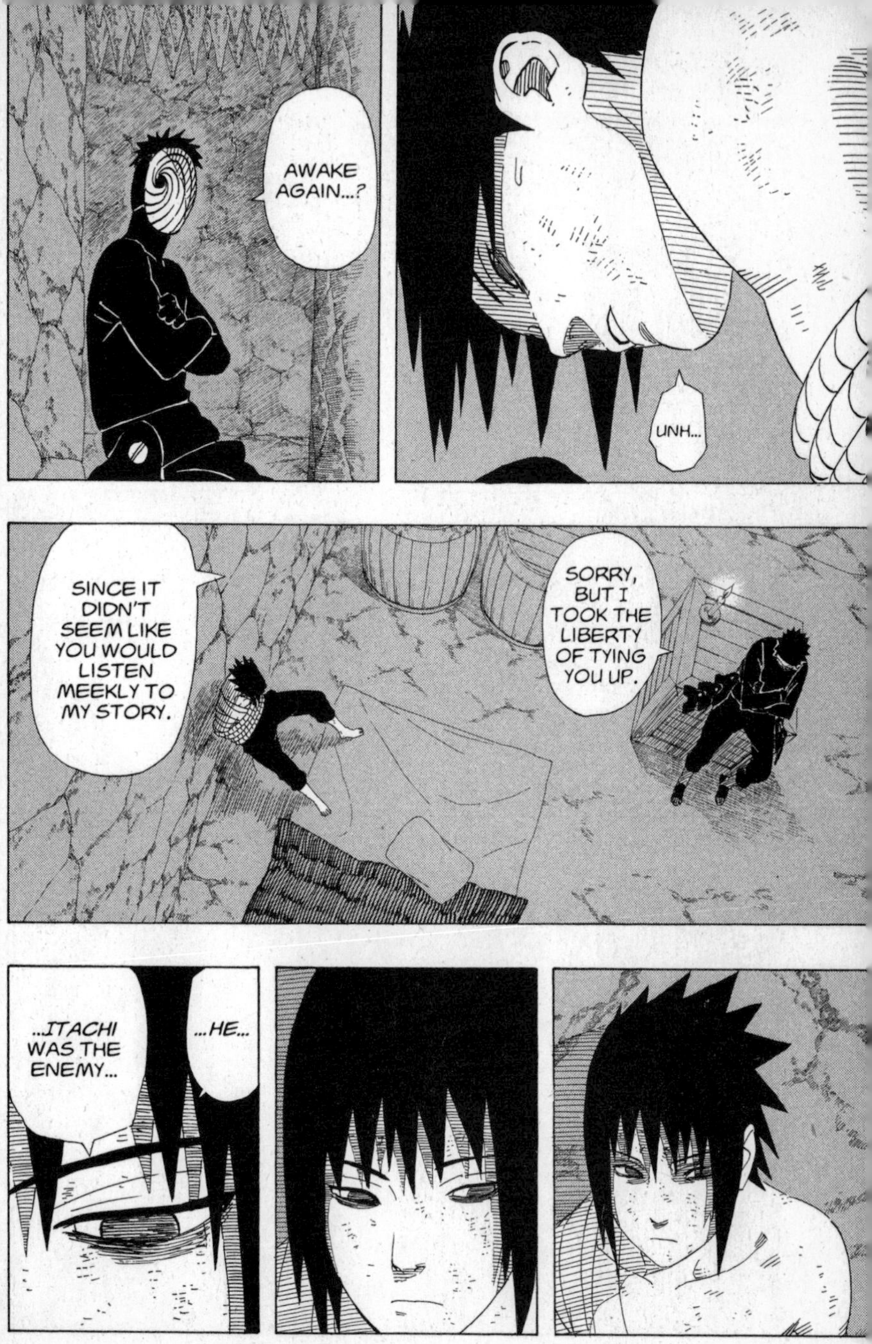
UNH...
AWAKE AGAIN...?
SORRY, BUT I TOOK THE LIBERTY OF TYING YOU UP.
SINCE IT DIDN'T SEEM LIKE YOU WOULD LISTEN MEEKLY TO MY STORY.
...HE...
...ITACHI WAS THE ENEMY...

READ THIS WAY

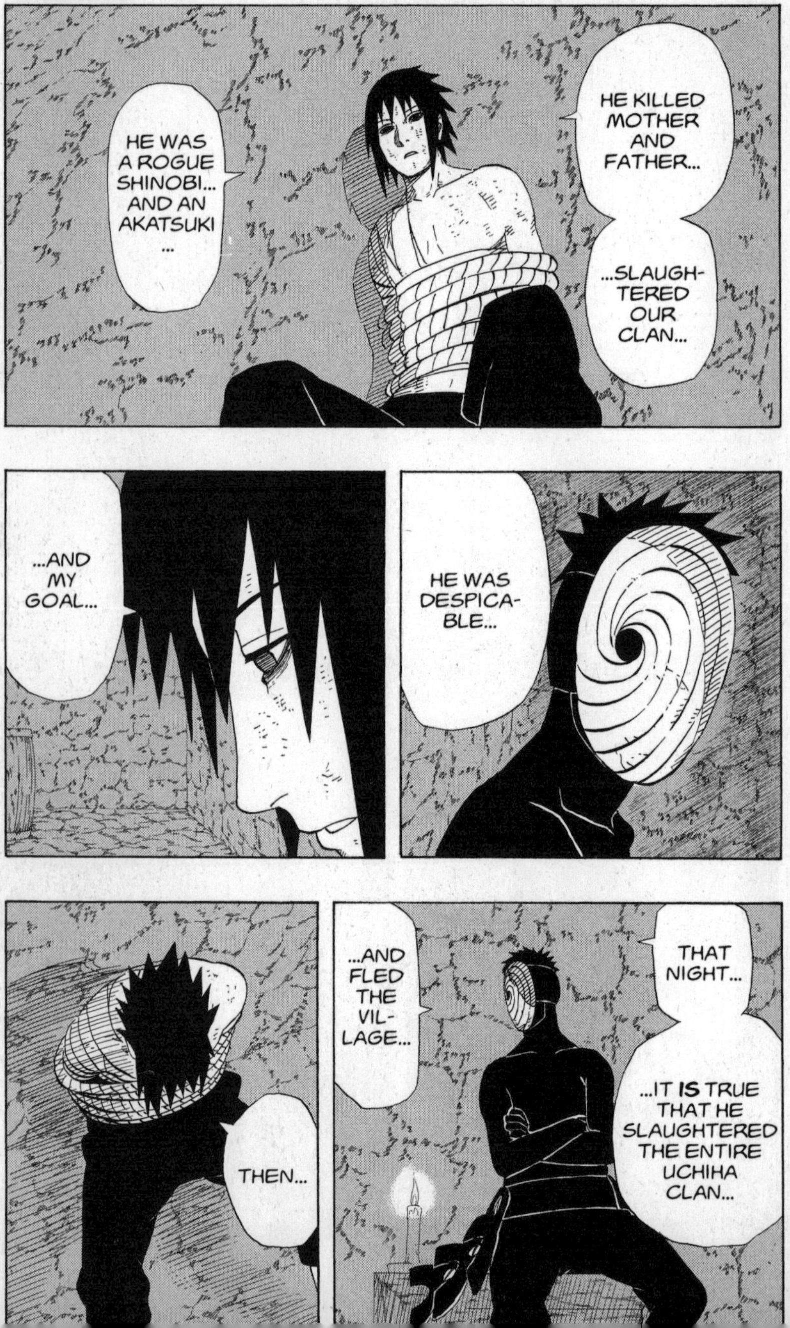
HE KILLED MOTHER AND FATHER...
...SLAUGHTERED OUR CLAN...
HE WAS A ROGUE SHINOBI... AND AN AKATSUKI ...
HE WAS DESPICABLE...
...AND MY GOAL...
THAT NIGHT...
...IT **IS** TRUE THAT HE SLAUGHTERED THE ENTIRE UCHIHA CLAN...
...AND FLED THE VILLAGE...
THEN...

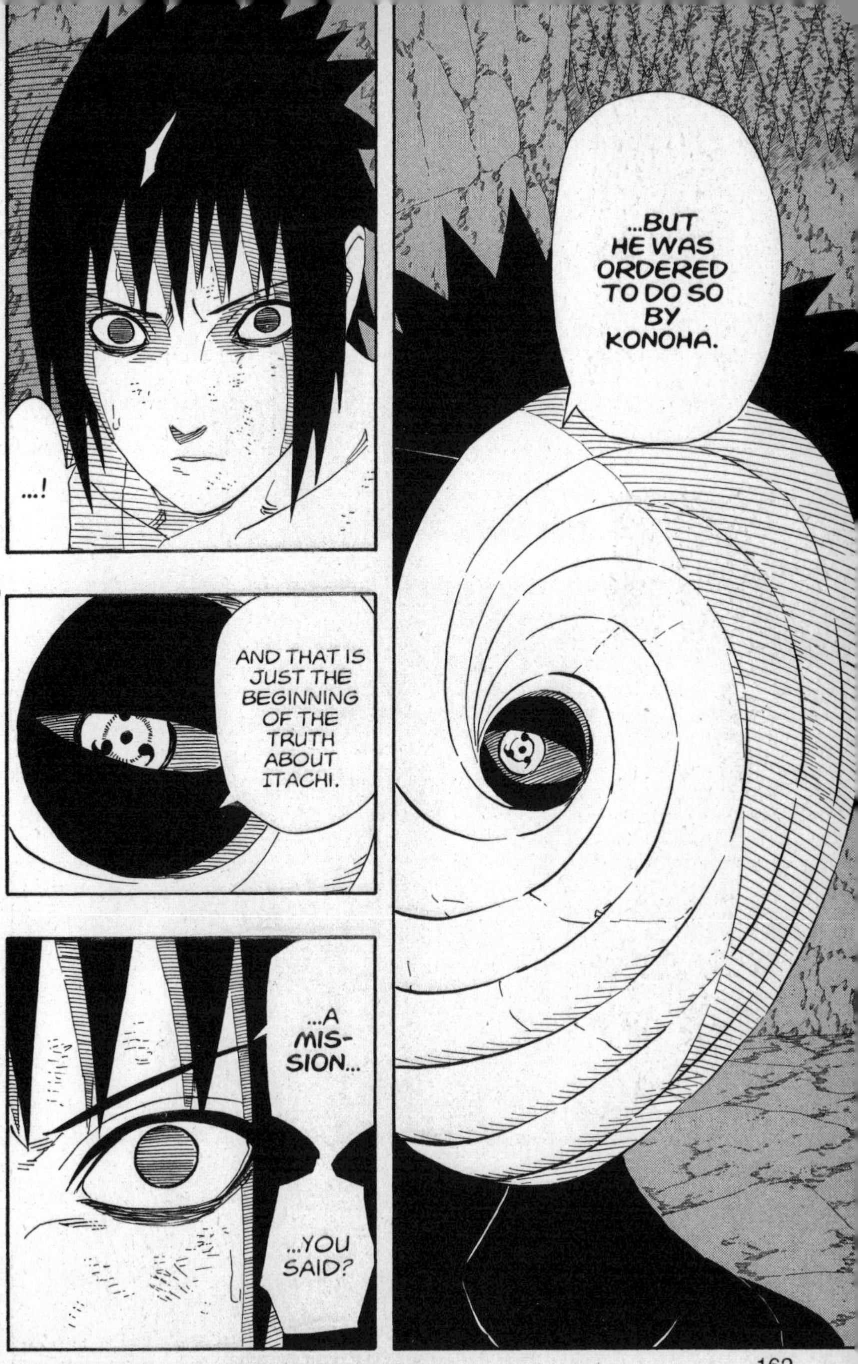
...BUT HE WAS ORDERED TO DO SO BY KONOHA.
...!
AND THAT IS JUST THE BEGINNING OF THE TRUTH ABOUT ITACHI.
...A MIS-SION...
...YOU SAID?

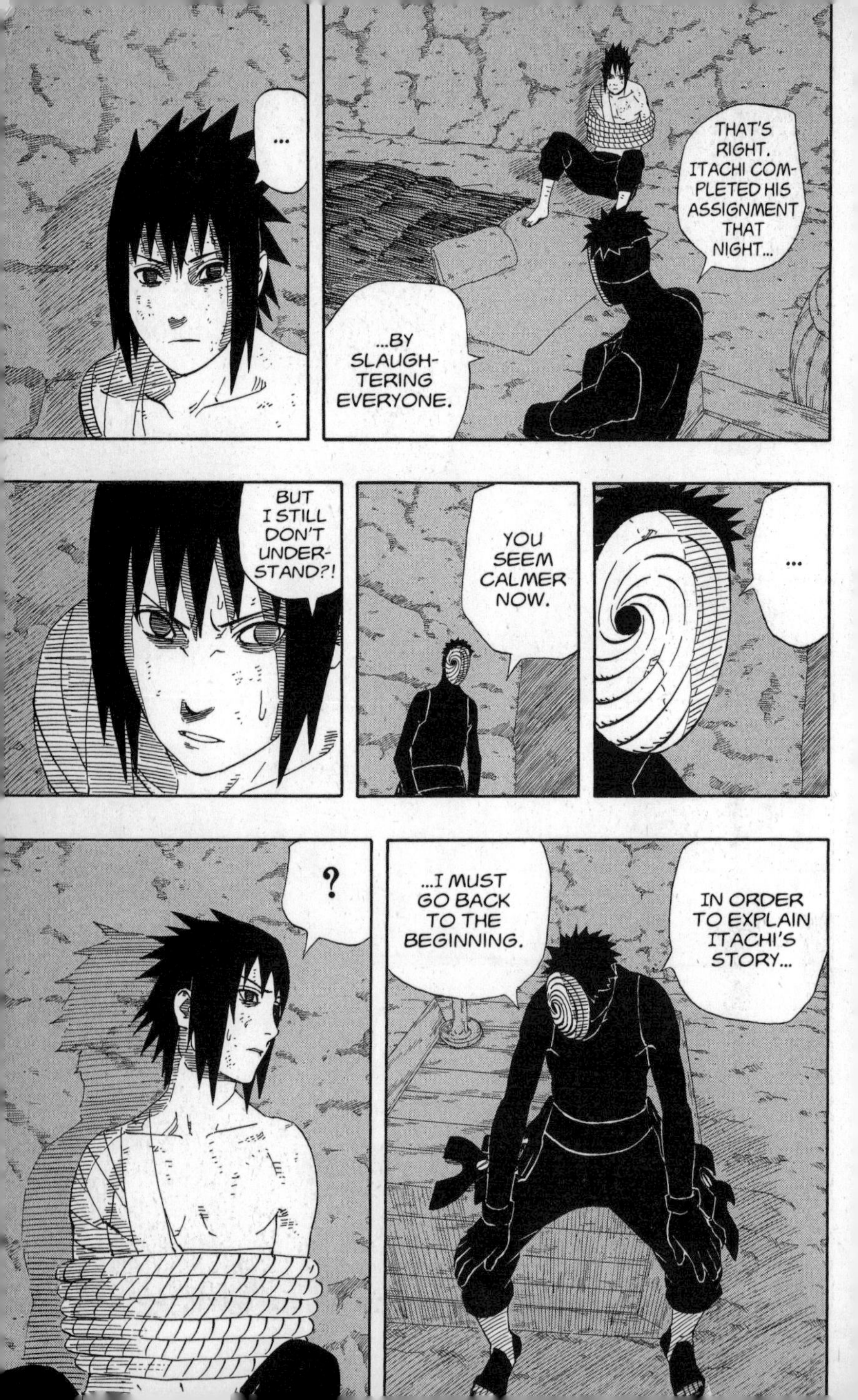

THAT'S RIGHT. ITACHI COMPLETED HIS ASSIGNMENT THAT NIGHT...
...BY SLAUGHTERING EVERYONE.
...
...
YOU SEEM CALMER NOW.
BUT I STILL DON'T UNDERSTAND?!
IN ORDER TO EXPLAIN ITACHI'S STORY...
...I MUST GO BACK TO THE BEGINNING.
?

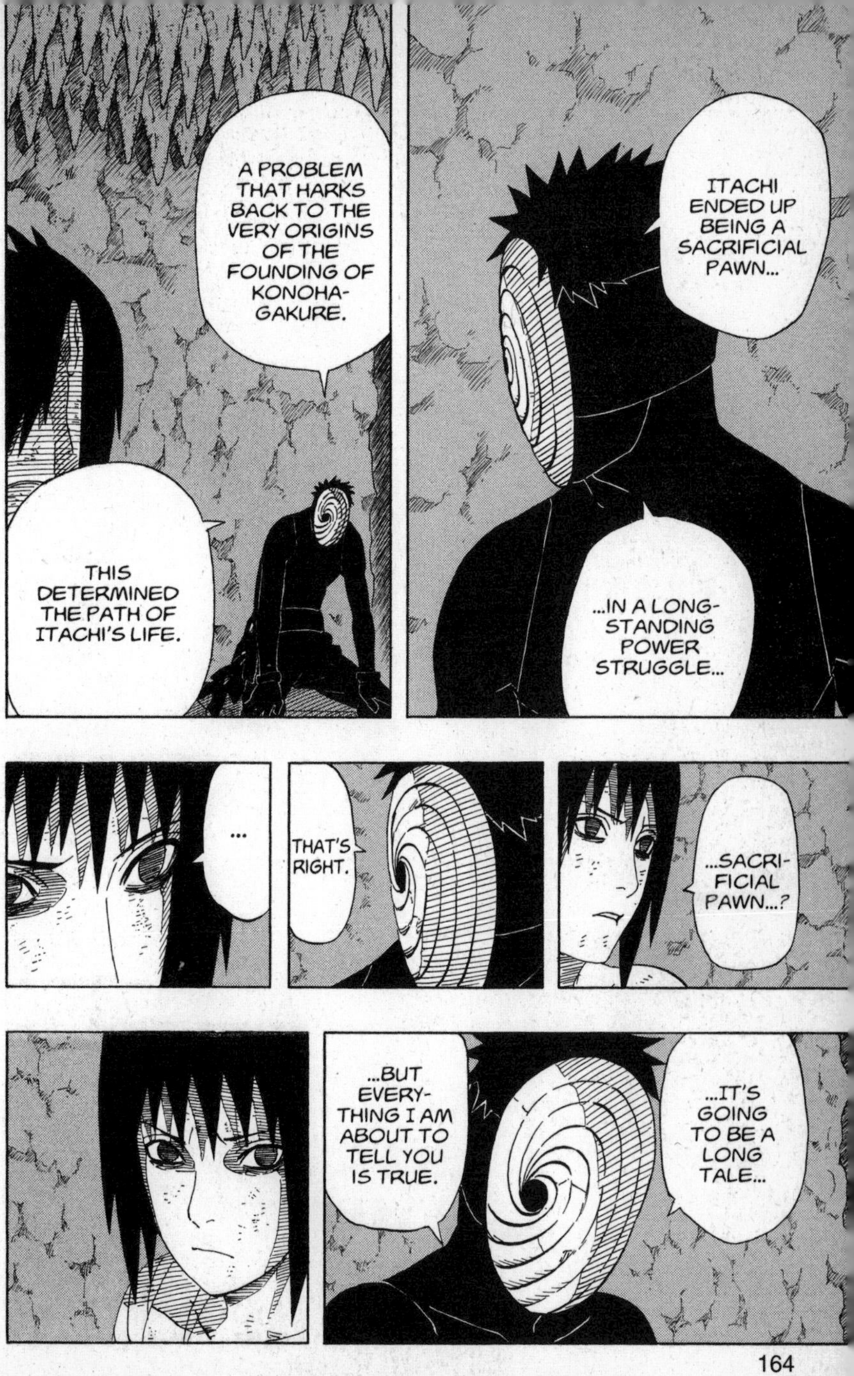
ITACHI ENDED UP BEING A SACRIFICIAL PAWN...
...IN A LONG-STANDING POWER STRUGGLE...
A PROBLEM THAT HARKS BACK TO THE VERY ORIGINS OF THE FOUNDING OF KONOHA-GAKURE.
THIS DETERMINED THE PATH OF ITACHI'S LIFE.
...SACRI-FICIAL PAWN...?
THAT'S RIGHT.
...
...IT'S GOING TO BE A LONG TALE...
...BUT EVERY-THING I AM ABOUT TO TELL YOU IS TRUE.

READ THIS WAY

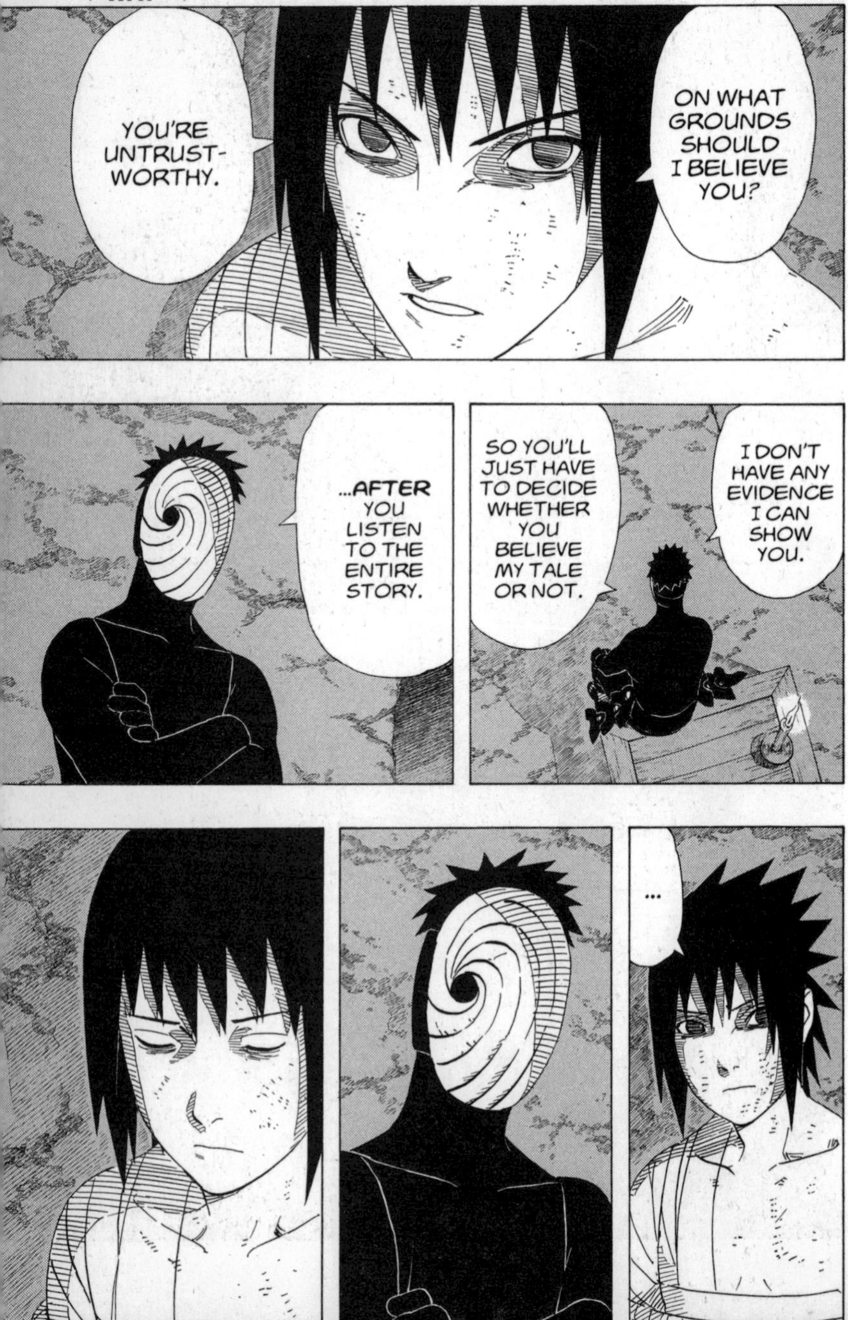

ON WHAT GROUNDS SHOULD I BELIEVE YOU?
YOU'RE UNTRUST-WORTHY.
I DON'T HAVE ANY EVIDENCE I CAN SHOW YOU.
SO YOU'LL JUST HAVE TO DECIDE WHETHER YOU BELIEVE MY TALE OR NOT.
...AFTER YOU LISTEN TO THE ENTIRE STORY.
...

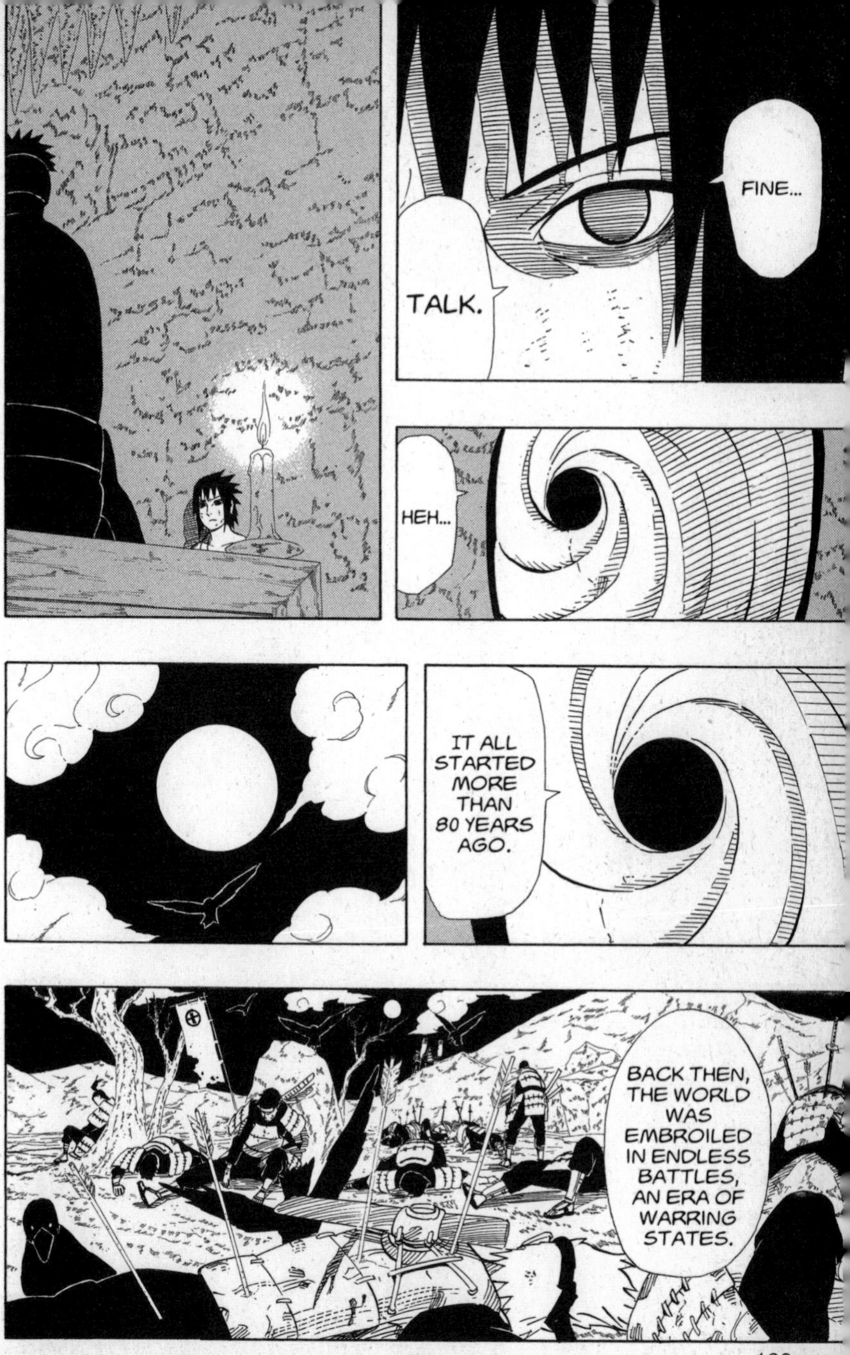
FINE...
TALK.
HEH...
IT ALL STARTED MORE THAN 80 YEARS AGO.
BACK THEN, THE WORLD WAS EMBROILED IN ENDLESS BATTLES, AN ERA OF WARRING STATES.

READ THIS WAY

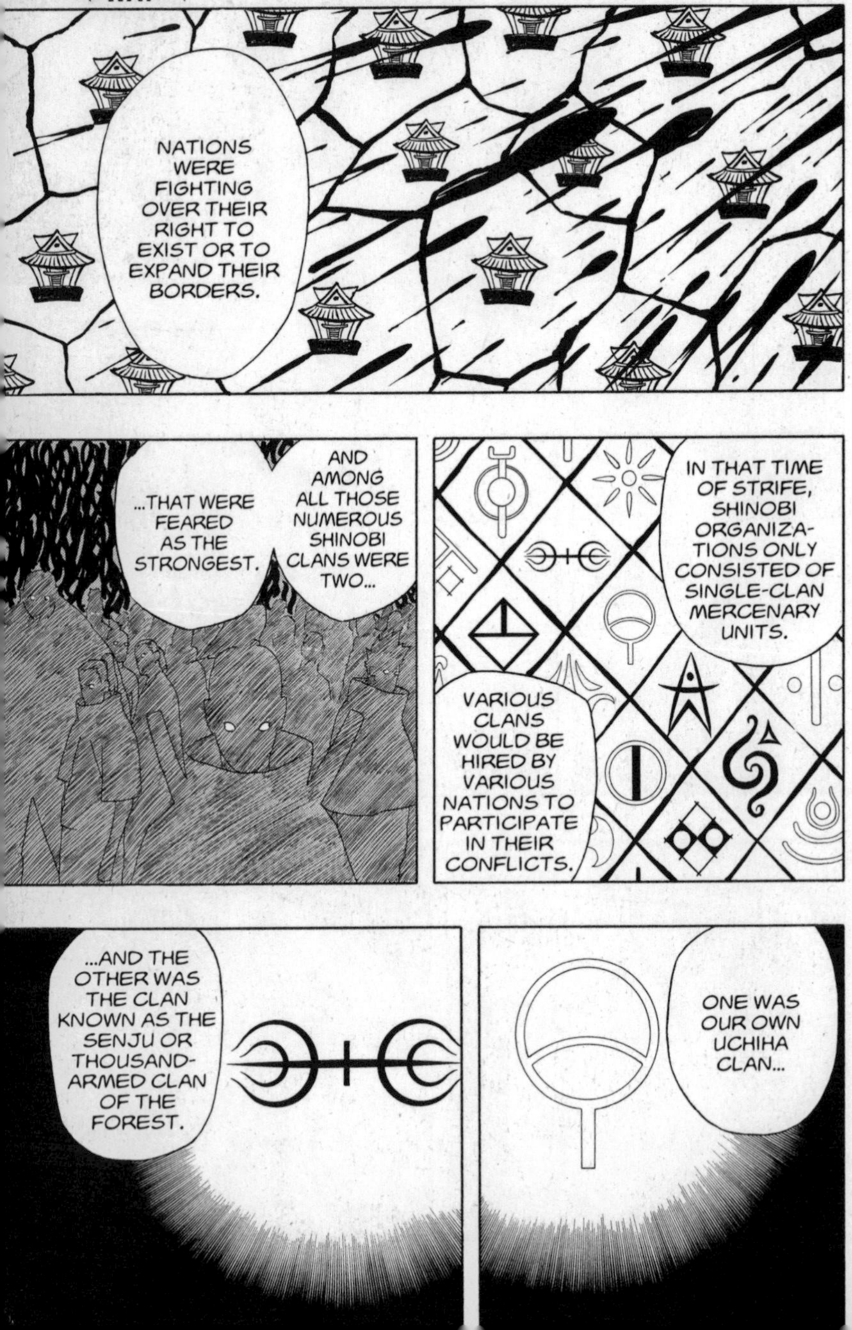
NATIONS WERE FIGHTING OVER THEIR RIGHT TO EXIST OR TO EXPAND THEIR BORDERS.
IN THAT TIME OF STRIFE, SHINOBI ORGANIZA-TIONS ONLY CONSISTED OF SINGLE-CLAN MERCENARY UNITS.
VARIOUS CLANS WOULD BE HIRED BY VARIOUS NATIONS TO PARTICIPATE IN THEIR CONFLICTS.
AND AMONG ALL THOSE NUMEROUS SHINOBI CLANS WERE TWO...
...THAT WERE FEARED AS THE STRONGEST.
ONE WAS OUR OWN UCHIHA CLAN...
...AND THE OTHER WAS THE CLAN KNOWN AS THE SENJU OR THOUSAND-ARMED CLAN OF THE FOREST.

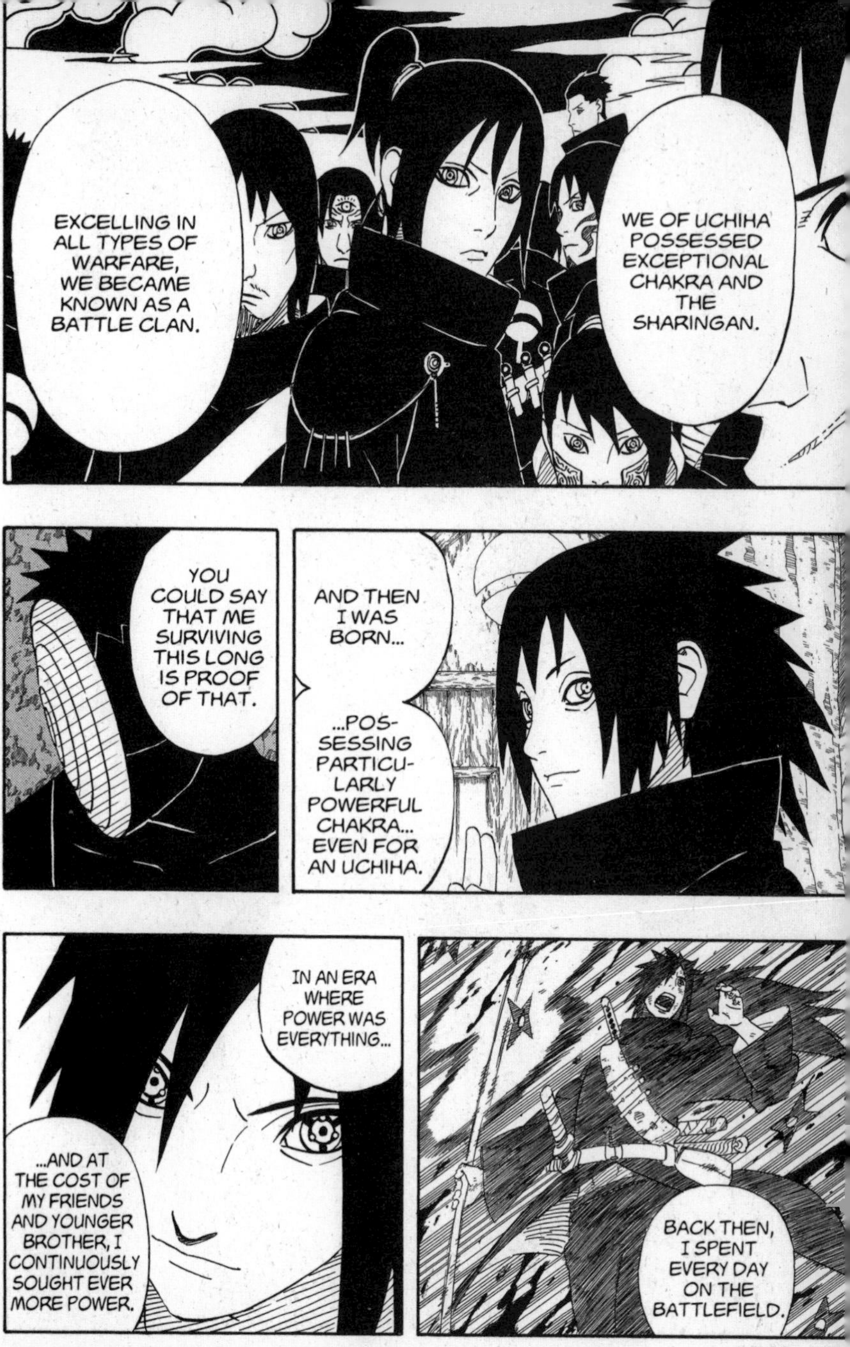
WE OF UCHIHA POSSESSED EXCEPTIONAL CHAKRA AND THE SHARINGAN.
EXCELLING IN ALL TYPES OF WARFARE, WE BECAME KNOWN AS A BATTLE CLAN.
AND THEN I WAS BORN...
...POSSESSING PARTICULARLY POWERFUL CHAKRA... EVEN FOR AN UCHIHA.
YOU COULD SAY THAT ME SURVIVING THIS LONG IS PROOF OF THAT.
BACK THEN, I SPENT EVERY DAY ON THE BATTLEFIELD.
IN AN ERA WHERE POWER WAS EVERYTHING...
...AND AT THE COST OF MY FRIENDS AND YOUNGER BROTHER, I CONTINUOUSLY SOUGHT EVER MORE POWER.

READ THIS WAY

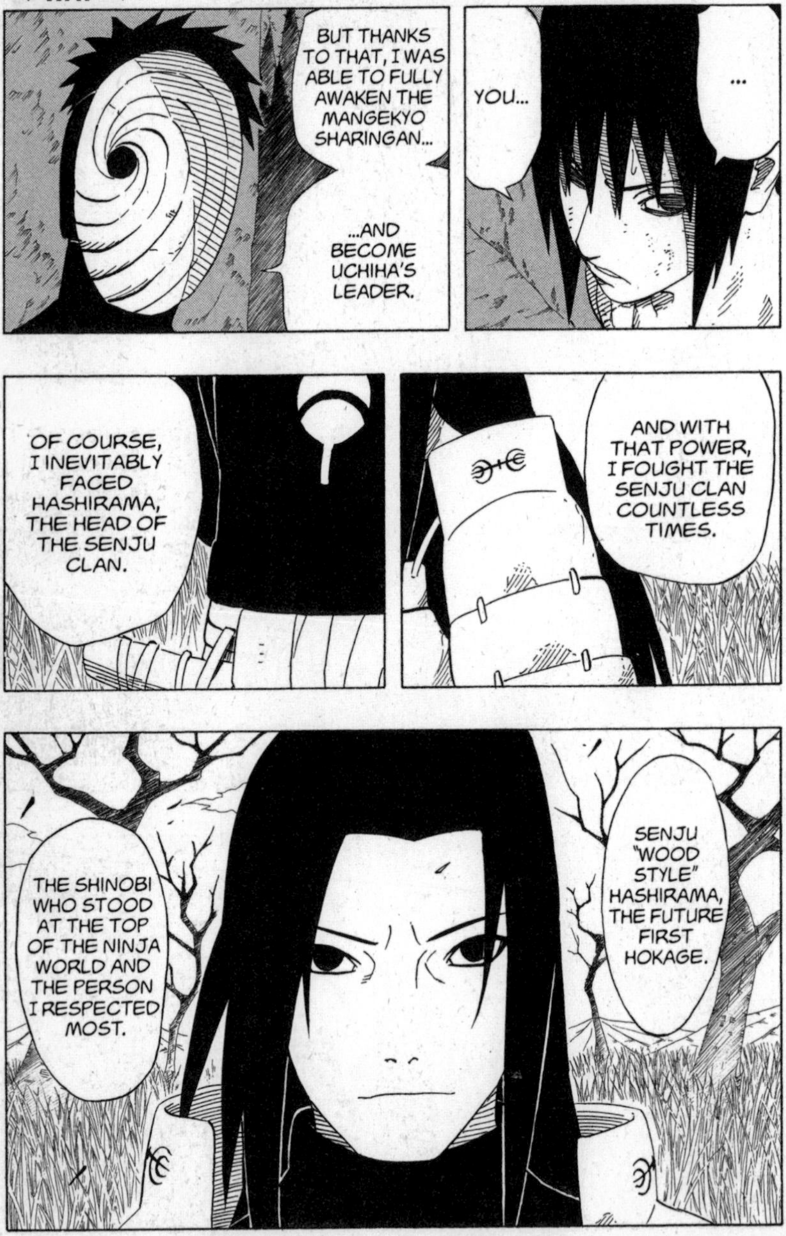
...
YOU...
BUT THANKS TO THAT, I WAS ABLE TO FULLY AWAKEN THE MANGEKYO SHARINGAN...
...AND BECOME UCHIHA'S LEADER.
AND WITH THAT POWER, I FOUGHT THE SENJU CLAN COUNTLESS TIMES.
OF COURSE, I INEVITABLY FACED HASHIRAMA, THE HEAD OF THE SENJU CLAN.
SENJU "WOOD STYLE" HASHIRAMA, THE FUTURE FIRST HOKAGE.
THE SHINOBI WHO STOOD AT THE TOP OF THE NINJA WORLD AND THE PERSON I RESPECTED MOST.

NARUTO

Number 399: How It All Begins!!

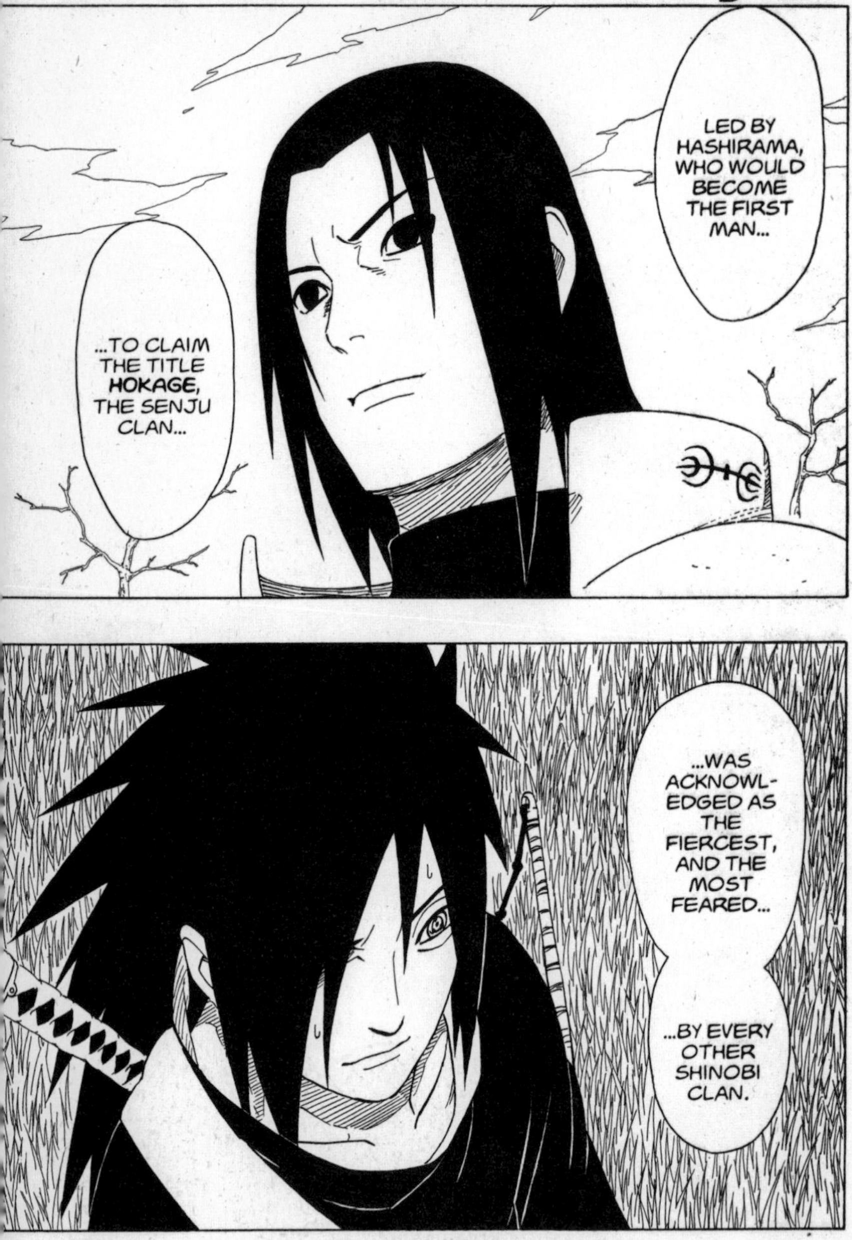
LED BY HASHIRAMA, WHO WOULD BECOME THE FIRST MAN...
...TO CLAIM THE TITLE **HOKAGE**, THE SENJU CLAN...
...WAS ACKNOWL-EDGED AS THE FIERCEST, AND THE MOST FEARED...
...BY EVERY OTHER SHINOBI CLAN.

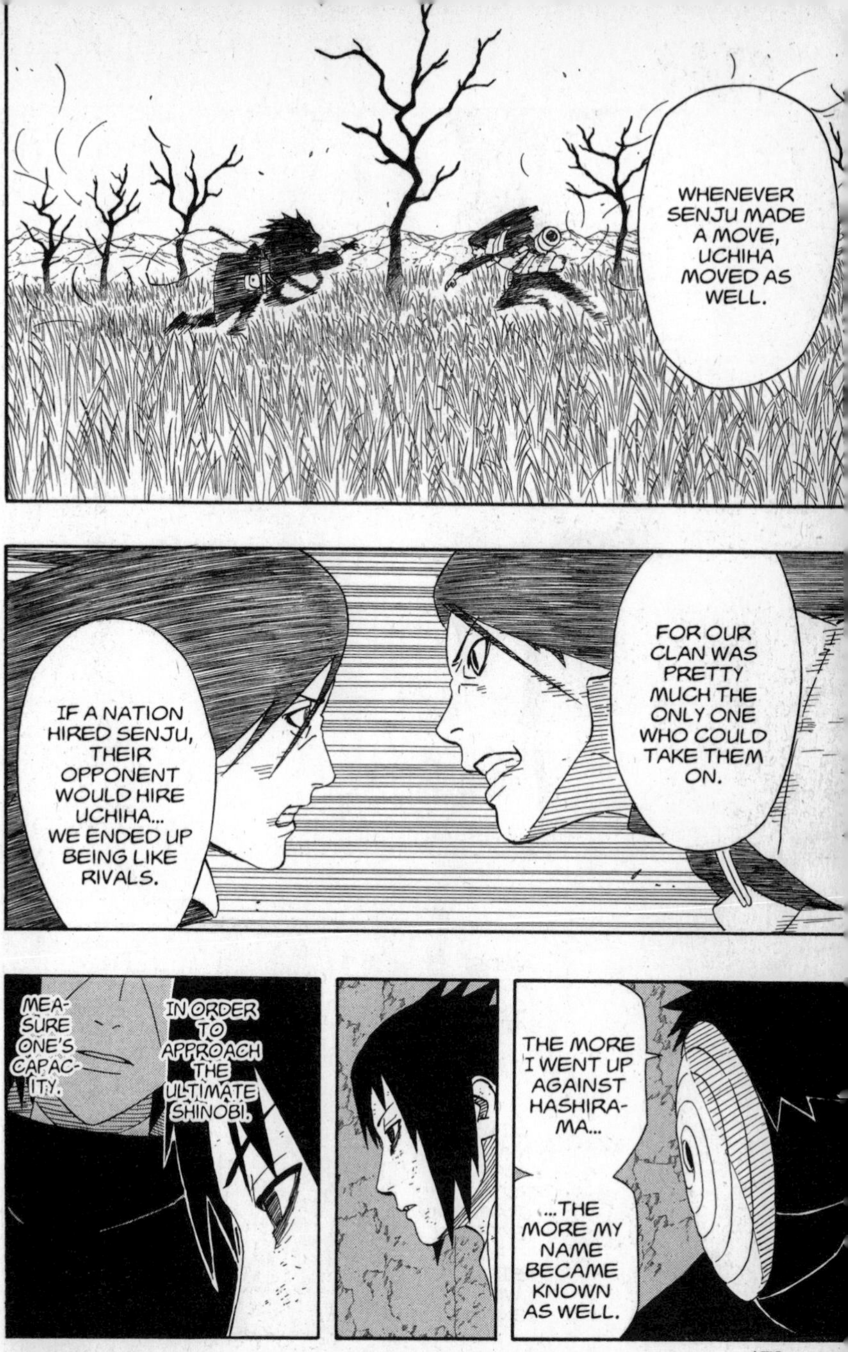
WHENEVER SENJU MADE A MOVE, UCHIHA MOVED AS WELL.
FOR OUR CLAN WAS PRETTY MUCH THE ONLY ONE WHO COULD TAKE THEM ON.
IF A NATION HIRED SENJU, THEIR OPPONENT WOULD HIRE UCHIHA... WE ENDED UP BEING LIKE RIVALS.
THE MORE I WENT UP AGAINST HASHIRAMA...
...THE MORE MY NAME BECAME KNOWN AS WELL.
IN ORDER TO APPROACH THE ULTIMATE SHINOBI.
MEASURE ONE'S CAPACITY.

READ THIS WAY

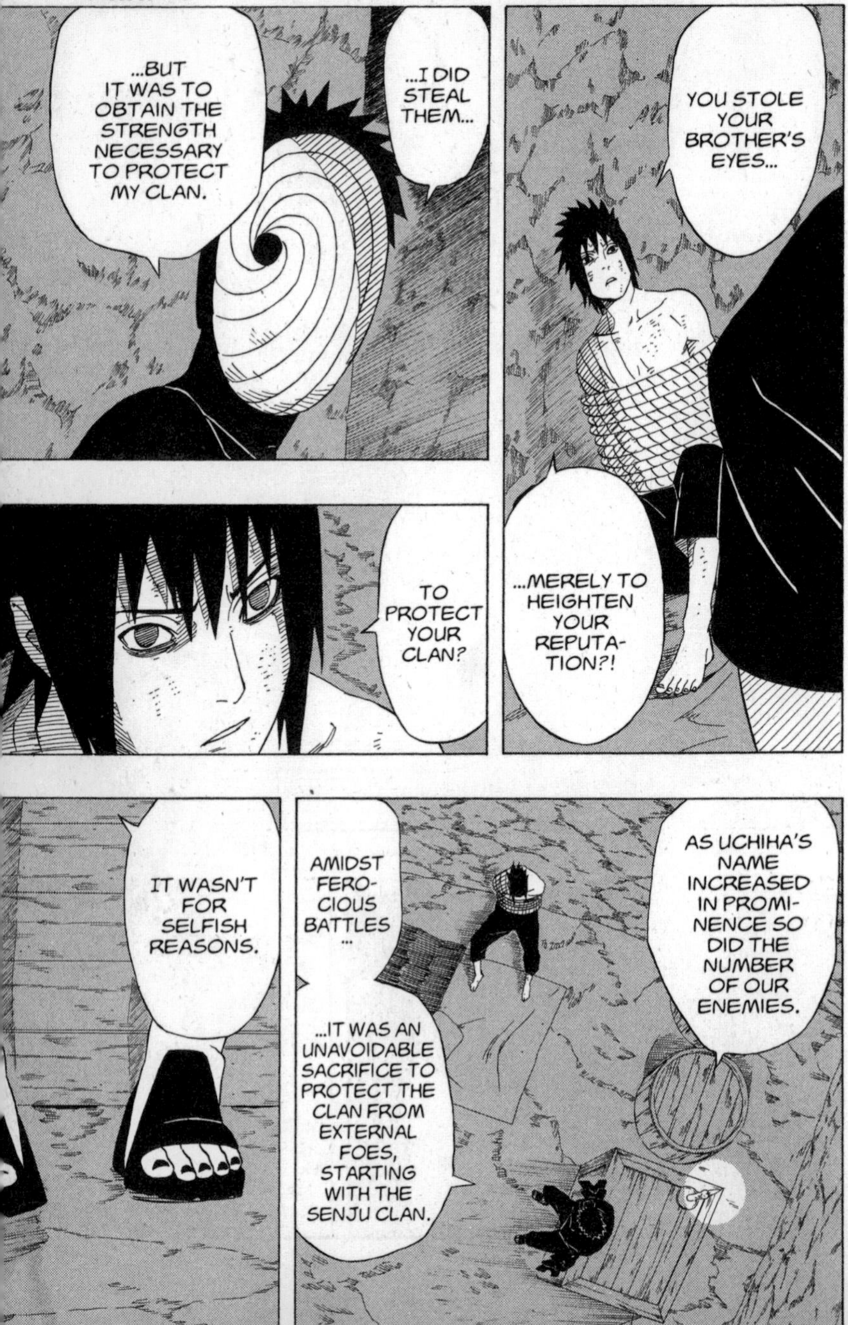
YOU STOLE YOUR BROTHER'S EYES...
...MERELY TO HEIGHTEN YOUR REPUTATION?!
...I DID STEAL THEM...
...BUT IT WAS TO OBTAIN THE STRENGTH NECESSARY TO PROTECT MY CLAN.
TO PROTECT YOUR CLAN?
AS UCHIHA'S NAME INCREASED IN PROMINENCE SO DID THE NUMBER OF OUR ENEMIES.
AMIDST FEROCIOUS BATTLES...
...IT WAS AN UNAVOIDABLE SACRIFICE TO PROTECT THE CLAN FROM EXTERNAL FOES, STARTING WITH THE SENJU CLAN.
IT WASN'T FOR SELFISH REASONS.

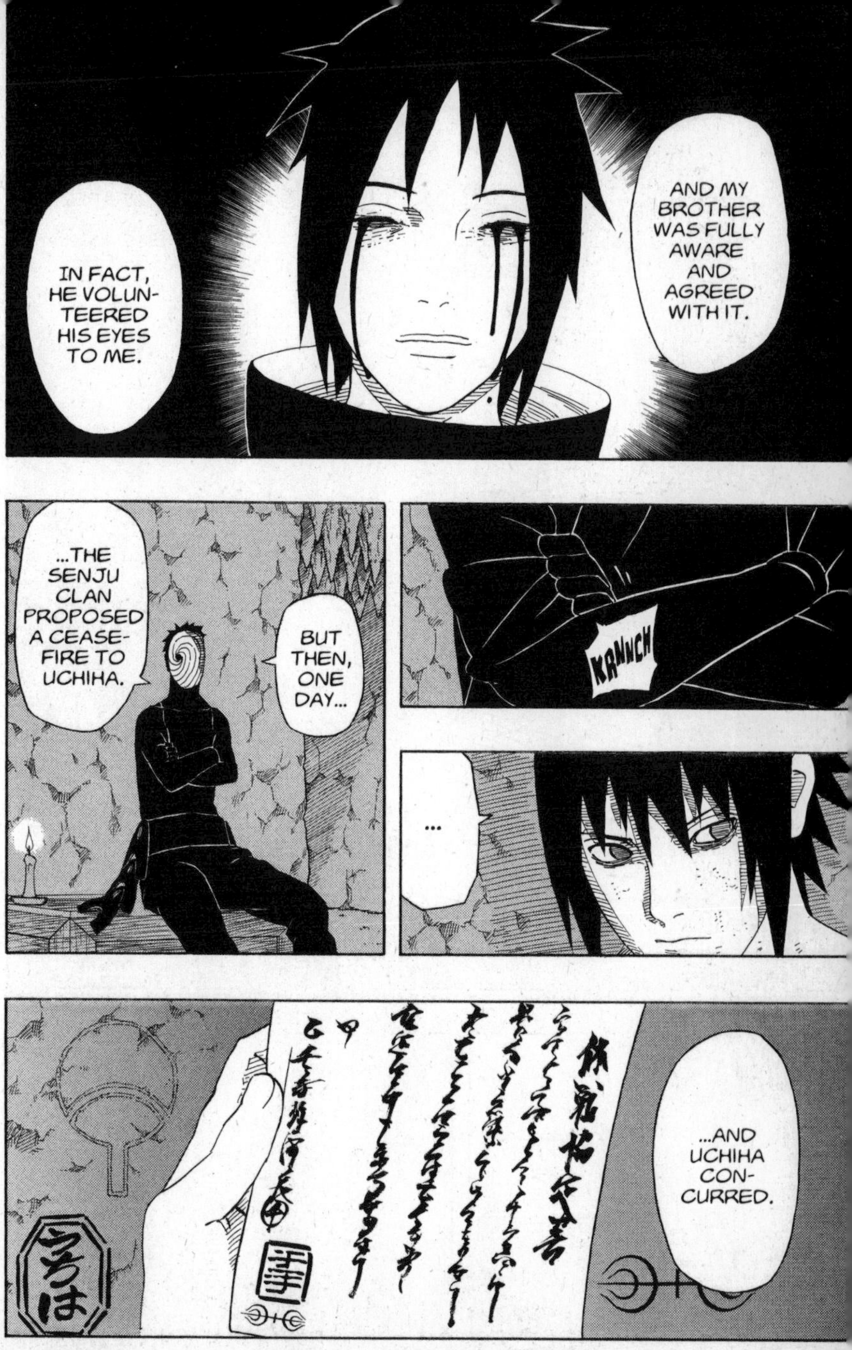
AND MY BROTHER WAS FULLY AWARE AND AGREED WITH IT.
IN FACT, HE VOLUNTEERED HIS EYES TO ME.
KRNNCH
...
BUT THEN, ONE DAY...
...THE SENJU CLAN PROPOSED A CEASE-FIRE TO UCHIHA.
...AND UCHIHA CONCURRED.
うちは

READ THIS WAY

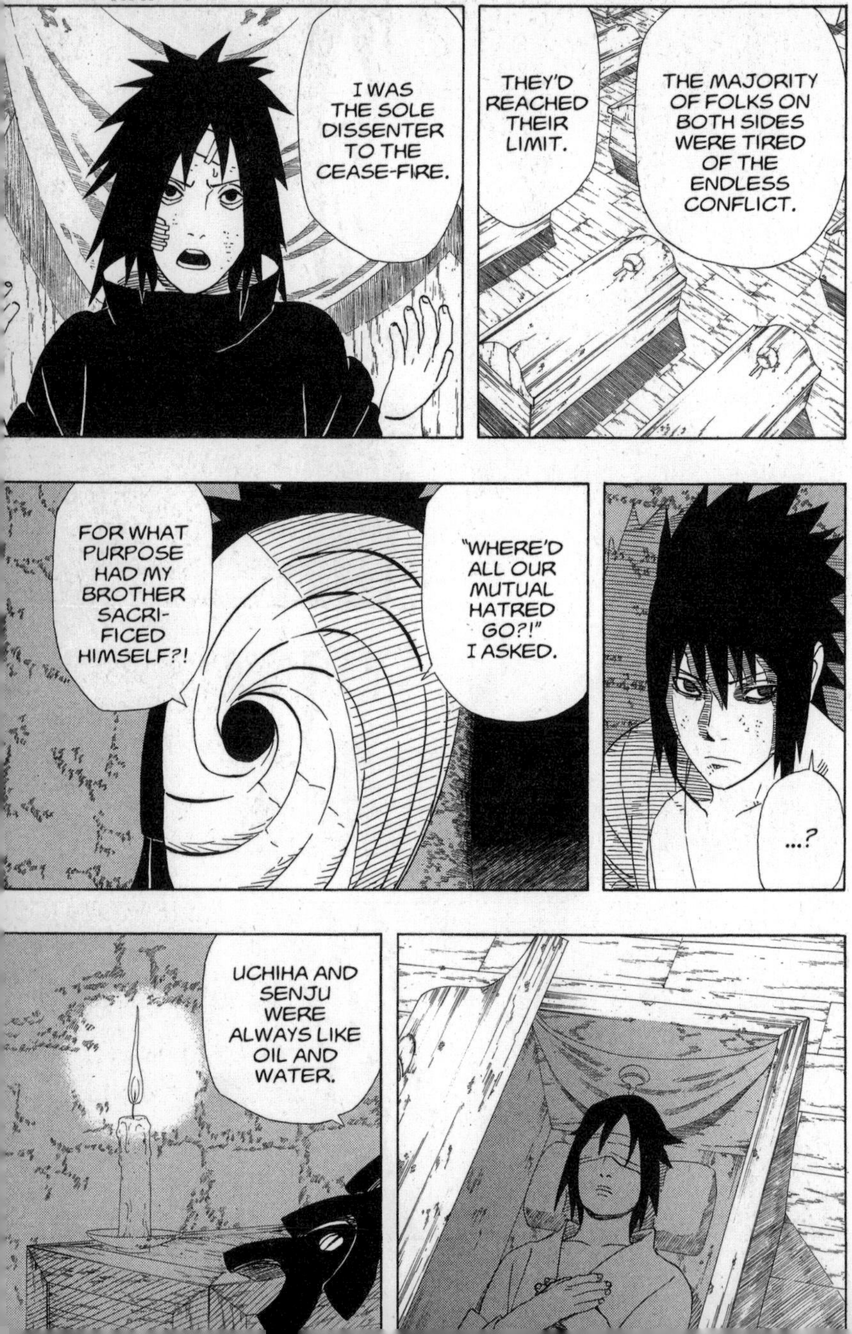
THE MAJORITY OF FOLKS ON BOTH SIDES WERE TIRED OF THE ENDLESS CONFLICT.
THEY'D REACHED THEIR LIMIT.
I WAS THE SOLE DISSENTER TO THE CEASE-FIRE.
...?
"WHERE'D ALL OUR MUTUAL HATRED GO?!" I ASKED.
FOR WHAT PURPOSE HAD MY BROTHER SACRI-FICED HIMSELF?!
UCHIHA AND SENJU WERE ALWAYS LIKE OIL AND WATER.

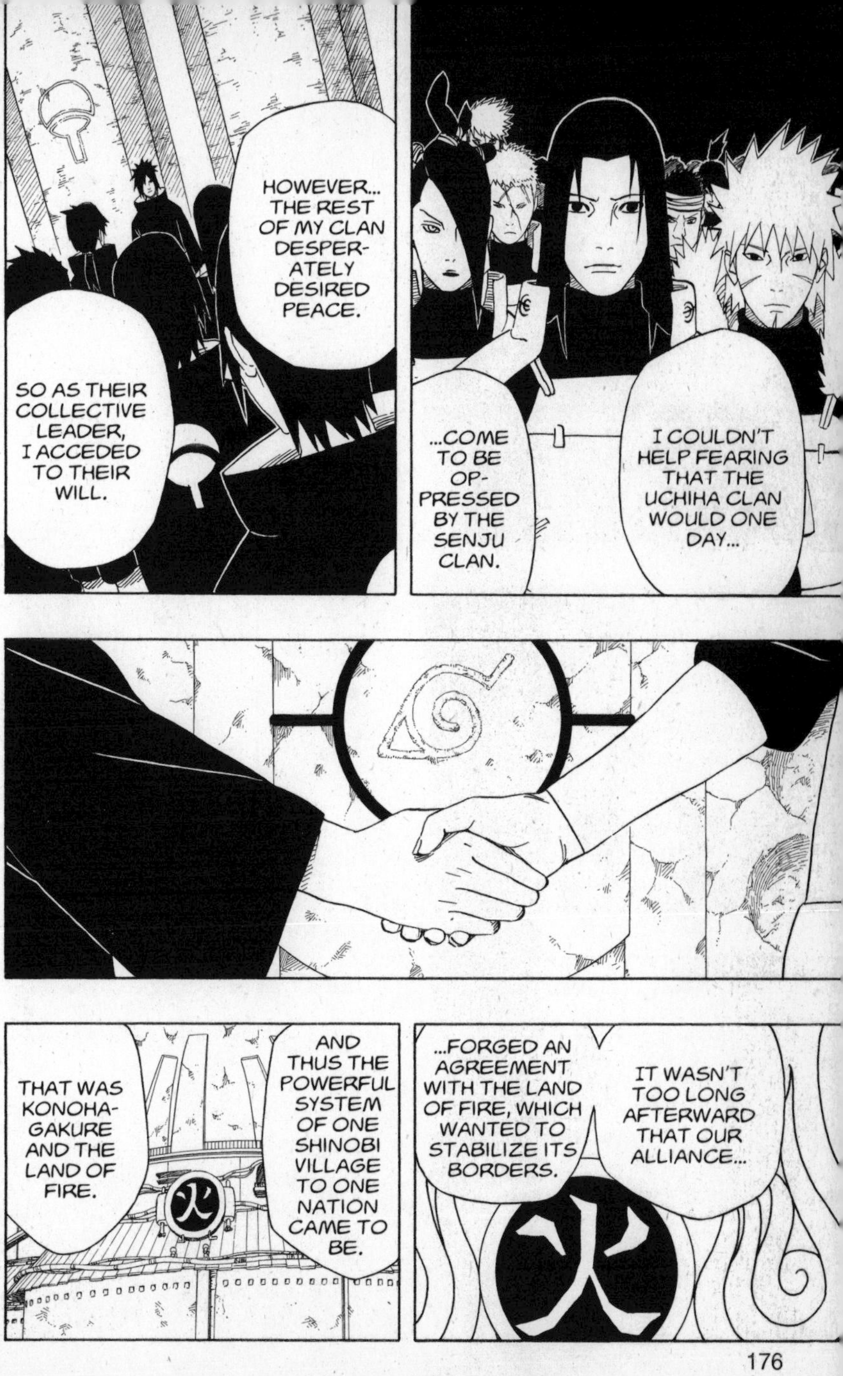
I COULDN'T HELP FEARING THAT THE UCHIHA CLAN WOULD ONE DAY...
...COME TO BE OPPRESSED BY THE SENJU CLAN.
HOWEVER... THE REST OF MY CLAN DESPERATELY DESIRED PEACE.
SO AS THEIR COLLECTIVE LEADER, I ACCEDED TO THEIR WILL.
IT WASN'T TOO LONG AFTERWARD THAT OUR ALLIANCE...
...FORGED AN AGREEMENT WITH THE LAND OF FIRE, WHICH WANTED TO STABILIZE ITS BORDERS.
AND THUS THE POWERFUL SYSTEM OF ONE SHINOBI VILLAGE TO ONE NATION CAME TO BE.
THAT WAS KONOHAGAKURE AND THE LAND OF FIRE.

READ THIS WAY

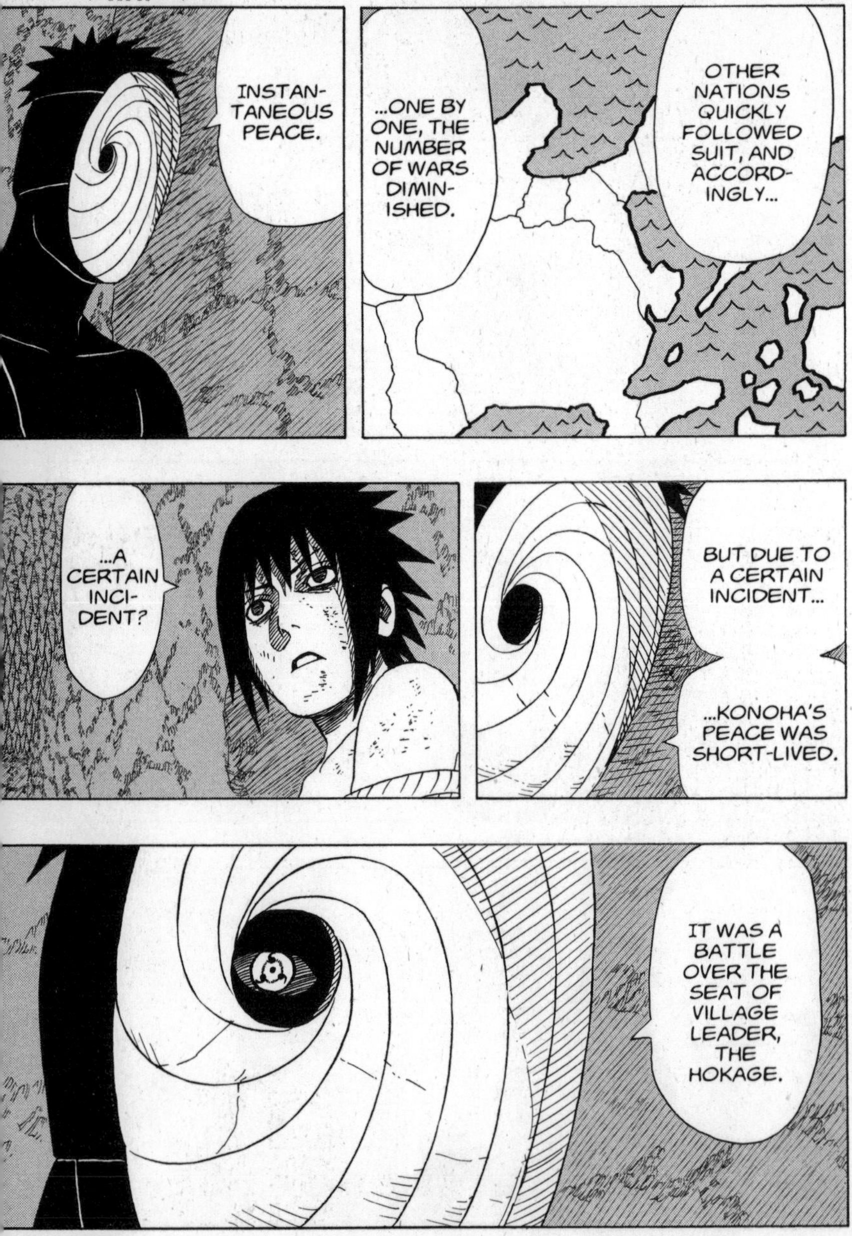
OTHER NATIONS QUICKLY FOLLOWED SUIT, AND ACCORD-INGLY...
...ONE BY ONE, THE NUMBER OF WARS DIMIN-ISHED.
INSTAN-TANEOUS PEACE.
BUT DUE TO A CERTAIN INCIDENT...
...KONOHA'S PEACE WAS SHORT-LIVED.
...A CERTAIN INCI-DENT?
IT WAS A BATTLE OVER THE SEAT OF VILLAGE LEADER, THE HOKAGE.

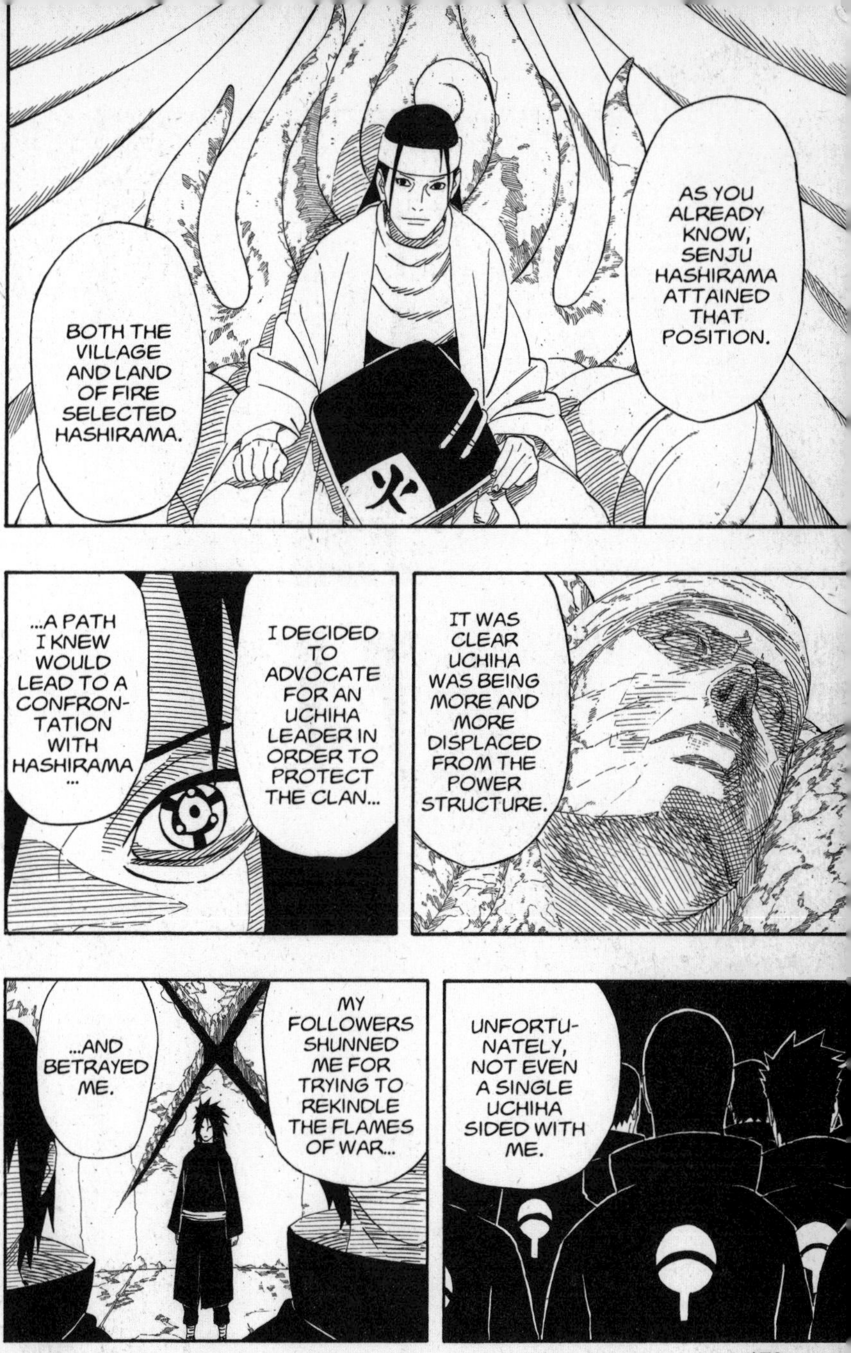
AS YOU ALREADY KNOW, SENJU HASHIRAMA ATTAINED THAT POSITION.
BOTH THE VILLAGE AND LAND OF FIRE SELECTED HASHIRAMA.
IT WAS CLEAR UCHIHA WAS BEING MORE AND MORE DISPLACED FROM THE POWER STRUCTURE.
I DECIDED TO ADVOCATE FOR AN UCHIHA LEADER IN ORDER TO PROTECT THE CLAN...
...A PATH I KNEW WOULD LEAD TO A CONFRONTATION WITH HASHIRAMA...
UNFORTUNATELY, NOT EVEN A SINGLE UCHIHA SIDED WITH ME.
MY FOLLOWERS SHUNNED ME FOR TRYING TO REKINDLE THE FLAMES OF WAR...
...AND BETRAYED ME.

READ THIS WAY

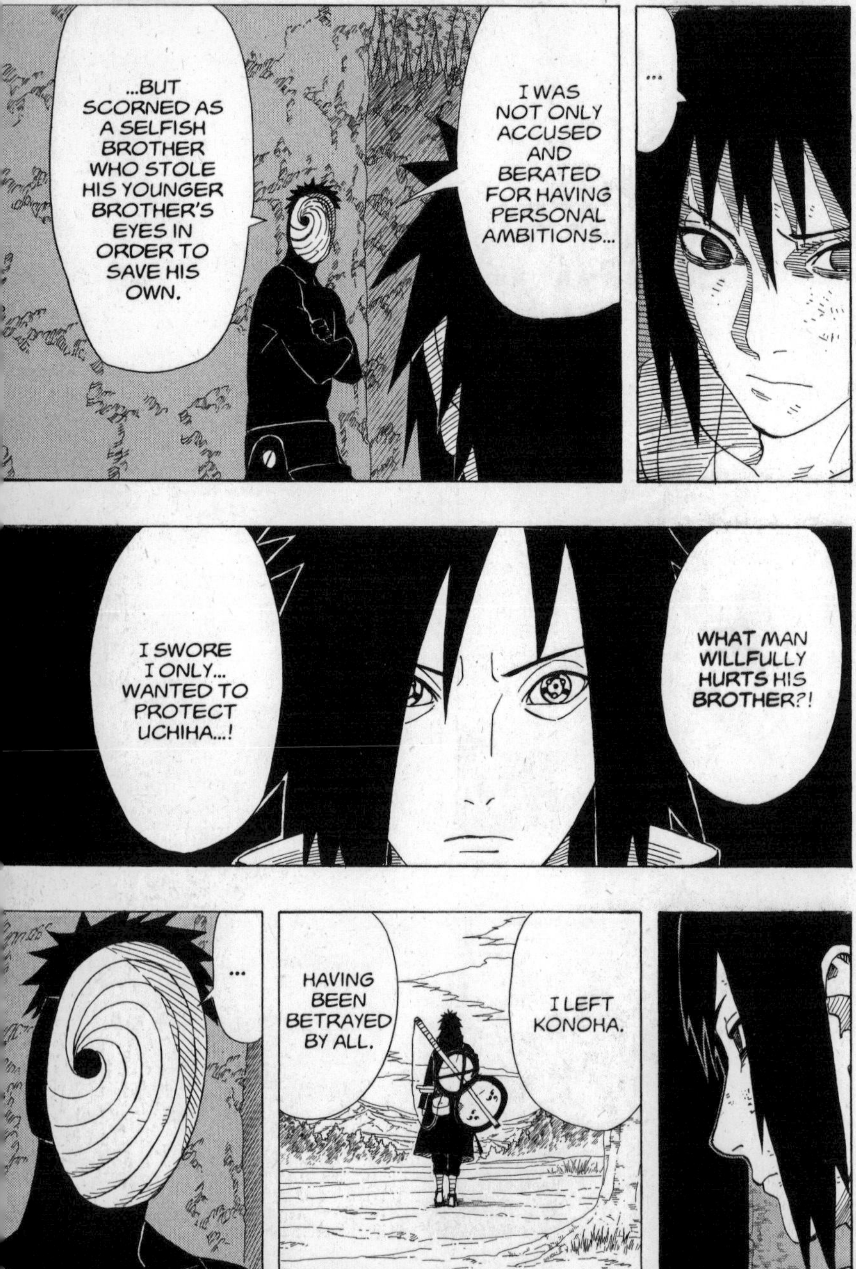
...
I WAS NOT ONLY ACCUSED AND BERATED FOR HAVING PERSONAL AMBITIONS...
...BUT SCORNED AS A SELFISH BROTHER WHO STOLE HIS YOUNGER BROTHER'S EYES IN ORDER TO SAVE HIS OWN.
WHAT MAN WILLFULLY HURTS HIS BROTHER?!
I SWORE I ONLY... WANTED TO PROTECT UCHIHA...!
I LEFT KONOHA.
HAVING BEEN BETRAYED BY ALL.
...

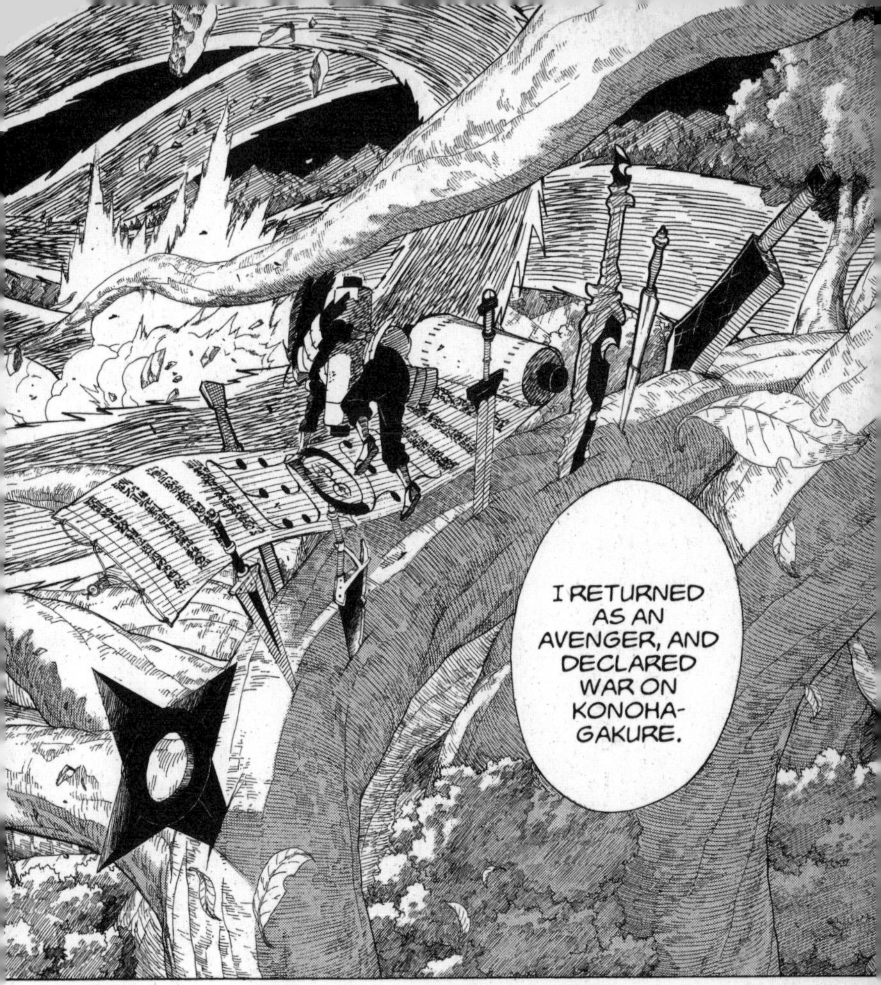
I RETURNED AS AN AVENGER, AND DECLARED WAR ON KONOHA-GAKURE.
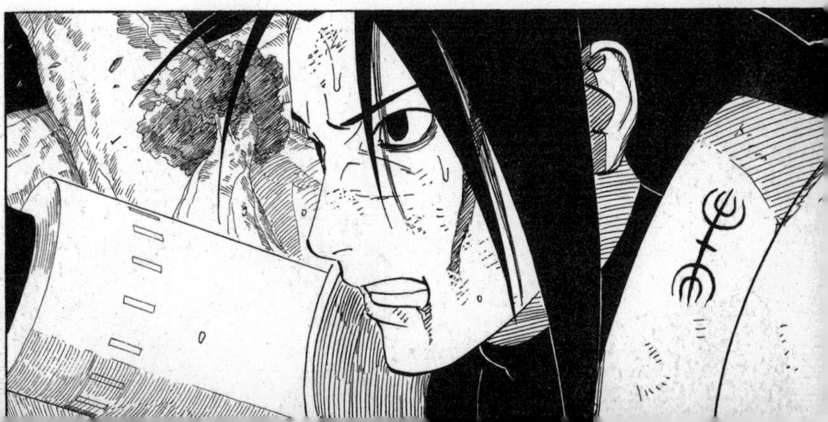

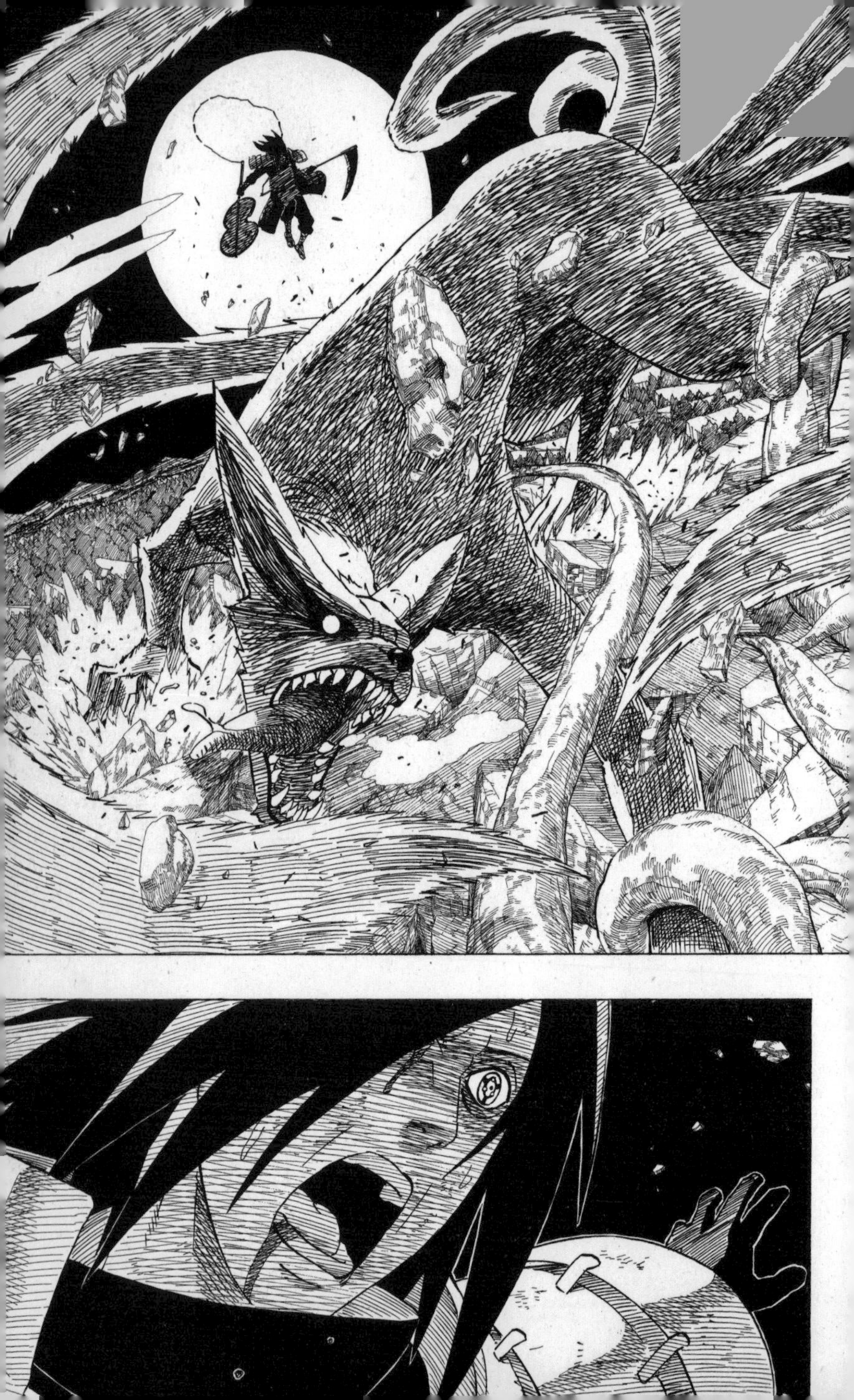

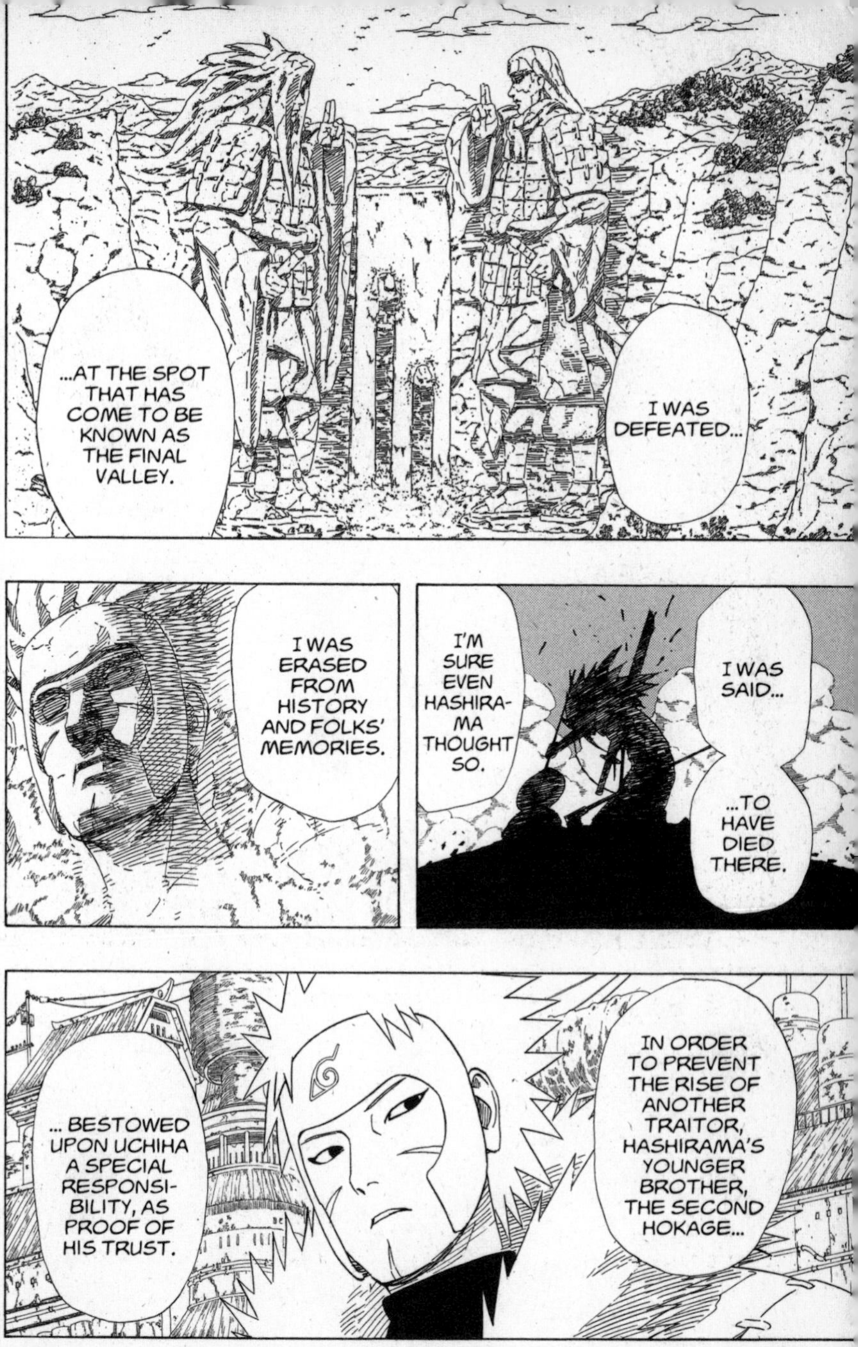
I WAS DEFEATED...
...AT THE SPOT THAT HAS COME TO BE KNOWN AS THE FINAL VALLEY.
I WAS SAID...
...TO HAVE DIED THERE.
I'M SURE EVEN HASHIRAMA THOUGHT SO.
I WAS ERASED FROM HISTORY AND FOLKS' MEMORIES.
IN ORDER TO PREVENT THE RISE OF ANOTHER TRAITOR, HASHIRAMA'S YOUNGER BROTHER, THE SECOND HOKAGE...
... BESTOWED UPON UCHIHA A SPECIAL RESPONSIBILITY, AS PROOF OF HIS TRUST.

READ THIS WAY

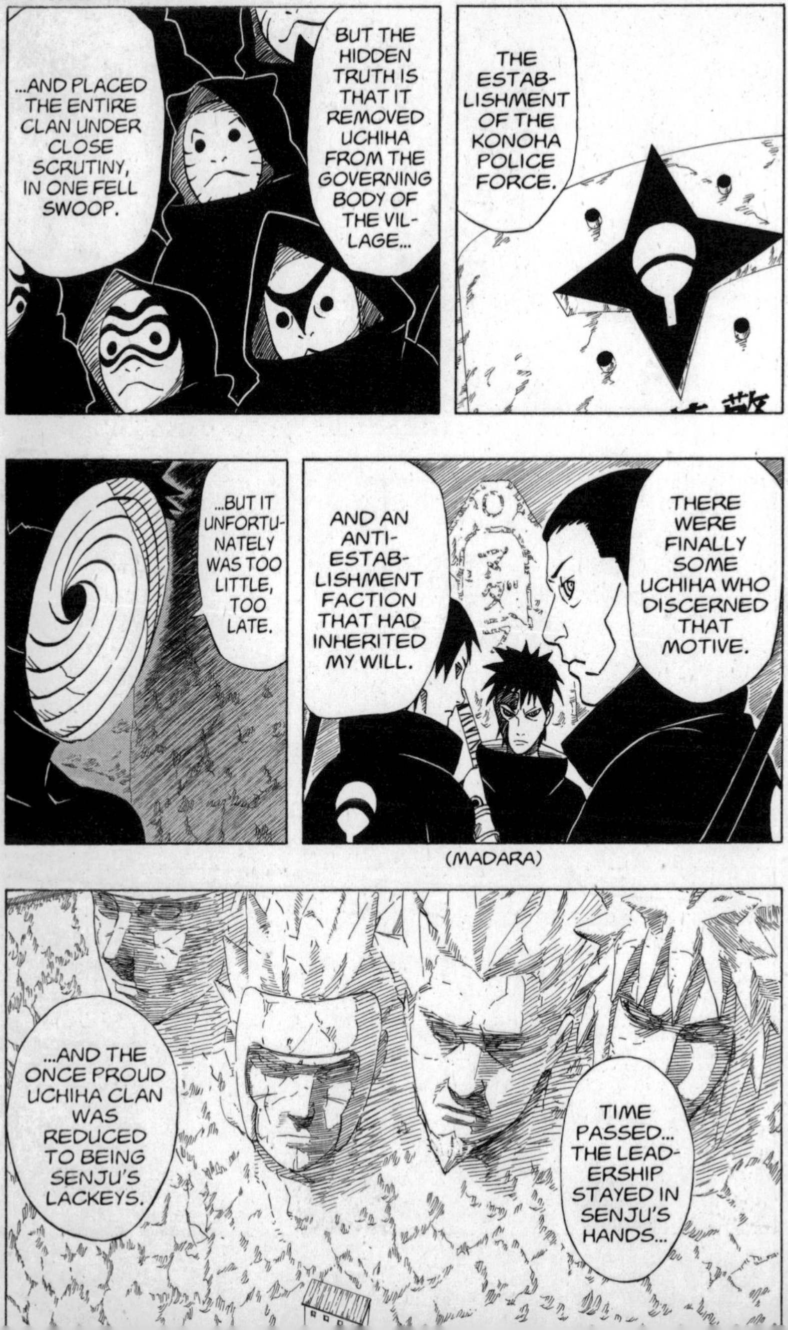
THE ESTAB-LISHMENT OF THE KONOHA POLICE FORCE.
BUT THE HIDDEN TRUTH IS THAT IT REMOVED UCHIHA FROM THE GOVERNING BODY OF THE VIL-LAGE...
...AND PLACED THE ENTIRE CLAN UNDER CLOSE SCRUTINY, IN ONE FELL SWOOP.
THERE WERE FINALLY SOME UCHIHA WHO DISCERNED THAT MOTIVE.
AND AN ANTI-ESTAB-LISHMENT FACTION THAT HAD INHERITED MY WILL.
(MADARA)
...BUT IT UNFORTU-NATELY WAS TOO LITTLE, TOO LATE.
TIME PASSED... THE LEAD-ERSHIP STAYED IN SENJU'S HANDS...
...AND THE ONCE PROUD UCHIHA CLAN WAS REDUCED TO BEING SENJU'S LACKEYS.

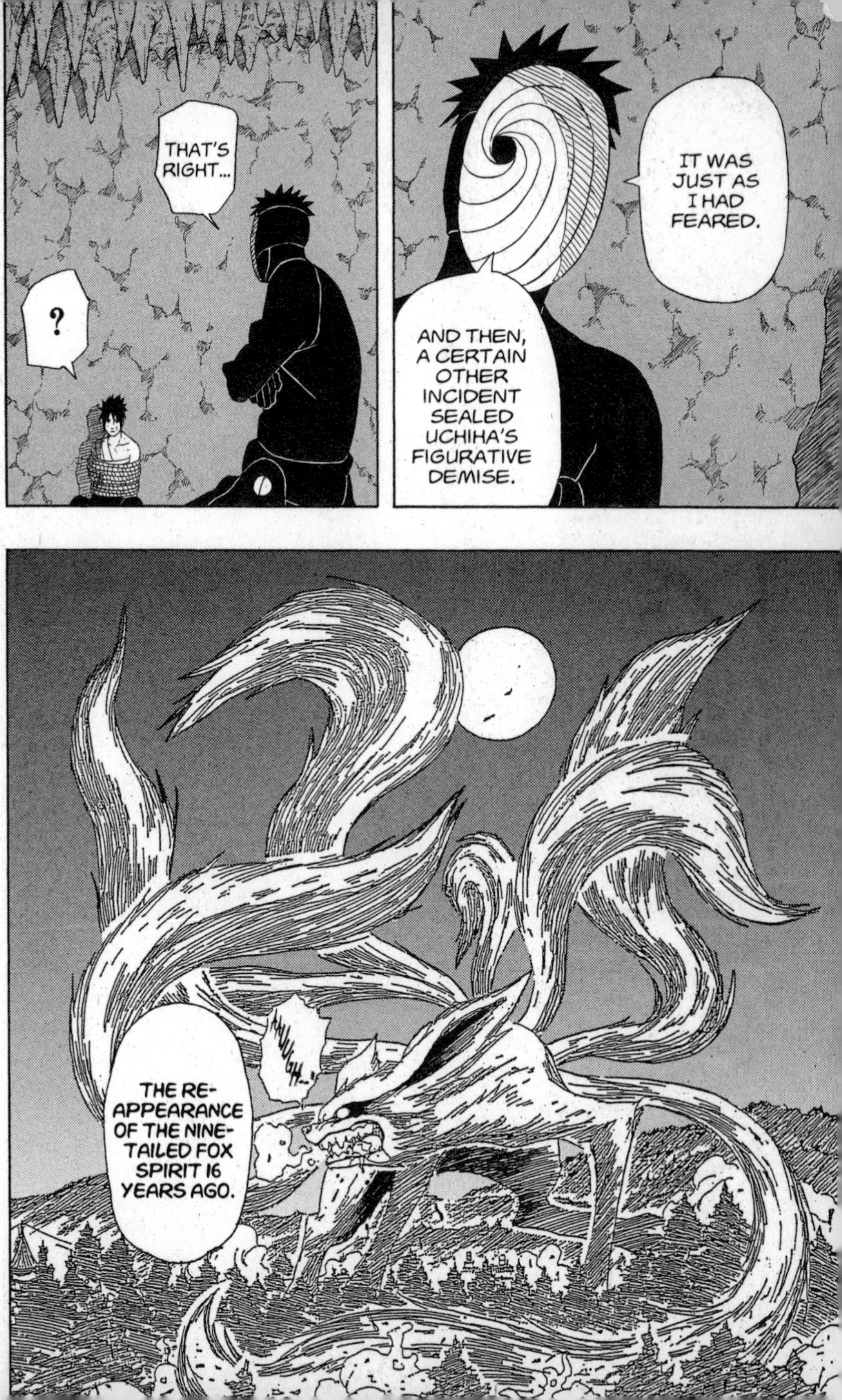
IT WAS JUST AS I HAD FEARED.
AND THEN, A CERTAIN OTHER INCIDENT SEALED UCHIHA'S FIGURATIVE DEMISE.
THAT'S RIGHT...
?
THE RE-APPEARANCE OF THE NINE-TAILED FOX SPIRIT 16 YEARS AGO.

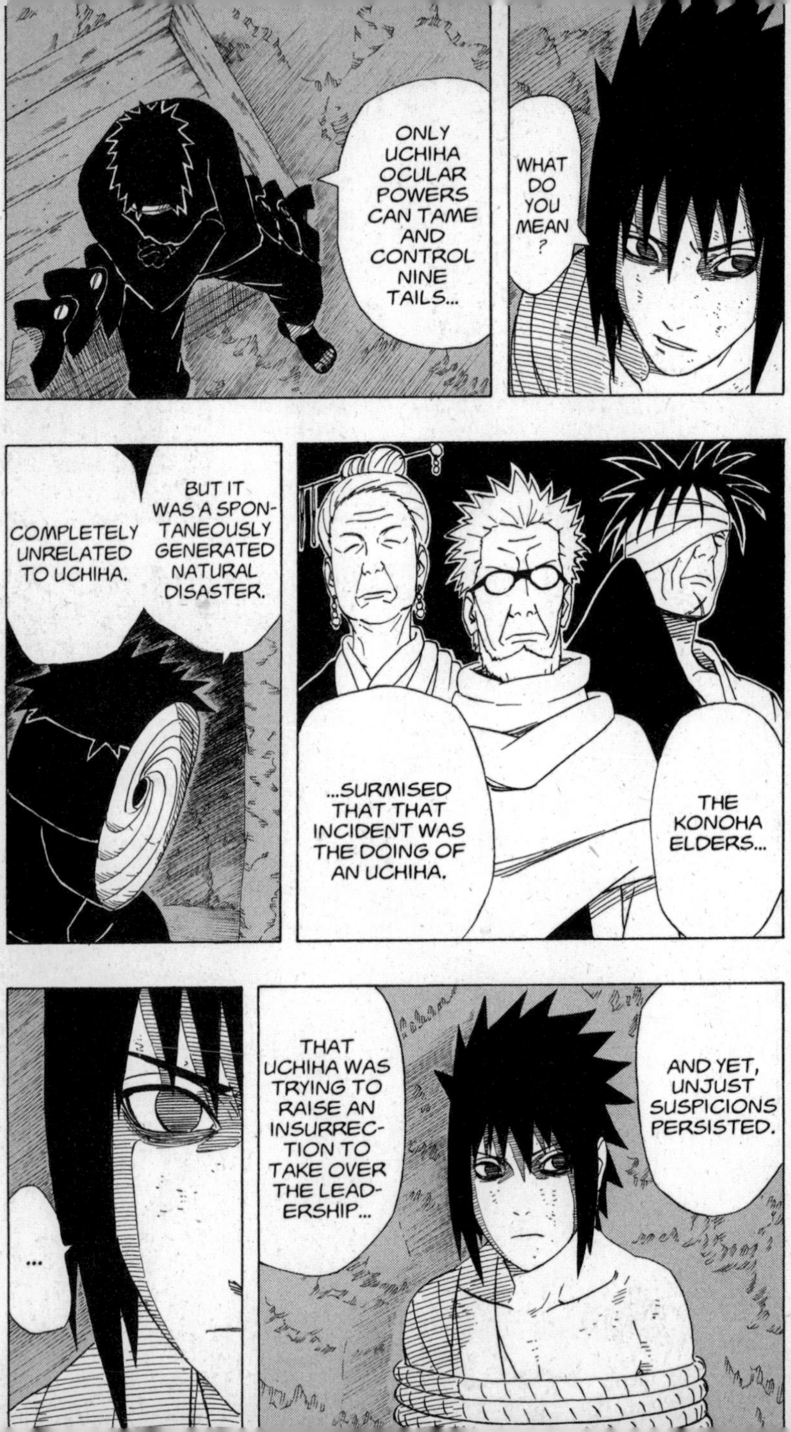
WHAT DO YOU MEAN?
ONLY UCHIHA OCULAR POWERS CAN TAME AND CONTROL NINE TAILS...
THE KONOHA ELDERS...
...SURMISED THAT THAT INCIDENT WAS THE DOING OF AN UCHIHA.
BUT IT WAS A SPON-TANEOUSLY GENERATED NATURAL DISASTER.
COMPLETELY UNRELATED TO UCHIHA.
AND YET, UNJUST SUSPICIONS PERSISTED.
THAT UCHIHA WAS TRYING TO RAISE AN INSURREC-TION TO TAKE OVER THE LEAD-ERSHIP...
...

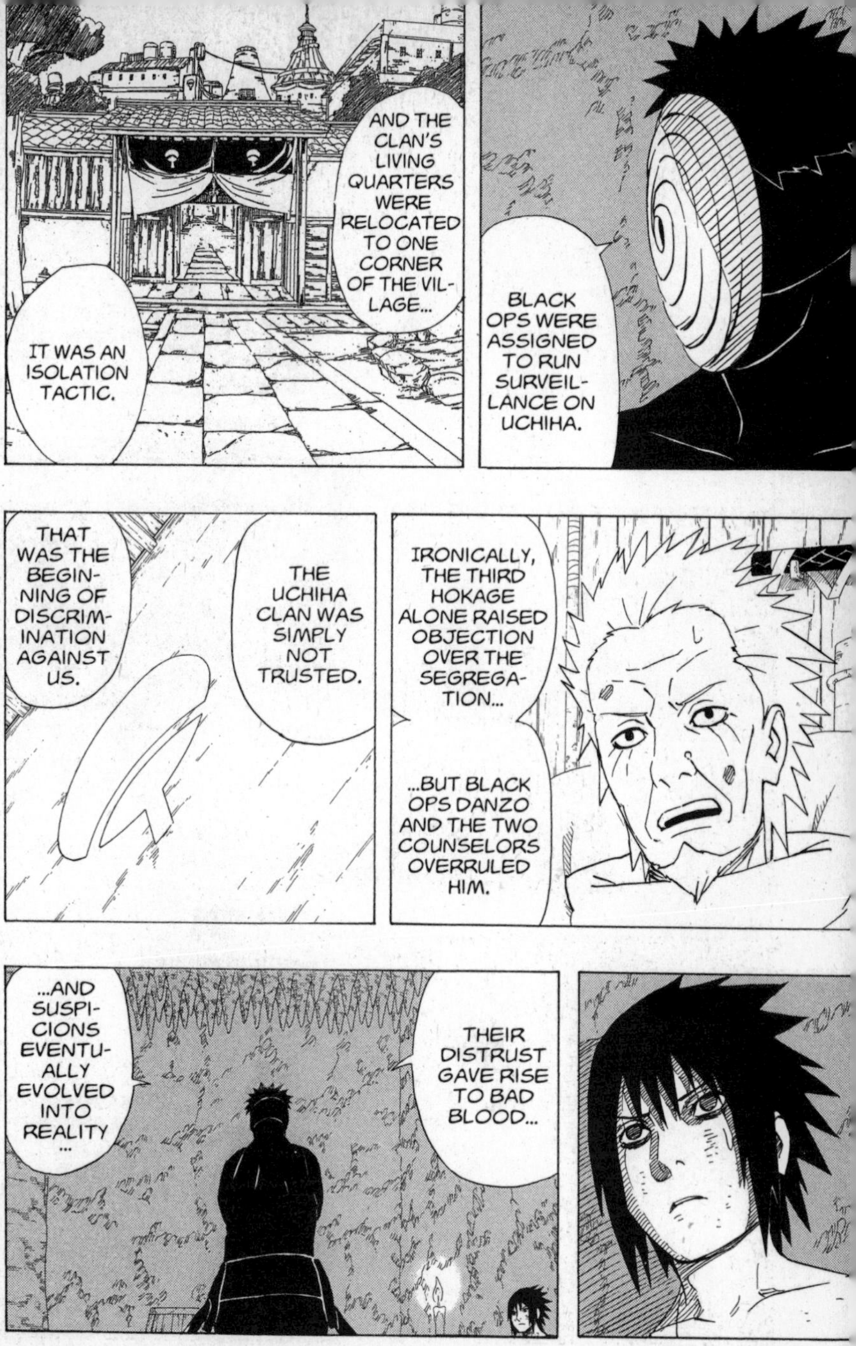
BLACK OPS WERE ASSIGNED TO RUN SURVEIL-LANCE ON UCHIHA.
AND THE CLAN'S LIVING QUARTERS WERE RELOCATED TO ONE CORNER OF THE VIL-LAGE...
IT WAS AN ISOLATION TACTIC.
IRONICALLY, THE THIRD HOKAGE ALONE RAISED OBJECTION OVER THE SEGREGA-TION...
...BUT BLACK OPS DANZO AND THE TWO COUNSELORS OVERRULED HIM.
THE UCHIHA CLAN WAS SIMPLY NOT TRUSTED.
THAT WAS THE BEGIN-NING OF DISCRIM-INATION AGAINST US.
THEIR DISTRUST GAVE RISE TO BAD BLOOD...
...AND SUSPI-CIONS EVENTU-ALLY EVOLVED INTO REALITY...

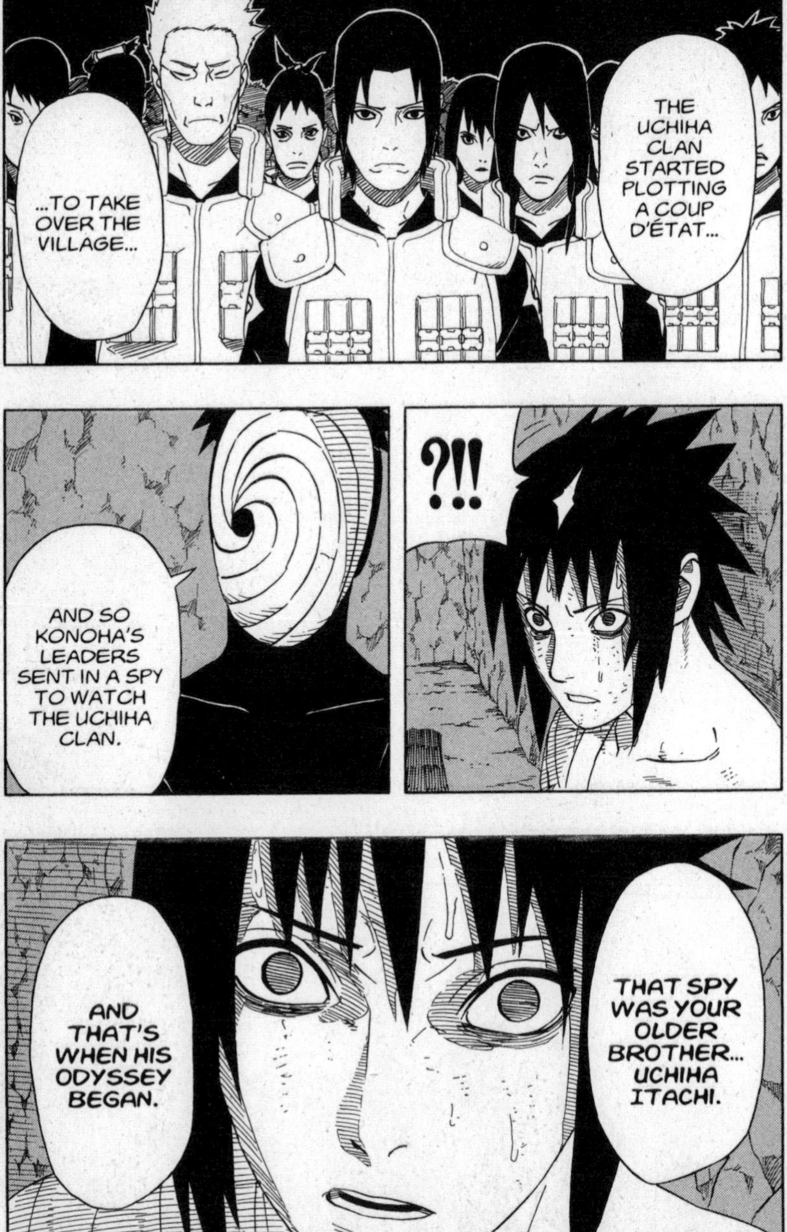
THE UCHIHA CLAN STARTED PLOTTING A COUP D'ÉTAT...
...TO TAKE OVER THE VILLAGE...
?!!
AND SO KONOHA'S LEADERS SENT IN A SPY TO WATCH THE UCHIHA CLAN.
THAT SPY WAS YOUR OLDER BROTHER... UCHIHA ITACHI.
AND THAT'S WHEN HIS ODYSSEY BEGAN.

NARUTO

Number 400: Living a Nightmare

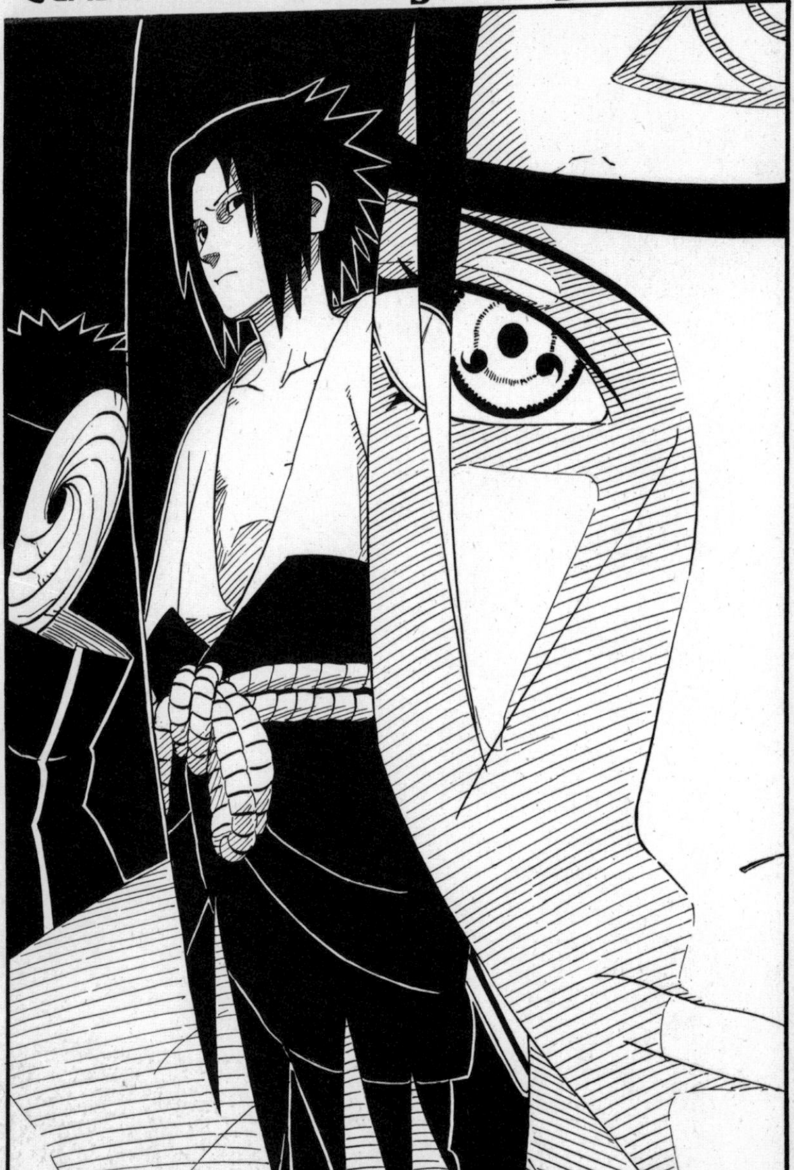

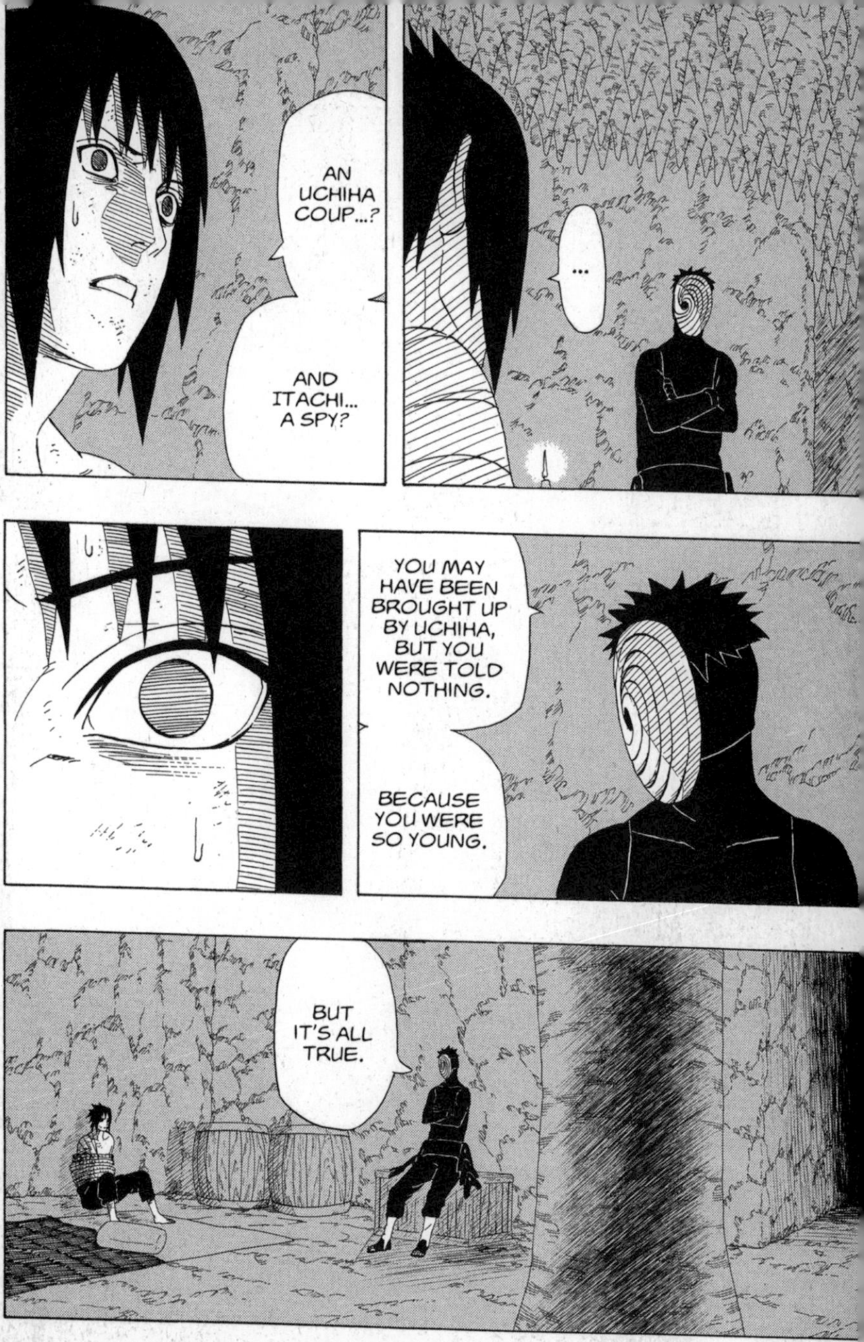
...
AN UCHIHA COUP...?
AND ITACHI... A SPY?
YOU MAY HAVE BEEN BROUGHT UP BY UCHIHA, BUT YOU WERE TOLD NOTHING.
BECAUSE YOU WERE SO YOUNG.
BUT IT'S ALL TRUE.

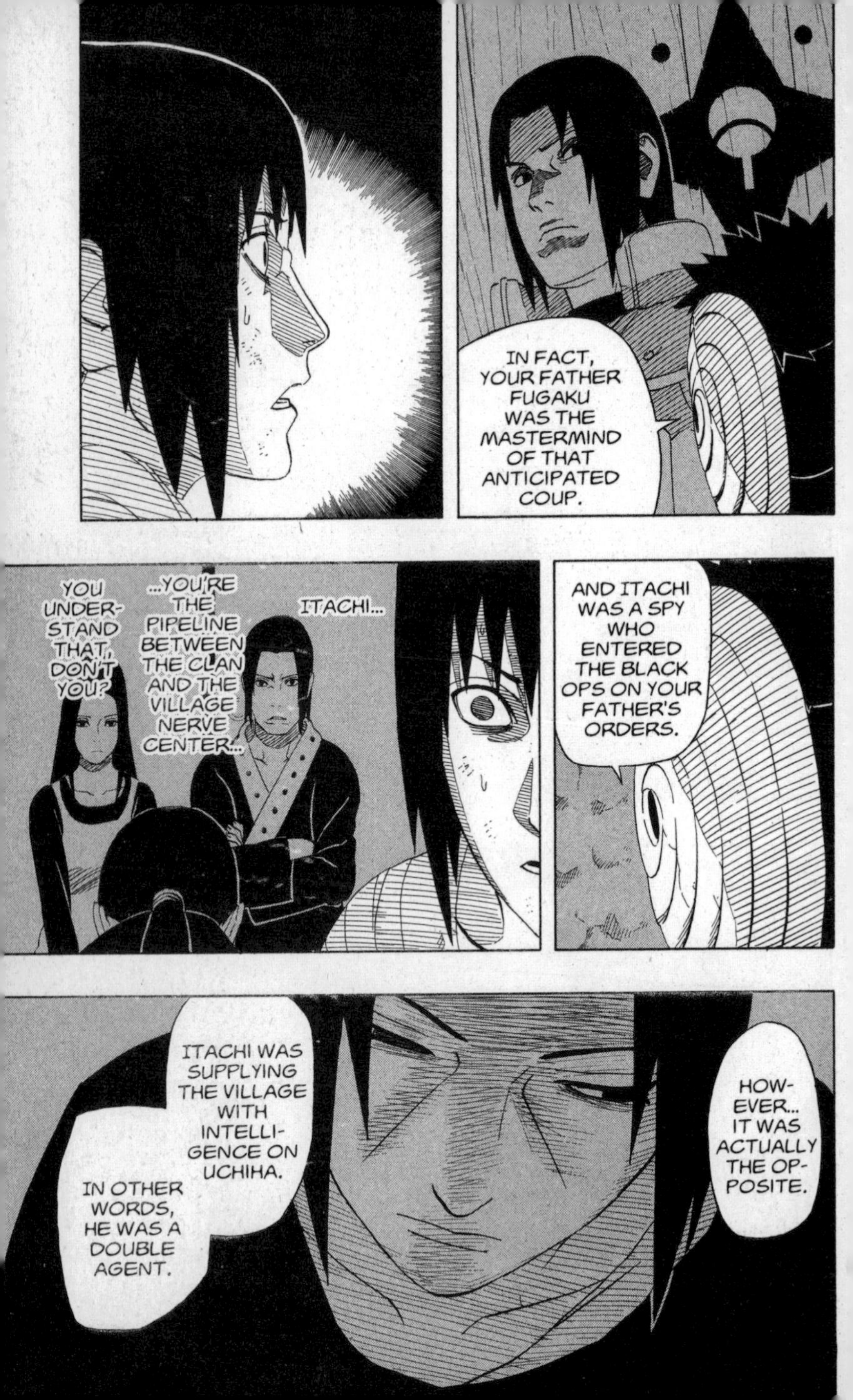
IN FACT, YOUR FATHER FUGAKU WAS THE MASTERMIND OF THAT ANTICIPATED COUP.
AND ITACHI WAS A SPY WHO ENTERED THE BLACK OPS ON YOUR FATHER'S ORDERS.
ITACHI...
...YOU'RE THE PIPELINE BETWEEN THE CLAN AND THE VILLAGE NERVE CENTER...
YOU UNDER-STAND THAT, DON'T YOU?
HOW-EVER... IT WAS ACTUALLY THE OP-POSITE.
ITACHI WAS SUPPLYING THE VILLAGE WITH INTELLI-GENCE ON UCHIHA.
IN OTHER WORDS, HE WAS A DOUBLE AGENT.

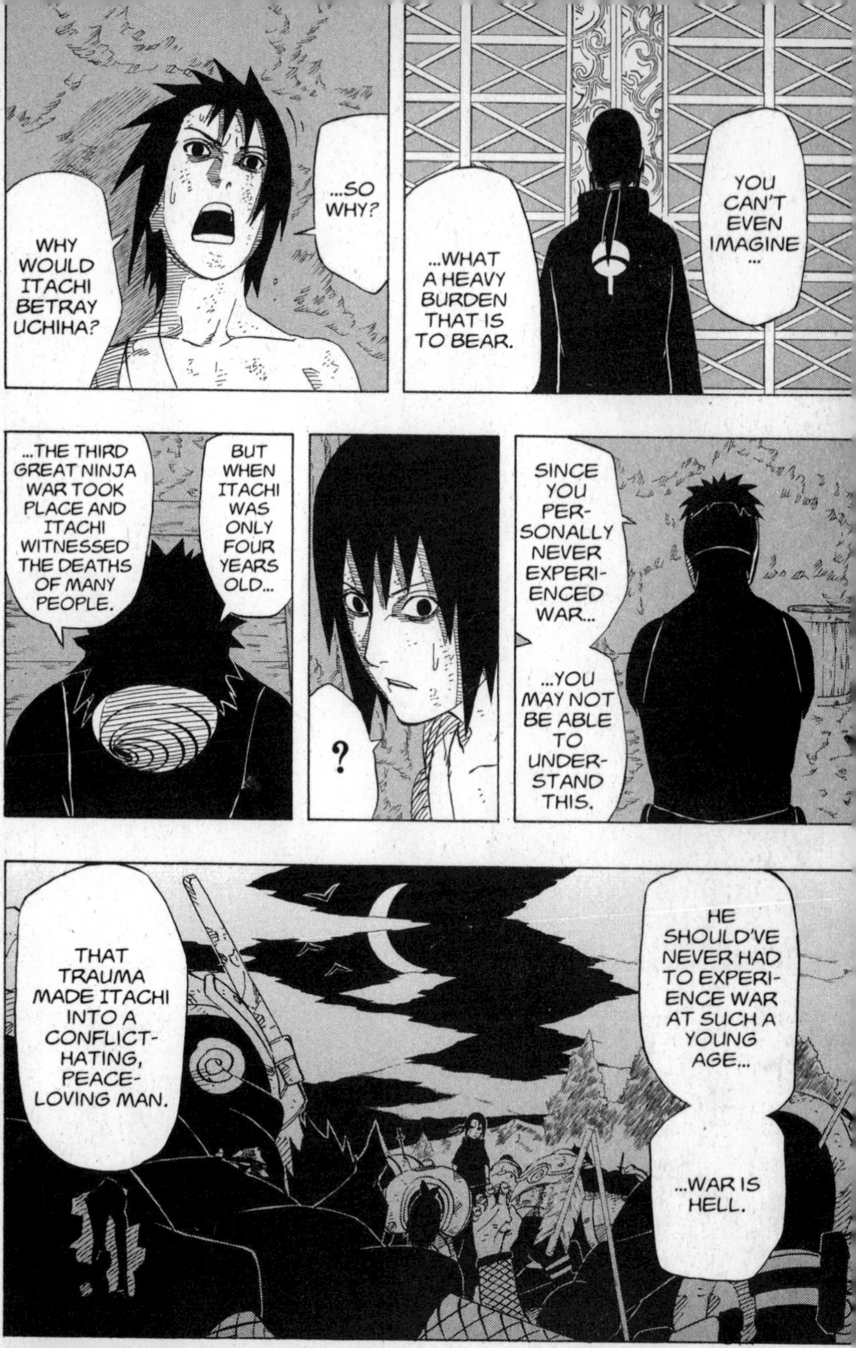
YOU CAN'T EVEN IMAGINE...
...WHAT A HEAVY BURDEN THAT IS TO BEAR.
...SO WHY?
WHY WOULD ITACHI BETRAY UCHIHA?
SINCE YOU PERSONALLY NEVER EXPERIENCED WAR...
...YOU MAY NOT BE ABLE TO UNDERSTAND THIS.
?
BUT WHEN ITACHI WAS ONLY FOUR YEARS OLD...
...THE THIRD GREAT NINJA WAR TOOK PLACE AND ITACHI WITNESSED THE DEATHS OF MANY PEOPLE.
HE SHOULD'VE NEVER HAD TO EXPERIENCE WAR AT SUCH A YOUNG AGE...
...WAR IS HELL.
THAT TRAUMA MADE ITACHI INTO A CONFLICT-HATING, PEACE-LOVING MAN.

READ THIS WAY

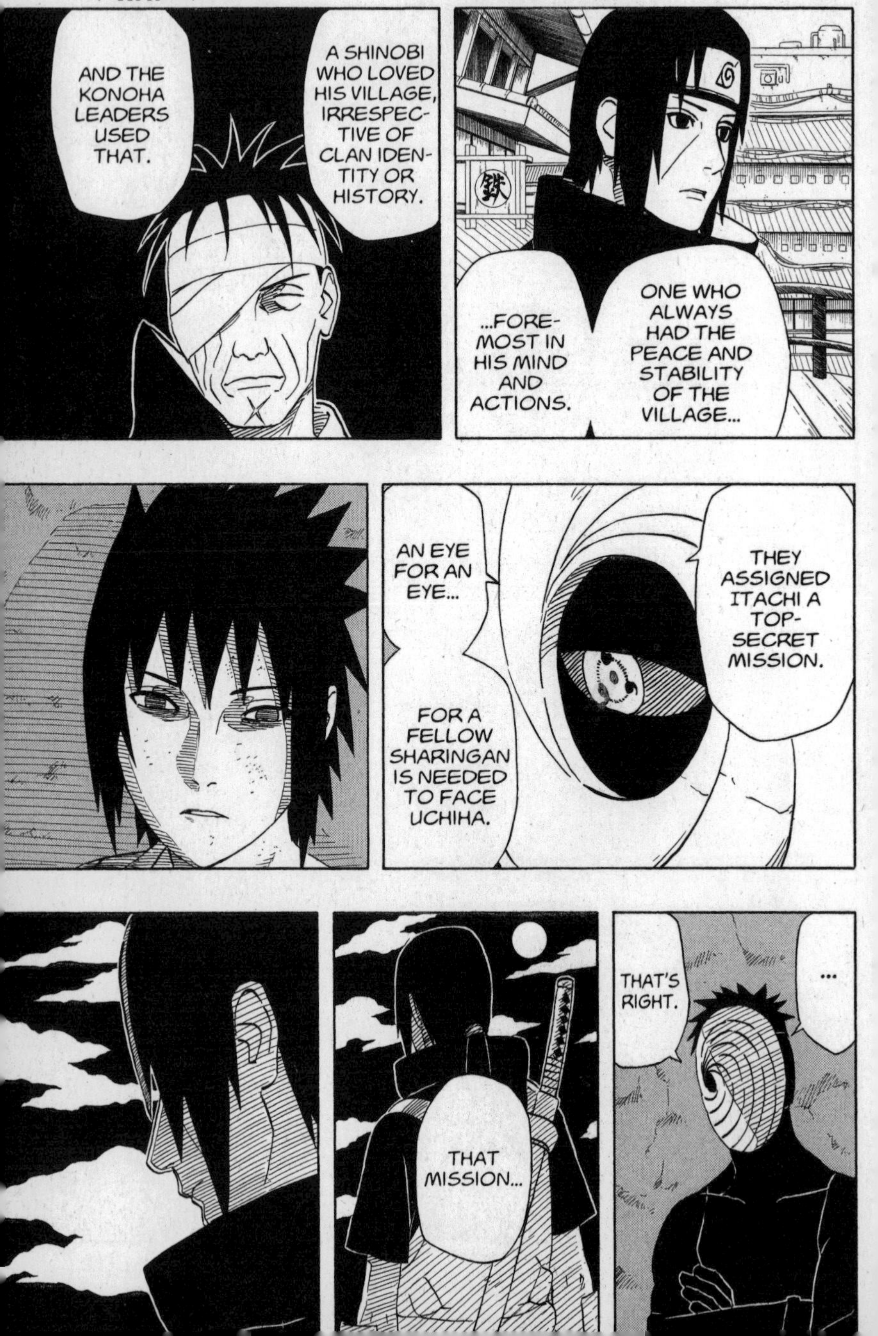

ONE WHO ALWAYS HAD THE PEACE AND STABILITY OF THE VILLAGE...
...FOREMOST IN HIS MIND AND ACTIONS.
A SHINOBI WHO LOVED HIS VILLAGE, IRRESPECTIVE OF CLAN IDENTITY OR HISTORY.
AND THE KONOHA LEADERS USED THAT.
THEY ASSIGNED ITACHI A TOP-SECRET MISSION.
AN EYE FOR AN EYE...
FOR A FELLOW SHARINGAN IS NEEDED TO FACE UCHIHA.
...
THAT'S RIGHT.
THAT MISSION...

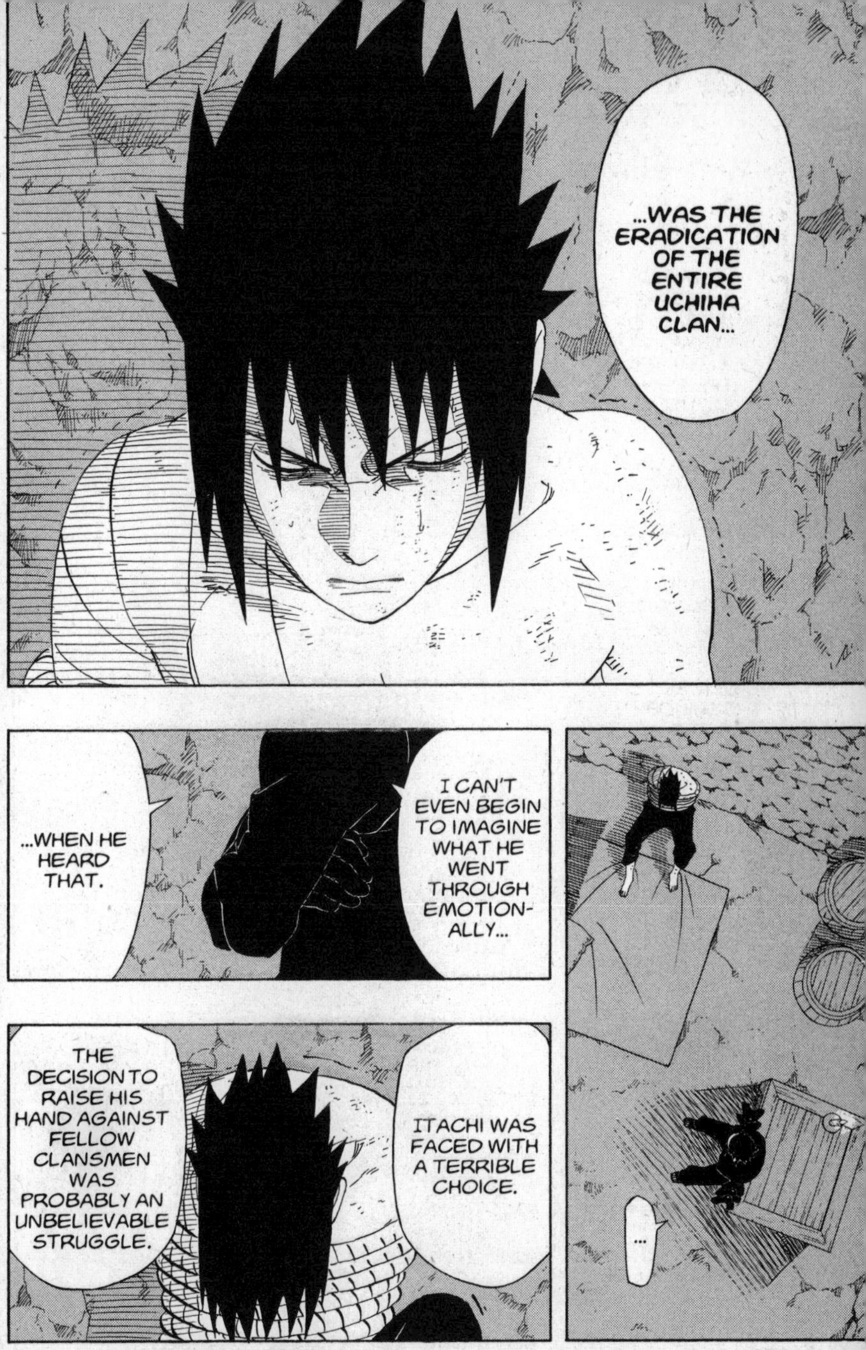
...WAS THE ERADICATION OF THE ENTIRE UCHIHA CLAN...
I CAN'T EVEN BEGIN TO IMAGINE WHAT HE WENT THROUGH EMOTION-ALLY...
...WHEN HE HEARD THAT.
ITACHI WAS FACED WITH A TERRIBLE CHOICE.
THE DECISION TO RAISE HIS HAND AGAINST FELLOW CLANSMEN WAS PROBABLY AN UNBELIEVABLE STRUGGLE.
...

READ THIS WAY

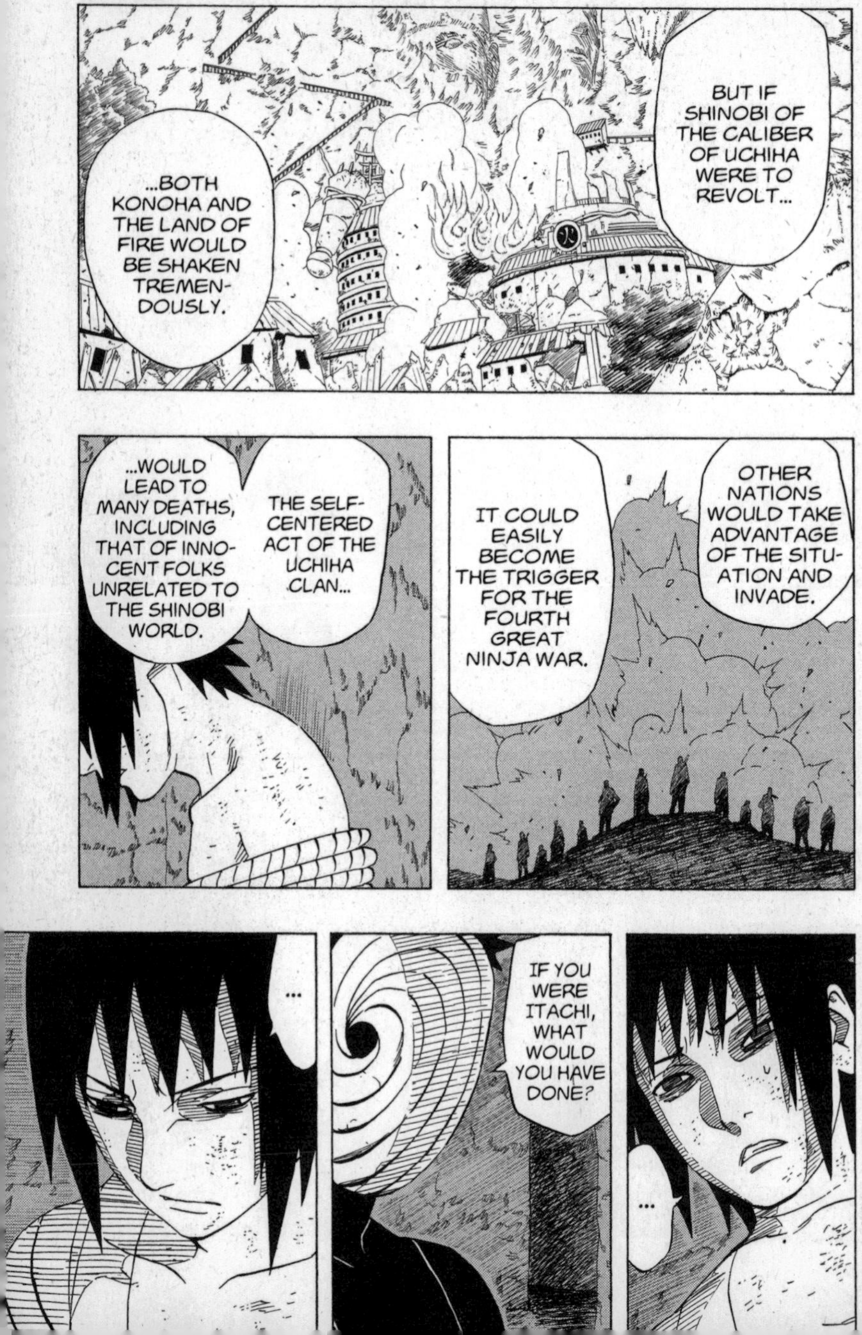
BUT IF SHINOBI OF THE CALIBER OF UCHIHA WERE TO REVOLT...
...BOTH KONOHA AND THE LAND OF FIRE WOULD BE SHAKEN TREMENDOUSLY.
OTHER NATIONS WOULD TAKE ADVANTAGE OF THE SITUATION AND INVADE.
IT COULD EASILY BECOME THE TRIGGER FOR THE FOURTH GREAT NINJA WAR.
THE SELF-CENTERED ACT OF THE UCHIHA CLAN...
...WOULD LEAD TO MANY DEATHS, INCLUDING THAT OF INNOCENT FOLKS UNRELATED TO THE SHINOBI WORLD.
...
IF YOU WERE ITACHI, WHAT WOULD YOU HAVE DONE?
...

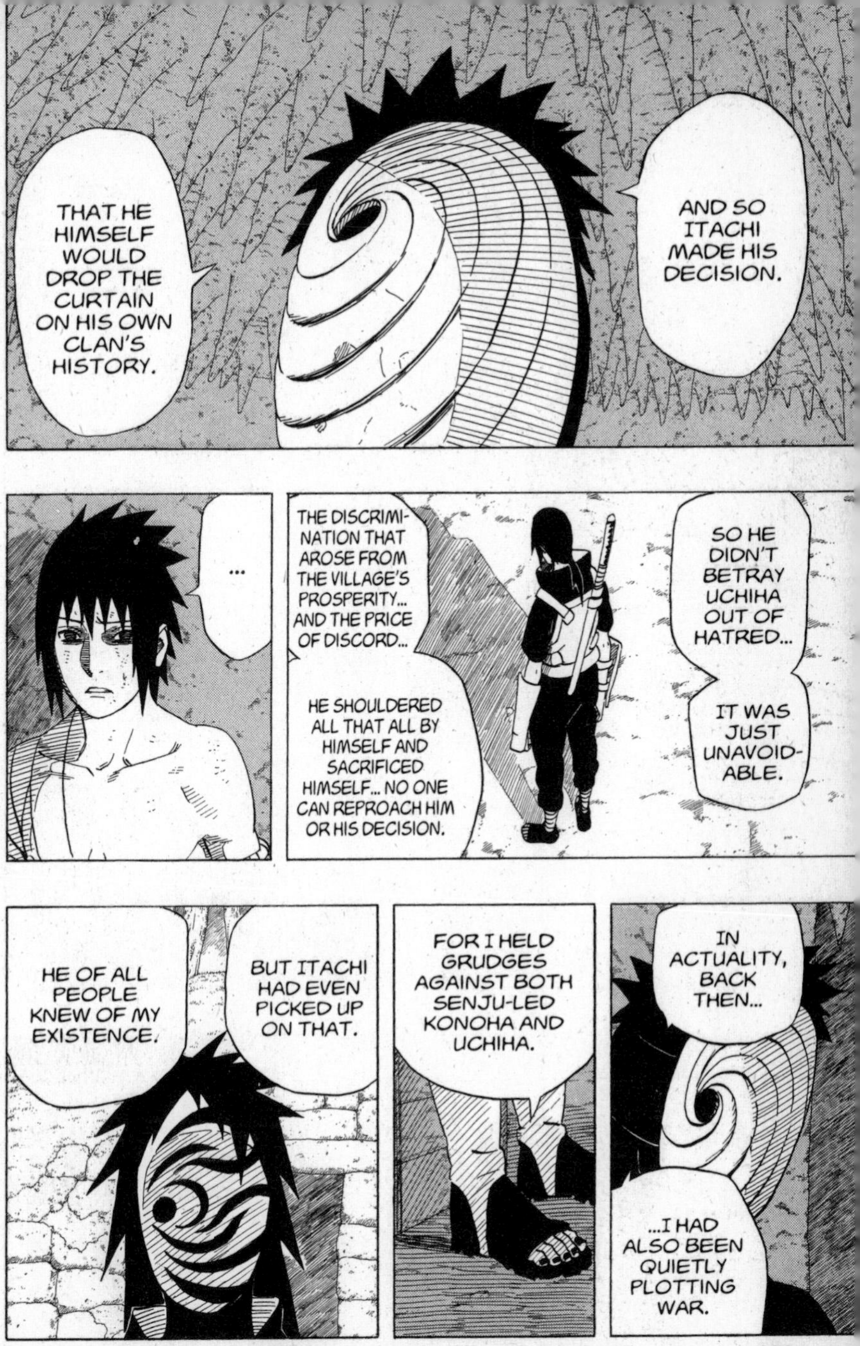
AND SO ITACHI MADE HIS DECISION.
THAT HE HIMSELF WOULD DROP THE CURTAIN ON HIS OWN CLAN'S HISTORY.
SO HE DIDN'T BETRAY UCHIHA OUT OF HATRED...
IT WAS JUST UNAVOIDABLE.
THE DISCRIMINATION THAT AROSE FROM THE VILLAGE'S PROSPERITY... AND THE PRICE OF DISCORD...
HE SHOULDERED ALL THAT ALL BY HIMSELF AND SACRIFICED HIMSELF... NO ONE CAN REPROACH HIM OR HIS DECISION.
...
IN ACTUALITY, BACK THEN...
...I HAD ALSO BEEN QUIETLY PLOTTING WAR.
FOR I HELD GRUDGES AGAINST BOTH SENJU-LED KONOHA AND UCHIHA.
BUT ITACHI HAD EVEN PICKED UP ON THAT.
HE OF ALL PEOPLE KNEW OF MY EXISTENCE.

READ THIS WAY

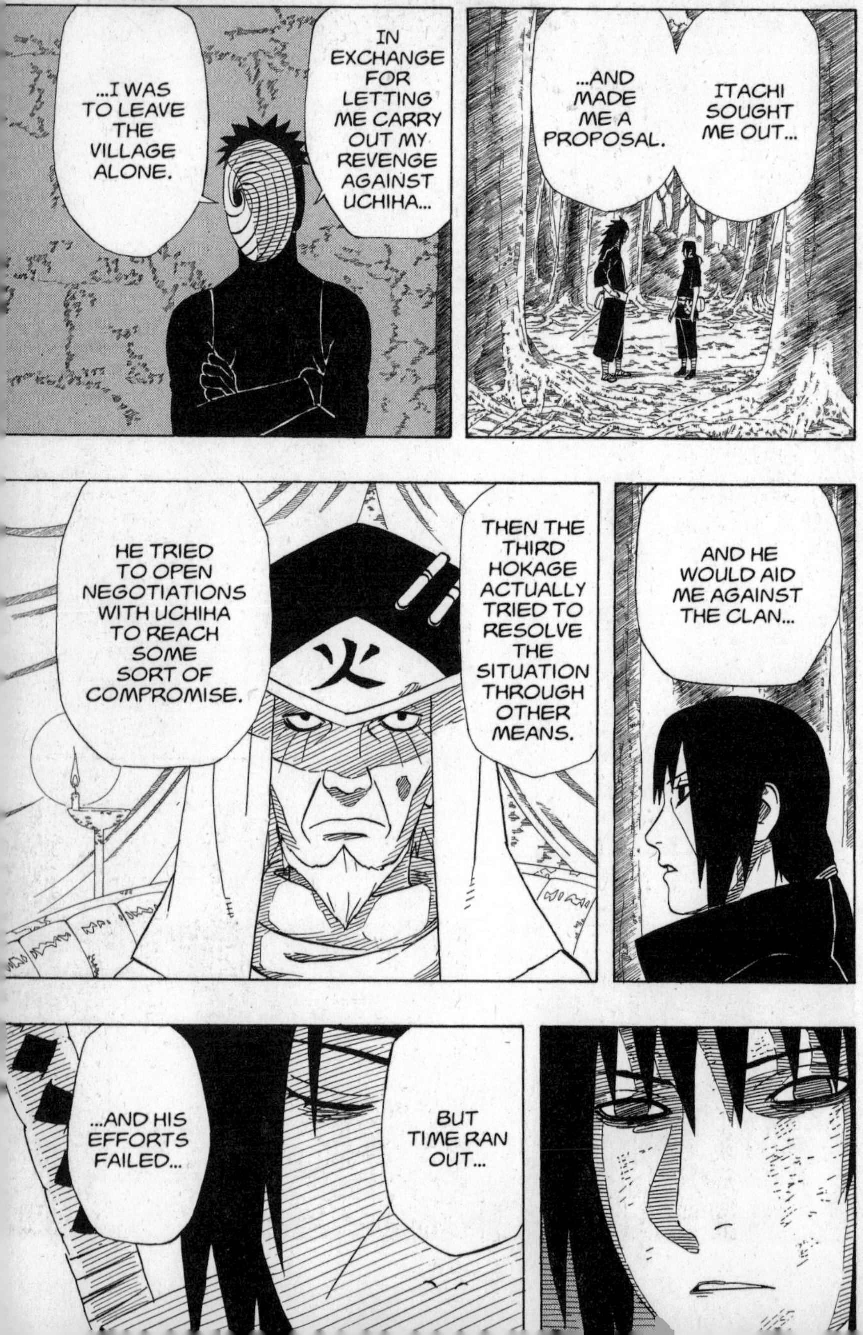
ITACHI SOUGHT ME OUT...
...AND MADE ME A PROPOSAL.
IN EXCHANGE FOR LETTING ME CARRY OUT MY REVENGE AGAINST UCHIHA...
...I WAS TO LEAVE THE VILLAGE ALONE.
AND HE WOULD AID ME AGAINST THE CLAN...
THEN THE THIRD HOKAGE ACTUALLY TRIED TO RESOLVE THE SITUATION THROUGH OTHER MEANS.
火
HE TRIED TO OPEN NEGOTIATIONS WITH UCHIHA TO REACH SOME SORT OF COMPROMISE.
BUT TIME RAN OUT...
...AND HIS EFFORTS FAILED...

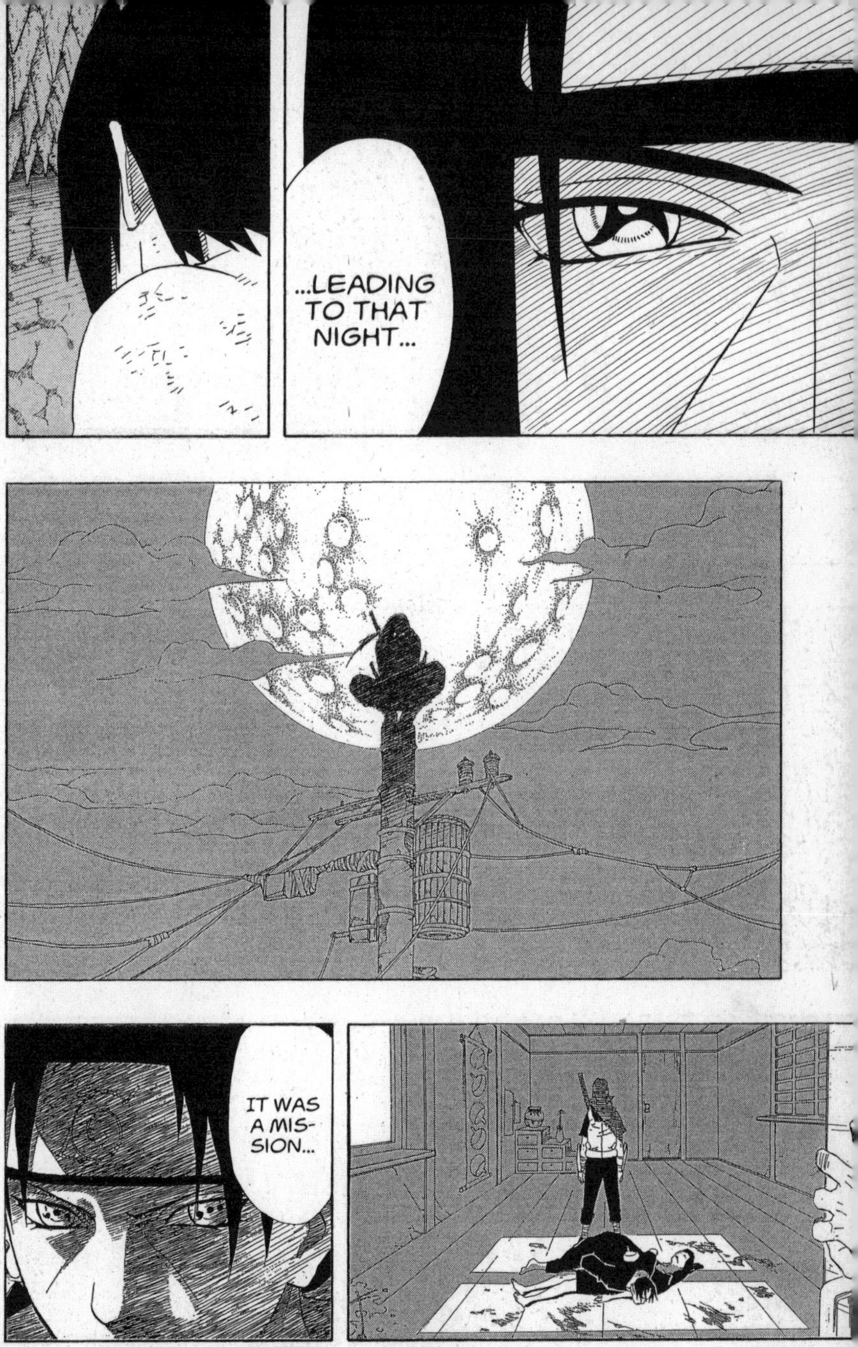
...LEADING TO THAT NIGHT...
IT WAS A MIS- SION...

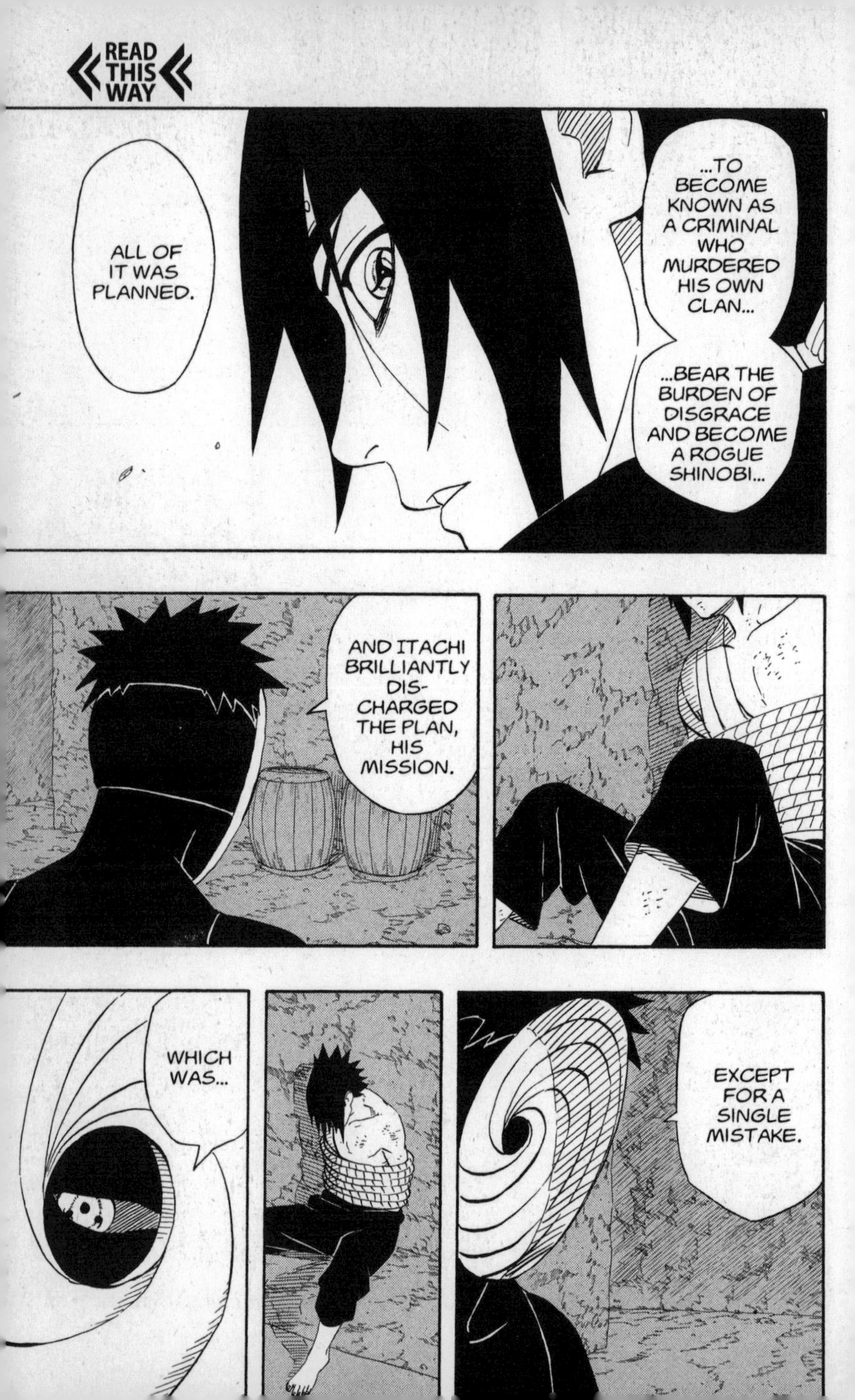READ THIS WAY
...TO BECOME KNOWN AS A CRIMINAL WHO MURDERED HIS OWN CLAN...
...BEAR THE BURDEN OF DISGRACE AND BECOME A ROGUE SHINOBI...
ALL OF IT WAS PLANNED.
AND ITACHI BRILLIANTLY DIS-CHARGED THE PLAN, HIS MISSION.
EXCEPT FOR A SINGLE MISTAKE.
WHICH WAS...

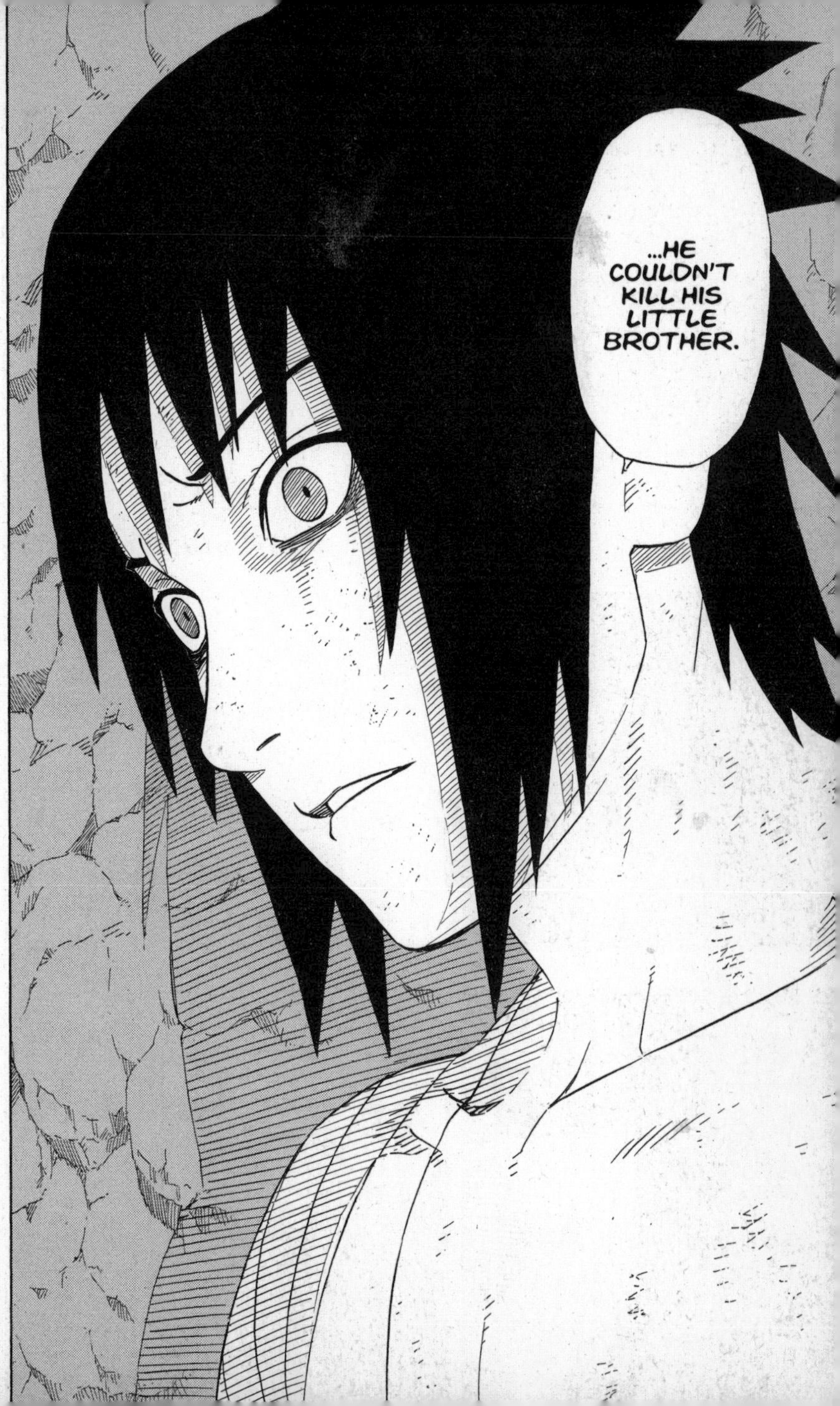
...HE COULDN'T KILL HIS LITTLE BROTHER.

READ THIS WAY

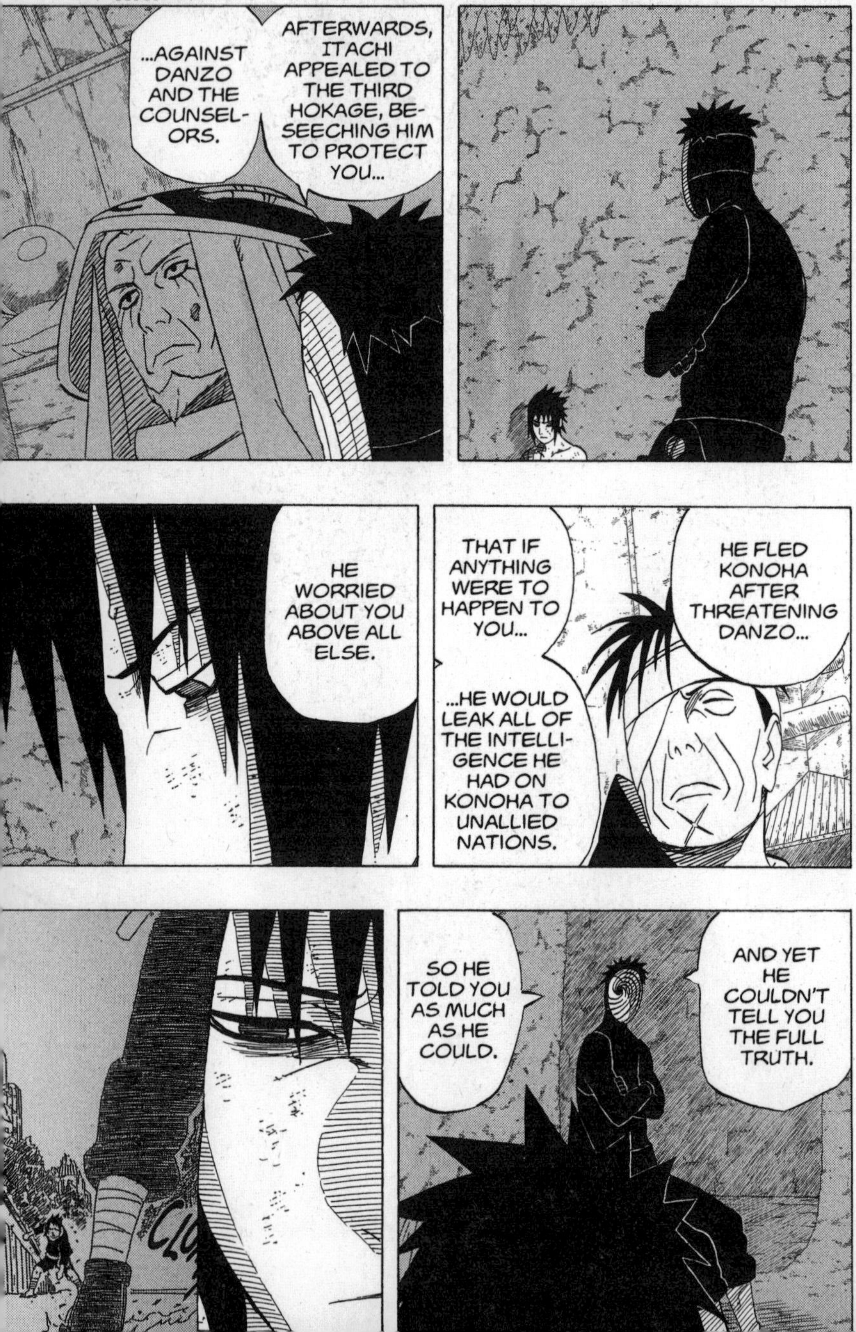

AFTERWARDS, ITACHI APPEALED TO THE THIRD HOKAGE, BE-SEECHING HIM TO PROTECT YOU...
...AGAINST DANZO AND THE COUNSEL-ORS.
HE FLED KONOHA AFTER THREATENING DANZO...
THAT IF ANYTHING WERE TO HAPPEN TO YOU...
...HE WOULD LEAK ALL OF THE INTELLI-GENCE HE HAD ON KONOHA TO UNALLIED NATIONS.
HE WORRIED ABOUT YOU ABOVE ALL ELSE.
AND YET HE COULDN'T TELL YOU THE FULL TRUTH.
SO HE TOLD YOU AS MUCH AS HE COULD.

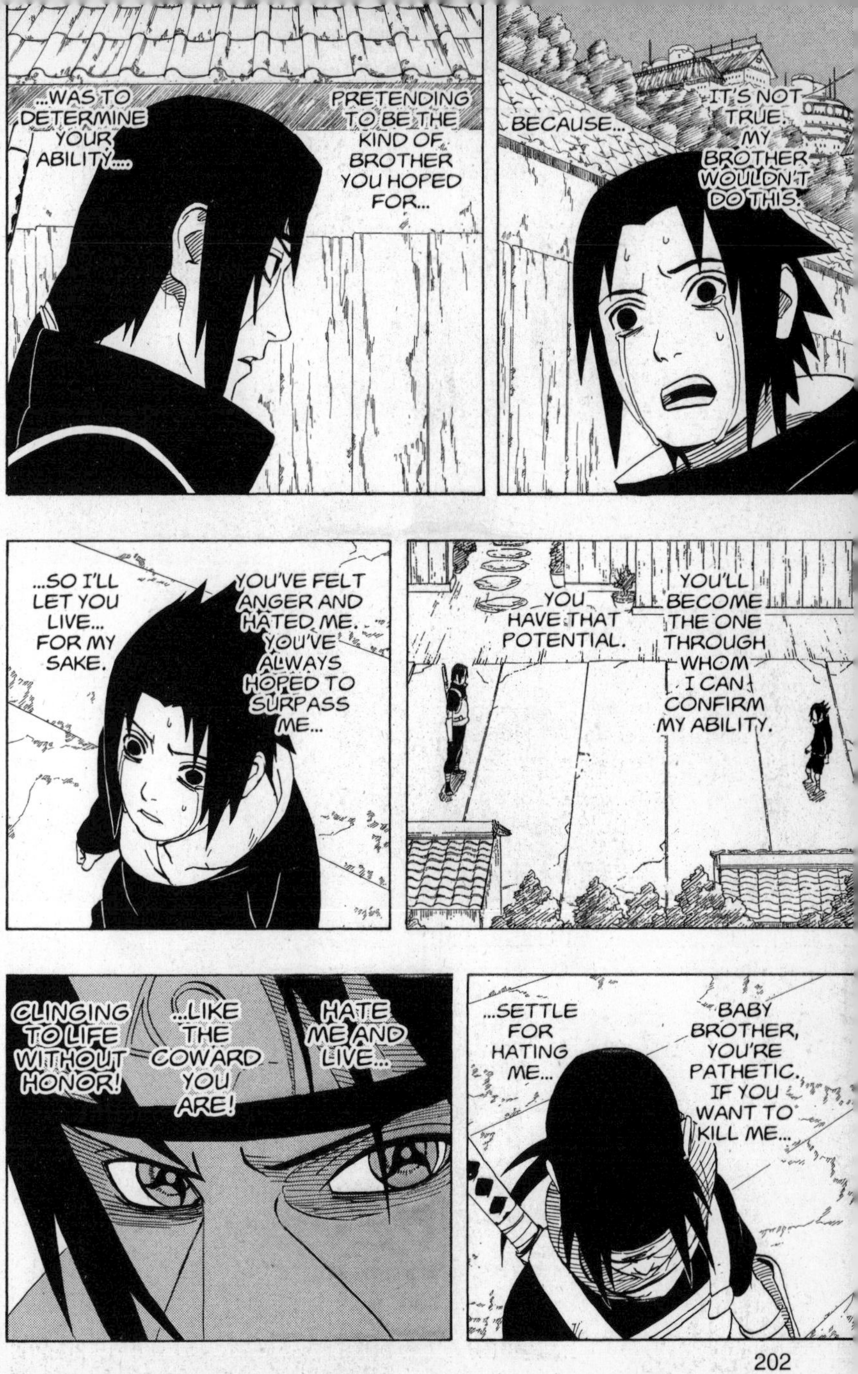
IT'S NOT TRUE. MY BROTHER WOULDN'T DO THIS.
BECAUSE...
PRETENDING TO BE THE KIND OF BROTHER YOU HOPED FOR...
...WAS TO DETERMINE YOUR ABILITY....
YOU'LL BECOME THE ONE THROUGH WHOM I CAN CONFIRM MY ABILITY.
YOU HAVE THAT POTENTIAL.
YOU'VE FELT ANGER AND HATED ME. YOU'VE ALWAYS HOPED TO SURPASS ME...
...SO I'LL LET YOU LIVE... FOR MY SAKE.
BABY BROTHER, YOU'RE PATHETIC. IF YOU WANT TO KILL ME...
...SETTLE FOR HATING ME...
HATE ME AND LIVE...
...LIKE THE COWARD YOU ARE!
CLINGING TO LIFE WITHOUT HONOR!

READ THIS WAY

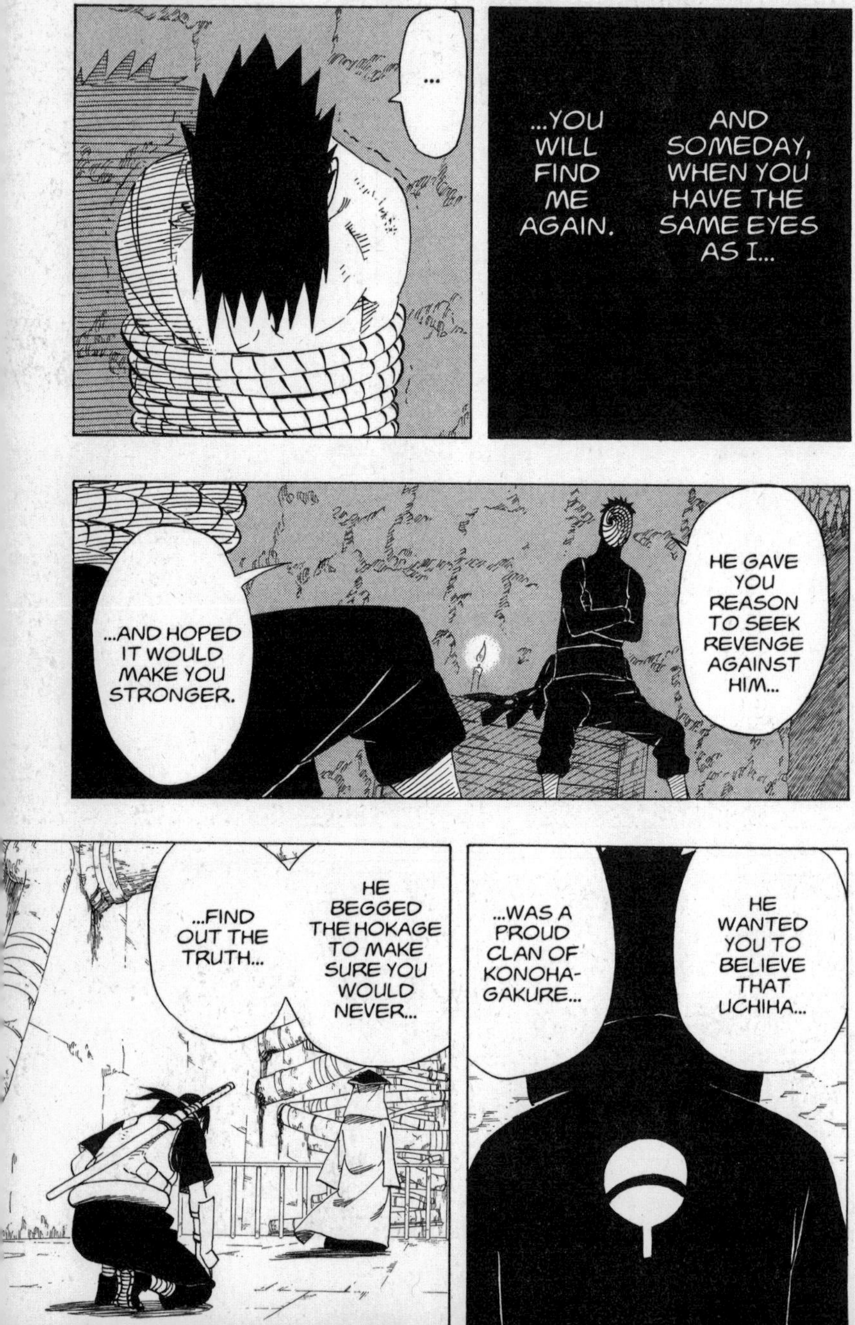
AND SOMEDAY, WHEN YOU HAVE THE SAME EYES AS I...
...YOU WILL FIND ME AGAIN.
...
HE GAVE YOU REASON TO SEEK REVENGE AGAINST HIM...
...AND HOPED IT WOULD MAKE YOU STRONGER.
HE WANTED YOU TO BELIEVE THAT UCHIHA...
...WAS A PROUD CLAN OF KONOHA-GAKURE...
HE BEGGED THE HOKAGE TO MAKE SURE YOU WOULD NEVER...
...FIND OUT THE TRUTH...

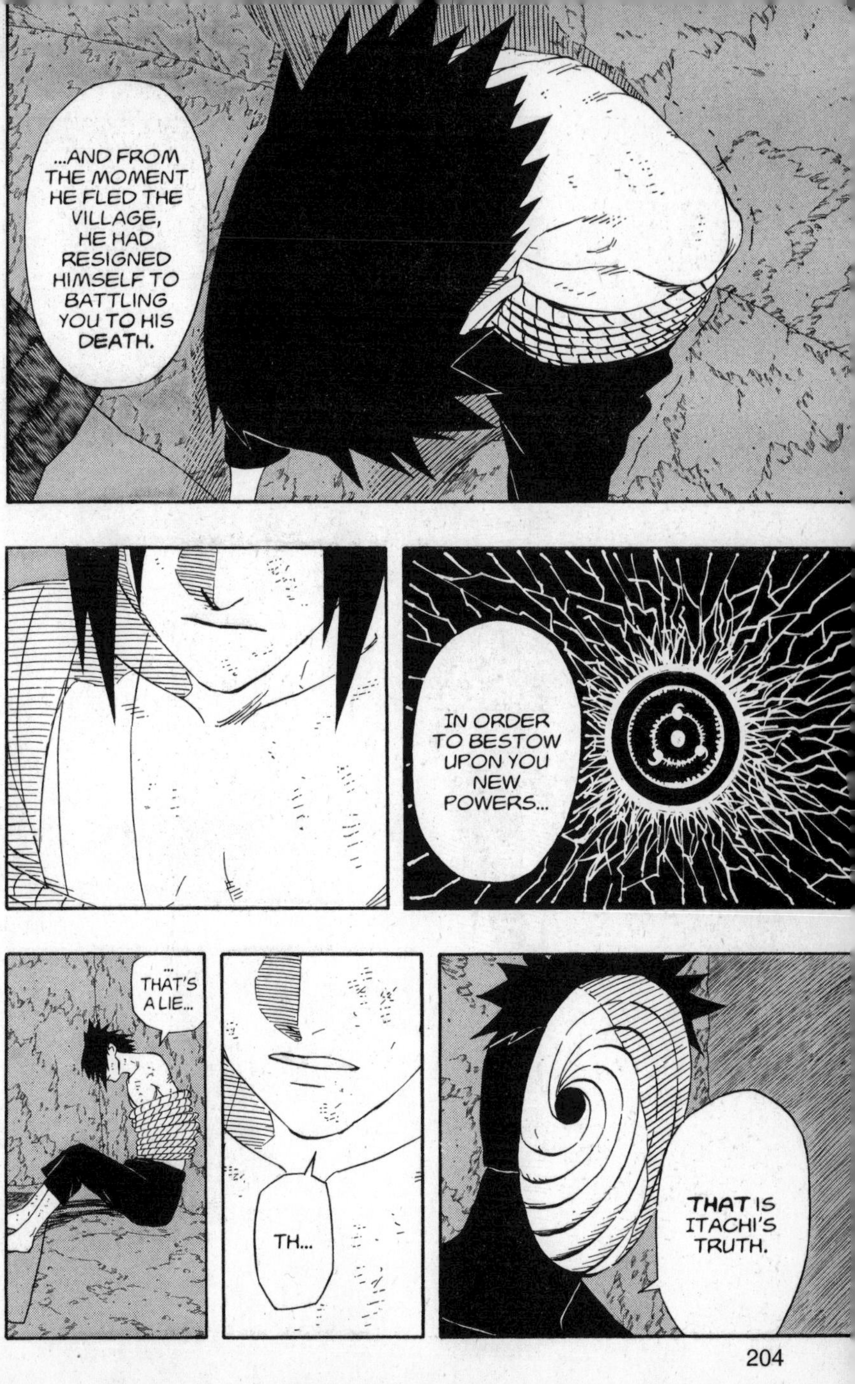
...AND FROM THE MOMENT HE FLED THE VILLAGE, HE HAD RESIGNED HIMSELF TO BATTLING YOU TO HIS DEATH.
IN ORDER TO BESTOW UPON YOU NEW POWERS...
THAT IS ITACHI'S TRUTH.
TH...
... THAT'S A LIE...

READ THIS WAY

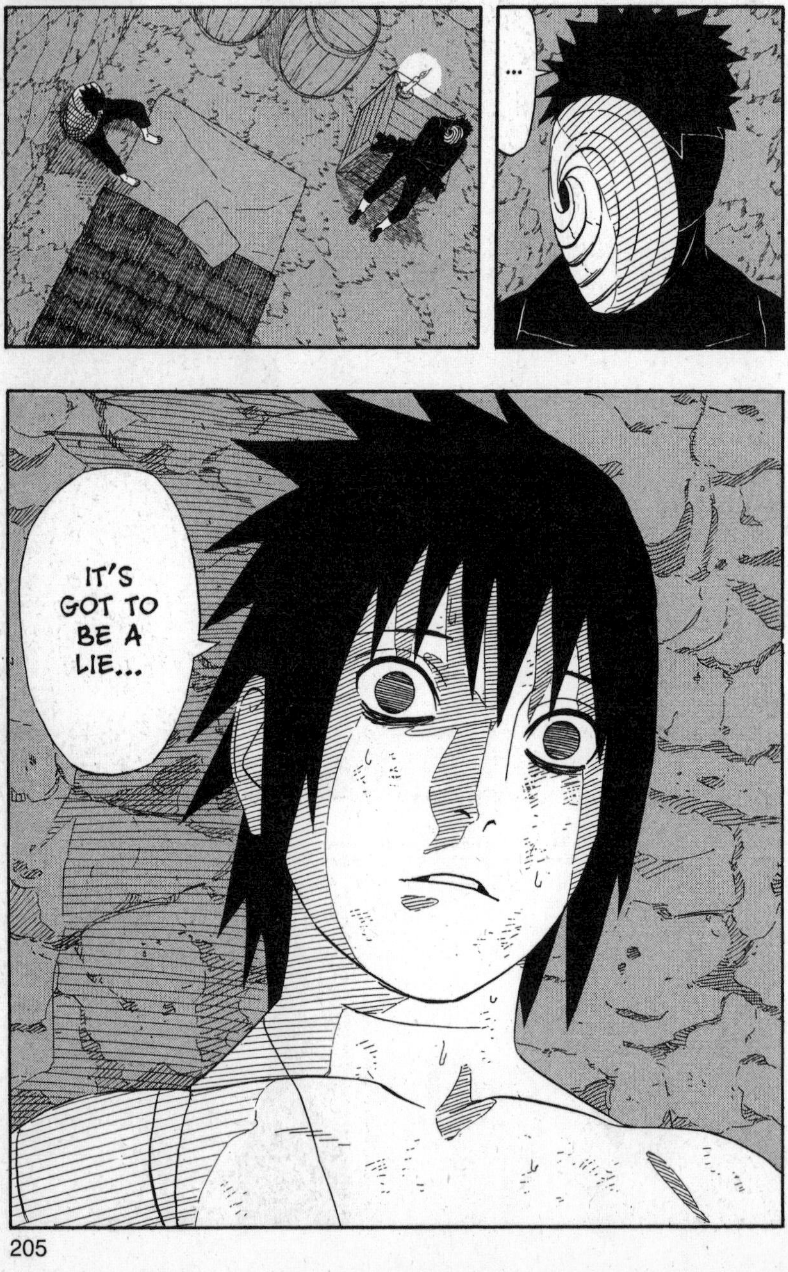
...
IT'S GOT TO BE A LIE...

NARUTO

Number 401: Illusions

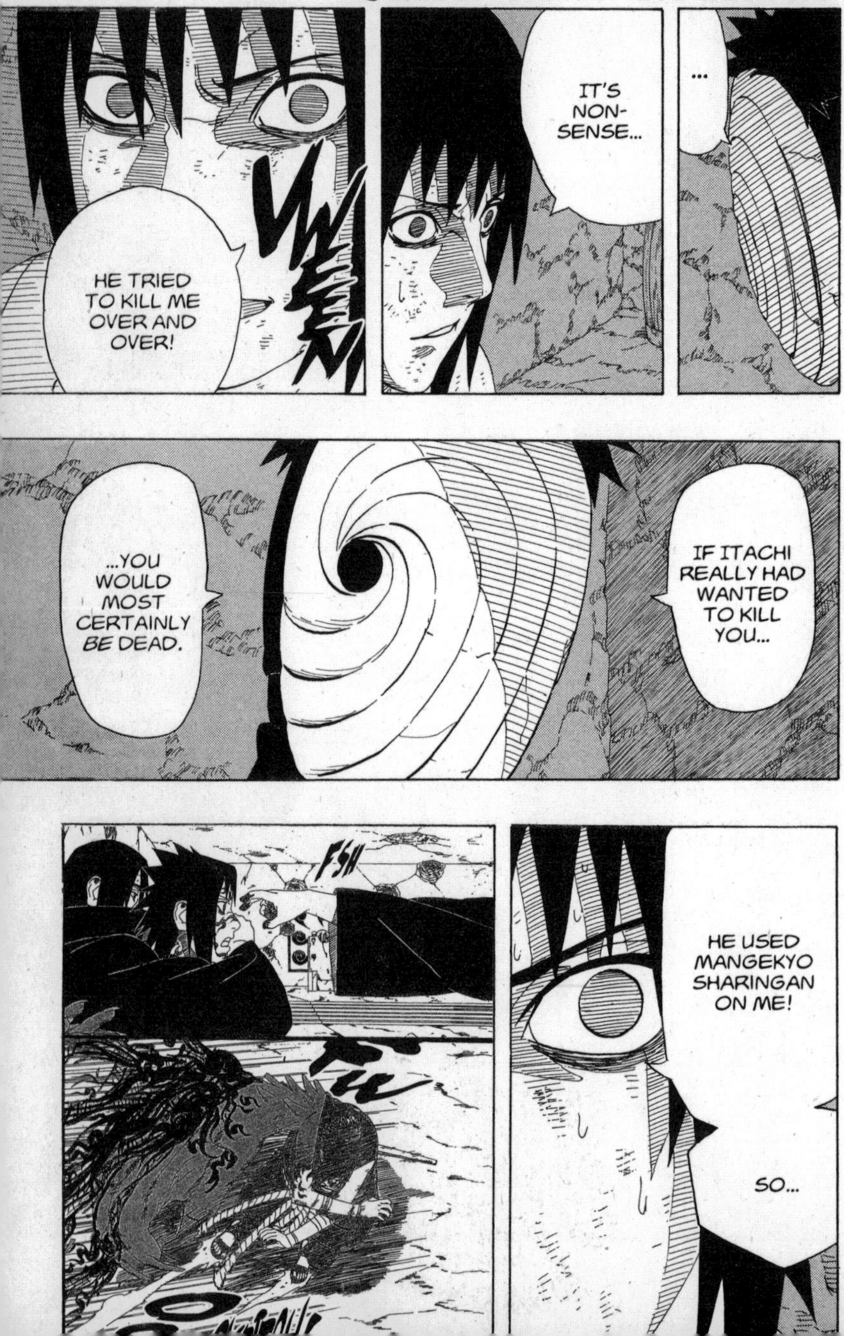
...
IT'S NON-SENSE...
HE TRIED TO KILL ME OVER AND OVER!
IF ITACHI REALLY HAD WANTED TO KILL YOU...
...YOU WOULD MOST CERTAINLY BE DEAD.
HE USED MANGEKYO SHARINGAN ON ME!
SO...
FSH

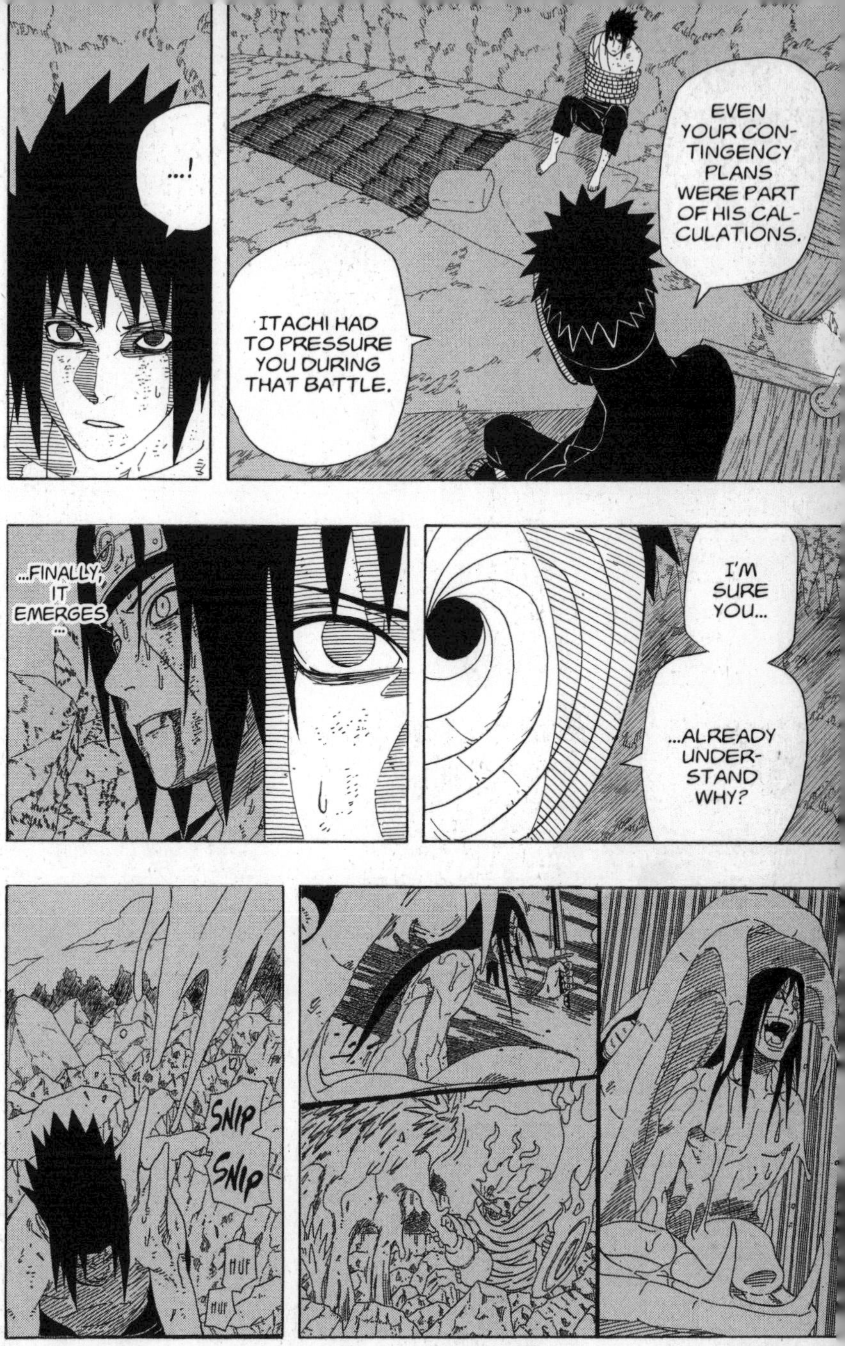

EVEN YOUR CONTINGENCY PLANS WERE PART OF HIS CALCULATIONS.
ITACHI HAD TO PRESSURE YOU DURING THAT BATTLE.
...!
I'M SURE YOU...
...ALREADY UNDERSTAND WHY?
...FINALLY, IT EMERGES...
SNIP
SNIP
HUF
HUF

READ THIS WAY

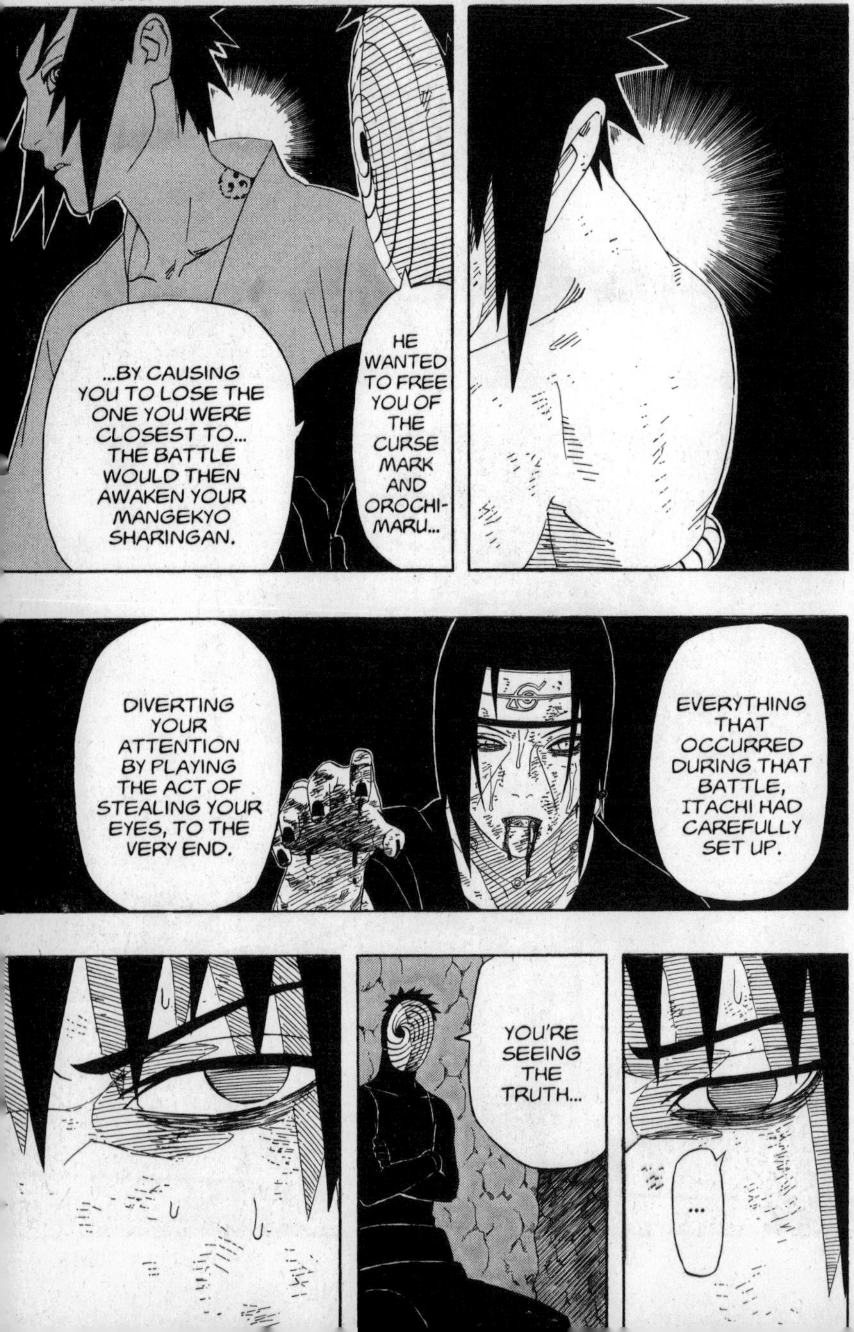
HE WANTED TO FREE YOU OF THE CURSE MARK AND OROCHI-MARU...
...BY CAUSING YOU TO LOSE THE ONE YOU WERE CLOSEST TO... THE BATTLE WOULD THEN AWAKEN YOUR MANGEKYO SHARINGAN.
EVERYTHING THAT OCCURRED DURING THAT BATTLE, ITACHI HAD CAREFULLY SET UP.
DIVERTING YOUR ATTENTION BY PLAYING THE ACT OF STEALING YOUR EYES, TO THE VERY END.
...
YOU'RE SEEING THE TRUTH...

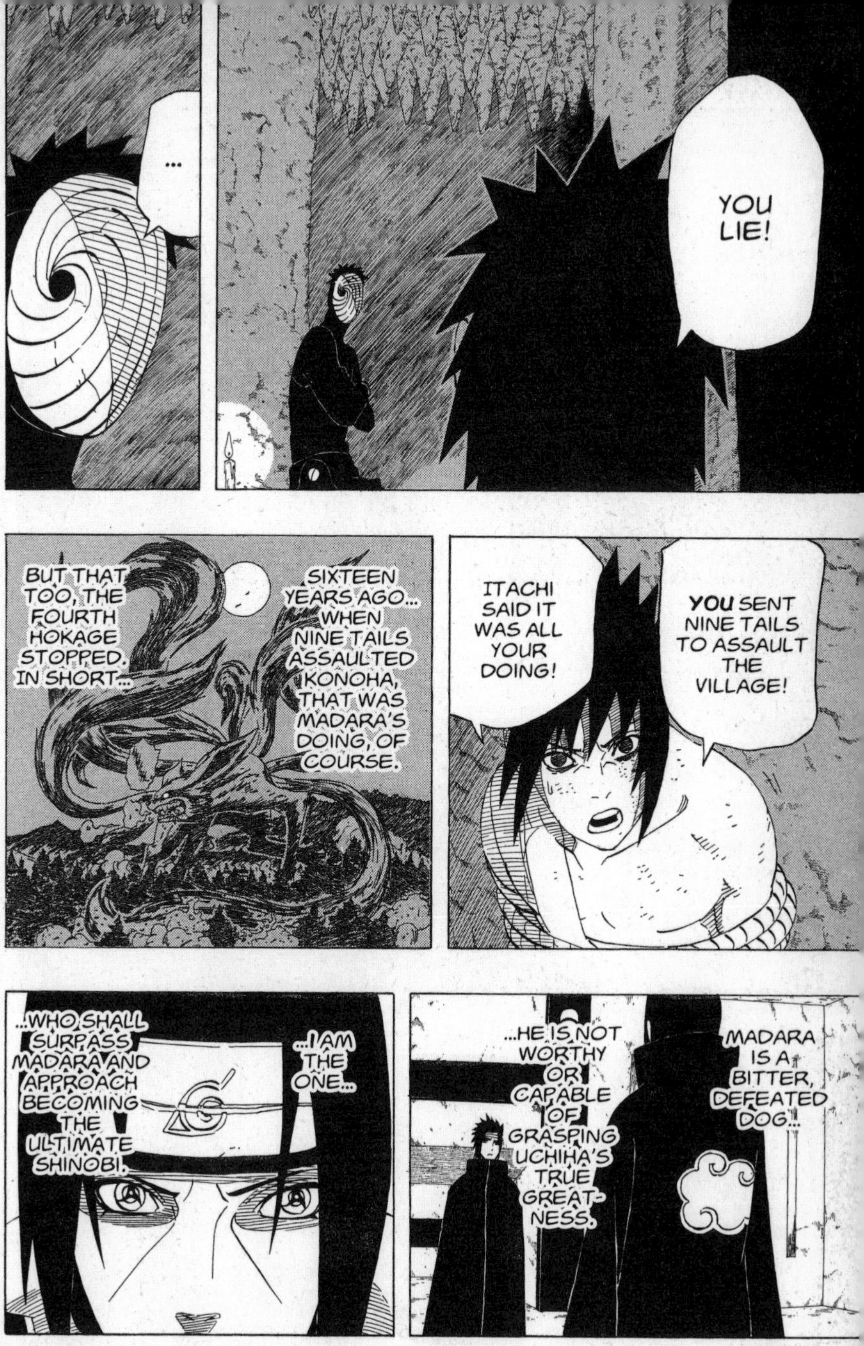
YOU LIE!
...
YOU SENT NINE TAILS TO ASSAULT THE VILLAGE!
ITACHI SAID IT WAS ALL YOUR DOING!
SIXTEEN YEARS AGO... WHEN NINE TAILS ASSAULTED KONOHA, THAT WAS MADARA'S DOING, OF COURSE.
BUT THAT TOO, THE FOURTH HOKAGE STOPPED. IN SHORT...
MADARA IS A BITTER, DEFEATED DOG...
...HE IS NOT WORTHY OR CAPABLE OF GRASPING UCHIHA'S TRUE GREAT-NESS.
...I AM THE ONE...
...WHO SHALL SURPASS MADARA AND APPROACH BECOMING THE ULTIMATE SHINOBI.

READ THIS WAY

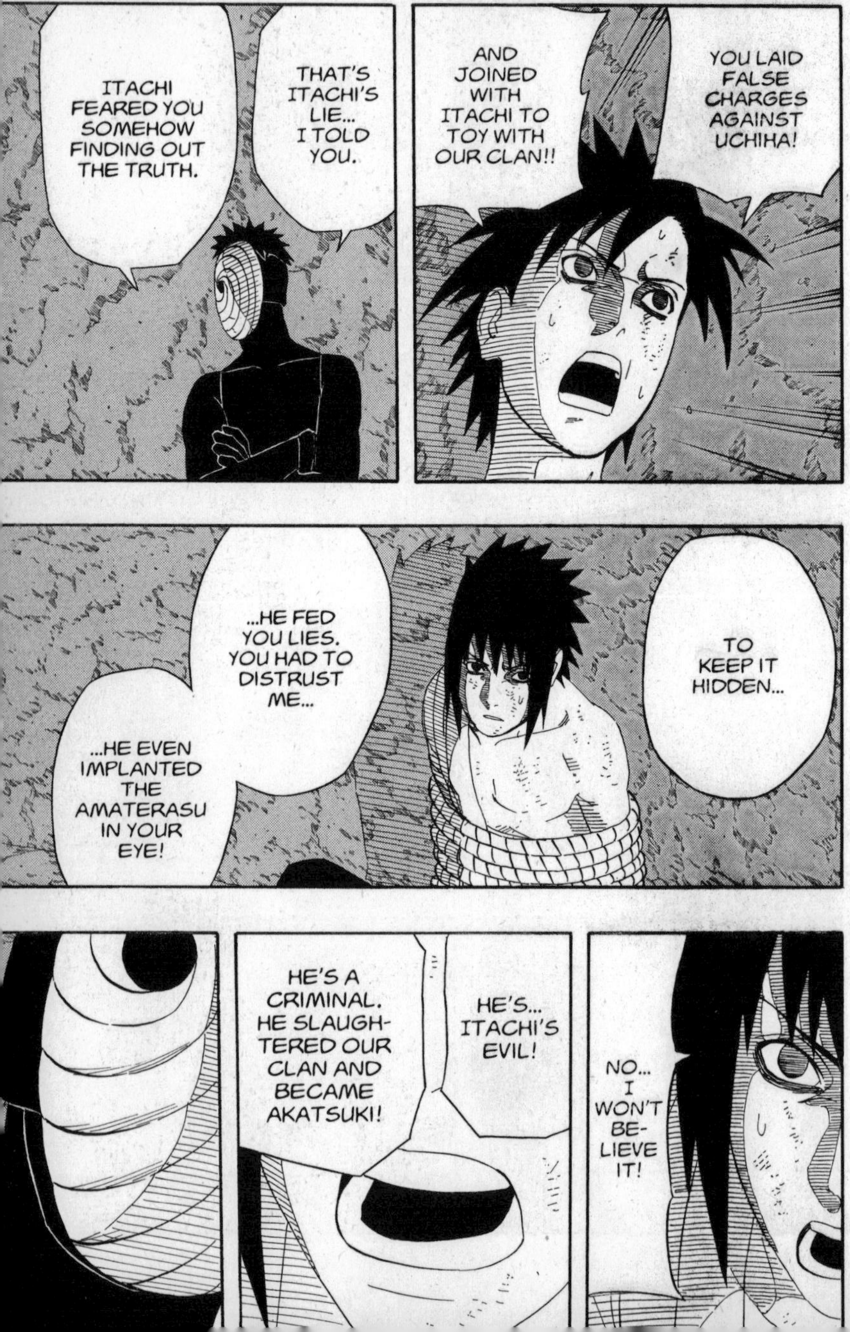
YOU LAID FALSE CHARGES AGAINST UCHIHA!
AND JOINED WITH ITACHI TO TOY WITH OUR CLAN!!
THAT'S ITACHI'S LIE... I TOLD YOU.
ITACHI FEARED YOU SOMEHOW FINDING OUT THE TRUTH.
TO KEEP IT HIDDEN...
...HE FED YOU LIES. YOU HAD TO DISTRUST ME...
...HE EVEN IMPLANTED THE AMATERASU IN YOUR EYE!
NO... I WON'T BE-LIEVE IT!
HE'S... ITACHI'S EVIL!
HE'S A CRIMINAL. HE SLAUGH-TERED OUR CLAN AND BECAME AKATSUKI!

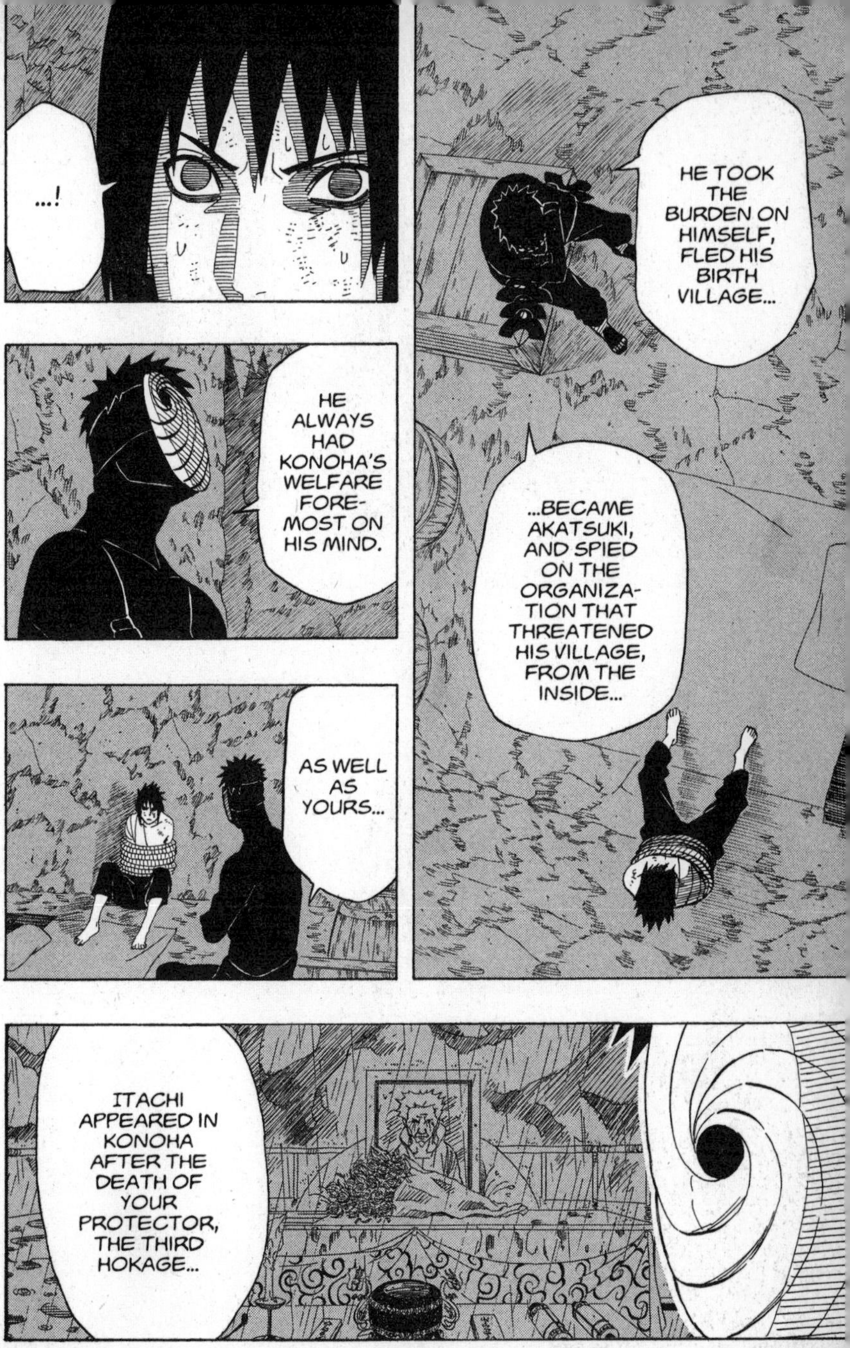
HE TOOK THE BURDEN ON HIMSELF, FLED HIS BIRTH VILLAGE...
...BECAME AKATSUKI, AND SPIED ON THE ORGANIZATION THAT THREATENED HIS VILLAGE, FROM THE INSIDE...
...!
HE ALWAYS HAD KONOHA'S WELFARE FOREMOST ON HIS MIND.
AS WELL AS YOURS...
ITACHI APPEARED IN KONOHA AFTER THE DEATH OF YOUR PROTECTOR, THE THIRD HOKAGE...

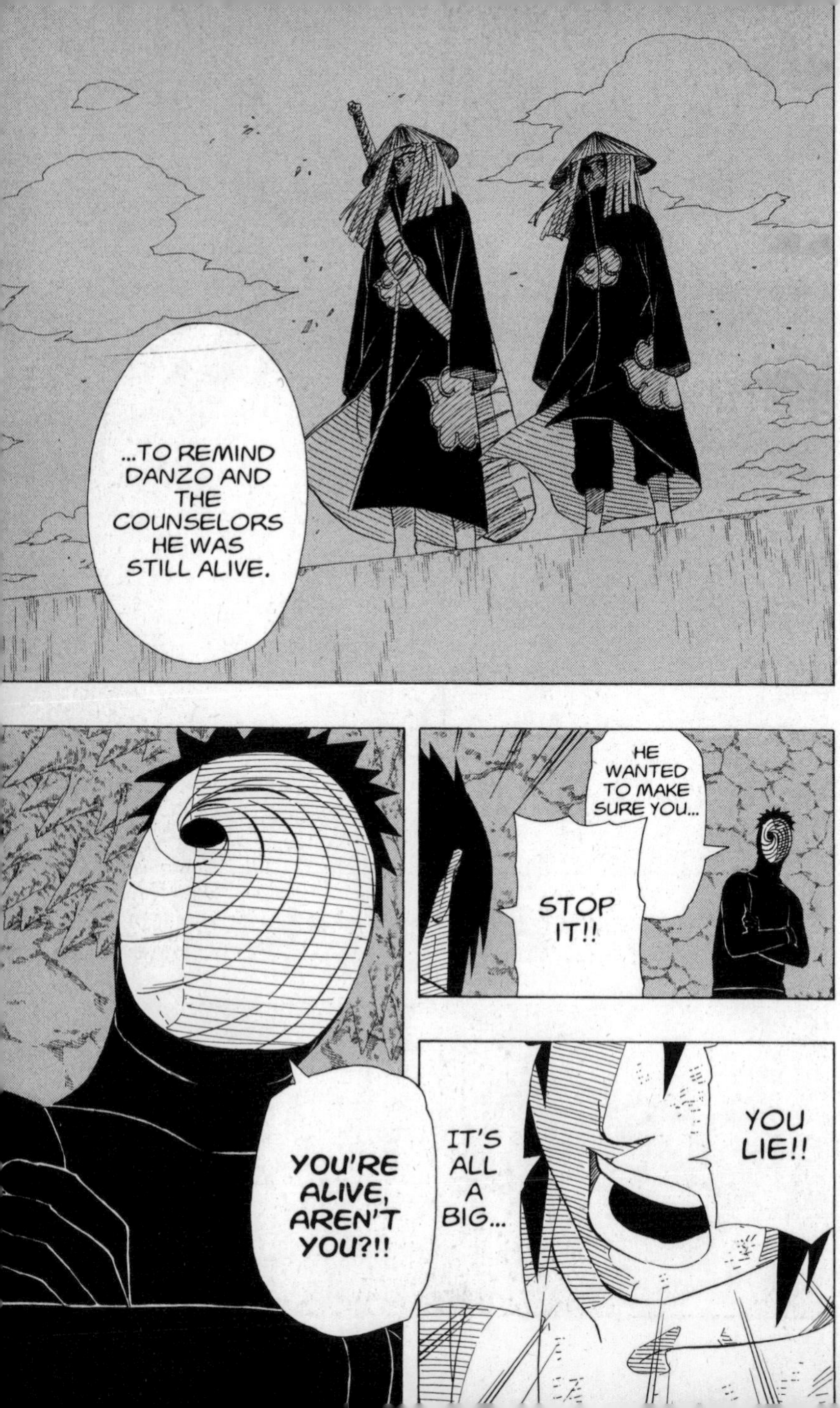
...TO REMIND DANZO AND THE COUNSELORS HE WAS STILL ALIVE.
HE WANTED TO MAKE SURE YOU...
STOP IT!!
YOU LIE!!
IT'S ALL A BIG...
YOU'RE ALIVE, AREN'T YOU?!!

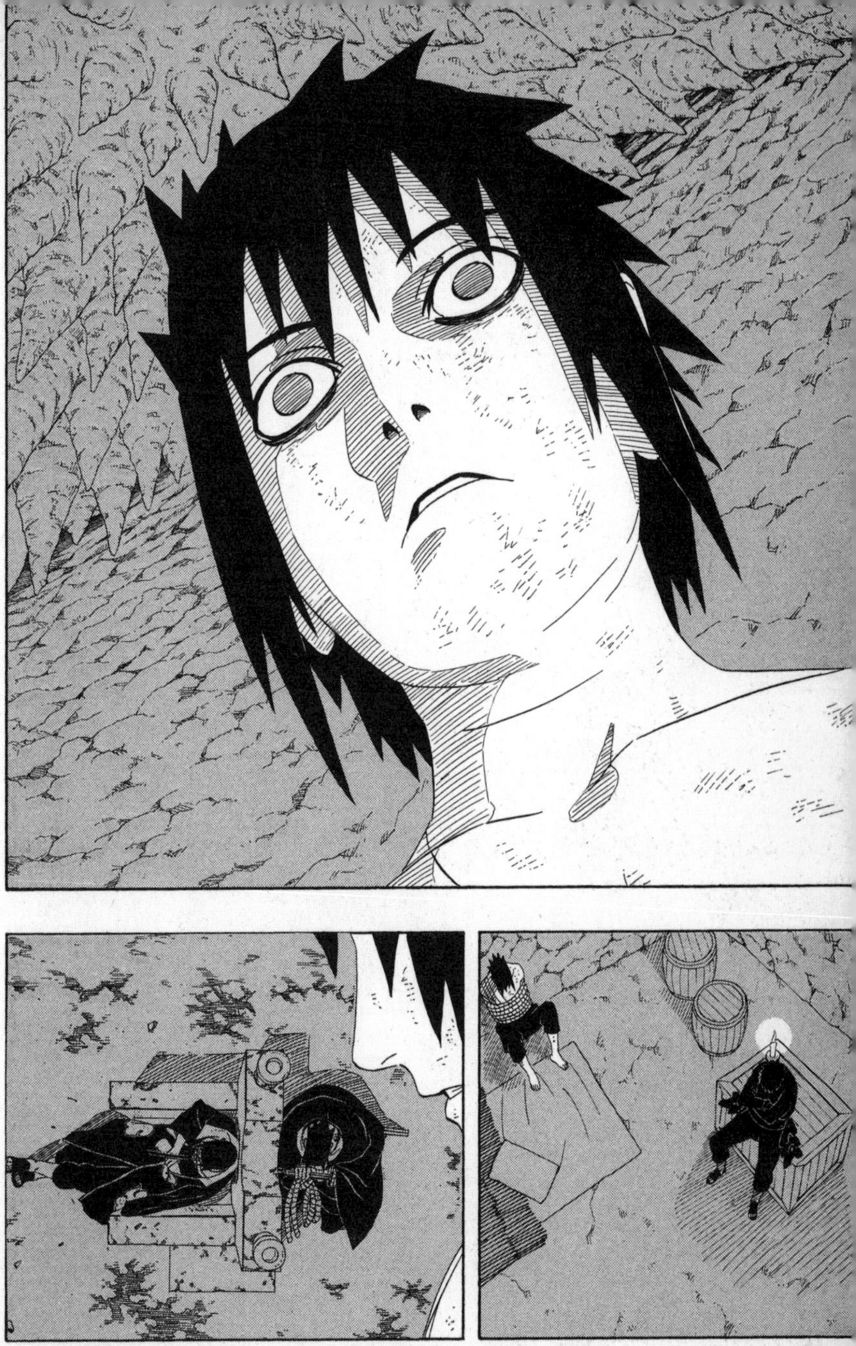

READ THIS WAY

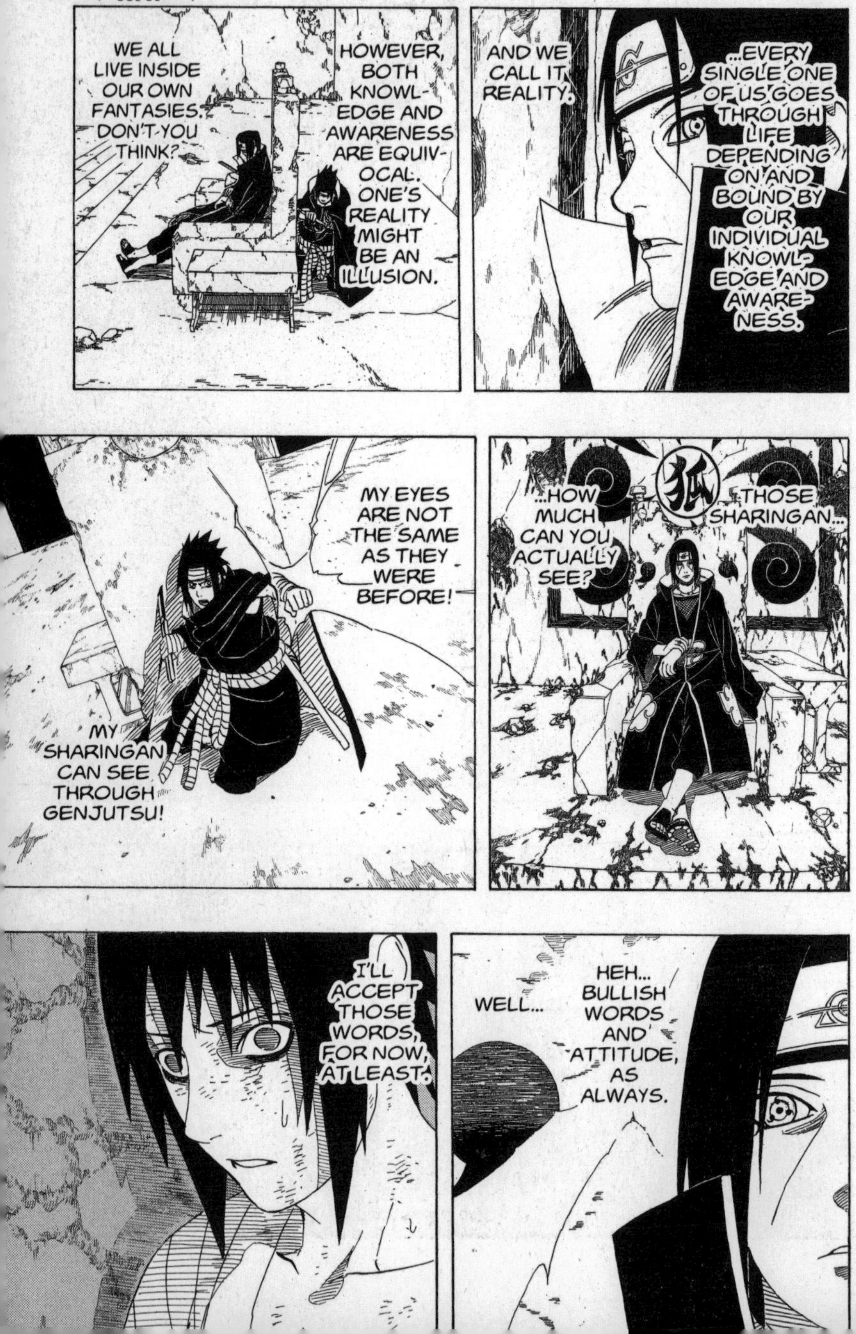
...EVERY SINGLE ONE OF US GOES THROUGH LIFE DEPENDING ON AND BOUND BY OUR INDIVIDUAL KNOWLEDGE AND AWARENESS.
AND WE CALL IT REALITY.
HOWEVER, BOTH KNOWLEDGE AND AWARENESS ARE EQUIVOCAL. ONE'S REALITY MIGHT BE AN ILLUSION.
WE ALL LIVE INSIDE OUR OWN FANTASIES. DON'T YOU THINK?
THOSE SHARINGAN...
...HOW MUCH CAN YOU ACTUALLY SEE?
MY EYES ARE NOT THE SAME AS THEY WERE BEFORE!
MY SHARINGAN CAN SEE THROUGH GENJUTSU!
HEH... BULLISH WORDS AND ATTITUDE, AS ALWAYS.
WELL...
I'LL ACCEPT THOSE WORDS, FOR NOW, AT LEAST.

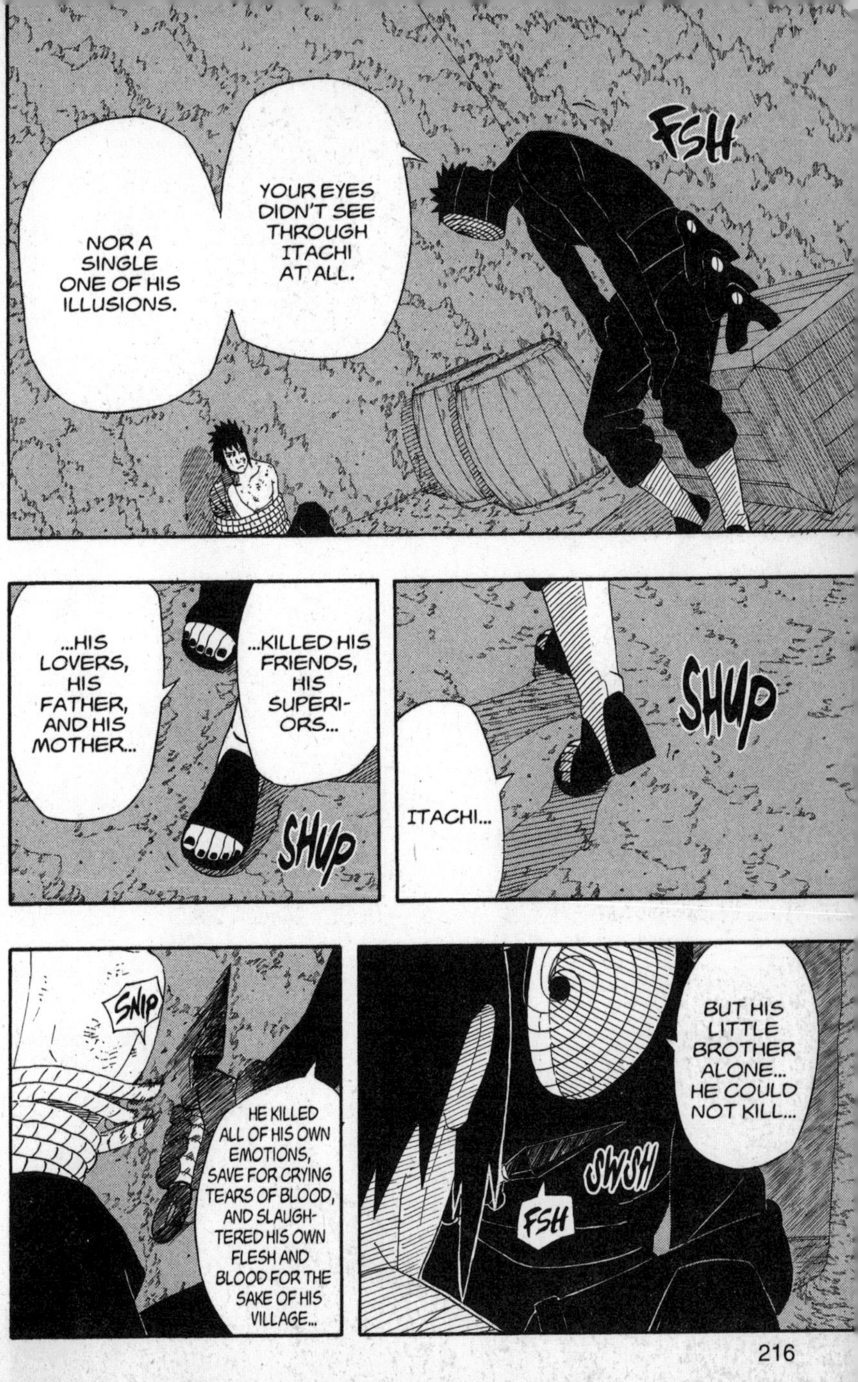
FSH
YOUR EYES DIDN'T SEE THROUGH ITACHI AT ALL.
NOR A SINGLE ONE OF HIS ILLUSIONS.
SHUP
ITACHI...
...KILLED HIS FRIENDS, HIS SUPERIORS...
...HIS LOVERS, HIS FATHER, AND HIS MOTHER...
SHUP
BUT HIS LITTLE BROTHER ALONE... HE COULD NOT KILL...
SWSH
FSH
SNIP
HE KILLED ALL OF HIS OWN EMOTIONS, SAVE FOR CRYING TEARS OF BLOOD, AND SLAUGHTERED HIS OWN FLESH AND BLOOD FOR THE SAKE OF HIS VILLAGE...

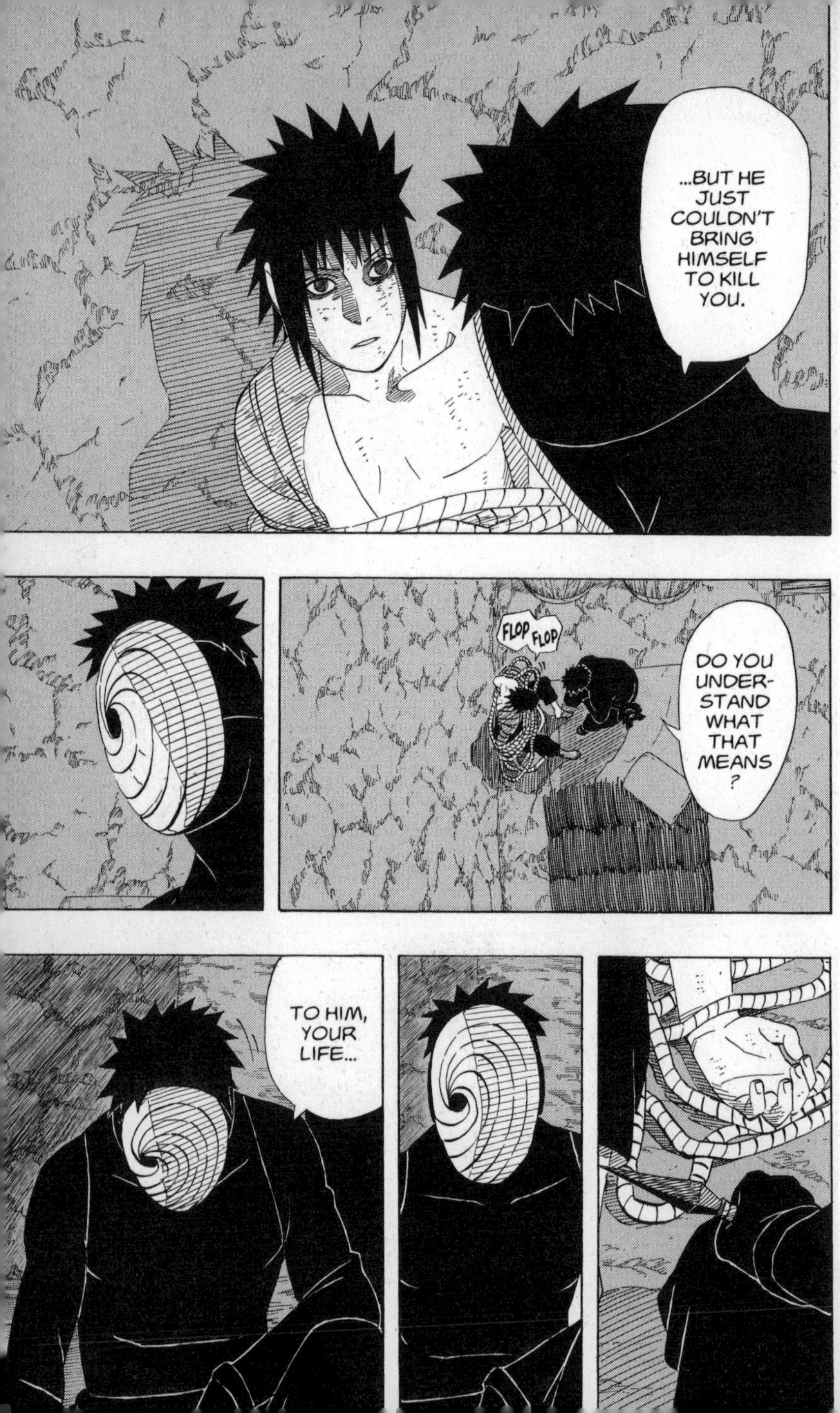
...BUT HE JUST COULDN'T BRING HIMSELF TO KILL YOU.
DO YOU UNDER-STAND WHAT THAT MEANS?
FLOP FLOP
TO HIM, YOUR LIFE...

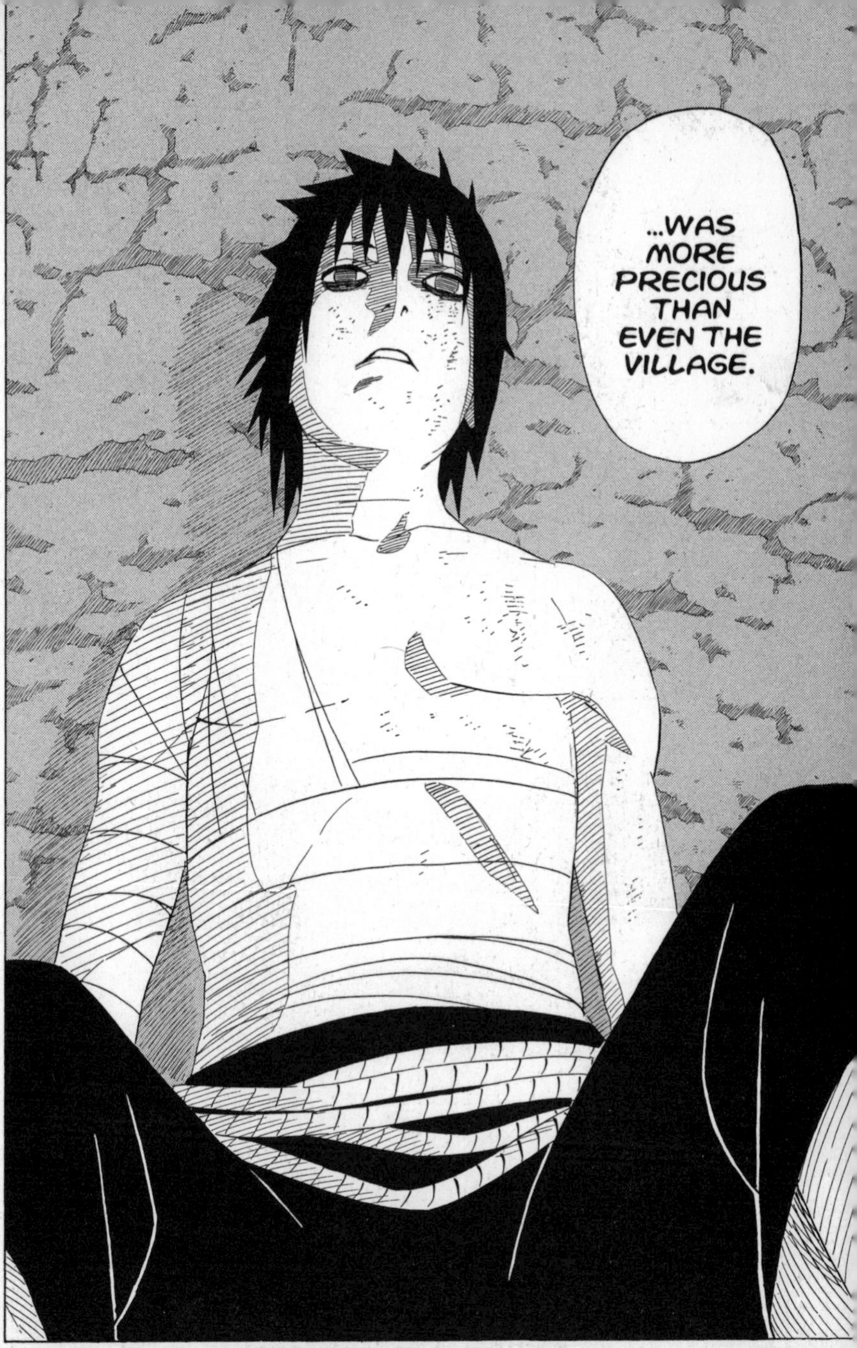
...WAS MORE PRECIOUS THAN EVEN THE VILLAGE.

READ THIS WAY

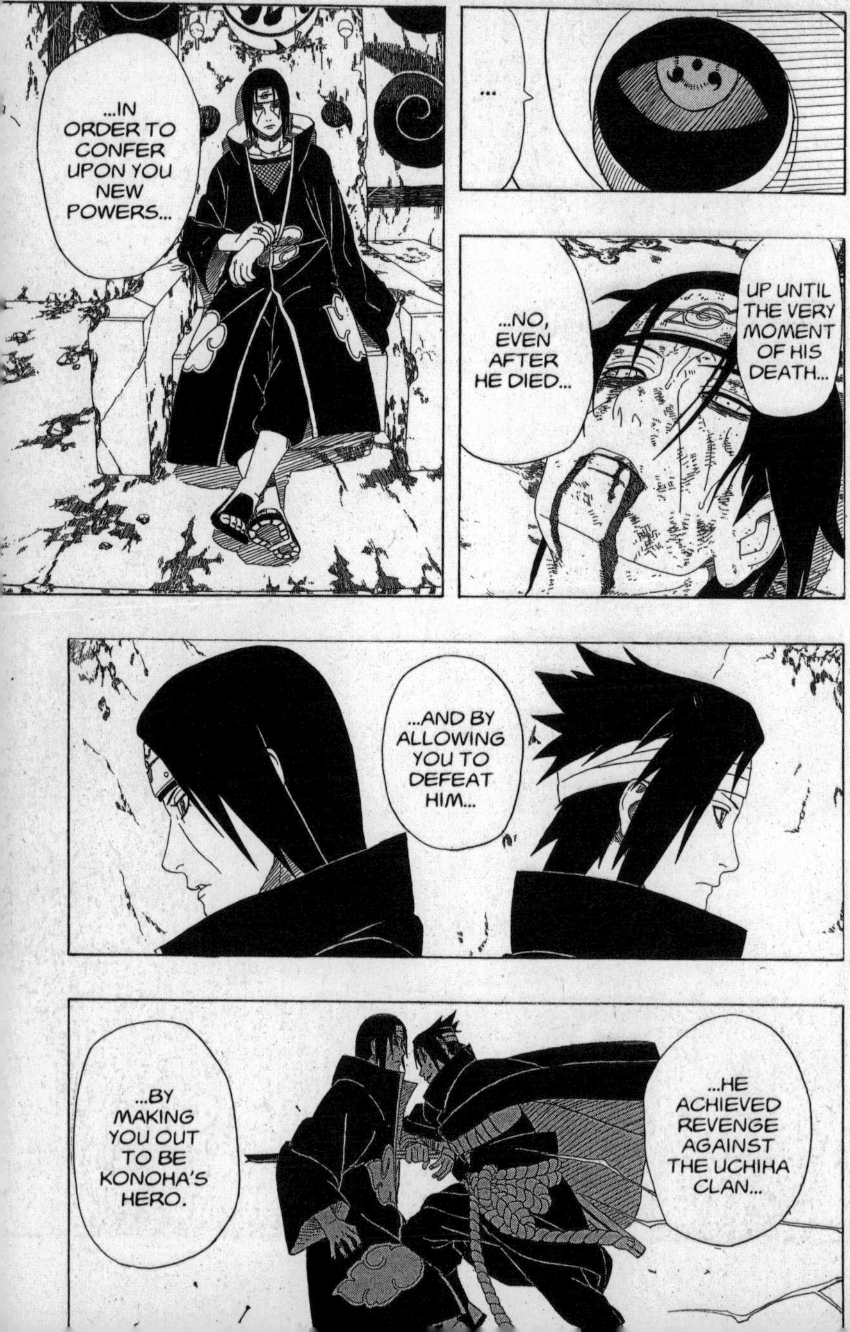
...
UP UNTIL THE VERY MOMENT OF HIS DEATH...
...NO, EVEN AFTER HE DIED...
...IN ORDER TO CONFER UPON YOU NEW POWERS...
...AND BY ALLOWING YOU TO DEFEAT HIM...
...HE ACHIEVED REVENGE AGAINST THE UCHIHA CLAN...
...BY MAKING YOU OUT TO BE KONOHA'S HERO.

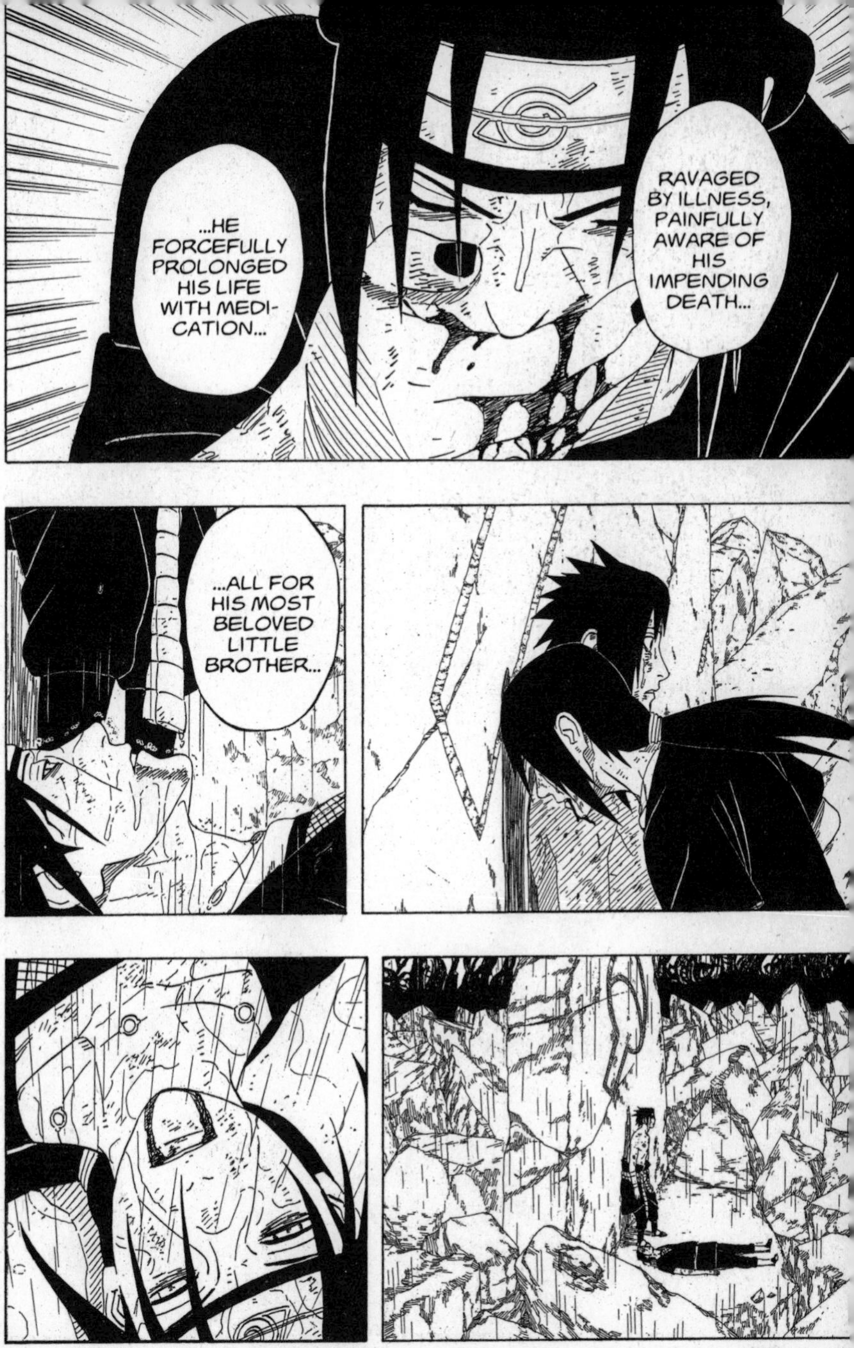
RAVAGED BY ILLNESS, PAINFULLY AWARE OF HIS IMPENDING DEATH...
...HE FORCEFULLY PROLONGED HIS LIFE WITH MEDI-CATION...
...ALL FOR HIS MOST BELOVED LITTLE BROTHER...

READ THIS WAY

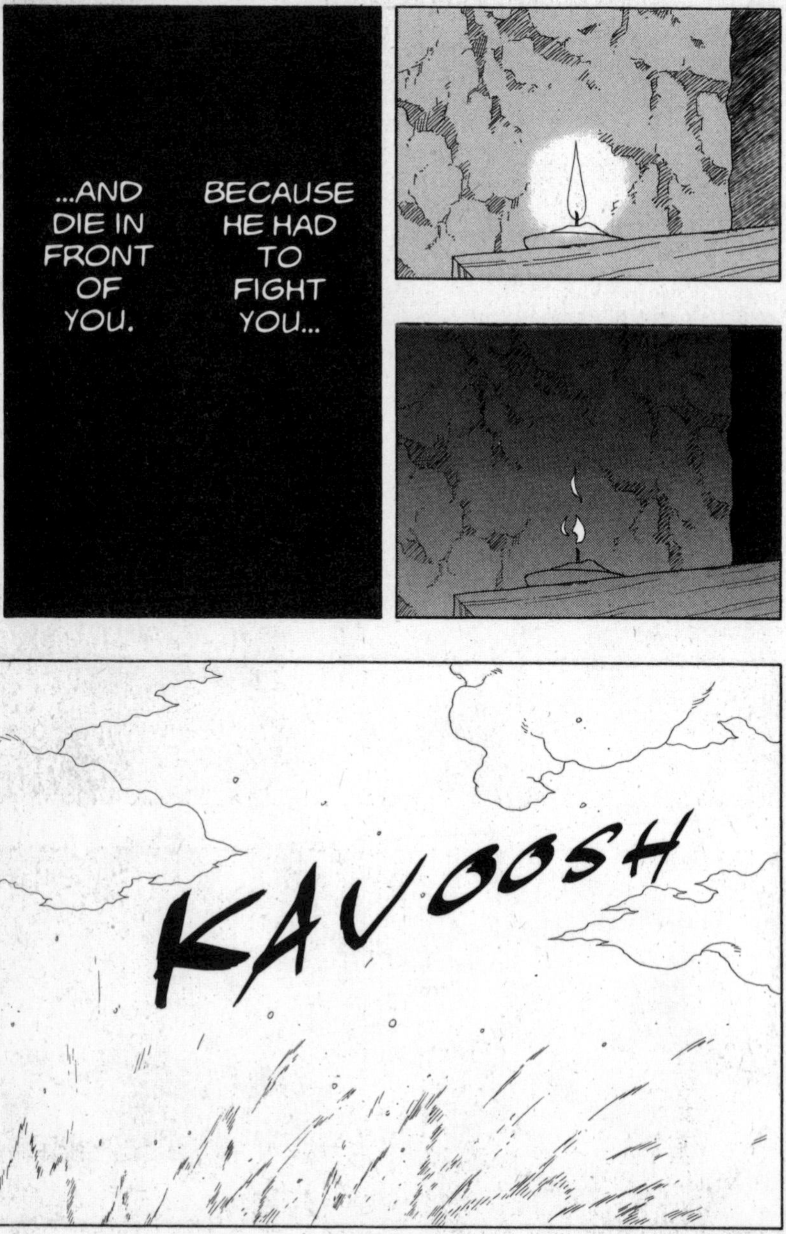
BECAUSE HE HAD TO FIGHT YOU...
...AND DIE IN FRONT OF YOU.
KAVOOSH

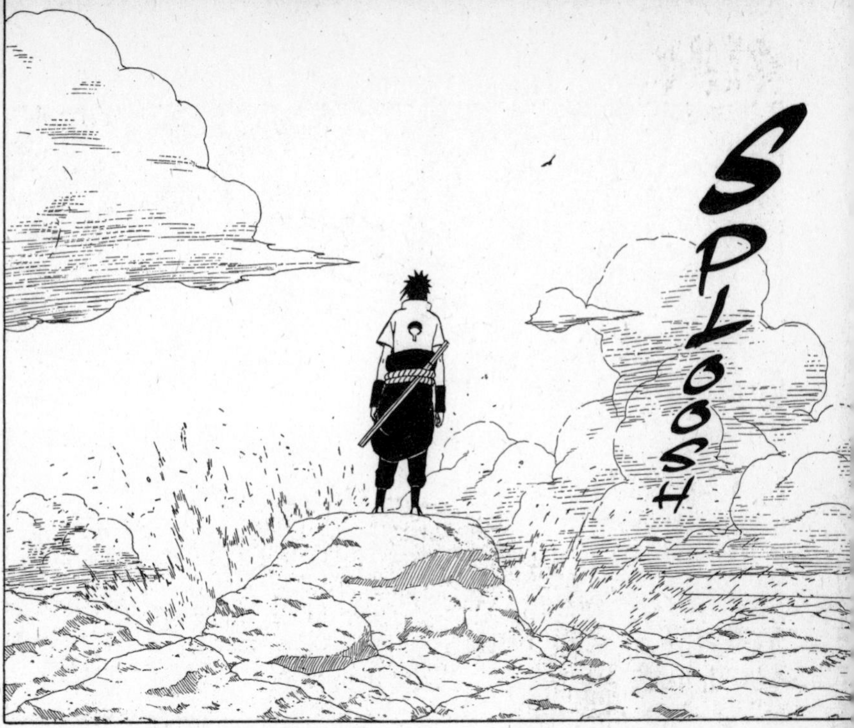
SPLOOSH

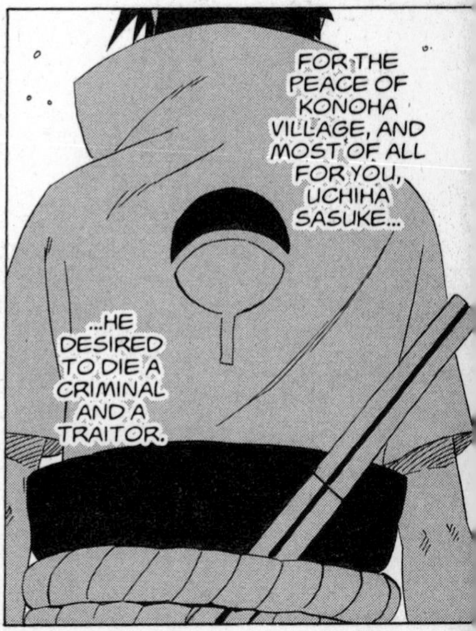
FOR THE PEACE OF KONOHA VILLAGE, AND MOST OF ALL FOR YOU, UCHIHA SASUKE...
...HE DESIRED TO DIE A CRIMINAL AND A TRAITOR.

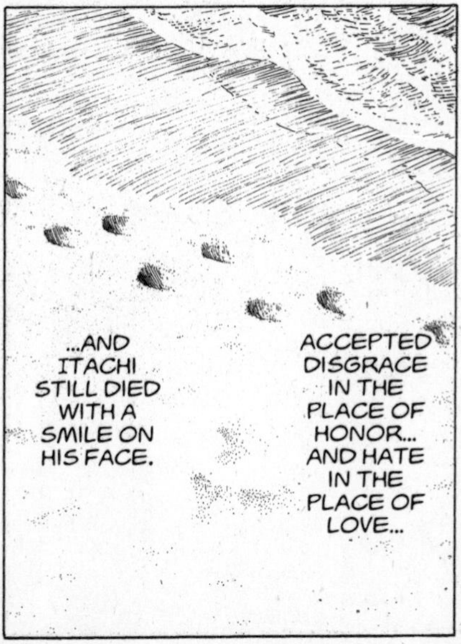
ACCEPTED DISGRACE IN THE PLACE OF HONOR... AND HATE IN THE PLACE OF LOVE...
...AND ITACHI STILL DIED WITH A SMILE ON HIS FACE.

READ THIS WAY

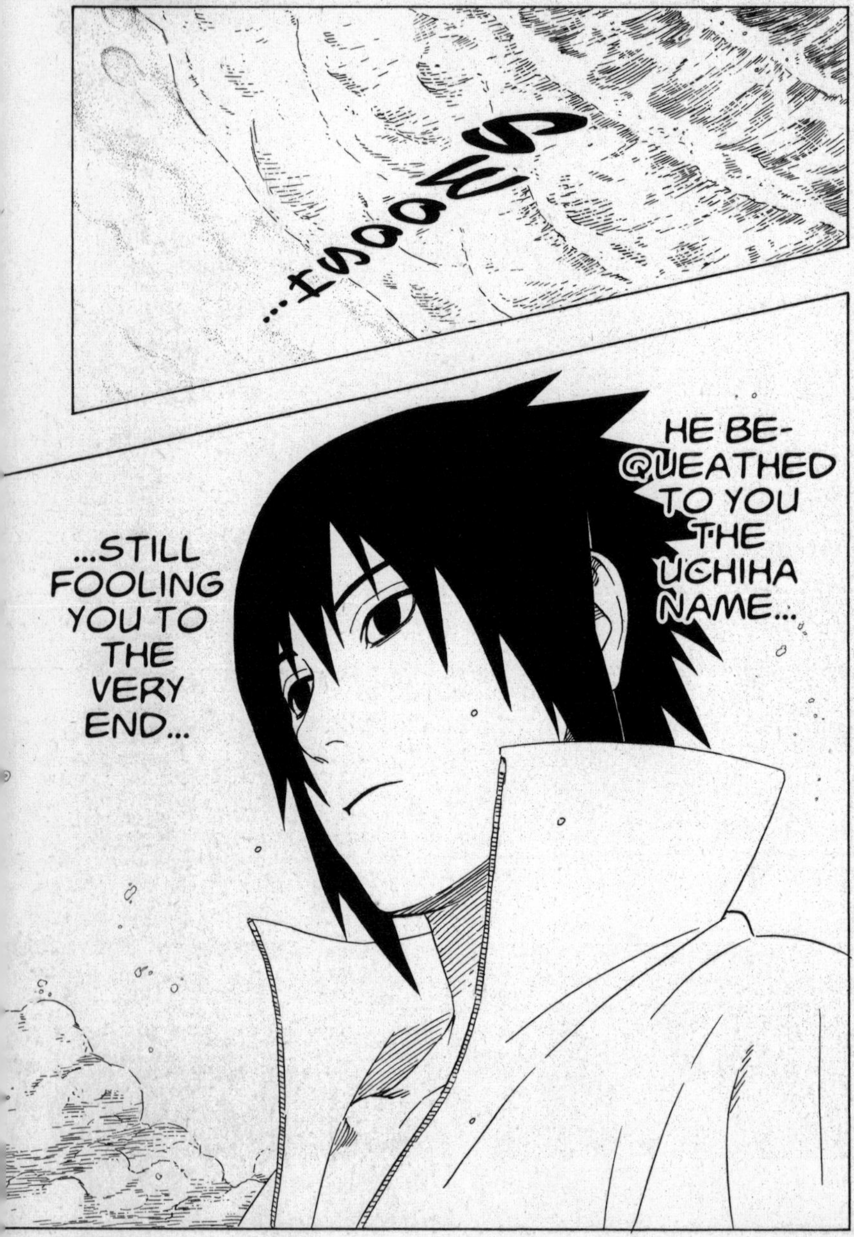
SWOOSH...
HE BEQUEATHED TO YOU THE UCHIHA NAME...
...STILL FOOLING YOU TO THE VERY END...

NARUTO

Number 402: Final Words

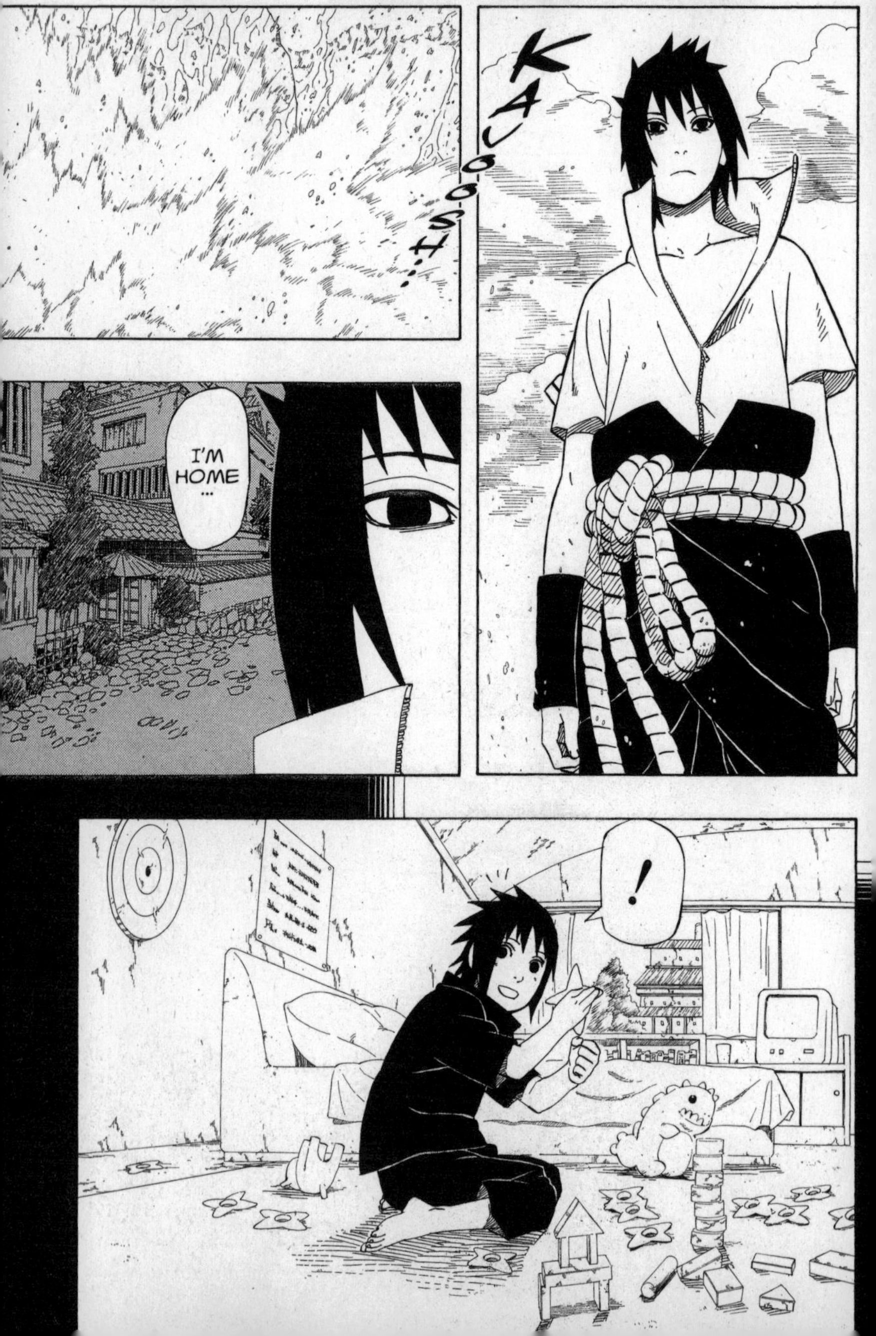
KAJOOOSH...
I'M HOME ...
!

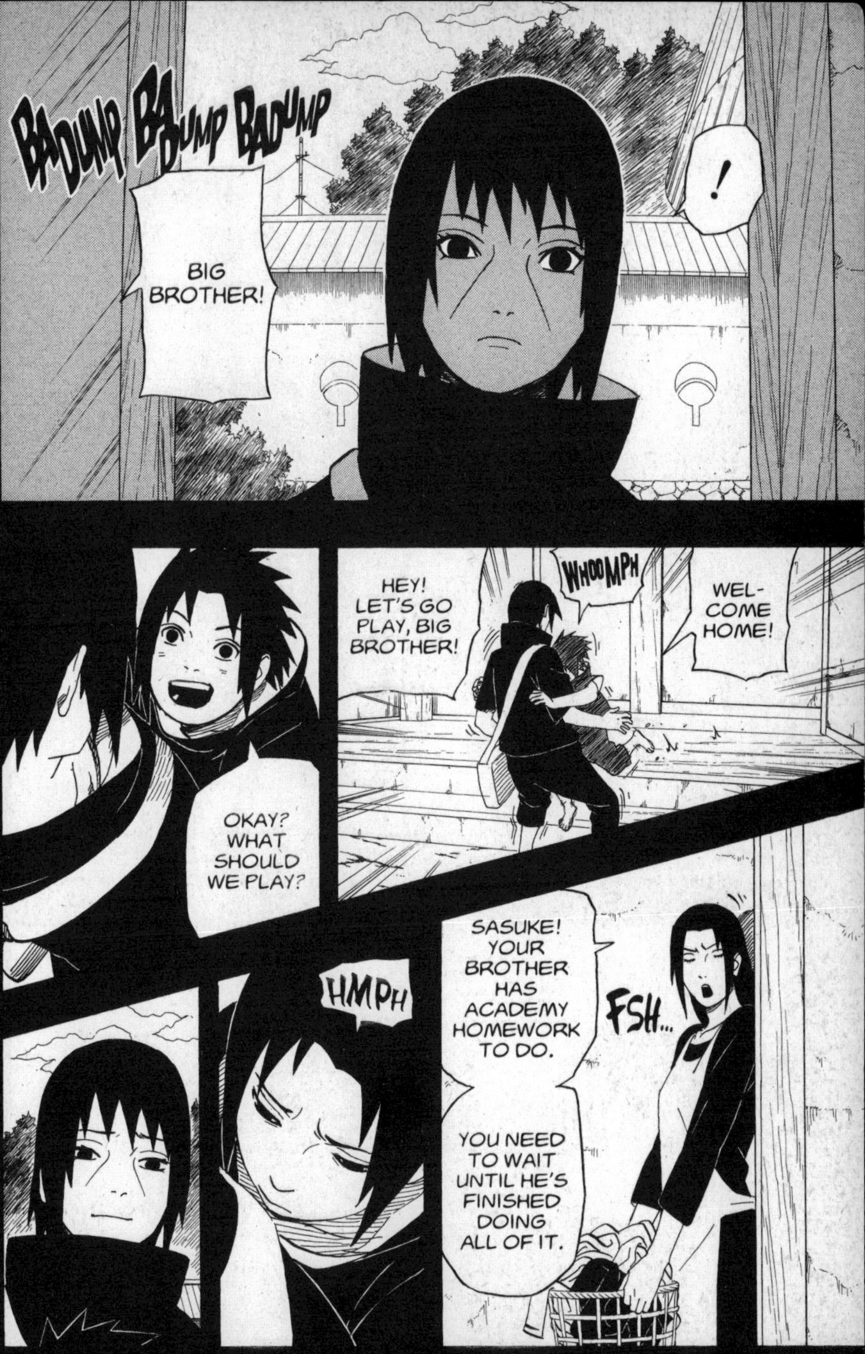
!
BADUMP BADUMP BADUMP
BIG BROTHER!
WEL-COME HOME!
WHOOMPH
HEY! LET'S GO PLAY, BIG BROTHER!
OKAY? WHAT SHOULD WE PLAY?
FSH...
SASUKE! YOUR BROTHER HAS ACADEMY HOMEWORK TO DO.
YOU NEED TO WAIT UNTIL HE'S FINISHED DOING ALL OF IT.
HMPH

READ THIS WAY

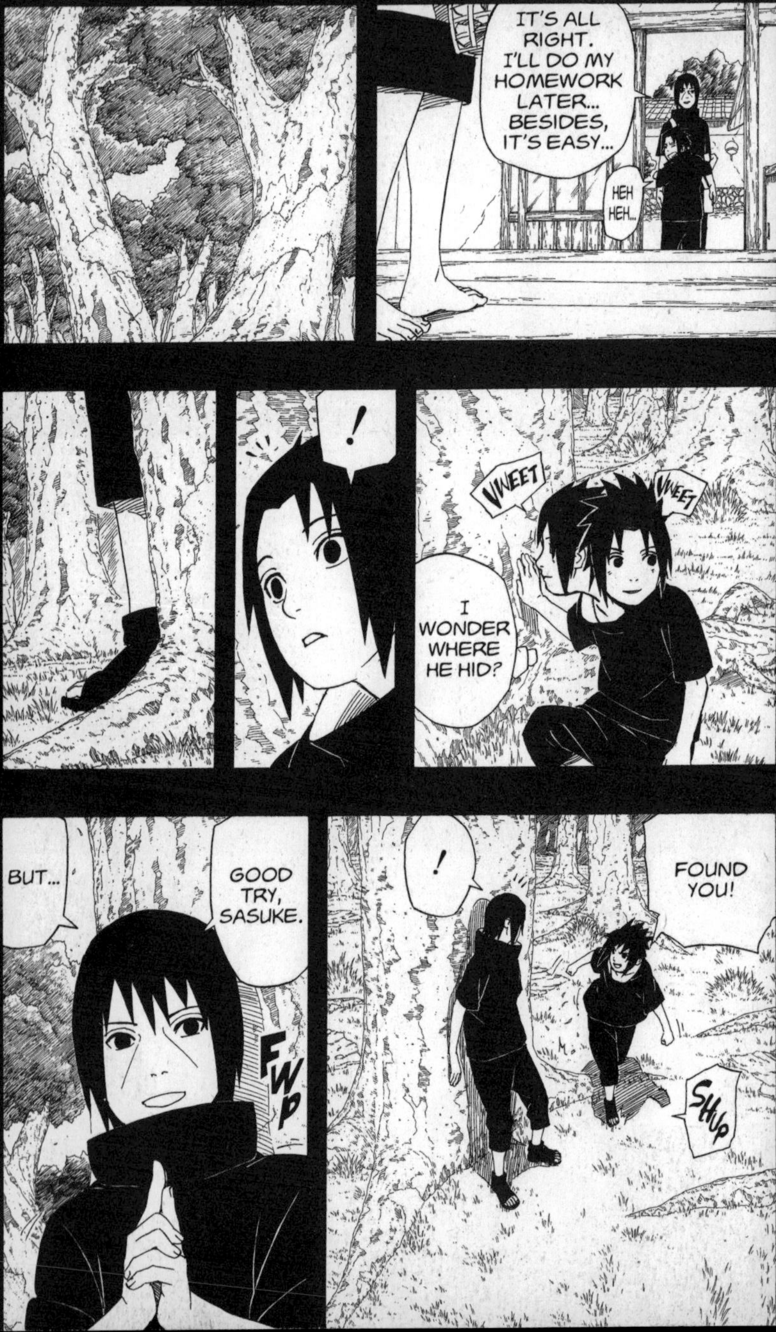
IT'S ALL RIGHT. I'LL DO MY HOMEWORK LATER... BESIDES, IT'S EASY...
HEH HEH...
VWEET
VWEET
I WONDER WHERE HE HID?
!
!
FOUND YOU!
SHUP
GOOD TRY, SASUKE.
BUT...
FWP

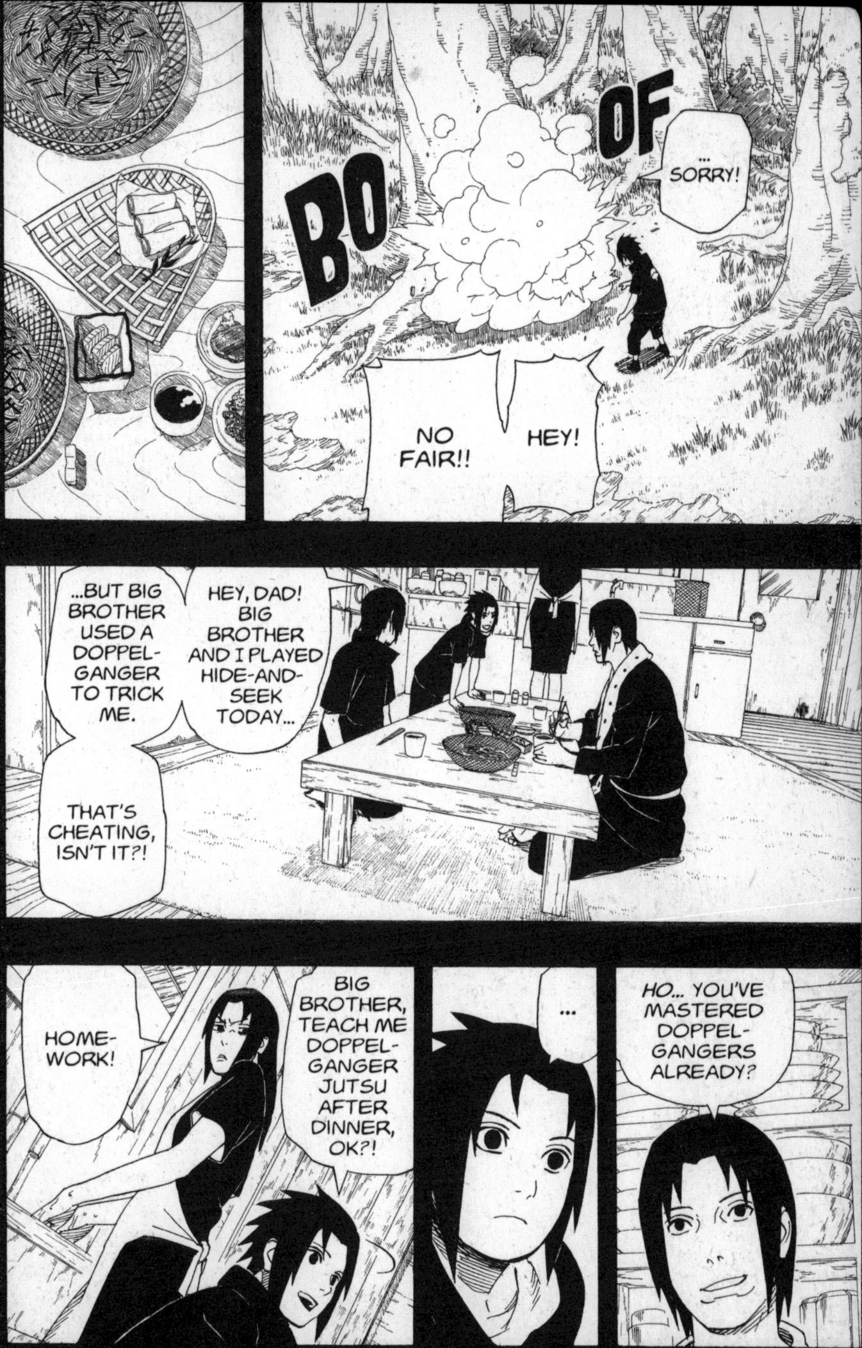
... SORRY!
BOOF
HEY!
NO FAIR!!
HEY, DAD! BIG BROTHER AND I PLAYED HIDE-AND-SEEK TODAY...
...BUT BIG BROTHER USED A DOPPELGANGER TO TRICK ME.
THAT'S CHEATING, ISN'T IT?!
HO... YOU'VE MASTERED DOPPELGANGERS ALREADY?
...
BIG BROTHER, TEACH ME DOPPELGANGER JUTSU AFTER DINNER, OK?!
HOMEWORK!

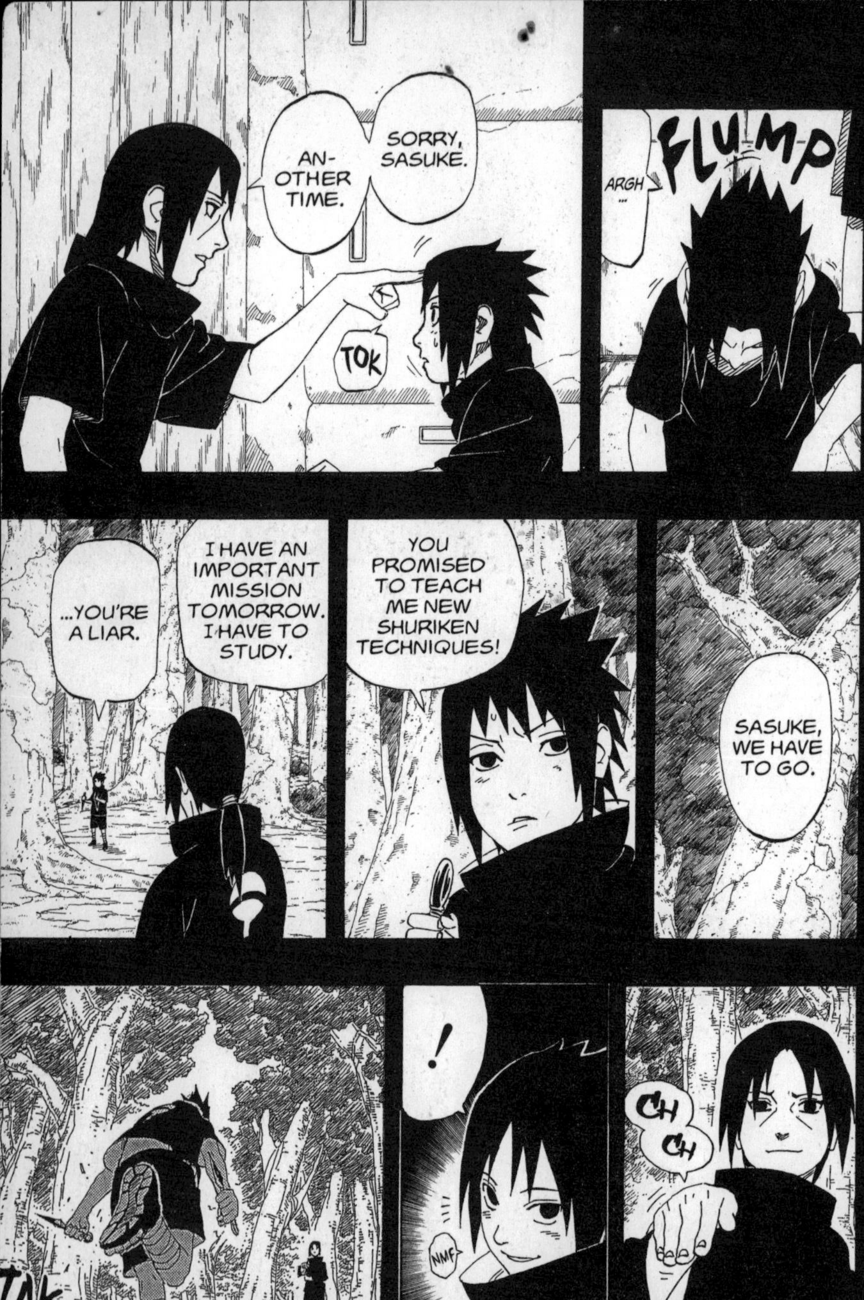

FLUMP
ARGH ...
SORRY, SASUKE.
AN-OTHER TIME.
TOK
SASUKE, WE HAVE TO GO.
YOU PROMISED TO TEACH ME NEW SHURIKEN TECHNIQUES!
I HAVE AN IMPORTANT MISSION TOMORROW. I HAVE TO STUDY.
...YOU'RE A LIAR.
CH
CH
!
NMF
TAK

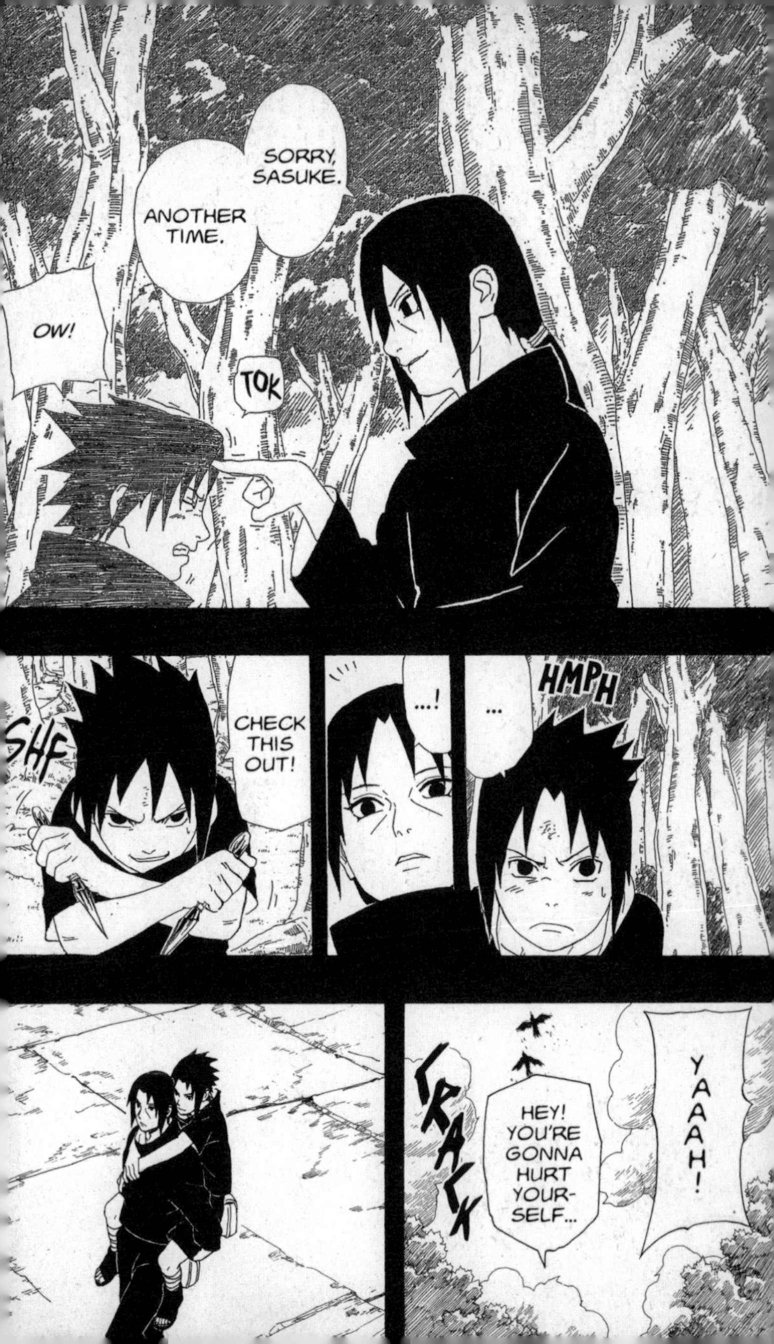
SORRY, SASUKE.
ANOTHER TIME.
TOK
OW!
HMPH
...
...!
CHECK THIS OUT!
SHF
YAAAH!
HEY! YOU'RE GONNA HURT YOUR-SELF...
CRACK

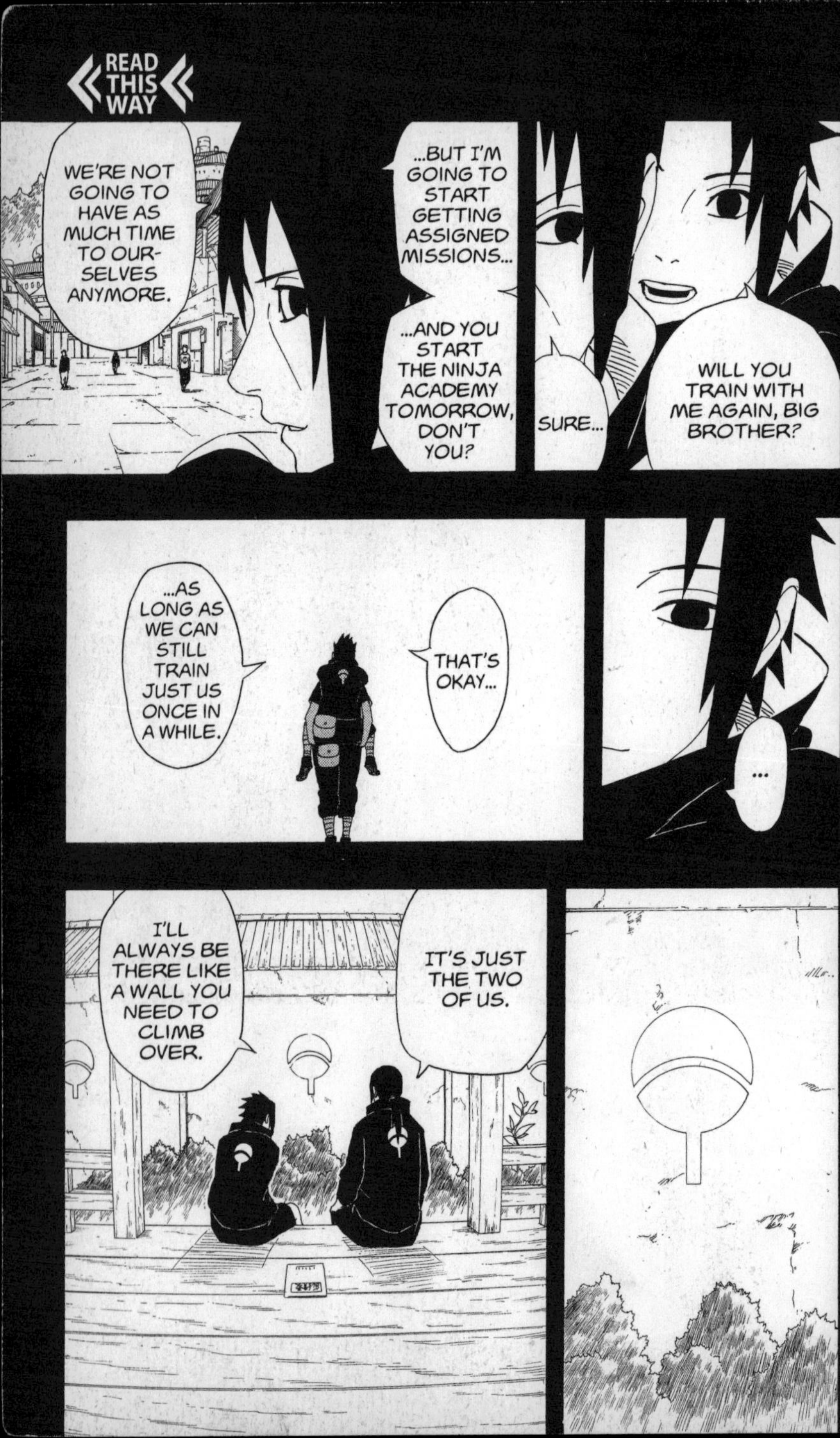
READ THIS WAY
WILL YOU TRAIN WITH ME AGAIN, BIG BROTHER?
SURE...
...BUT I'M GOING TO START GETTING ASSIGNED MISSIONS...
...AND YOU START THE NINJA ACADEMY TOMORROW, DON'T YOU?
WE'RE NOT GOING TO HAVE AS MUCH TIME TO OUR-SELVES ANYMORE.
...
THAT'S OKAY...
...AS LONG AS WE CAN STILL TRAIN JUST US ONCE IN A WHILE.
IT'S JUST THE TWO OF US.
I'LL ALWAYS BE THERE LIKE A WALL YOU NEED TO CLIMB OVER.

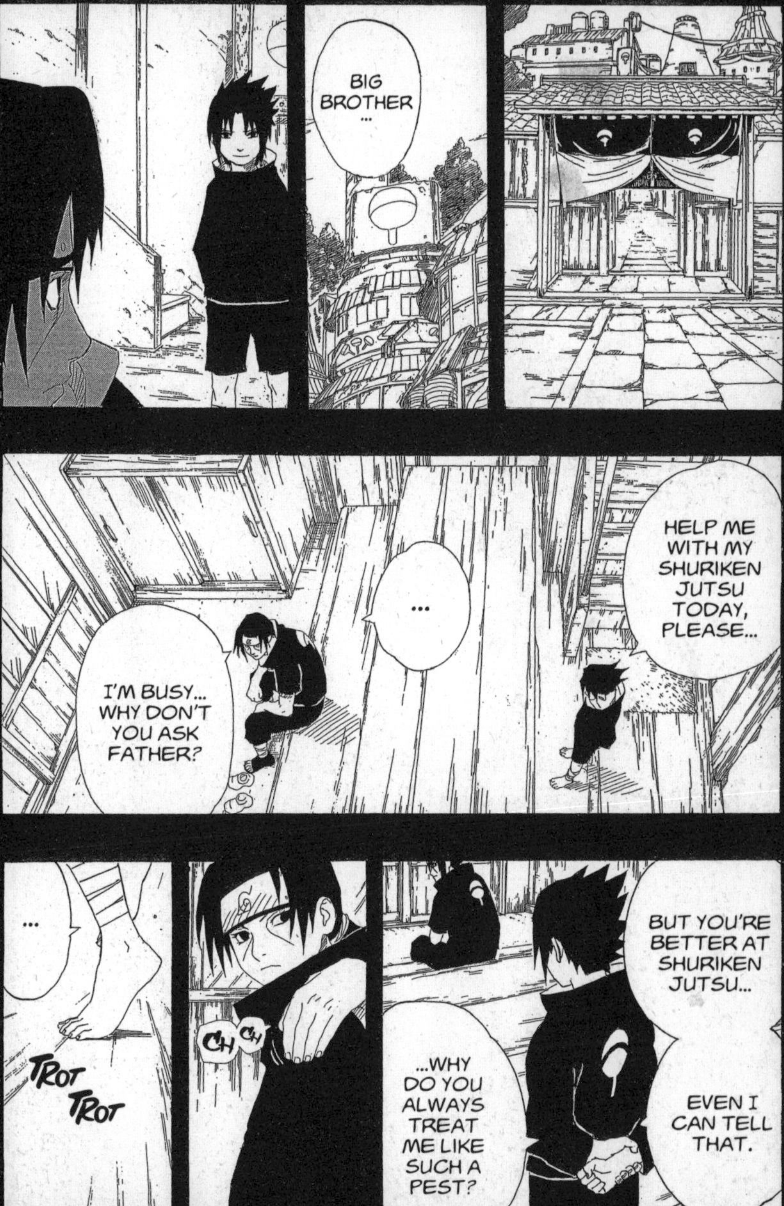
BIG BROTHER ...
HELP ME WITH MY SHURIKEN JUTSU TODAY, PLEASE...
...
I'M BUSY... WHY DON'T YOU ASK FATHER?
BUT YOU'RE BETTER AT SHURIKEN JUTSU...
EVEN I CAN TELL THAT.
...WHY DO YOU ALWAYS TREAT ME LIKE SUCH A PEST?
CH CH
...
TROT TROT

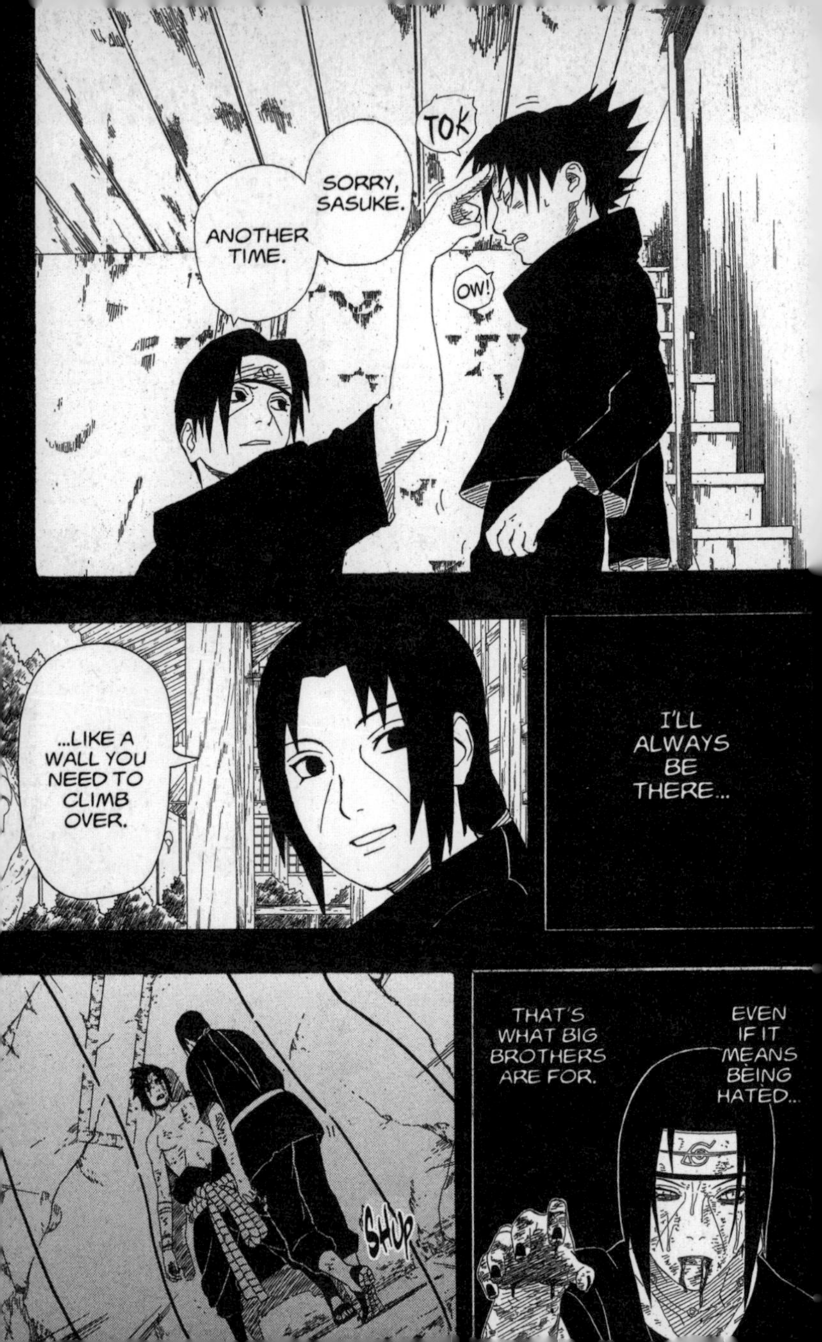
TOK
SORRY, SASUKE.
ANOTHER TIME.
OW!
I'LL ALWAYS BE THERE...
...LIKE A WALL YOU NEED TO CLIMB OVER.
EVEN IF IT MEANS BEING HATED...
THAT'S WHAT BIG BROTHERS ARE FOR.
SHUP

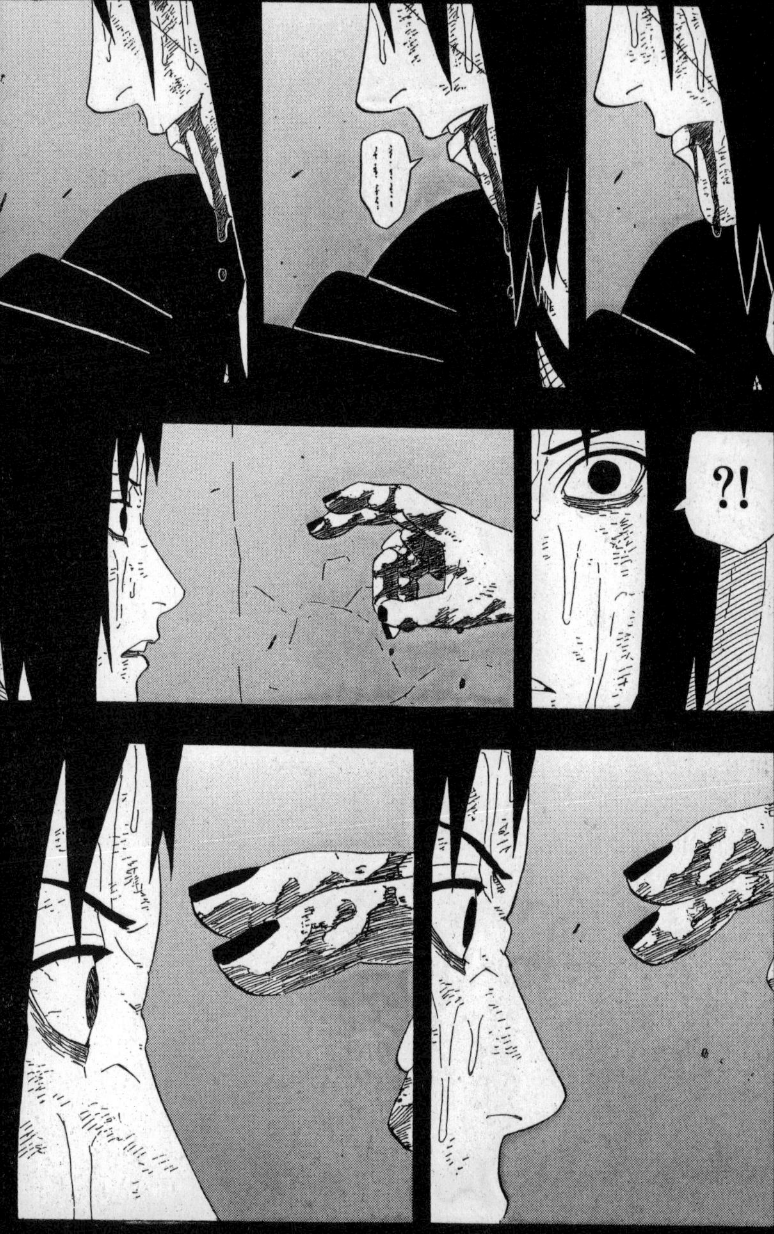
......
?!

READ THIS WAY

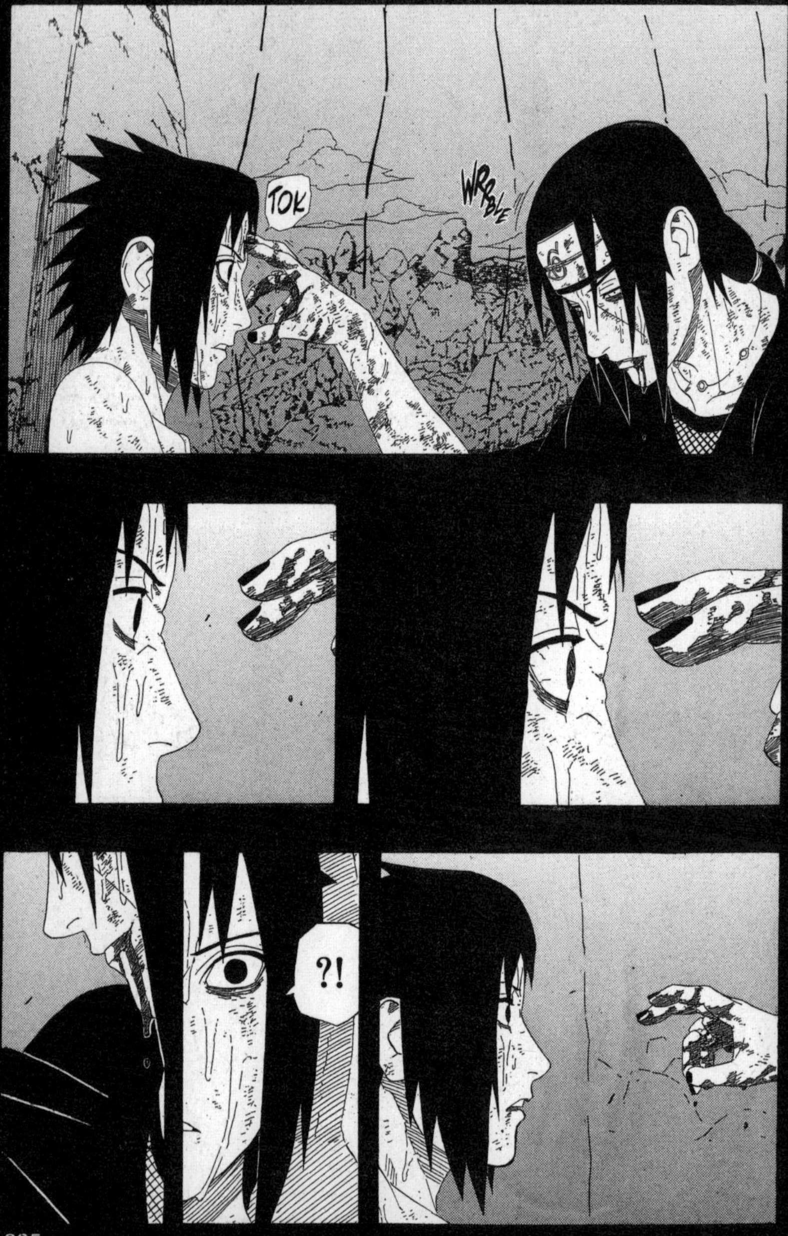
WRBBLE
TOK
?!

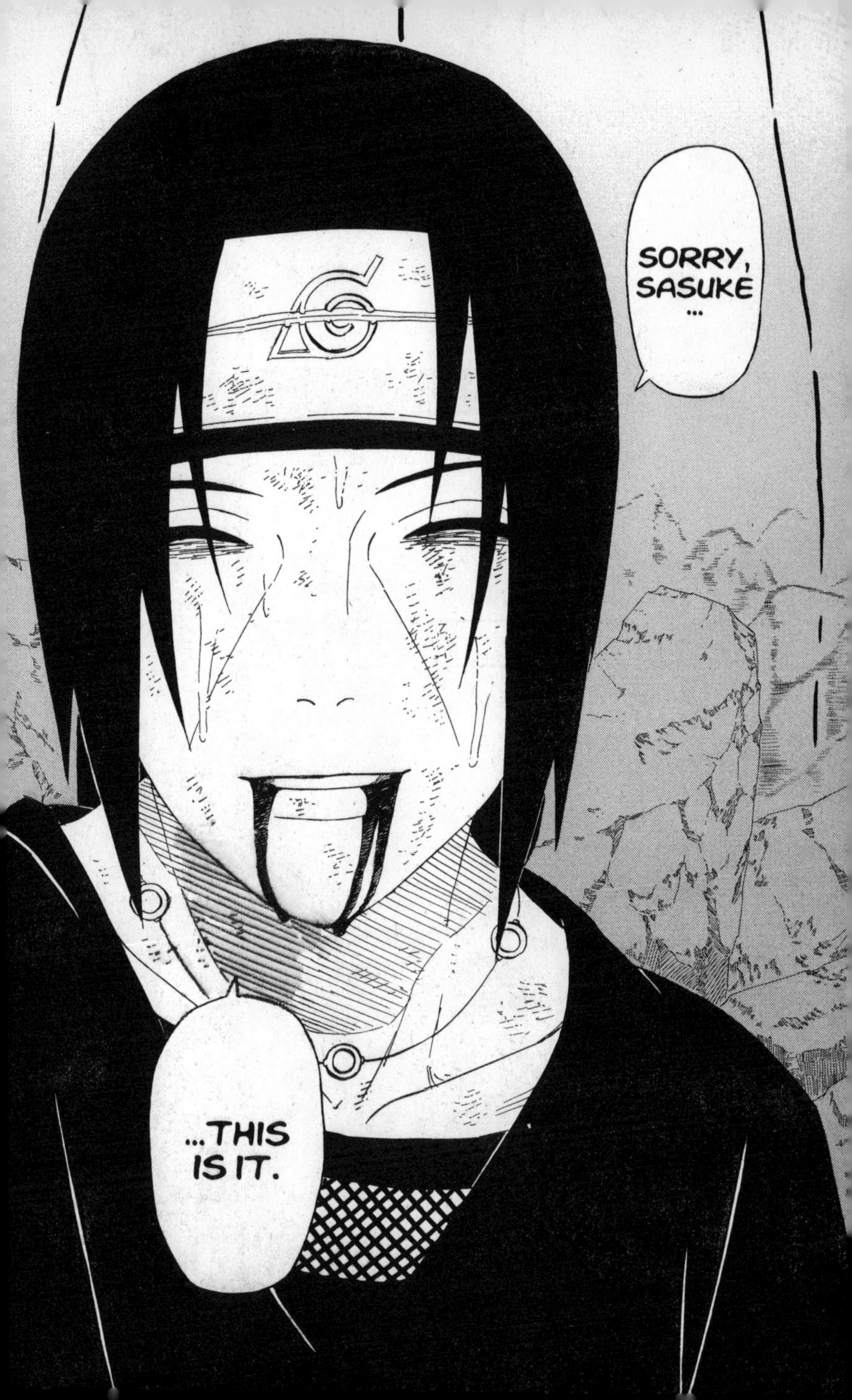
SORRY, SASUKE ...
...THIS IS IT.

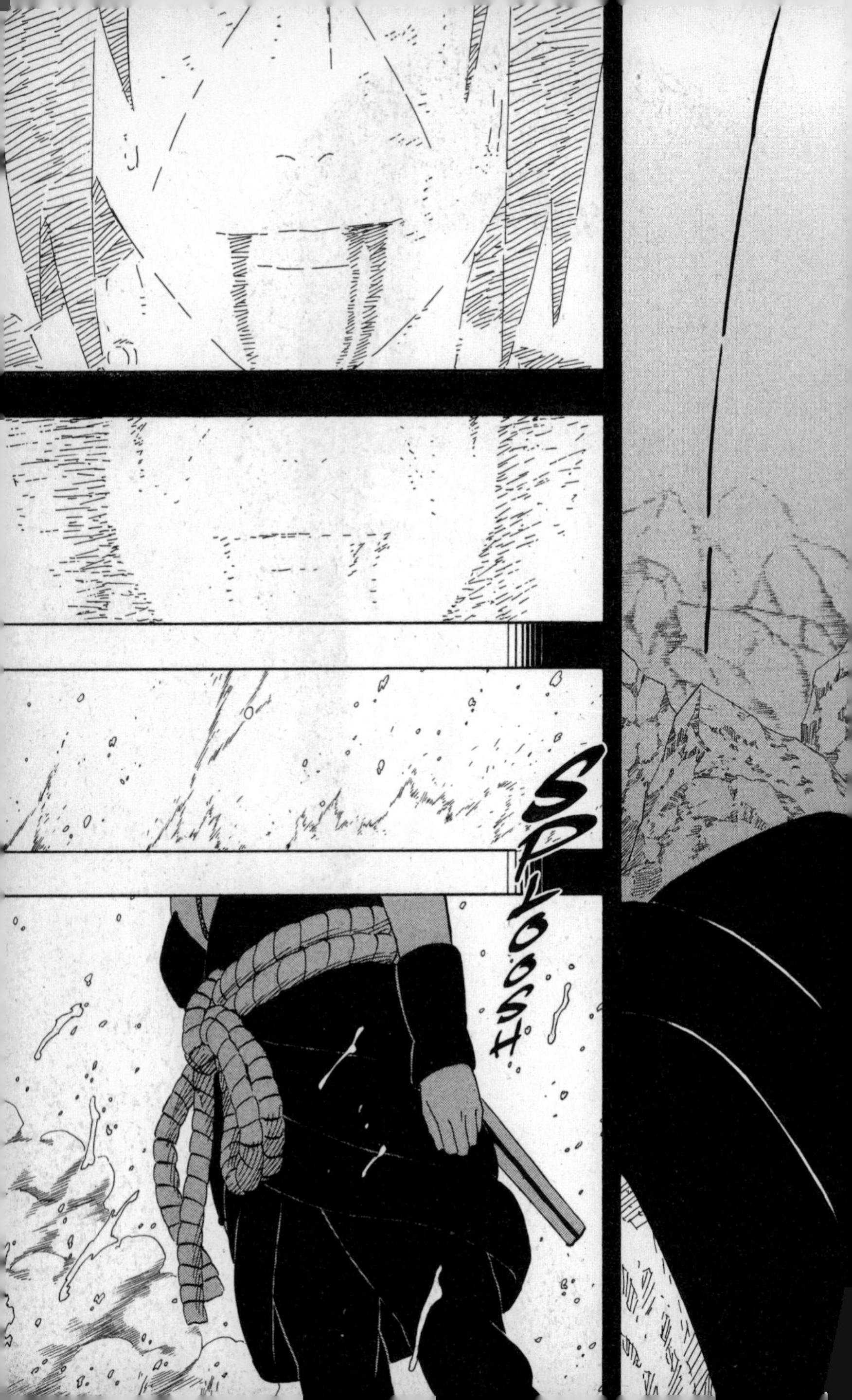
SPLOOSH

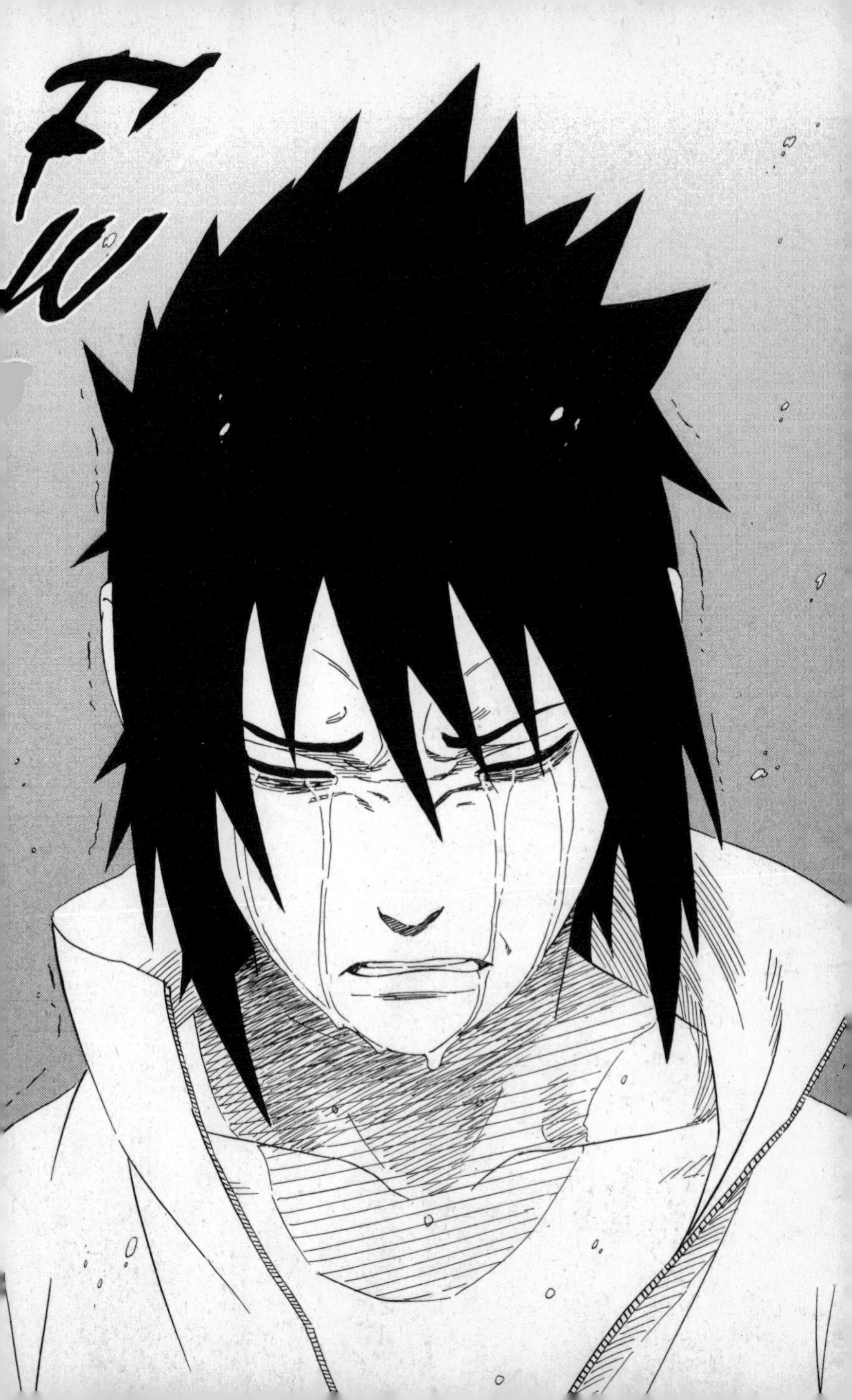

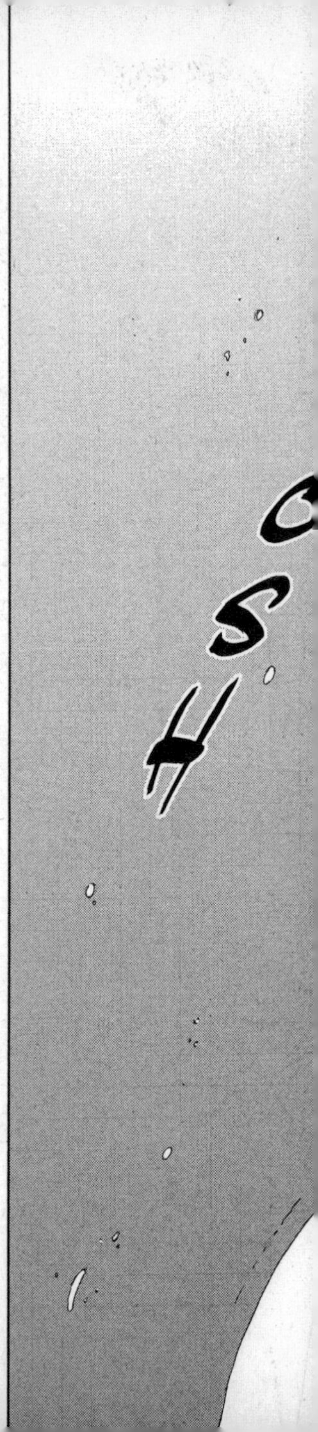
OSH

READ THIS WAY

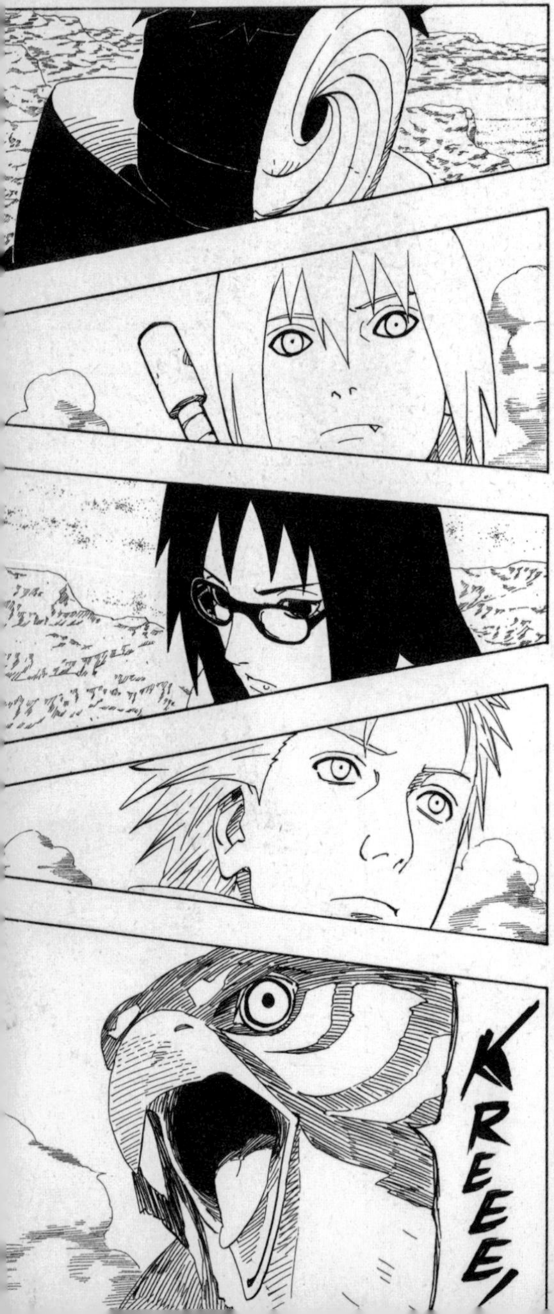
KREEE!

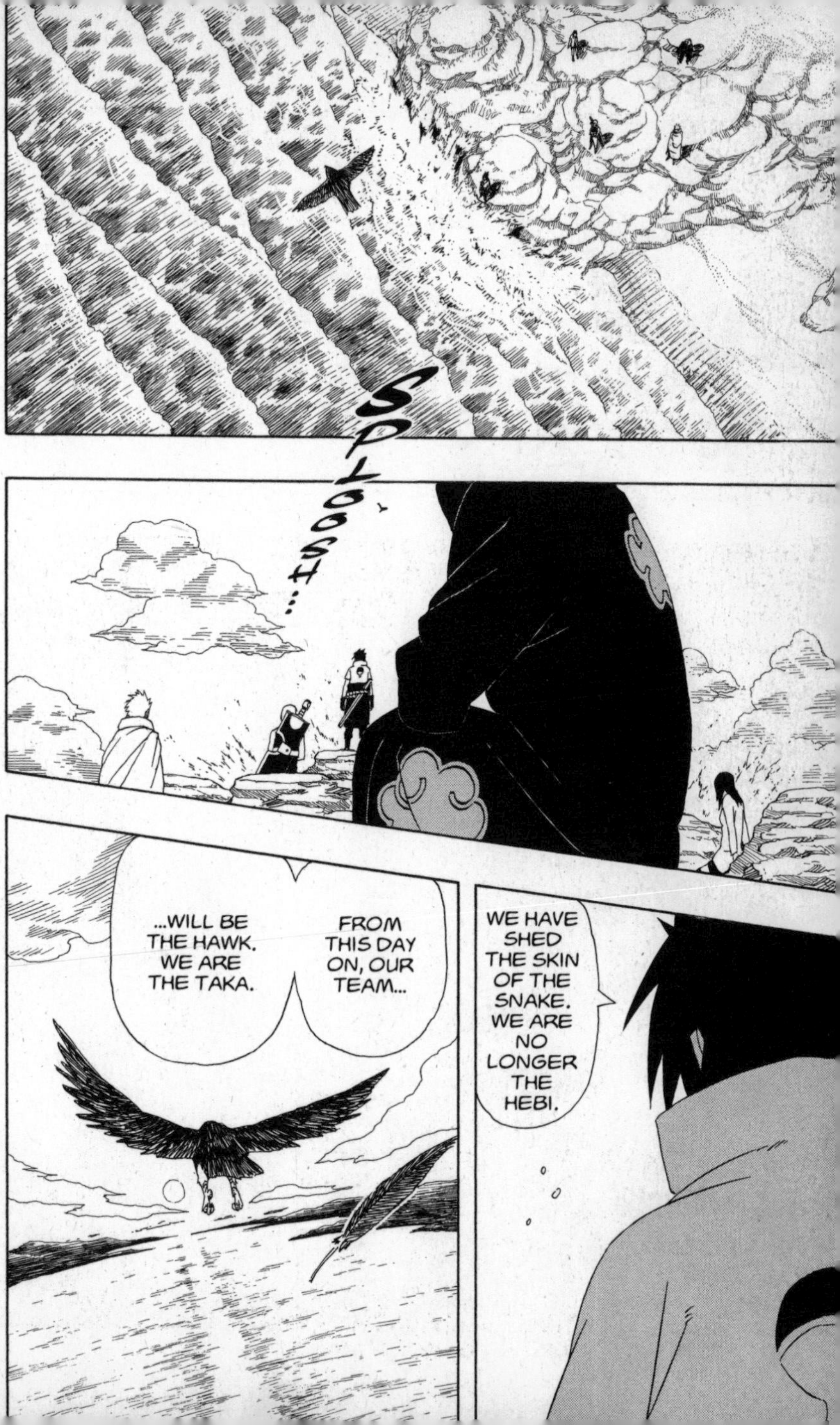
SPLOOSH...
WE HAVE SHED THE SKIN OF THE SNAKE. WE ARE NO LONGER THE HEBI.
FROM THIS DAY ON, OUR TEAM...
...WILL BE THE HAWK. WE ARE THE TAKA.

READ THIS WAY

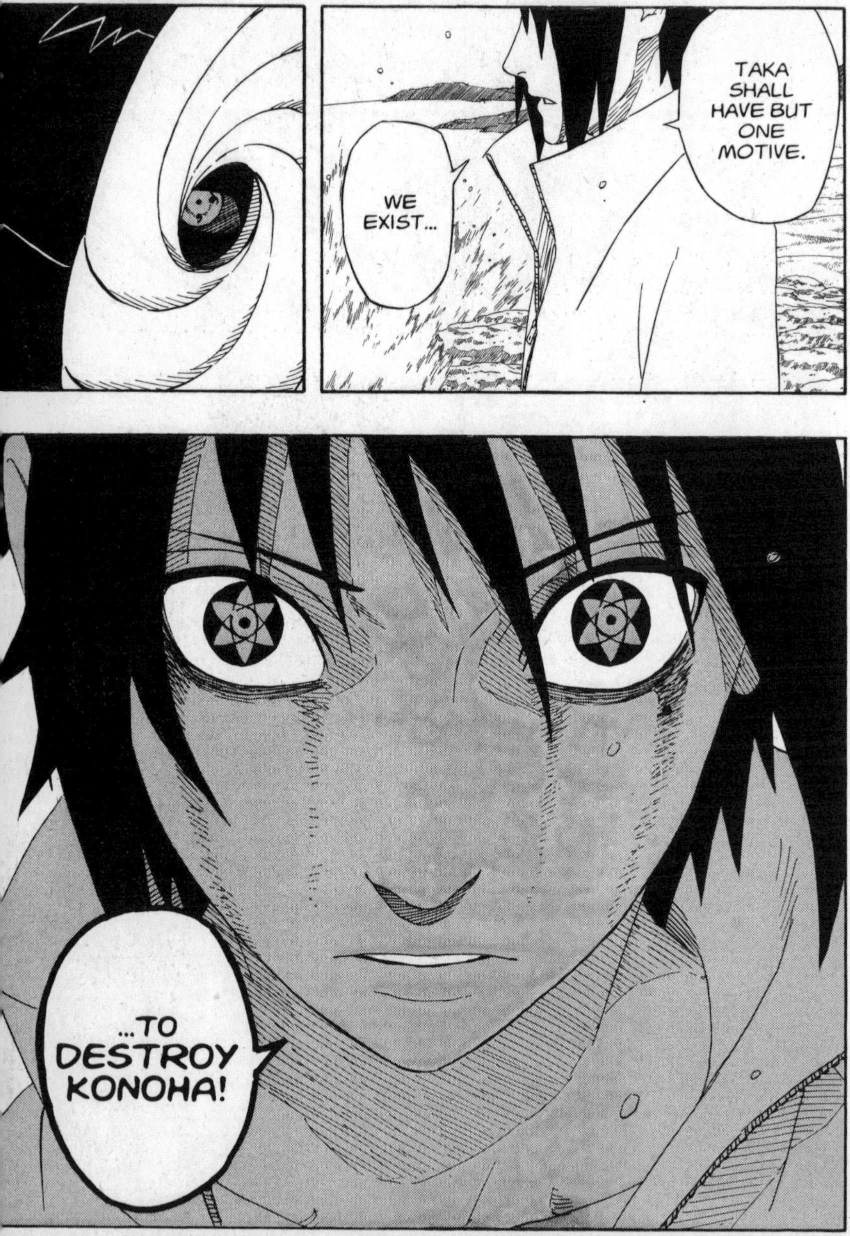

TAKA SHALL HAVE BUT ONE MOTIVE.
WE EXIST...
...TO DESTROY KONOHA!

 TO BE CONTINUED IN *NARUTO* VOLUME 44!

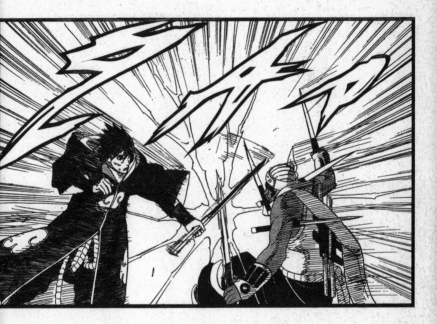

IN THE NEXT VOLUME...

INHERITANCE

Naruto must decipher the cryptic last words of his beloved mentor. What did Jiraiya find out about the leader of the Akatsuki that was so important he had to hide it in code? And does Naruto stand a fighting chance against those who managed to take down one of the Three Great Shinobi?

AVAILABLE NOW!

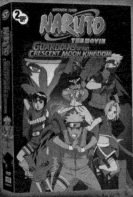
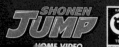

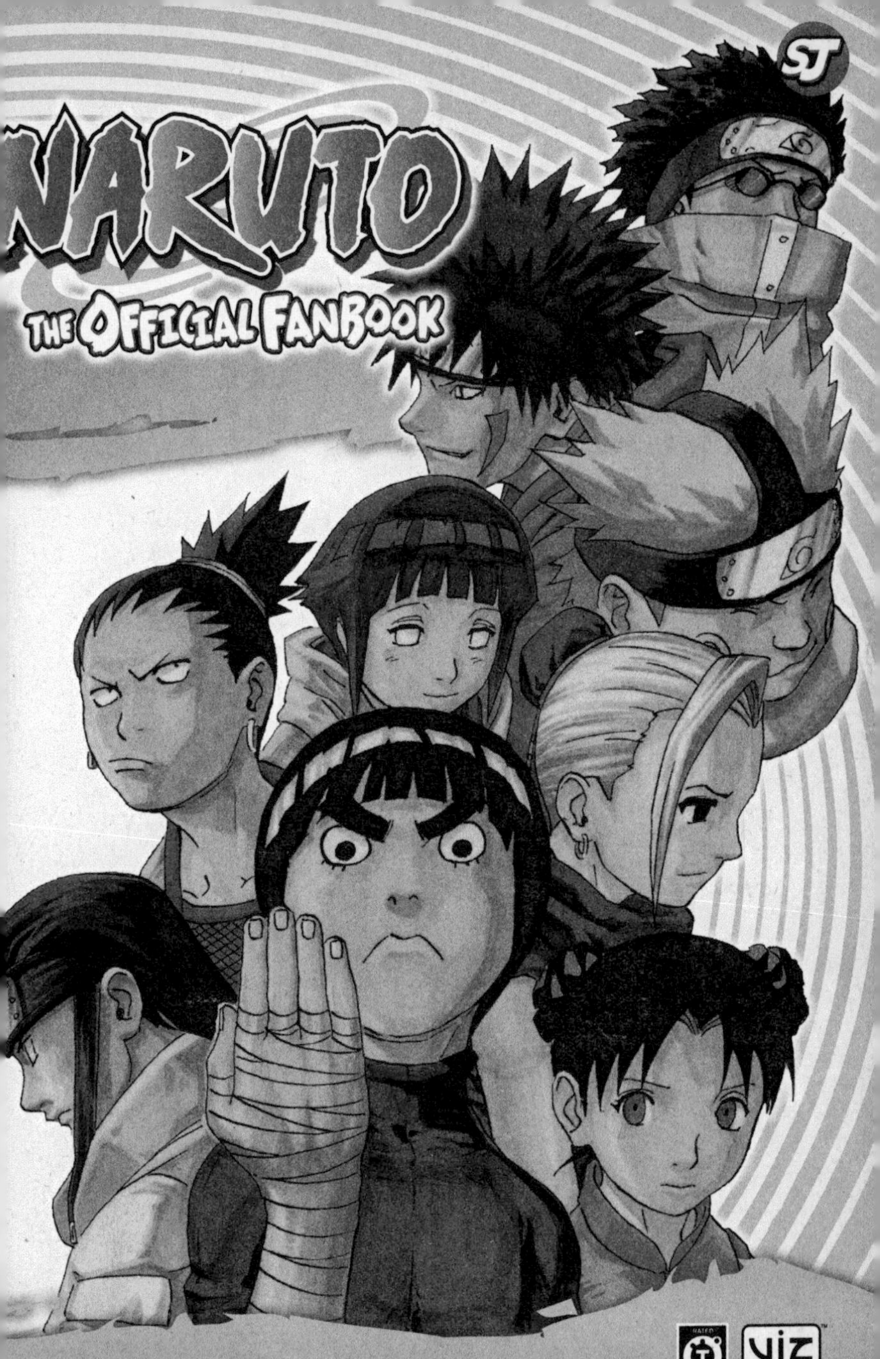
SJ
NARUTO
THE OFFICIAL FANBOOK

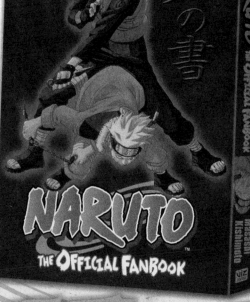
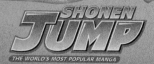

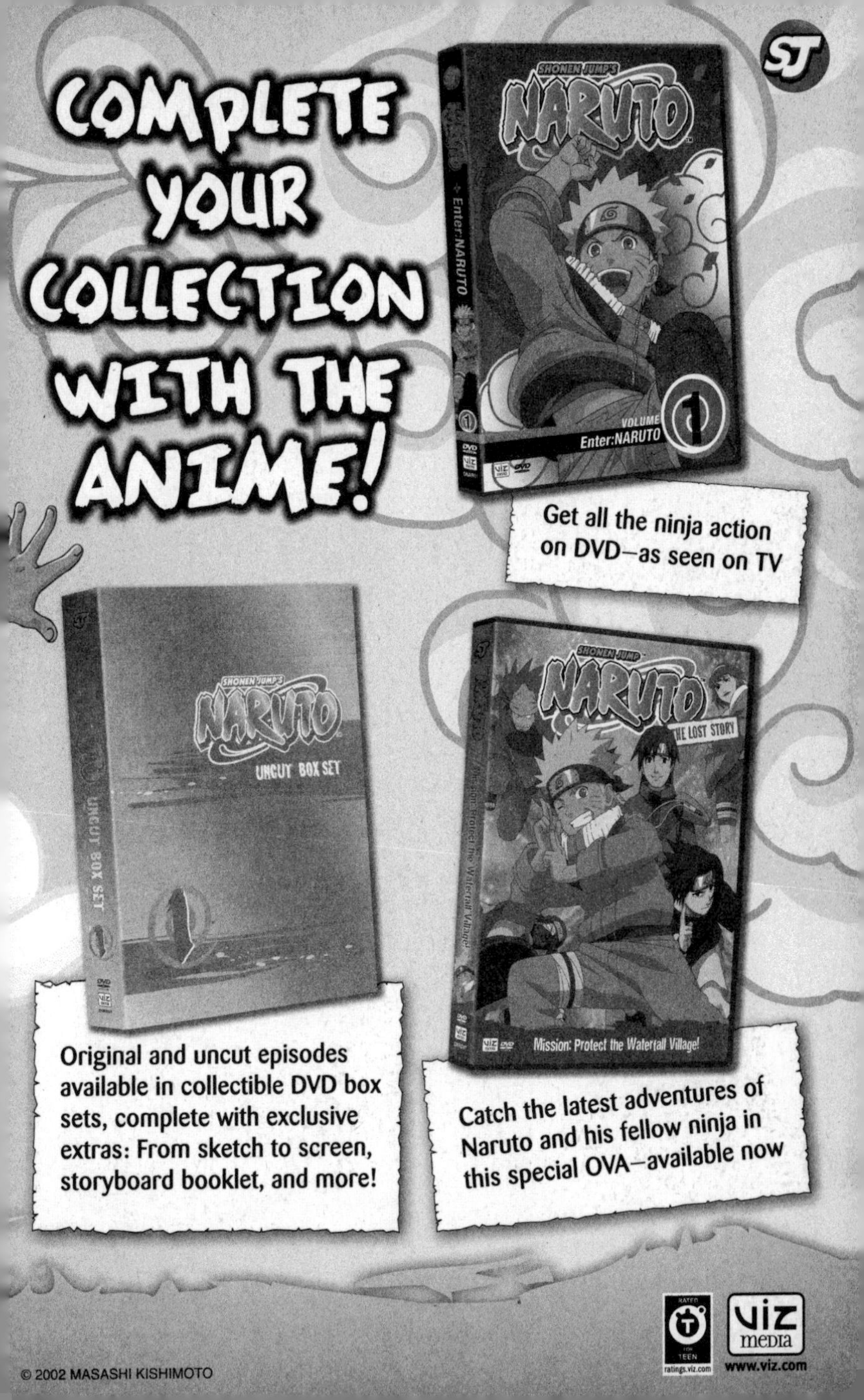
COMPLETE YOUR COLLECTION WITH THE ANIME!
SHONEN JUMP'S NARUTO
VOLUME 1
Enter:NARUTO
Get all the ninja action on DVD—as seen on TV
SHONEN JUMP'S NARUTO
UNCUT BOX SET
SHONEN JUMP NARUTO
THE LOST STORY
Mission: Protect the Waterfall Village!
Original and uncut episodes available in collectible DVD box sets, complete with exclusive extras: From sketch to screen, storyboard booklet, and more!
Catch the latest adventures of Naruto and his fellow ninja in this special OVA—available now
RATED T FOR TEEN
ratings.viz.com
VIZ media
www.viz.com
© 2002 MASASHI KISHIMOTO

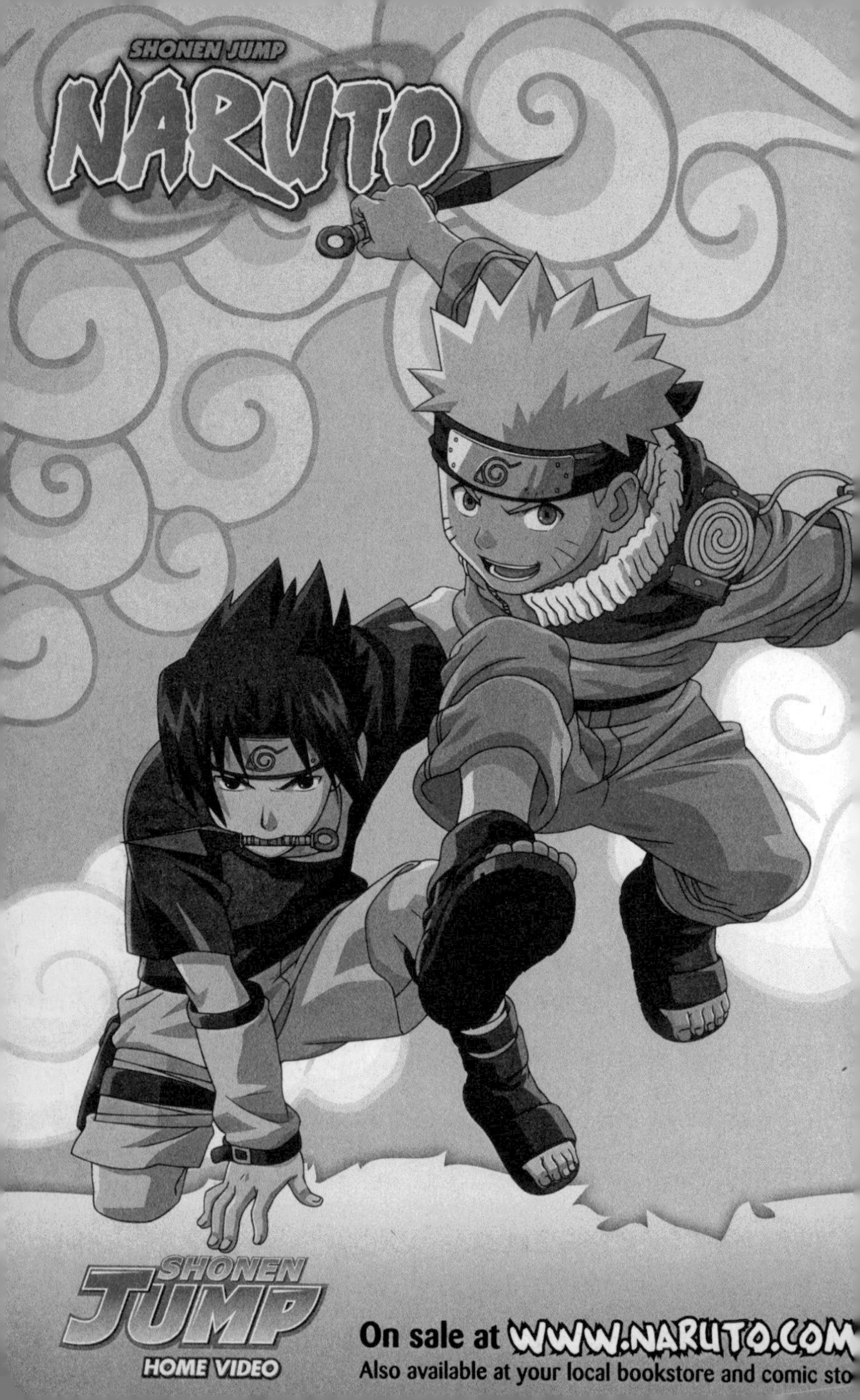
SHONEN JUMP
NARUTO
SHONEN JUMP
HOME VIDEO
On sale at WWW.NARUTO.COM
Also available at your local bookstore and comic sto

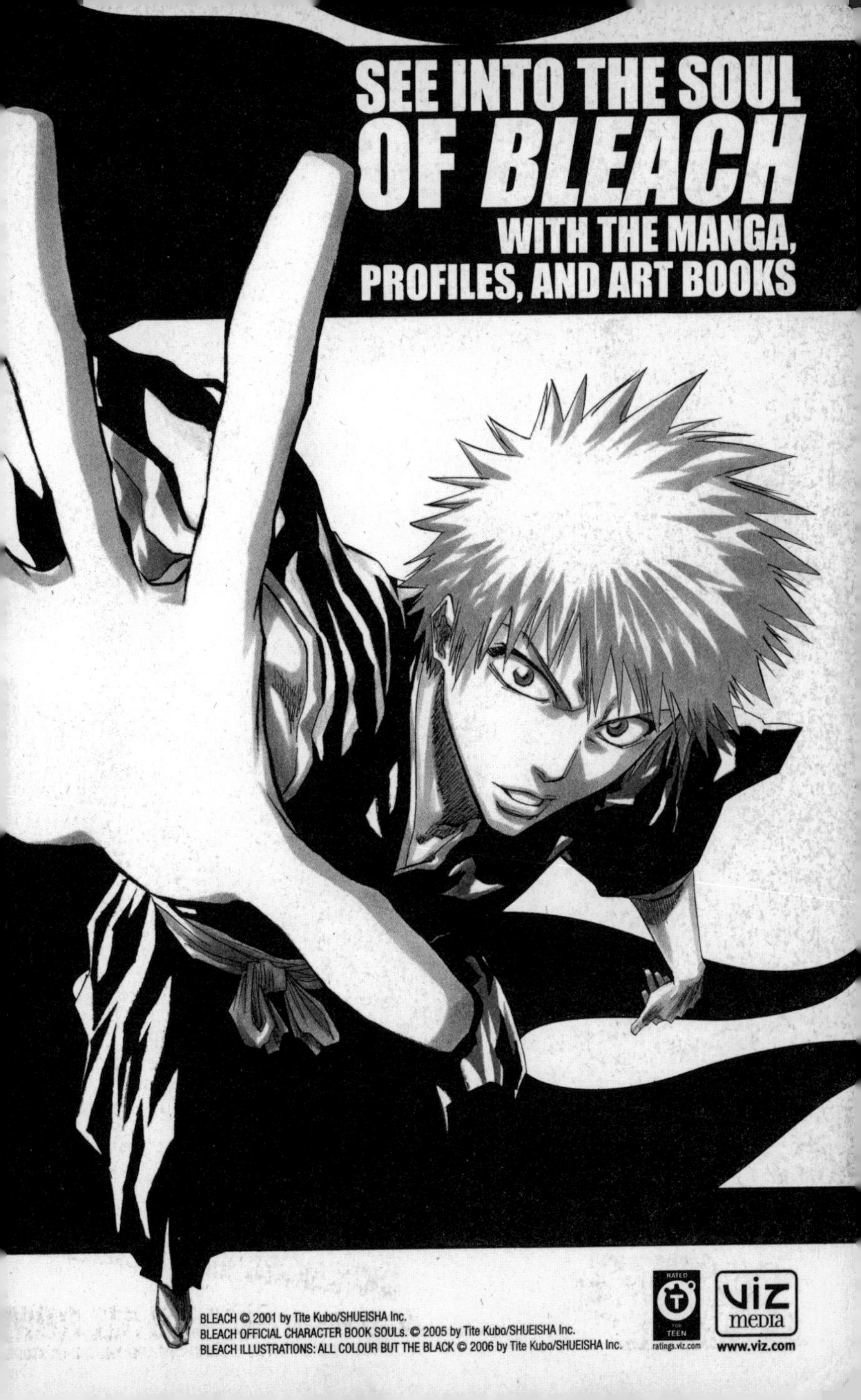
SEE INTO THE SOUL
OF BLEACH
WITH THE MANGA,
PROFILES, AND ART BOOKS
BLEACH © 2001 by Tite Kubo/SHUEISHA Inc.
BLEACH OFFICIAL CHARACTER BOOK SOULs. © 2005 by Tite Kubo/SHUEISHA Inc.
BLEACH ILLUSTRATIONS: ALL COLOUR BUT THE BLACK © 2006 by Tite Kubo/SHUEISHA Inc.
RATED T FOR TEEN
ratings.viz.com
viz media
www.viz.com

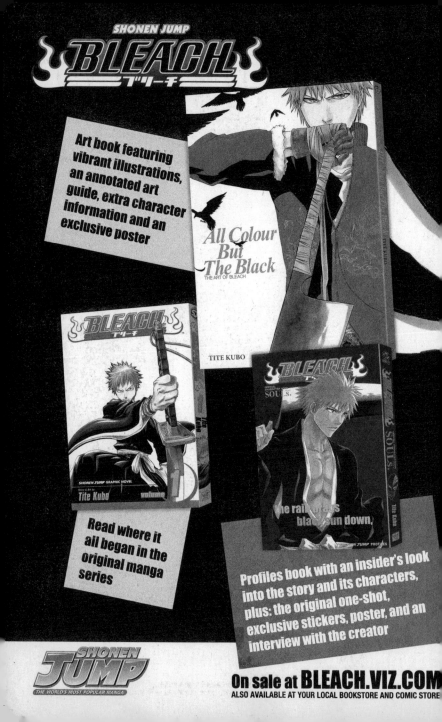

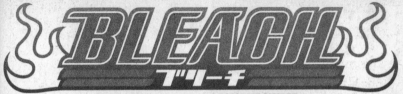

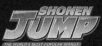

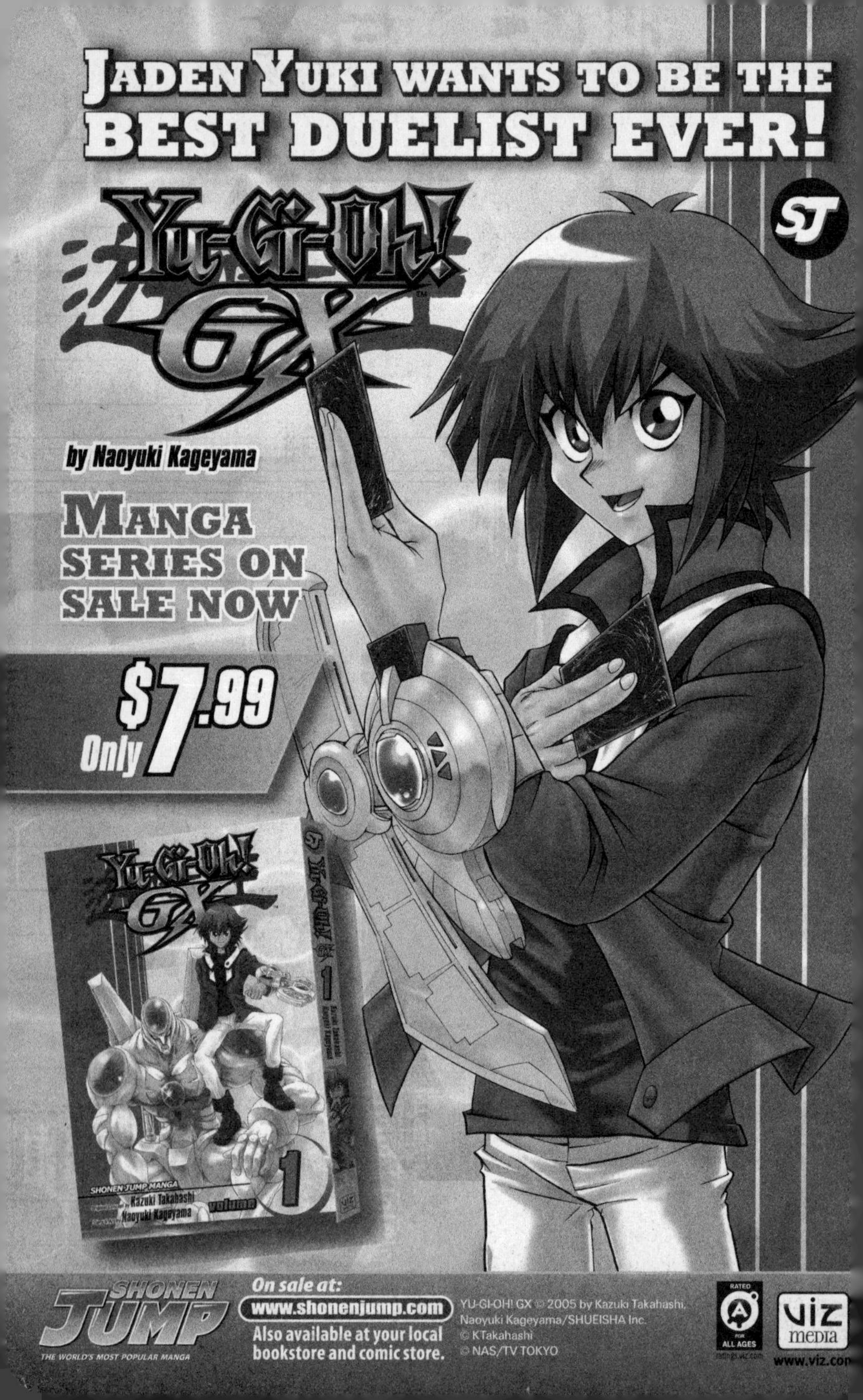
JADEN YUKI WANTS TO BE THE
BEST DUELIST EVER!
SJ
YU-GI-OH! GX™
by Naoyuki Kageyama
MANGA
SERIES ON
SALE NOW
Only $7.99
YU-GI-OH! GX
SJ YU-GI-OH! GX 1
SHONEN JUMP MANGA
Kazuki Takahashi
Naoyuki Kageyama
volume 1
SHONEN JUMP
THE WORLD'S MOST POPULAR MANGA
On sale at:
www.shonenjump.com
Also available at your local
bookstore and comic store.
YU-GI-OH! GX © 2005 by Kazuki Takahashi,
Naoyuki Kageyama/SHUEISHA Inc.
© KTakahashi
© NAS/TV TOKYO
RATED A FOR ALL AGES
VIZ media
www.viz.com

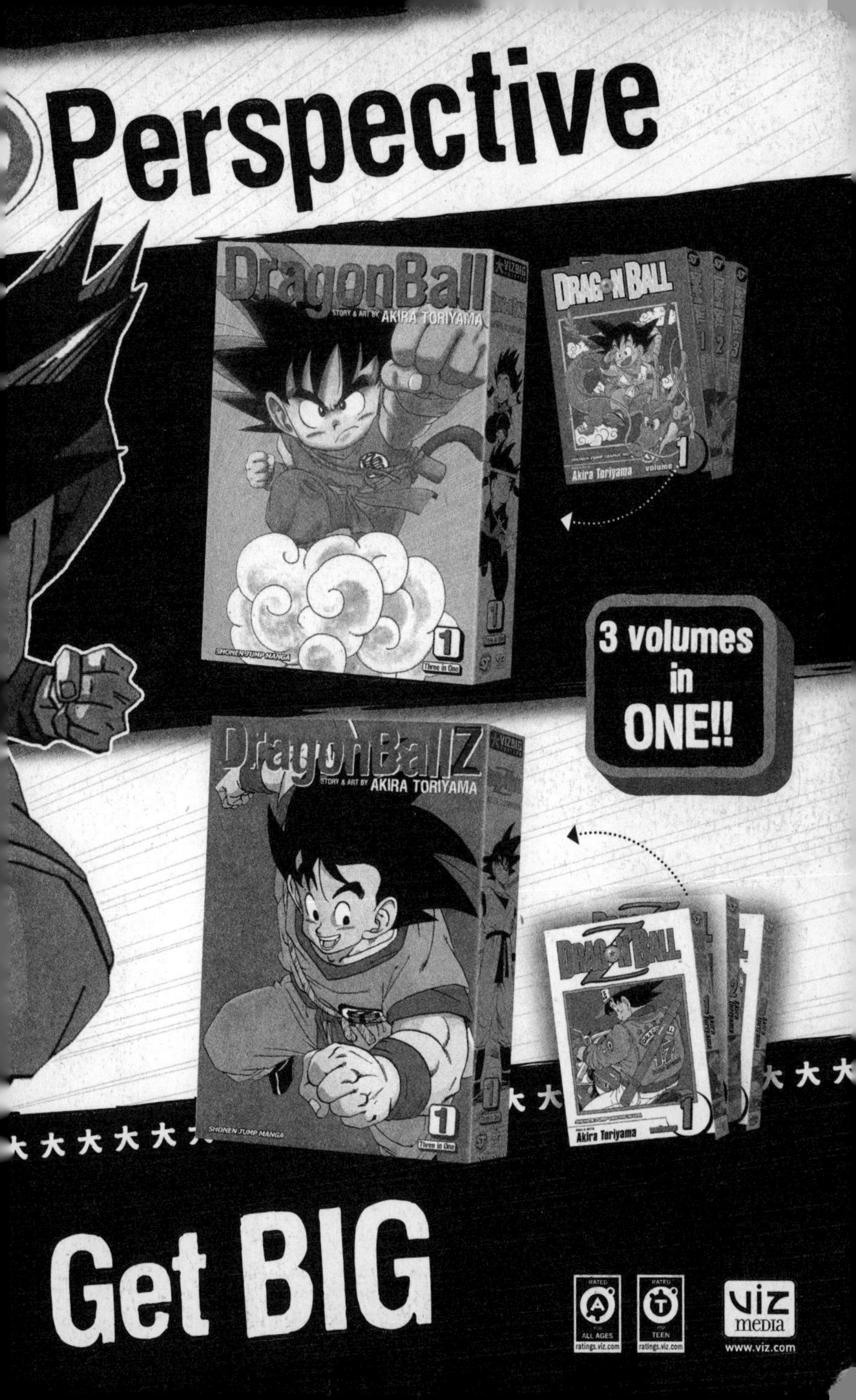
Perspective
DragonBall
STORY & ART BY AKIRA TORIYAMA
SHONEN JUMP MANGA
1
Three in One
DRAGON BALL
Akira Toriyama
volume 1
3 volumes in ONE!!
DragonBall Z
STORY & ART BY AKIRA TORIYAMA
SHONEN JUMP MANGA
1
Three in One
DRAGON BALL Z
Akira Toriyama
Get BIG
RATED A FOR ALL AGES
ratings.viz.com
RATED T FOR TEEN
ratings.viz.com
viz media
www.viz.com

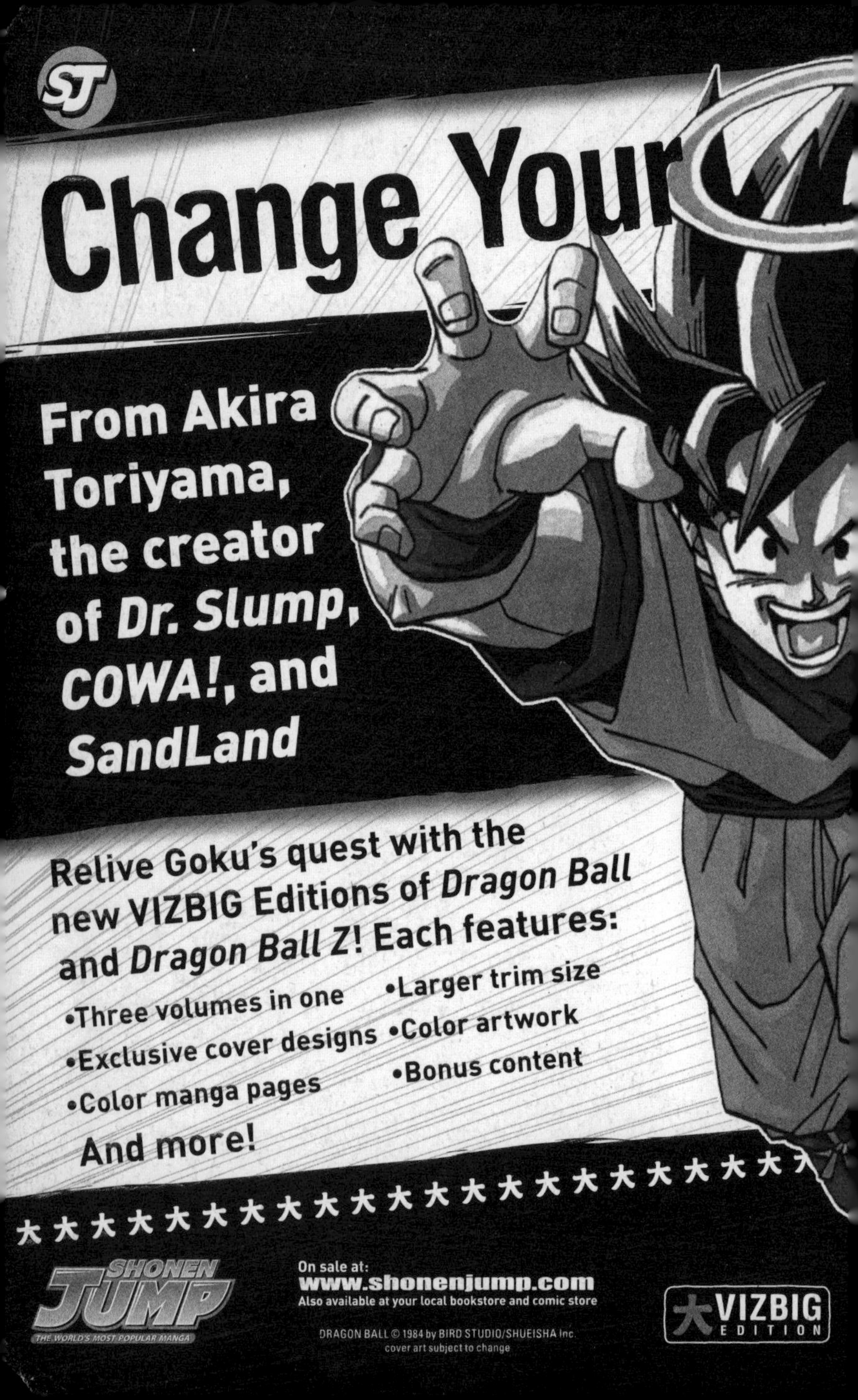
SJ
Change Your
From Akira Toriyama, the creator of Dr. Slump, COWA!, and SandLand
Relive Goku's quest with the new VIZBIG Editions of Dragon Ball and Dragon Ball Z! Each features:
•Three volumes in one
•Exclusive cover designs
•Color manga pages
•Larger trim size
•Color artwork
•Bonus content
And more!
SHONEN JUMP
THE WORLD'S MOST POPULAR MANGA
On sale at:
www.shonenjump.com
Also available at your local bookstore and comic store
DRAGON BALL © 1984 by BIRD STUDIO/SHUEISHA Inc.
cover art subject to change
大 VIZBIG EDITION

Tell us what you think about SHONEN JUMP manga!

Our survey is now available online.
Go to: www.SHONENJUMP.com/mangasurvey

Help us make our product offering better!

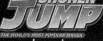

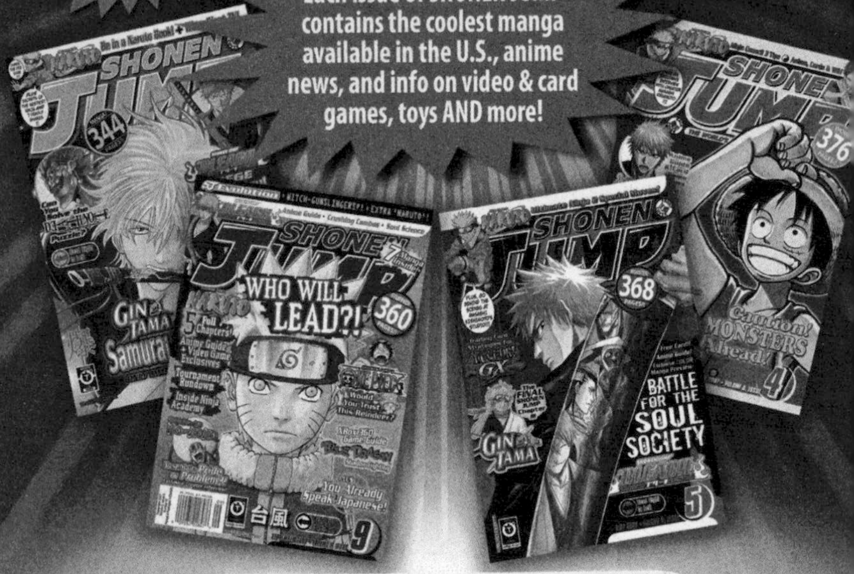

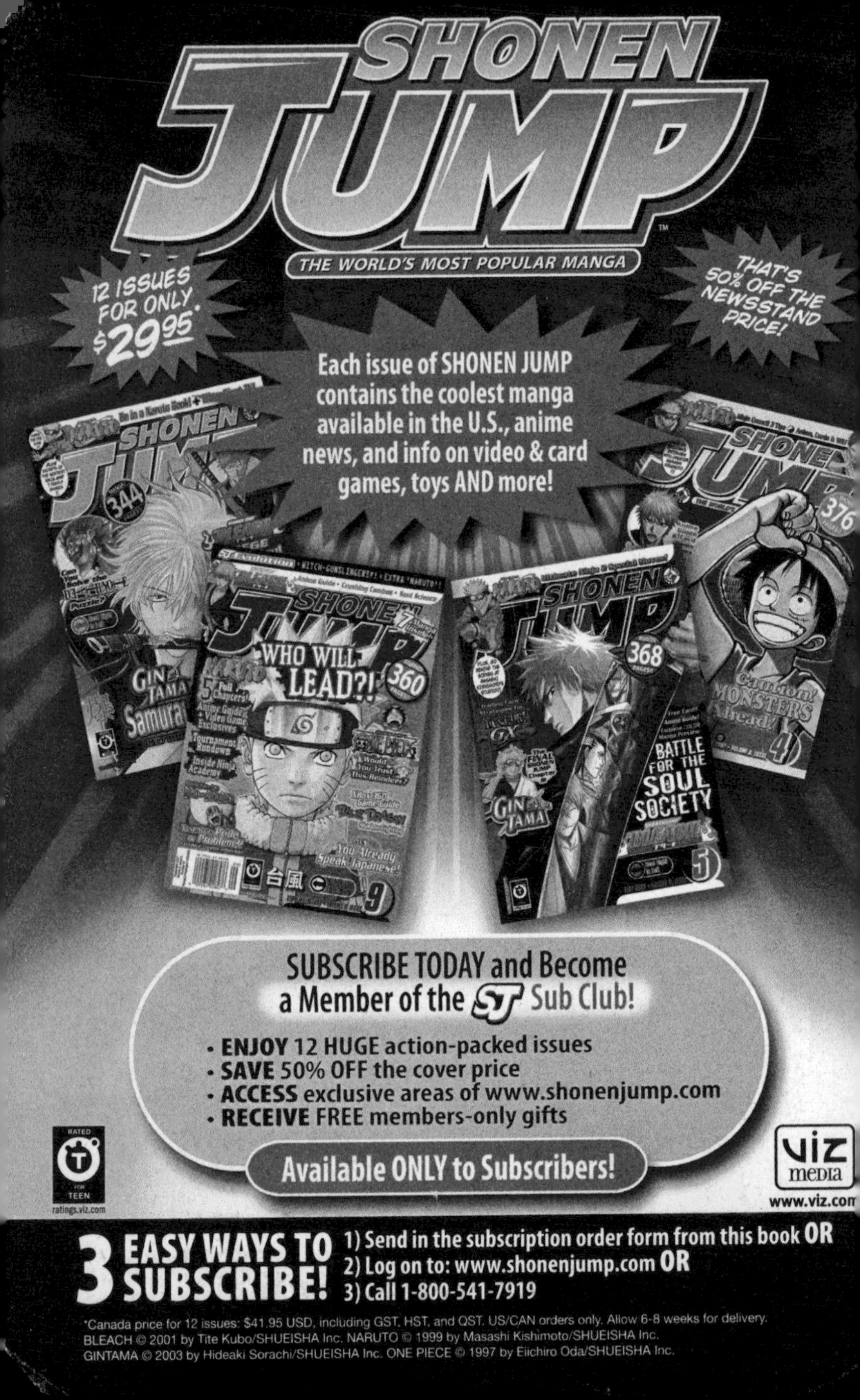